P. VERGILI MARONIS

AENEIDOS
LIBER SEXTVS

P. VERGILI MARONIS

AENEIDOS

LIBER SEXTVS

WITH A COMMENTARY

BY

R. G. AUSTIN

OXFORD

AT THE CLARENDON PRESS

1977

Oxford University Press, Walton Street, Oxford OX2 6DP

OXFORD LONDON GLASGOW
NEW YORK TORONTO MELBOURNE WELLINGTON
IBADAN NAIROBI DAR ES SALAAM LUSAKA CAPE TOWN
KUALA LUMPUR SINGAPORE JAKARTA HONG KONG TOKYO
DELHI BOMBAY CALCUTTA MADRAS KARACHI

British Library Cataloguing in Publication Data
Virgil
    P. Vergili Maronis Aeneidos, liber sextus
    Bibl. – Index
    ISBN 0–19–872077–7
    1. Aeneid. Book 6
    873'. 01   PA6801
    Latin poetry

*Printed in Great Britain
at the University Press, Oxford
by Vivian Ridler
Printer to the University*

PREFACE

ROLAND AUSTIN died on 5 October 1974. He completed the revised draft of his commentary of *Aeneid* VI a couple of days before his death. He had known for some months that he might not live to finish the book, and had asked me to take charge of the manuscript should this prove necessary. In fact he succeeded in putting the commentary virtually into its final shape, and his meticulous memoranda suggest that the edition would not have been substantially changed except for the addition of an Introduction. I have followed his wishes in printing the commentary as he left it, apart from a few minor corrections and additions, and in making only such changes of substance as were necessitated by the incorporation of the topographical and archaeological material which Mr. Colin Hardie had agreed with him to contribute. After some thought and discussion it was decided not to add an Introduction from another source.

In addition to providing the Appendix, Mr. Hardie is largely responsible for the choice and preparation of the maps and illustrations and has also contributed to some of the notes, particularly that on the Cave of the Sibyl. He has written part or the bulk of the notes on lines 2 *oris*, 7 f., 8, 9 *arces*, 10 *procul*, 13 *tecta*, 19 *templa*, 42 ff., 201 *lacus Auernus*, 237 ff. *spelunca*, 239 ff., 899 *uiam secat*.

I am most grateful to Mr. Hardie and Mr. L. M. Styler for their help in reading all the proofs, and to others who offered, out of simple *pietas*, to do the same. Mr. D. A. Russell and Mr. J. K. Cordy were generous with help and encouragement in the final stages of the book, and I much regret that there is no full record of the many who had discussed points of detail with Roland Austin and whose assistance he would have wished to acknowledge. We are grateful to Professor Raymond J. Clark of the Memorial University of Newfoundland for permission to publish what

is essentially his plan of the Cave of the Sibyl, designed to
accompany an article which is due to appear in *Latomus*
in 1977.

It is inevitable that a book which its author had com-
pleted under such circumstances and with such courage and
devotion should be in the nature of a memorial, and in the
case of Roland Austin this is not inappropriate. His com-
mentaries reflect his personality to an unusual degree and
will communicate to those who knew him, and to others
too, a measure of that humanity which infused his life and
scholarship and won him the deep affection of generations
of pupils, colleagues, and friends.

Oxford, June 1976   L. D. REYNOLDS

CONTENTS

BIBLIOGRAPHY

(Specialized bibliographical references will be found at their relevant points in the Commentary)

BAILEY, C., *Religion in Virgil*, Oxford, 1935.

BUTLER, H. E., *The Sixth Book of the Aeneid*, Blackwell, Oxford, 1920.

CAMPS, W. A., 'The Role of the Sixth Book in the Aeneid', *Proceedings of the Virgil Society* vii, 1967–8, 22–30.

—— *An Introduction to Virgil's Aeneid*, Oxford, 1969.

CUMONT, F., *Lux Perpetua*, Paris, 1949.

DIETERICH, A., *Nekyia*², Berlin, 1913.

DODDS, E. R., *The Greeks and the Irrational*, Berkeley, 1951.

FLETCHER, Sir F., *Virgil Aeneid VI*, Oxford, 1941.

FOWLER, W. W., *Religious Experience of the Roman People*, London, 1911.

FRAZER, Sir J. G., Apollodorus (Loeb series, London, 1921).

GUTHRIE, W. K. C., *Orpheus and Greek Religion*², London, 1952.

HEINZE, R., *Virgils epische Technik*³, Leipzig, 1915 (repr. 1957).

LINFORTH, I. M., *The Arts of Orpheus*, Berkeley, 1941.

MAIURI, A., *The Phlegraean Fields*⁴, Rome, 1969.

MERKELBACH, R., 'Aeneas in Cumae', *Museum Helveticum* xviii, 1961, 83–99.

NETTLESHIP, H., 'Suggestions Introductory to a Study of the Aeneid', *Lectures and Essays*, Oxford, 1885, 97–142.

NORDEN, E., *P. Vergilius Maro Aeneis Buch VI*⁵ (reprint of ed. 4, containing the *Nachträge* of eds. 2 and 3), Stuttgart, 1970.

NORWOOD, F., 'The Tripartite Eschatology of Aeneid 6', *Classical Philology* xlix, 1954, 15–26.

OGILVIE, R. M., *A Commentary on Livy Books 1–5*, Oxford, 1965.

OTIS, B., *Virgil, A Study in Civilized Poetry*, Oxford, 1963.

SETAIOLI, A., *Alcuni aspetti del VI libro dell'Eneide*, Bologna, 1972.

SOLMSEN, F., 'Greek Ideas of the Hereafter in Virgil's Roman Epic', *Proceedings of the American Philosophical Society* cxii, 1968, 8–14.

SOLMSEN F., 'The World of the Dead in Book 6 of the Aeneid', *Classical Philology* lxvii, 1972, 31–41.

SOUBIRAN, J., *L'Élision dans la poésie latine*, Paris, 1966.

TOYNBEE, J. M. C., *Death and Burial in the Roman World*, London, 1971.

WEST, M. L., Hesiod, *Theogony*, Oxford, 1966.

WILLIAMS, G., *Tradition and Originality in Roman Poetry*, Oxford, 1968.

WILLIAMS, R. D., 'The Sixth Book of the Aeneid', *Greece & Rome*, second series xi, 1964, 48–63.

ABBREVIATIONS

References to periodicals follow the system of *L'Année philologique*.

ALL	*Archiv für lateinische Lexicographie.*
HSz	Hofmann–Szantyr, *Lateinische Syntax und Stilistik*, Munich, 1965.
K–S	Kühner–Stegmann, *Ausführliche Grammatik der lateinischen Sprache*², Hanover, 1912–14.
Thes.L.L.	*Thesaurus Linguae Latinae.*

NOTE ON THE TEXT

I AM grateful for permission to use the plates of Sir Roger Mynors's Oxford Classical Text (reprinted with corrections, 1972). I have, however, changed the punctuation at lines 60–2, 336, 376, 377, 389, 429–30, 575, 747, 811, 882, 898. I have also had the advantage of consulting the text of M. Geymonat (Paravia, Turin, 1973).

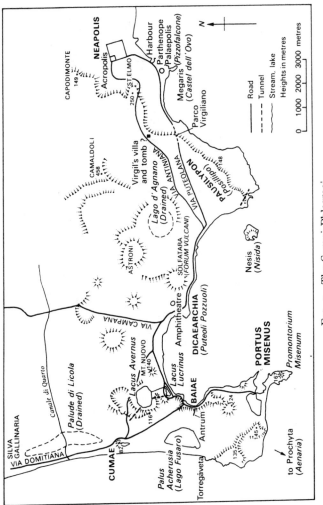

FIG. 1. The Campi Phlegraei

SILVA
VIA DOMITIANA
Canale di Quarto
Palude di Licola
(Drained)
CUMAE
Palus
Acherusia
(Lago Fusaro)
Torregàveta
Lacus Avernus
MT. NUOVO
116 140
Lacus Lucrinus
BAIAE
Antrum
to Prochyta
(Aenaria)
135
145
124
PORTUS
MISENUS
Promontorium
Misenum
161
VIA CAMPANA
Amphitheatre
DICAEARCHIA
(Puteoli Pozzuoli)
SOLFATARA
(FORUM VULCANI)
ASTRONI
CAMALDOLI
458
Lago d'Agnano
(Drained)
VIA PUTEOLANA
Virgil's villa
and tomb ?
ANTINIANA
CRYPTA
POSILLIPO)
148
PAUSILYPON
Nesis
(Nisida)
Parco
Virgiliano
Megaris
(Castel dell' Ovo)
Palaepolis
Parthenope
Pizzofalcone)
Harbour
ST. ELMO
250
CAPODIMONTE
149
Acropolis
NEAPOLIS
N

Road
Tunnel
Stream, lake
Heights in metres

0   1000   2000   3000 metres

SIGLA CODICVM

F	Vaticanus lat. 3225	saec. iv
G	Sangallensis 1394	saec. v
M	Florentinus Laur. xxxix. 1	saec. v
P	Vaticanus Palatinus lat. 1631	saec. iv/v
R	Vaticanus lat. 3867	saec. v
$M^2 P^2 R^2$	corrector aliquis antiquus	

Codices saeculi noni:

a	Bernensis 172 cum Parisino lat. 7929
b	Bernensis 165
c	Bernensis 184
d	Bernensis 255+239
e	Bernensis 167
f	Oxoniensis Bodl. Auct. F. 2. 8
h	Valentianensis 407
r	Parisinus lat. 7926
s	Parisinus lat. 7928
t	Parisinus lat. 13043
u	Parisinus lat. 13044
v	Vaticanus lat. 1570
ω	consensus horum lue omnium uel quotquot non separatim nominantur
γ	Guelferbytanus Gudianus lat. 2°. 70
def.	deficit (uel mutilus est uel legi non potest)
recc.	codices saec. nono recentiores

P. VERGILI MARONIS
AENEIDOS
LIBER VI

Sic fatur lacrimans, classique immittit habenas
et tandem Euboicis Cumarum adlabitur oris.
obuertunt pelago proras; tum dente tenaci
ancora fundabat nauis et litora curuae
praetexunt puppes. ·iuuenum manus emicat ardens   5
litus in Hesperium; quaerit pars semina flammae
abstrusa in uenis silicis, pars densa ferarum
tecta rapit siluas inuentaque flumina monstrat.
at pius Aeneas arces quibus altus Apollo
praesidet horrendaeque procul secreta Sibyllae,   10
antrum immane, petit, magnam cui mentem animumque
Delius inspirat uates aperitque futura.
iam subeunt Triuiae lucos atque aurea tecta.

Daedalus, ut fama est, fugiens Minoia regna
praepetibus pennis ausus se credere caelo   15
insuetum per iter gelidas enauit ad Arctos,
Chalcidicaque leuis tandem super astitit arce.
redditus his primum terris tibi, Phoebe, sacrauit
remigium alarum posuitque immania templa.
in foribus letum Androgeo; tum pendere poenas   20
Cecropidae iussi (miserum!) septena quotannis
corpora natorum; stat ductis sortibus urna.
contra elata mari respondet Cnosia tellus:
hic crudelis amor tauri suppostaque furto
Pasiphae mixtumque genus prolesque biformis   25

1-25 *MPR*   17 arcaem *M¹*: arca *R*   20 Androgeo *actv*,
Gramm., Seru. ad A. ii 371, *DSeru. ad A.* ii 392: -gei *MPRb?def*(-ge
f¹)*hr*, 'aliqui' *ap. Probum* 227. 34

Minotaurus inest, Veneris monimenta nefandae,
hic labor ille domus et inextricabilis error;
magnum reginae sed enim miseratus amorem
Daedalus ipse dolos tecti ambagesque resoluit,
caeca regens filo uestigia. tu quoque magnam   30
partem opere in tanto, sineret dolor, Icare, haberes.
bis conatus erat casus effingere in auro,
bis patriae cecidere manus. quin protinus omnia
perlegerent oculis, ni iam praemissus Achates
adforet atque una Phoebi Triuiaeque sacerdos,   35
Deiphobe Glauci, fatur quae talia regi:
'non hoc ista sibi tempus spectacula poscit;
nunc grege de intacto septem mactare iuuencos
praestiterit, totidem lectas ex more bidentis.'
talibus adfata Aenean (nec sacra morantur   40
iussa uiri) Teucros uocat alta in templa sacerdos.
    Excisum Euboicae latus ingens rupis in antrum,
quo lati ducunt aditus centum, ostia centum,
unde ruunt totidem uoces, responsa Sibyllae.
uentum erat ad limen, cum uirgo 'poscere fata   45
tempus' ait; 'deus ecce deus!' cui talia fanti
ante fores subito non uultus, non color unus,
non comptae mansere comae; sed pectus anhelum,
et rabie fera corda tument, maiorque uideri
nec mortale sonans, adflata est numine quando   50
iam propiore dei. 'cessas in uota precesque,
Tros' ait 'Aenea? cessas? neque enim ante dehiscent
attonitae magna ora domus.' et talia fata
conticuit. gelidus Teucris per dura cucurrit
ossa tremor, funditque preces rex pectore ab imo: 55
'Phoebe, grauis Troiae semper miserate labores,
Dardana qui Paridis derexti tela manusque

    26–50 FMPR; 51–7 MPR   33 omne Rb?eh   34 pelligerent
Quint. viii 3. 25 (pollicerent codd.), Scaurus 26. 9   37 poscunt
MR, respuit Seru.   39 ex Fc: de (A. iv 57 al.) MPRω, Seru.
51 deo cerv   57 derexti Ribbeck: dir- codd.

corpus in Aeacidae, magnas obeuntia terras
tot maria intraui duce te penitusque repostas
Massylum gentis praetentaque Syrtibus arua;   60
iam tandem Italiae fugientis prendimus oras:
hac Troiana tenus fuerit fortuna secuta.
uos quoque Pergameae iam fas est parcere genti,
dique deaeque omnes, quibus obstitit Ilium et ingens
gloria Dardaniae. tuque, o sanctissima uates,   65
praescia uenturi, da (non indebita posco
regna meis fatis) Latio considere Teucros
errantisque deos agitataque numina Troiae.
tum Phoebo et Triuiae solido de marmore templum
instituam festosque dies de nomine Phoebi.   70
te quoque magna manent regnis penetralia nostris:
hic ego namque tuas sortis arcanaque fata
dicta meae genti ponam, lectosque sacrabo,
alma, uiros. foliis tantum ne carmina manda,
ne turbata uolent rapidis ludibria uentis;   75
ipsa canas oro.' finem dedit ore loquendi.

    At Phoebi nondum patiens immanis in antro
bacchatur uates, magnum si pectore possit
excussisse deum; tanto magis ille fatigat
os rabidum, fera corda domans, fingitque premendo.   80
ostia iamque domus patuere ingentia centum
sponte sua uatisque ferunt responsa per auras:
'o tandem magnis pelagi defuncte periclis
(sed terrae grauiora manent), in regna Lauini
Dardanidae uenient (mitte hanc de pectore curam),   85
sed non et uenisse uolent. bella, horrida bella,
et Thybrim multo spumantem sanguine cerno.
non Simois tibi nec Xanthus nec Dorica castra
defuerint; alius Latio iam partus Achilles,
natus et ipse dea; nec Teucris addita Iuno   90

58–90 *MPR*   67 consistere *R*   69 templum *MRh*: templa
Pω   78 posset *R*   84 terrae *MPt*: terra *Rω*, *'unum tamen
est' iudice Seru.*   Lauini] Latini *'alii' ap. Seru.*

usquam aberit, cum tu supplex in rebus egenis
quas gentis Italum aut quas non oraueris urbes!
causa mali tanti coniunx iterum hospita Teucris
externique iterum thalami.
tu ne cede malis, sed contra audentior ito, 95
qua tua te Fortuna sinet. uia prima salutis
(quod minime reris) Graia pandetur ab urbe.'
    Talibus ex adyto dictis Cumaea Sibylla
horrendas canit ambages antroque remugit,
obscuris uera inuoluens: ea frena furenti 100
concutit et stimulos sub pectore uertit Apollo.
ut primum cessit furor et rabida ora quierunt,
incipit Aeneas heros: 'non ulla laborum,
o uirgo, noua mi facies inopinaue surgit;
omnia praecepi atque animo mecum ante peregi. 105
unum oro: quando hic inferni ianua regis
dicitur et tenebrosa palus Acheronte refuso,
ire ad conspectum cari genitoris et ora
contingat; doceas iter et sacra ostia pandas.
illum ego per flammas et mille sequentia tela 110
eripui his umeris medioque ex hoste recepi;
ille meum comitatus iter maria omnia mecum
atque omnis pelagique minas caelique ferebat,
inualidus, uiris ultra sortemque senectae.
quin, ut te supplex peterem et tua limina adirem, 115
idem orans mandata dabat. gnatique patrisque,
alma, precor, miserere (potes namque omnia, nec te
nequiquam lucis Hecate praefecit Auernis),
si potuit manis accersere coniugis Orpheus
Threicia fretus cithara fidibusque canoris, 120
si fratrem Pollux alterna morte redemit

91–121 *MPR*   96 qua *b²* (*cf. A.* ii 387): quam *codd., codd.*
Senecae ep. 82. 18 (*cui* sinet *sententiae finis*), *Seru.*   102 rapida *R*
105 percepi *br*   109 contingam *PR*   113 caelique minas
pelagique *M*   115 et *MP²acert?*: om. *P¹Rbdfhv*   119 accersere
MP¹Rac, Macrob. iv 5. 3, *Char.* 227. 7 (arcersere *P²*): arcessere *ω*,
Seru., Isid. i 37. 35 (*cf. A.* v 746)

itque reditque uiam totiens. quid Thesea, magnum
quid memorem Alciden? et mi genus ab Ioue summo.'
   Talibus orabat dictis arasque tenebat,
cum sic orsa loqui uates: 'sate sanguine diuum,   125
Tros Anchisiade, facilis descensus Auerno:
noctes atque dies patet atri ianua Ditis;
sed reuocare gradum superasque euadere ad auras,
hoc opus, hic labor est. pauci, quos aequus amauit
Iuppiter aut ardens euexit ad aethera uirtus,   130
dis geniti potuere. tenent media omnia siluae,
Cocytusque sinu labens circumuenit atro.
quod si tantus amor menti, si tanta cupido est
bis Stygios innare lacus, bis nigra uidere
Tartara, et insano iuuat indulgere labori,   135
accipe quae peragenda prius. latet arbore opaca
aureus et foliis et lento uimine ramus,
Iunoni infernae dictus sacer; hunc tegit omnis
lucus et obscuris claudunt conuallibus umbrae.
sed non ante datur telluris operta subire   140
auricomos quam quis decerpserit arbore fetus.
hoc sibi pulchra suum ferri Proserpina munus
instituit. primo auulso non deficit alter
aureus, et simili frondescit uirga metallo.
ergo alte uestiga oculis et rite repertum   145
carpe manu; namque ipse uolens facilisque sequetur,
si te fata uocant; aliter non uiribus ullis
uincere nec duro poteris conuellere ferro.
praeterea iacet exanimum tibi corpus amici
(heu nescis) totamque incestat funere classem,   150
dum consulta petis nostroque in limine pendes.
sedibus hunc refer ante suis et conde sepulcro.
duc nigras pecudes; ea prima piacula sunto.

122–53 *MPR*   126 Auerno *M¹P¹br* (-no est *M²*): Auerni
P²Rω, utrumque agnoscit Seru.   133 est *M¹Rω: om.*
M²P   141 quis] qui *M*   144 similis *M*   147 non]
nec *R*

sic demum lucos Stygis et regna inuia uiuis
aspicies.' dixit, pressoque obmutuit ore.   155
  Aeneas maesto defixus lumina uultu
ingreditur linquens antrum, caecosque uolutat
euentus animo secum. cui fidus Achates
it comes et paribus curis uestigia figit.
multa inter sese uario sermone serebant,   160
quem socium exanimum uates, quod corpus humandum
diceret. atque illi Misenum in litore sicco,
ut uenere, uident indigna morte peremptum,
Misenum Aeoliden, quo non praestantior alter
aere ciere uiros Martemque accendere cantu.   165
Hectoris hic magni fuerat comes, Hectora circum
et lituo pugnas insignis obibat et hasta.
postquam illum uita uictor spoliauit Achilles,
Dardanio Aeneae sese fortissimus heros
addiderat socium, non inferiora secutus.   170
sed tum, forte caua dum personat aequora concha,
demens, et cantu uocat in certamina diuos,
aemulus exceptum Triton, si credere dignum est,
inter saxa uirum spumosa immerserat unda.
ergo omnes magno circum clamore fremebant,   175
praecipue pius Aeneas. tum iussa Sibyllae,
haud mora, festinant flentes aramque sepulcri
congerere arboribus caeloque educere certant.
itur in antiquam siluam, stabula alta ferarum;
procumbunt piceae, sonat icta securibus ilex   180
fraxineaeque trabes cuneis et fissile robur
scinditur, aduoluunt ingentis montibus ornos.
  Nec non Aeneas opera inter talia primus
hortatur socios paribusque accingitur armis.
atque haec ipse suo tristi cum corde uolutat   185

154–85 *MPR*   154 Stygis *M²P¹t, Seru.*(?): Stygiis *M¹R*:
Stygios *P²ω*   et *om. efhruv*   156 deflexus *P¹*   177 sepulchri
(*ut Sil. Ital.* xv 387) *MRω, Non.* 298. 15, *Seru.*: sepulchro *Pab?r, Tib.*
182 ac uoluunt *ehuv*

aspectans siluam immensam, et sic forte precatur:
'si nunc se nobis ille aureus arbore ramus
ostendat nemore in tanto! quando omnia uere
heu nimium de te uates, Misene, locuta est.'
uix ea fatus erat, geminae cum forte columbae   190
ipsa sub ora uiri caelo uenere uolantes,
et uiridi sedere solo. tum maximus heros
maternas agnouit auis laetusque precatur:
'este duces, o, si qua uia est, cursumque per auras
derigite in lucos ubi pinguem diues opacat   195
ramus humum. tuque, o, dubiis ne defice rebus,
diua parens.' sic effatus uestigia pressit
obseruans quae signa ferant, quo tendere pergant.
pascentes illae tantum prodire uolando
quantum acie possent oculi seruare sequentum.   200
inde ubi uenere ad fauces graue olentis Auerni,
tollunt se celeres liquidumque per aëra lapsae
sedibus optatis gemina super arbore sidunt,
discolor unde auri per ramos aura refulsit.
quale solet siluis brumali frigore uiscum   205
fronde uirere noua, quod non sua seminat arbos,
et croceo fetu teretis circumdare truncos,
talis erat species auri frondentis opaca
ilice, sic leni crepitabat brattea uento.
corripit Aeneas extemplo auidusque refringit   210
cunctantem, et uatis portat sub tecta Sibyllae.
  Nec minus interea Misenum in litore Teucri
flebant et cineri ingrato suprema ferebant.
principio pinguem taedis et robore secto
ingentem struxere pyram, cui frondibus atris   215
intexunt latera et feralis ante cupressos
constituunt, decorantque super fulgentibus armis.

186–217 MPR   186 forte] uoce (A. ix 403, xi 784) R
193 agnouit Ma (cf. u. 498, A. x 874): agnoscit PRω   195 di-
rigite Mω   200 acies M¹   sequentur P¹   203 geminae R
209 crepitabant ω(praeter d)γ

pars calidos latices et aëna undantia flammis
expediunt, corpusque lauant frigentis et unguunt.
fit gemitus. tum membra toro defleta reponunt   220
purpureasque super uestis, uelamina nota,
coniciunt. pars ingenti.subiere feretro,
triste ministerium, et subiectam more parentum
auersi tenuere facem. congesta cremantur
turea dona, dapes, fuso crateres oliuo.   225
postquam conlapsi cineres et flamma quieuit,
reliquias uino et bibulam lauere fauillam,
ossaque lecta cado texit Corynaeus aëno.
idem ter socios pura circumtulit unda
spargens rore leui et ramo felicis oliuae,   230
lustrauitque uiros dixitque nouissima uerba.
at pius Aeneas ingenti mole sepulcrum
imponit suaque arma uiro remumque tubamque
monte sub aërio, qui nunc Misenus ab illo
dicitur aeternumque tenet per saecula nomen.   235
   His actis propere exsequitur praecepta Sibyllae.
spelunca alta fuit uastoque immanis hiatu,
scrupea, tuta lacu nigro nemorumque tenebris,
quam super haud ullae poterant impune uolantes
tendere iter pennis: talis sese halitus atris   240
faucibus effundens supera ad conuexa ferebat.
[unde locum Grai dixerunt nomine Aornum.]
quattuor hic primum nigrantis terga iuuencos
constituit frontique inuergit uina sacerdos,
et summas carpens media inter cornua saetas   245
ignibus imponit sacris, libamina prima,
uoce uocans Hecaten caeloque Ereboque potentem.
supponunt alii cultros tepidumque cruorem

218 *MPR*; 219–48 *FMPR*   223 subiecta *F¹P²*   224 faces *P²*
225 dapes] ferunt *P²* (*A.* v 101)   231 uiros *FMP²ω*: domos
P¹Rabr (domus *Tib.*)   241 super *M¹P¹R* (*cf. uu.* 750, 787, *A.*
vii 562, x 251)   242 *u. habent hic Rb, ante* 241 *γ, om. ceteri*
Aornum *γ*: Aornon *ed. Aldina an.* 1501: Auernum *Rb*

succipiunt pateris. ipse atri uelleris agnam
Aeneas matri Eumenidum magnaeque sorori   250
ense ferit, sterilemque tibi, Proserpina, uaccam;
tum Stygio regi nocturnas incohat aras
et solida imponit taurorum uiscera flammis,
pingue super oleum fundens ardentibus extis.
ecce autem primi sub limina solis et ortus   255
sub pedibus mugire solum et iuga coepta moueri
siluarum, uisaeque canes ululare per umbram
aduentante dea. 'procul, o procul este, profani,'
conclamat uates, 'totoque absistite luco;
tuque inuade uiam uaginaque eripe ferrum: 260
nunc animis opus, Aenea, nunc pectore firmo.'
tantum effata furens antro se immisit aperto;
ille ducem haud timidis uadentem passibus aequat.

   Di, quibus imperium est animarum, umbraeque silentes
et Chaos et Phlegethon, loca nocte tacentia late,   265
sit mihi fas audita loqui, sit numine uestro
pandere res alta terra et caligine mersas.

   Ibant obscuri sola sub nocte per umbram
perque domos Ditis uacuas et inania regna:
quale per incertam lunam sub luce maligna   270
est iter in siluis, ubi caelum condidit umbra
Iuppiter, et rebus nox abstulit atra colorem.
uestibulum ante ipsum primisque in faucibus Orci
Luctus et ultrices posuere cubilia Curae,
pallentesque habitant Morbi tristisque Senectus,   275
et Metus et malesuada Fames ac turpis Egestas,
terribiles uisu formae, Letumque Labosque;
tum consanguineus Leti Sopor et mala mentis

   249–72 *FMPR*; 273–8 *MPR*   249 succipiunt *FPbt, Seru.*
(*cf. A.* i 175): suscipiunt *MRω, Tib.*   254 super *recc. aliquot* (*cf. A.*
i 668): superque *codd.*   infundens *M*   255 limina *FMah*:
lumina *PRω* (lumine *b*), *Char.* 236. 9, *Seru.*   265 tacentia] silen-
tia *M²*(*in margine*)*ω*(*praeter abcr*), *Seru.*   267 altas *M¹*
268 umbras *ω*(*praeter abc*)   270 incertam *F*(-tum *F¹*)*MPRω*,
'*alii*' *ap. Seru., ipse ad G.* ii 179, *DSeru. ad A.* iii 203: inceptam *beuv,*
Seru.   273 primis (*om.* -que) *Pc*

Gaudia, mortiferumque aduerso in limine Bellum,
ferreique Eumenidum thalami et Discordia demens   280
uipereum crinem uittis innexa cruentis.
in medio ramos annosaque bracchia pandit
ulmus opaca, ingens, quam sedem Somnia uulgo
uana tenere ferunt, foliisque sub omnibus haerent.
multaque praeterea uariarum monstra ferarum,   285
Centauri in foribus stabulant Scyllaeque biformes
et centumgeminus Briareus ac belua Lernae
horrendum stridens, flammisque armata Chimaera,
Gorgones Harpyiaeque et forma tricorporis umbrae.
corripit hic subita trepidus formidine ferrum   290
Aeneas strictamque aciem uenientibus offert,
et ni docta comes tenuis sine corpore uitas
admoneat uolitare caua sub imagine formae,
inruat et frustra ferro diuerberet umbras.

Hinc uia Tartarei quae fert Acherontis ad undas.   295
turbidus hic caeno uastaque uoragine gurges
aestuat atque omnem Cocyto eructat harenam.
portitor has horrendus aquas et flumina seruat
terribili squalore Charon, cui plurima mento
canities inculta iacet, stant lumina flamma,   300
sordidus ex umeris nodo dependet amictus.
ipse ratem conto subigit uelisque ministrat
et ferruginea subuectat corpora cumba,
iam senior, sed cruda deo uiridisque senectus.
huc omnis turba ad ripas effusa ruebat,   305
matres atque uiri defunctaque corpora uita
magnanimum heroum, pueri innuptaeque puellae,
impositique rogis iuuenes ante ora parentum:
quam multa in siluis autumni frigore primo
lapsa cadunt folia, aut ad terram gurgite ab alto   310

279–310 *MPR*   281 innixa *Rb*   289 *uide praefationem, p. xii*
297 Cocyti ω(*praeter etuv*)   300 flamma *M²P¹rt, Seru. ad E.*
vii 53, *A.* i 646, *DSeru. ad A.* ii 333: flammae *M¹P²Rω, DSeru. ad A.* i
646   301 dependit *aeuv*

quam multae glomerantur aues, ubi frigidus annus
trans pontum fugat et terris immittit apricis.
stabant orantes primi transmittere cursum
tendebantque manus ripae ulterioris amore.
nauita sed tristis nunc hos nunc accipit illos,   315
ast alios longe summotos arcet harena.
Aeneas miratus enim motusque tumultu
'dic,' ait, 'o uirgo, quid uult concursus ad amnem?
quidue petunt animae? uel quo discrimine ripas
hae linquunt, illae remis uada liuida uerrunt?'   320
olli sic breuiter fata est longaeua sacerdos:
'Anchisa generate, deum certissima proles,
Cocyti stagna alta uides Stygiamque paludem,
di cuius iurare timent et fallere numen.
haec omnis, quam cernis, inops inhumataque turba est;   325
portitor ille Charon; hi, quos uehit unda, sepulti.
nec ripas datur horrendas et rauca fluenta
transportare prius quam sedibus ossa quierunt.
centum errant annos uolitantque haec litora circum;
tum demum admissi stagna exoptata reuisunt.'   330
constitit Anchisa satus et uestigia pressit
multa putans sortemque animo miseratus iniquam.
cernit ibi maestos et mortis honore carentis
Leucaspim et Lyciae ductorem classis Oronten,
quos simul a Troia uentosa per aequora uectos   335
obruit Auster, aqua inuoluens nauemque uirosque.
    Ecce gubernator sese Palinurus agebat,
qui Libyco nuper cursu, dum sidera seruat,
exciderat puppi mediis effusus in undis.
hunc ubi uix multa maestum cognouit in umbra,   340
sic prior adloquitur: 'quis te, Palinure, deorum
eripuit nobis medioque sub aequore mersit?
dic age. namque mihi, fallax haud ante repertus,
hoc uno responso animum delusit Apollo,

311–44 MPR   320 uertunt P   332 animi (A. x 686) M¹
336 uirumque P¹

qui fore te ponto incolumem finisque canebat   345
uenturum Ausonios. en haec promissa fides est?'
ille autem: 'neque te Phoebi cortina fefellit,
dux Anchisiade, nec me deus aequore mersit.
namque gubernaclum multa ui forte reuulsum,
cui datus haerebam custos cursusque regebam,   350
praecipitans traxi mecum. maria aspera iuro
non ullum pro me tantum cepisse timorem,
quam tua ne spoliata armis, excussa magistro,
deficeret tantis nauis surgentibus undis.
tris Notus hibernas immensa per aequora noctes   355
uexit me uiolentus aqua; uix lumine quarto
prospexi Italiam summa sublimis ab unda.
paulatim adnabam terrae; iam tuta tenebam,
ni gens crudelis madida cum ueste grauatum
prensantemque uncis manibus capita aspera montis   360
ferro inuasisset praedamque ignara putasset.
nunc me fluctus habet uersantque in litore uenti.
quod te per caeli iucundum lumen et auras,
per genitorem oro, per spes surgentis Iuli,
eripe me his, inuicte, malis: aut tu mihi terram   365
inice, namque potes, portusque require Velinos;
aut tu, si qua uia est, si quam tibi diua creatrix
ostendit (neque enim, credo, sine numine diuum
flumina tanta paras Stygiamque innare paludem),
da dextram misero et tecum me tolle per undas,   370
sedibus ut saltem placidis in morte quiescam.'
talia fatus erat coepit cum talia uates:
'unde haec, o Palinure, tibi tam dira cupido?
tu Stygias inhumatus aquas amnemque seuerum
Eumenidum aspicies, ripamue iniussus adibis?   375
desine fata deum flecti sperare precando.

345-76 *MPR*   349 ui forte] uix arte (*A*. v 270) *P*   350 ge-
rebam *P*   352 illum *M*¹ (*A*. iv 227)   353 ni *Rufin.* 56. 7
358 iam] et iam *R*   375 ripamque *aeuv*   adibis *MPRb?cfhru*,
'*alii*' *ap. Seru.*: abibis *adtv* (abis *e*), *Seru. hic et ad A*. iv 106, *Tib.*

sed cape dicta memor, duri solacia casus:
nam tua finitimi, longe lateque per urbes
prodigiis acti caelestibus, ossa piabunt
et statuent tumulum et tumulo sollemnia mittent,   380
aeternumque locus Palinuri nomen habebit.'
his dictis curae emotae pulsusque parumper
corde dolor tristi; gaudet cognomine terra.

    Ergo iter inceptum peragunt fluuioque propinquant.
nauita quos iam inde ut Stygia prospexit ab unda   385
per tacitum nemus ire pedemque aduertere ripae,
sic prior adgreditur dictis atque increpat ultro:
'quisquis es, armatus qui nostra ad flumina tendis,
fare age quid uenias, iam istinc, et comprime gressum.
umbrarum hic locus est, somni noctisque soporae: 390
corpora uiua nefas Stygia uectare carina.
nec uero Alciden me sum laetatus euntem
accepisse lacu, nec Thesea Pirithoumque,
dis quamquam geniti atque inuicti uiribus essent.
Tartareum ille manu custodem in uincla petiuit   395
ipsius a solio regis traxitque trementem;
hi dominam Ditis thalamo deducere adorti.'
quae contra breuiter fata est Amphrysia uates:
'nullae hic insidiae tales (absiste moueri),
nec uim tela ferunt; licet ingens ianitor antro   400
aeternum latrans exsanguis terreat umbras,
casta licet patrui seruet Proserpina limen.
Troius Aeneas, pietate insignis et armis,
ad genitorem imas Erebi descendit ad umbras.
si te nulla mouet tantae pietatis imago,   405
at ramum hunc' (aperit ramum qui ueste latebat)
'agnoscas.' tumida ex ira tum corda residunt;
nec plura his. ille admirans uenerabile donum
fatalis uirgae longo post tempore uisum

377–92 *MPR*; 393–409 *FMPR*   383 terra *Seru.*: terrae *codd.*,
Non. 378. 17   385 conspexit *M*   387 adloquitur *Rb*
388 tendes *P*   390 est] et *R*   399 hinc *F²aeuv*

caeruleam aduertit puppim ripaeque propinquat.　　410
inde alias animas, quae per iuga longa sedebant,
deturbat laxatque foros; simul accipit alueo
ingentem Aenean. gemuit sub pondere cumba
sutilis et multam accepit rimosa paludem.
tandem trans fluuium incolumis uatemque uirumque　415
informi limo glaucaque exponit in ulua.
　Cerberus haec ingens latratu regna trifauci
personat aduerso recubans immanis in antro.
cui uates horrere uidens iam colla colubris
melle soporatam et medicatis frugibus offam　　　420
obicit. ille fame rabida tria guttura pandens
corripit obiectam, atque immania terga resoluit
fusus humi totoque ingens extenditur antro.
occupat Aeneas aditum custode sepulto
euaditque celer ripam inremeabilis undae.　　　　425
　Continuo auditae uoces uagitus et ingens
infantumque animae flentes, in limine primo
quos dulcis uitae exsortis et ab ubere raptos
abstulit atra dies et funere mersit acerbo.
hos iuxta falso damnati crimine mortis;　　　　430
nec uero hae sine sorte datae, sine iudice, sedes:
quaesitor Minos urnam mouet; ille silentum
consiliumque uocat uitasque et crimina discit.
proxima deinde tenent maesti loca, qui sibi letum
insontes peperere manu lucemque perosi　　　　435
proiecere animas. quam uellent aethere in alto
nunc et pauperiem et duros perferre labores!
fas obstat, tristisque palus inamabilis undae
alligat et nouies Styx interfusa coercet.
nec procul hinc partem fusi monstrantur in omnem　440

410–23 *FMPR*; 424–40 *MPR*　　　428 uita *P*²　　　433 consiliumque
P, ps.Ascon. in Cic. Verr. ii 1, *Tib. in lemmate*: conc- (*A*.x2) *MR*ω,
Seru., Tib.　　　438 fas obstat *MPabrt* (optat *R*), *Aug. c.d.* i 19: fata
obstant (*A.* iv 440) ω, *Seru.*　　tristisque *PRabr* (trisque *M*), *Aug.*,
respuit Seru.: tristique ω, *Seru., Tib.*　　undae *MPR*¹*a, Aug.*: unda (*G.*
iv 479) *R*²ω, *Seru., Tib.*　　440 hic *MR*

Lugentes campi; sic illos nomine dicunt.
hic quos durus amor crudeli tabe peredit
secreti celant calles et myrtea circum
silua tegit; curae non ipsa in morte relinquunt.
his Phaedram Procrinque locis maestamque Eriphylen   445
crudelis nati monstrantem uulnera cernit,
Euadnenque et Pasiphaen; his Laodamia
it comes et iuuenis quondam, nunc femina, Caeneus
rursus et in ueterem fato reuoluta figuram.
inter quas Phoenissa recens a uulnere Dido   450
errabat silua in magna; quam Troius heros
ut primum iuxta stetit agnouitque per umbras
obscuram, qualem primo qui surgere mense
aut uidet aut uidisse putat per nubila lunam,
demisit lacrimas dulcique adfatus amore est: 455
'infelix Dido, uerus mihi nuntius ergo
uenerat exstinctam ferroque extrema secutam?
funeris heu tibi causa fui? per sidera iuro,
per superos et si qua fides tellure sub ima est,
inuitus, regina, tuo de litore cessi.   460
sed me iussa deum, quae nunc has ire per umbras,
per loca senta situ cogunt noctemque profundam,
imperiis egere suis; nec credere quiui
hunc tantum tibi me discessu ferre dolorem.
siste gradum teque aspectu ne subtrahe nostro.   465
quem fugis? extremum fato quod te adloquor hoc est.'
talibus Aeneas ardentem et torua tuentem
lenibat dictis animum lacrimasque ciebat.
illa solo fixos oculos auersa tenebat
nec magis incepto uultum sermone mouetur   470
quam si dura silex aut stet Marpesia cautes.
tandem corripuit sese atque inimica refugit
in nemus umbriferum, coniunx ubi pristinus illi
respondet curis aequatque Sychaeus amorem.

441-74 *MPR*   442 peremit *M¹*   449 reuocata *R*   452 um-
bram *M²*(umbra *M¹*)ω, *Tib.*   455 dimisit *M*   474 respondit *Rbfγ*

nec minus Aeneas casu percussus iniquo   475
prosequitur lacrimis longe et miseratur euntem.
    Inde datum molitur iter. iamque arua tenebant
ultima, quae bello clari secreta frequentant.
hic illi occurrit Tydeus, hic inclutus armis
Parthenopaeus et Adrasti pallentis imago,   480
hic multum fleti ad superos belloque caduci
Dardanidae, quos ille omnis longo ordine cernens
ingemuit, Glaucumque Medontaque Thersilochumque,
tris Antenoridas Cererique sacrum Polyboeten,
Idaeumque etiam currus, etiam arma tenentem.   485
circumstant animae dextra laeuaque frequentes,
nec uidisse semel satis est; iuuat usque morari
et conferre gradum et ueniendi discere causas.
at Danaum proceres Agamemnoniaeque phalanges
ut uidere uirum fulgentiaque arma per umbras,   490
ingenti trepidare metu; pars uertere terga,
ceu quondam petiere rates, pars tollere uocem
exiguam: inceptus clamor frustratur hiantis.
    Atque hic Priamiden laniatum corpore toto
Deiphobum uidet et lacerum crudeliter ora,   495
ora manusque ambas, populataque tempora raptis
auribus et truncas inhonesto uulnere naris.
uix adeo agnouit pauitantem ac dira tegentem
supplicia, et notis compellat uocibus ultro:
'Deiphobe armipotens, genus alto a sanguine Teucri,   500
quis tam crudelis optauit sumere poenas?
cui tantum de te licuit? mihi fama suprema
nocte tulit fessum uasta te caede Pelasgum
procubuisse super confusae stragis aceruum.

    475–90 MPR; 491–504 FMPR   475 percussus Rω, Tib.:
concussus (A. v 700) MP   476 lacrimis PRbt, Seru.: lacrimans
M²(-mas M¹)ω   477 tenebat Pd   481 hic PRcdefht: hi
Mabruv, Seru. ad A. ii 4   484 Polyboten P¹   486 frementis
P¹(-tes P²)   488 discere] poscere (A. i 414) R   495 uidet
et N. Heinsius: uidit et M¹: uidit F¹P¹ω, Seru.: uidet F²M²P²Rabr,
P. Colt 2   498 ac MP: et FRωγ, Tib.   500 a om. F¹: ab P¹br

tunc egomet tumulum Rhoeteo in litore inanem   505
constitui et magna manis ter uoce uocaui.
nomen et arma locum seruant; te, amice, nequiui
conspicere et patria decedens ponere terra.'
ad quae Priamides: 'nihil o tibi, amice, relictum;
omnia Deiphobo soluisti et funeris umbris.   510
sed me fata mea et scelus exitiale Lacaenae
his mersere malis; illa haec monimenta reliquit.
namque ut supremam falsa inter gaudia noctem
egerimus, nosti: et nimium meminisse necesse est.
cum fatalis equus saltu super ardua uenit   515
Pergama et armatum peditem grauis attulit aluo,
illa chorum simulans euhantis orgia circum
ducebat Phrygias; flammam media ipsa tenebat
ingentem et summa Danaos ex arce uocabat.
tum me confectum curis somnoque grauatum   520
infelix habuit thalamus, pressitque iacentem
dulcis et alta quies placidaeque simillima morti.
egregia interea coniunx arma omnia tectis
emouet, et fidum capiti subduxerat ensem:
intra tecta uocat Menelaum et limina pandit,   525
scilicet id magnum sperans fore munus amanti,
et famam exstingui ueterum sic posse malorum.
quid moror? inrumpunt thalamo, comes additus una
hortator scelerum Aeolides. di, talia Grais
instaurate, pio si poenas ore reposco.   530
sed te qui uiuum casus, age fare uicissim,
attulerint. pelagine uenis erroribus actus
an monitu diuum? an quae te fortuna fatigat,
ut tristis sine sole domos, loca turbida, adires?'

505–34 *FMPR*   505 in *MP²ω, Seru. hic et ad u.* 325: *om. FP¹Rr*
509 ad quae *FRb²*(atque *b¹r*), atquae (*quod idem ualet*) *M¹P*: atque
hic *M²aγ*: atque haec *ω*   516 alueo *MRa?*   520 tunc
Pb   524 emouet *F¹Rω, Tib.* (et mouet *P¹*): amouet *F²MP²bt*
528 thalamos *R, P. Colt 2*   additus *PRabh?*: additur *FMω, Tib.*
529 Aeolides *R*, Eol- *tu*, Eoliades *F*: Oelides *MPω, 'alii' ap. Seru.*
532 attulerit *M¹*

Hac uice sermonum roseis Aurora quadrigis   535
iam medium aetherio cursu traiecerat axem;
et fors omne datum traherent per talia tempus,
sed comes admonuit breuiterque adfata Sibylla est:
'nox ruit, Aenea; nos flendo ducimus horas.
hic locus est, partis ubi se uia findit in ambas: 540
dextera quae Ditis magni sub moenia tendit,
hac iter Elysium nobis; at laeua malorum
exercet poenas et ad impia Tartara mittit.'
Deiphobus contra: 'ne saeui, magna sacerdos;
discedam, explebo numerum reddarque tenebris.   545
i decus, i, nostrum; melioribus utere fatis.'
tantum effatus, et in uerbo uestigia torsit.

Respicit Aeneas subito et sub rupe sinistra
moenia lata uidet triplici circumdata muro,
quae rapidus flammis ambit torrentibus amnis,   550
Tartareus Phlegethon, torquetque sonantia saxa.
porta aduersa ingens solidoque adamante columnae,
uis ut nulla uirum, non ipsi exscindere bello
caelicolae ualeant; stat ferrea turris ad auras,
Tisiphoneque sedens palla succincta cruenta   555
uestibulum exsomnis seruat noctesque diesque.
hinc exaudiri gemitus et saeua sonare
uerbera, tum stridor ferri tractaeque catenae.
constitit Aeneas strepitumque exterritus hausit.
'quae scelerum facies? o uirgo, effare; quibusue   560
urgentur poenis? quis tantus plangor ad auras?'
tum uates sic orsa loqui: 'dux inclute Teucrum,
nulli fas casto sceleratum insistere limen;
sed me cum lucis Hecate praefecit Auernis,
ipsa deum poenas docuit perque omnia duxit.   565

535–59 *FMPR*; 560–5 *MPR*   542 hic *R*   547 torsit
FPω: pressit (*u.* 197) *MRa?*   553 bello *FPRa?brt*: ferro *Mω*
(*cf. A.* ix 137), *Seru.*:   556 insomnis *R*   559 strepituque *MP*²
hausit *F²P¹ω*, *Seru.*: haesit (*A.* iii 597, xi 699) *F¹MP²R*   561 quis
MP²ω: qui *P¹Rbr*   clangor (*ita Seru. ad u.* 554) ad auris *P* (*A.* iv
668, ix 395)   562 tunc *Pbr*   sic] hinc *PR*

Cnosius haec Rhadamanthus habet durissima regna
castigatque auditque dolos subigitque fateri
quae quis apud superos furto laetatus inani
distulit in seram commissa piacula mortem.
continuo sontis ultrix accincta flagello   570
Tisiphone quatit insultans, toruosque sinistra
intentans anguis uocat agmina saeua sororum.
tum demum horrisono stridentes cardine sacrae
panduntur portae. cernis custodia qualis
uestibulo sedeat, facies quae limina seruet :   575
quinquaginta atris immanis hiatibus Hydra
saeuior intus habet sedem. tum Tartarus ipse
bis patet in praeceps tantum tenditque sub umbras
quantus ad aetherium caeli suspectus Olympum.
hic genus antiquum Terrae, Titania pubes,   580
fulmine deiecti fundo uoluuntur in imo.
hic et Aloidas geminos immania uidi
corpora, qui manibus magnum rescindere caelum
adgressi superisque Iouem detrudere regnis.
uidi et crudelis dantem Salmonea poenas,   585
dum flammas Iouis et sonitus imitatur Olympi.
quattuor hic inuectus equis et lampada quassans
per Graium populos mediaeque per Elidis urbem
ibat ouans, diuumque sibi poscebat honorem,
demens, qui nimbos et non imitabile fulmen   590
aere et cornipedum pulsu simularet equorum.
at pater omnipotens densa inter nubila telum
contorsit, non ille faces nec fumea taedis
lumina, praecipitemque immani turbine adegit.
nec non et Tityon, Terrae omniparentis alumnum,   595
cernere erat, per tota nouem cui iugera corpus

566–88 *MPR*; 589–96 *FMPR*   571 tortosque *P²* (*cf. G.* iii
38)   580 pubes] proles (*A.* iv 258 *al.*) *R*   586 flammas
MP²Rω, Prisc. xi 34: flammam *P¹aefu*   sonitus] tonitrus *cehuv*
591 pulsu *FM¹P*: cursu *M²Rω*(curru *d*), *Tib.*   simularat *cfv*
595 omniparentis *M²Pω*: omnipotentis *FM¹R, Non.* 243. 4, *Arus.*
471. 29

porrigitur, rostroque immanis uultur obunco
immortale iecur tondens fecundaque poenis
uiscera rimaturque epulis habitatque sub alto
pectore, nec fibris requies datur ulla renatis.   600
quid memorem Lapithas, Ixiona Pirithoumque?
quos super atra silex iam iam lapsura cadentique
imminet adsimilis; lucent genialibus altis
aurea fulcra toris, epulaeque ante ora paratae
regifico luxu; Furiarum maxima iuxta   605
accubat et manibus prohibet contingere mensas,
exsurgitque facem attollens atque intonat ore.
hic, quibus inuisi fratres, dum uita manebat,
pulsatusue parens et fraus innexa clienti,
aut qui diuitiis soli incubuere repertis   610
nec partem posuere suis (quae maxima turba est),
quique ob adulterium caesi, quique arma secuti
impia nec ueriti dominorum fallere dextras,
inclusi poenam exspectant. ne quaere doceri
quam poenam, aut quae forma uiros fortunaue mersit. 615
saxum ingens uoluunt alii, radiisque rotarum
districti pendent; sedet aeternumque sedebit
infelix Theseus, Phlegyasque miserrimus omnis
admonet et magna testatur uoce per umbras:
"discite iustitiam moniti et non temnere diuos."   620
uendidit hic auro patriam dominumque potentem
imposuit; fixit leges pretio atque refixit;
hic thalamum inuasit natae uetitosque hymenaeos:
ausi omnes immane nefas ausoque potiti.
non, mihi si linguae centum sint oraque centum,   625
ferrea uox, omnis scelerum comprendere formas,
omnia poenarum percurrere nomina possim.'
   Haec ubi dicta dedit Phoebi longaeua sacerdos,

597–628 *FMPR*   597 obunco *Mω*, *Macrob.* v 7. 14: abunco
FRct: adunco *P*, *id.* iv 4. 15   602 quos *F²*(quod *F¹v*)*MPω*,
Macrob.: quo *Ru*   cadenti (*om.* -que) *R*, *P. Colt 2*   607 intonat]
increpat *P*   609 pulsatusque *ev*   et] aut *c*, *Non.* 372. 19, *Seru.*
617 districti *F¹acet*(distrincti *c¹*): destricti *F²MP²*(-te *P¹*)*Rbdfhrv*

'sed iam age, carpe uiam et susceptum perfice munus;
acceleremus' ait; 'Cyclopum educta caminis   630
moenia conspicio atque aduerso fornice portas,
haec ubi nos praecepta iubent deponere dona.'
dixerat et pariter gressi per opaca uiarum
corripiunt spatium medium foribusque propinquant.
occupat Aeneas aditum corpusque recenti   635
spargit aqua ramumque aduerso in limine figit.
   His demum exactis, perfecto munere diuae,
deuenere locos laetos et amoena uirecta
fortunatorum nemorum sedesque beatas.
largior hic campos aether et lumine uestit   640
purpureo, solemque suum, sua sidera norunt.
pars in gramineis exercent membra palaestris,
contendunt ludo et fulua luctantur harena;
pars pedibus plaudunt choreas et carmina dicunt.
nec non Threicius longa cum ueste sacerdos   645
obloquitur numeris septem discrimina uocum,
iamque eadem digitis, iam pectine pulsat eburno.
hic genus antiquum Teucri, pulcherrima proles,
magnanimi heroes nati melioribus annis,
Ilusque Assaracusque et Troiae Dardanus auctor.   650
arma procul currusque uirum miratur inanis;
stant terra defixae hastae passimque soluti
per campum pascuntur equi. quae gratia currum
armorumque fuit uiuis, quae cura nitentis
pascere equos, eadem sequitur tellure repostos.   655
conspicit, ecce, alios dextra laeuaque per herbam
uescentis laetumque choro paeana canentis
inter odoratum lauris nemus, unde superne

   629–54 *FMPR*; 655–9 *FGMPR*   629 sed] et *M*   630 e-
ducta *Mcefhrv, Seru., Tib.*: ducta *FPRabdt*   640 campos
F²MP²acdhrv: campus *F¹Rbeft*: campis *P¹*   651 miratur *PRω*:
mirantur *FMb²rt*(-entur *b¹*), *Tib.*   652 terra *MPRafr*: terrae
Fω (*cf. G.* ii 290)   653 campos *Rdv*   curruum *F²P¹, Tib., cf.
Prisc.* vii 90   656 herbas *aey*   658 lauris *G* (*cf. G.* iii 334, *A.*
ix 381): lauri *ceteri, Seru. ad A.* iv 132

plurimus Eridani per siluam uoluitur amnis.
hic manus ob patriam pugnando uulnera passi,   660
quique sacerdotes casti, dum uita manebat,
quique pii uates et Phoebo digna locuti,
inuentas aut qui uitam excoluere per artis
quique sui memores aliquos fecere merendo:
omnibus his niuea cinguntur tempora uitta.   665
quos circumfusos sic est adfata Sibylla,
Musaeum ante omnis (medium nam plurima turba
hunc habet atque umeris exstantem suspicit altis):
'dicite, felices animae tuque optime uates,
quae regio Anchisen, quis habet locus? illius ergo   670
uenimus et magnos Erebi tranauimus amnis.'
atque huic responsum paucis ita reddidit heros:
'nulli certa domus; lucis habitamus opacis,
riparumque toros et prata recentia riuis
incolimus. sed uos, si fert ita corde uoluntas,   675
hoc superate iugum, et facili iam tramite sistam.'
dixit, et ante tulit gressum camposque nitentis
desuper ostentat; dehinc summa cacumina linquunt.

  At pater Anchises penitus conualle uirenti
inclusas animas superumque ad lumen ituras   680
lustrabat studio recolens, omnemque suorum
forte recensebat numerum, carosque nepotes
fataque fortunasque uirum moresque manusque.
isque ubi tendentem aduersum per gramina uidit
Aenean, alacris palmas utrasque tetendit,   685
effusaeque genis lacrimae et uox excidit ore:
'uenisti tandem, tuaque exspectata parenti
uicit iter durum pietas? datur ora tueri,
nate, tua et notas audire et reddere uoces?
sic equidem ducebam animo rebarque futurum   690

660–73 *FMPR*; 674–84 *FGMPR*; 685–7 *FMPR*; 688–90 *FGMPR*
661 maneret *Non.* 267. 8, 440. 7   664 aliquos *F¹MPRabcr,
Don. ad Ter. Andr.* 331 *et Eun.* 458, *Seru.*: alios *F²defhtv, Macrob.
somn.* i 8. 6, *Don. ad Adelph.* 201, *Aug. c.d.* xxi 27   672 hic *M*
674 siluis *R*   678 dein *Ga*   685 alacris] lacrimans *P¹*

tempora dinumerans, nec me mea cura fefellit.
quas ego te terras et quanta per aequora uectum
accipio! quantis iactatum, nate, periclis!
quam metui ne quid Libyae tibi regna nocerent!'
ille autem: 'tua me, genitor, tua tristis imago   695
saepius occurrens haec limina tendere adegit;
stant sale Tyrrheno classes. da iungere dextram,
da, genitor, teque amplexu ne subtrahe nostro.'
sic memorans largo fletu simul ora rigabat.
ter conatus ibi collo dare bracchia circum;   700
ter frustra comprensa manus effugit imago,
par leuibus uentis uolucrique simillima somno.
  Interea uidet Aeneas in ualle reducta
seclusum nemus et uirgulta sonantia siluae,
Lethaeumque domos placidas qui praenatat amnem.   705
hunc circum innumerae gentes populique uolabant:
ac ueluti in pratis ubi apes aestate serena
floribus insidunt uariis et candida circum
lilia funduntur, strepit omnis murmure campus.
horrescit uisu subito causasque requirit   710
inscius Aeneas, quae sint ea flumina porro,
quiue uiri tanto complerint agmine ripas.
tum pater Anchises: 'animae, quibus altera fato
corpora debentur, Lethaei ad fluminis undam
securos latices et longa obliuia potant.   715
has equidem memorare tibi atque ostendere coram
iampridem, hanc prolem cupio enumerare meorum,
quo magis Italia mecum laetere reperta.'
'o pater, anne aliquas ad caelum hinc ire putandum est
sublimis animas iterumque ad tarda reuerti   720
corpora? quae lucis miseris tam dira cupido?'

691–721 *FGMPR*   692 te] per *R*   696 adire
coegit *d*   699 rigaebant *F¹P²*   701 compressa *Pbeu, Tib.*
702 (= *A*. ii 794) *om. Pbrt*   704 siluae *GM¹PRabc?rt, Seru.*: siluis
(*A*. iii 442) *FM²defhuv*   718 Italiam . . . repertam *F¹R*   laetare
MRcd   719 est *om. F*   721 cupido est *F¹d*

'dicam equidem nec te suspensum, nate, tenebo'
suscipit Anchises atque ordine singula pandit.

'Principio caelum ac terras camposque liquentis
lucentemque globum lunae Titaniaque astra   725
spiritus intus alit, totamque infusa per artus
mens agitat molem et magno se corpore miscet.
inde hominum pecudumque genus uitaeque uolantum
et quae marmoreo fert monstra sub aequore pontus.
igneus est ollis uigor et caelestis origo   730
seminibus, quantum non noxia corpora tardant
terrenique hebetant artus moribundaque membra.
hinc metuunt cupiuntque, dolent gaudentque, neque auras
dispiciunt clausae tenebris et carcere caeco.
quin et supremo cum lumine uita reliquit,   735
non tamen omne malum miseris nec funditus omnes
corporeae excedunt pestes, penitusque necesse est
multa diu concreta modis inolescere miris.
ergo exercentur poenis ueterumque malorum
supplicia expendunt: aliae panduntur inanes   740
suspensae ad uentos, aliis sub gurgite uasto
infectum eluitur scelus aut exuritur igni:
quisque suos patimur manis. exinde per amplum
mittimur Elysium et pauci laeta arua tenemus,
donec longa dies perfecto temporis orbe   745
concretam exemit labem, purumque relinquit
aetherium sensum atque aurai simplicis ignem:
has omnis, ubi mille rotam uoluere per annos,
Lethaeum ad fluuium deus euocat agmine magno,

722–24 FGMPR; 725–49 FMPR   723 suscipit FRacrtu:
suspicit GMPω   724 terras F²GMω (cf. A. iv 269), Minucius
Felix 19. 2, Seru. hic et ad G. iv 221: terram F¹PRb, utrumque Gramm.
725 lucentemque] ingentemque M¹   luna F¹   731 corpora noxia
P¹aefu   733 hic M¹bc   734 dispiciunt adhrtv, Tib.:
desp- FMPRb?cf: resp- esu, Seru.: susp- Aug. c.d. xiv 3, xxi 13
735 relinquit F¹bv   742 aut] adque F   746 tabem R,
agnoscit Tib.   relinquit F¹Mb: reliquit F²PRω, Seru. ad u. 340
747 aurai F²P¹ω, DSeru. ad A. vii 464: aura P²t: aurae F¹MRabdf,
Tib.

scilicet immemores supera ut conuexa reuisant   750
rursus, et incipiant in corpora uelle reuerti.'
    Dixerat Anchises natumque unaque Sibyllam
conuentus trahit in medios turbamque sonantem,
et tumulum capit unde omnis longo ordine posset
aduersos legere et uenientum discere uultus.   755
    'Nunc age, Dardaniam prolem quae deinde sequatur
gloria, qui maneant Itala de gente nepotes,
inlustris animas nostrumque in nomen ituras,
expediam dictis, et te tua fata docebo.
ille, uides, pura iuuenis qui nititur hasta,   760
proxima sorte tenet lucis loca, primus ad auras
aetherias Italo commixtus sanguine surget,
Siluius, Albanum nomen, tua postuma proles,
quem tibi longaeuo serum Lauinia coniunx
educet siluis regem regumque parentem,   765
unde genus Longa nostrum dominabitur Alba.
proximus ille Procas, Troianae gloria gentis,
et Capys et Numitor et qui te nomine reddet
Siluius Aeneas, pariter pietate uel armis
egregius, si umquam regnandam acceperit Albam.   770
qui iuuenes! quantas ostentant, aspice, uiris
atque umbrata gerunt ciuili tempora quercu!
hi tibi Nomentum et Gabios urbemque Fidenam,
hi Collatinas imponent montibus arces,
Pometios Castrumque Inui Bolamque Coramque;   775
haec tum nomina erunt, nunc sunt sine nomine terrae.
quin et auo comitem sese Mauortius addet
Romulus, Assaraci quem sanguinis Ilia mater
educet. uiden, ut geminae stant uertice cristae
et pater ipse suo superum iam signat honore?   780
en huius, nate, auspiciis illa incluta Roma

750–5 *FMPR*; 756–81 *MPR*   750 super *M*   aut *F*[1]
754 posset *MPRbcdtv*, *Seru. ad A.* ii 766: possent *Non.* 333. 7: possit
Faefhrsu, Tib.   762 surgit *M*   765 educit *M*[1]   766 nostrum
longa *M*[1]   768 reddat *Rc*   776 tunc *P*   terrae] gentes
M[1]

imperium terris, animos aequabit Olympo,
septemque una sibi muro circumdabit arces,
felix prole uirum: qualis Berecyntia mater
inuehitur curru Phrygias turrita per urbes   785
laeta deum partu, centum complexa nepotes,
omnis caelicolas, omnis supera alta tenentis.
huc geminas nunc flecte acies, hanc aspice gentem
Romanosque tuos. hic Caesar et omnis Iuli
progenies magnum caeli uentura sub axem.   790
hic uir, hic est, tibi quem promitti saepius audis,
Augustus Caesar, diui genus, aurea condet
saecula qui rursus Latio regnata per arua
Saturno quondam, super et Garamantas et Indos
proferet imperium; iacet extra sidera tellus,   795
extra anni solisque uias, ubi caelifer Atlas
axem umero torquet stellis ardentibus aptum.
huius in aduentum iam nunc et Caspia regna
responsis horrent diuum et Maeotia tellus,
et septemgemini turbant trepida ostia Nili.   800
nec uero Alcides tantum telluris obiuit,
fixerit aeripedem ceruam licet, aut Erymanthi
pacarit nemora et Lernam tremefecerit arcu;
nec qui pampineis uictor iuga flectit habenis
Liber, agens celso Nysae de uertice tigris.   805
et dubitamus adhuc uirtutem extendere factis,
aut metus Ausonia prohibet consistere terra?
quis procul ille autem ramis insignis oliuae
sacra ferens? nosco crinis incanaque menta
regis Romani primam qui legibus urbem   810
fundabit, Curibus paruis et paupere terra

782–811 *MPR*   787 supera (*u.* 241) *M²ω*: super *M¹PRabs*
793 arua] annos (*A.* ii 363) *R*   801 obiuit *ders*: obibit *MPRω*
802 fixerat *Rc*   803 pacarit *M²Pb?dhst, Seru.*: pacaret *M¹R*:
placarit *acefruv, Tib.*   806 uirtutem . . . factis *Mabfrt, Dosith.*
422. 17, *Seru.* (*cf. A.* x 468): uirtute . . . uires *PRcdesuv, P. Colt*
2, *utrumque agnoscit Tib.*: uirtutem . . . uires *hγ, Diom.* 417. 14
809 noscon *R*   810 primum *b*

missus in imperium magnum. cui deinde subibit
otia qui rumpet patriae residesque mouebit
Tullus in arma uiros et iam desueta triumphis
agmina. quem iuxta sequitur iactantior Ancus   815
nunc quoque iam nimium gaudens popularibus auris.
uis et Tarquinios reges animamque superbam
ultoris Bruti, fascisque uidere receptos?
consulis imperium hic primus saeuasque securis
accipiet, natosque pater noua bella mouentis   820
ad poenam pulchra pro libertate uocabit,
infelix, utcumque ferent ea facta minores:
uincet amor patriae laudumque immensa cupido.
quin Decios Drusosque procul saeuumque securi
aspice Torquatum et referentem signa Camillum.   825
illae autem paribus quas fulgere cernis in armis,
concordes animae nunc et dum nocte premuntur,
heu quantum inter se bellum, si lumina uitae
attigerint, quantas acies stragemque ciebunt,
aggeribus socer Alpinis atque arce Monoeci   830
descendens, gener aduersis instructus Eois!
ne, pueri, ne tanta animis adsuescite bella
neu patriae ualidas in uiscera uertite uiris;
tuque prior, tu parce, genus qui ducis Olympo,
proice tela manu, sanguis meus!—   835
ille triumphata Capitolia ad alta Corintho
uictor aget currum caesis insignis Achiuis.
eruet ille Argos Agamemnoniasque Mycenas
ipsumque Aeaciden, genus armipotentis Achilli,
ultus auos Troiae templa et temerata Mineruae.   840
quis te, magne Cato, tacitum aut te, Cosse, relinquat?
quis Gracchi genus aut geminos, duo fulmina belli,
Scipiadas, cladem Libyae, paruoque potentem

812–43 MPR   812 cui] qui M¹: quid R   819 primum M
824 Drusosque] Brutosque R   827 prementur P¹Rfhrtv:
premuntur MP²ω, Seru.   831 auersis M¹   837 currus
cefhsv, Tib. (cursus u)

Fabricium uel te sulco, Serrane, serentem?
quo fessum rapitis, Fabii? tu Maximus ille es,   845
unus qui nobis cunctando restituis rem.
excudent alii spirantia mollius aera
(credo equidem), uiuos ducent de marmore uultus,
orabunt causas melius, caelique meatus
describent radio et surgentia sidera dicent: 850
tu regere imperio populos, Romane, memento
(hae tibi erunt artes), pacique imponere morem,
parcere subiectis et debellare superbos.'
    Sic pater Anchises, atque haec mirantibus addit:
'aspice, ut insignis spoliis Marcellus opimis   855
ingreditur uictorque uiros supereminet omnis.
hic rem Romanam magno turbante tumultu
sistet eques, sternet Poenos Gallumque rebellem,
tertiaque arma patri suspendet capta Quirino.'
atque hic Aeneas (una namque ire uidebat   860
egregium forma iuuenem et fulgentibus armis,
sed frons laeta parum et deiecto lumina uultu)
'quis, pater, ille, uirum qui sic comitatur euntem?
filius, anne aliquis magna de stirpe nepotum?
qui strepitus circa comitum! quantum instar in ipso!   865
sed nox atra caput tristi circumuolat umbra.'
tum pater Anchises lacrimis ingressus obortis:
'o gnate, ingentem luctum ne quaere tuorum;
ostendent terris hunc tantum fata nec ultra
esse sinent. nimium uobis Romana propago   870
uisa potens, superi, propria haec si dona fuissent.
quantos ille uirum magnam Mauortis ad urbem
campus aget gemitus! uel quae, Tiberine, uidebis
funera, cum tumulum praeterlabere recentem!
nec puer Iliaca quisquam de gente Latinos   875

844–57 *MPR*; 858–72 *FMPR*; 873–75 *MPR*   845 gressum
R   tun *P*[1]   846 restitues *Rbcr*   848 credo (*A*. iv 12)
MP[2]*Rω*: cedo (*A*. ii 704) *P*[1] (caedo *d*), *Aug. c.d.* v 12   852 mores
Aug.   859 tristiaque *R*   865 qui *FPabceruv*: quis *MRdfhst*
ipso est *dəhrtuv*   869 nec *MRb*: neque *FPω*

in tantum spe tollet auos, nec Romula quondam
ullo se tantum tellus iactabit alumno.
heu pietas, heu prisca fides inuictaque bello
dextera! non illi se quisquam impune tulisset
obuius armato, seu cum pedes iret in hostem 880
seu spumantis equi foderet calcaribus armos.
heu, miserande puer, si qua fata aspera rumpas!
tu Marcellus eris. manibus date lilia plenis
purpureos spargam flores animamque nepotis
his saltem accumulem donis, et fungar inani 885
munere.' sic tota passim regione uagantur
aëris in campis latis atque omnia lustrant.
quae postquam Anchises natum per singula duxit
incenditque animum famae uenientis amore,
exim bella uiro memorat quae deinde gerenda, 890
Laurentisque docet populos urbemque Latini,
et quo quemque modo fugiatque feratque laborem.

Sunt geminae Somni portae, quarum altera fertur
cornea, qua ueris facilis datur exitus umbris,
altera candenti perfecta nitens elephanto, 895
sed falsa ad caelum mittunt insomnia Manes.
his ibi tum natum Anchises unaque Sibyllam
prosequitur dictis portaque emittit eburna.
ille uiam secat ad nauis sociosque reuisit.

Tum se ad Caietae recto fert limite portum. 900
ancora de prora iacitur; stant litore puppes.

876–8 MPR; 879–901 FMPR   885 inanis F¹M¹   889 ueni-
entis] melioris (A. iv 221) M   897 his ibi FP²(hibi P¹)Rω:
his ubi (A. v 816, vii 373) Mbct, Probus 248. 5, Tib.   898 inmit-
tit aeuγ   900 limite recc.: litore codd., Seru. ad A. iii 16, viii 57
901 (= A. iii 277) eiecit Bentley

COMMENTARY

1–13. *The Trojans land at Cumae: Aeneas goes straight to Apollo's temple, to seek a prophecy from the Sibyl.*

A brisk introduction. The crews attend to essentials, securing the ships, seeing to water-supplies and fuel. Aeneas has his own duty, and the apocalyptic function of the book is at once seen.

1. sic fatur: similarly *Il.* 7. 1 ὡς εἰπών, *Od.* 13. 1 ὡς ἔφαθ'; the reference is to Aeneas' grief for Palinurus (5. 870 f.); with *lacrimans* cf. *Il.* 1. 357 ὡς φάτο δάκρυ χέων.

Servius states, on 5. 871, that Virgil left this and the next line to conclude book 5, and that Tucca and Varius transferred them to the start of book 6; he adds (here) that 'Probus et alii' left them in their original place. If this is true, the change can only have been made with Virgil's approval, or in the knowledge that his own placing of the lines was tentative, pending a final shaping of the beginning of book 6; for it is probable that the Palinurus-episode which ends book 5 was composed later than the sixth book (see R. D. Williams, *Aen.* 5, xxv ff.). But it is an unsatisfactory story: why suppose that Virgil himself did not see at once that book 5 ends perfectly and beautifully without the two added lines, and that book 6 begins smoothly and naturally with them (as Servius realized)? Nettleship doubts the truth of it, with reason: he suggests that it was invented by Virgil's critics ('Probus et alii') to justify a pedantic rearrangement of their own. For a defence of Probus' action see Ribbeck, *Prolegomena*, 95.

immittit habenas: Aeneas (now at the helm of his own ship; see 5. 868) gives the fleet its head, as it were, slackening the sheets for speed before the wind: cf. 8. 707 f. 'ipsa uidebatur uentis regina uocatis / uela dare et laxos iam iamque immittere funis', Val. Flacc. 1. 687 'uolat immissis caua pinus habenis'. The metaphor is often used to express the release of energy: e.g. 5. 662 (of fire), 12. 499 (of anger), *G.* 2. 363 f. 'dum se laetus ad auras / palmes agit laxis per purum immissus habenis' (which looks back to Lucr. 5. 786 f. 'arboribusque datumst uariis exinde per auras / crescendi magnam immissis certamen habenis').

2. tandem: after all the dangers and all the longing: 'ad Aeneae desiderium retulit, olim ad Italiam uenire cupientis' (Servius).

Euboicis . . . oris : the epithet is transferred from *Cumarum*
to *oris*; cf. 9. 710 'Euboico Baiarum litore'. Such trans-
ference is a conscious stylistic ornament (occasionally also
in prose, e.g. Livy 2. 51. 7 'hesterna felicitate pugnae ferox'),
designed for variety and pleasure. Its practical advantage for
metre is obvious, especially where proper names are involved:
here *Euboicarum* could not have stood, and in 57 'Dardana
. . . Paridis . . . tela' the device resolves the impossibility of
Dardani. Sometimes it serves euphony, e.g. 8. 526 'Tyrrhe-
nusque tubae . . . clangor', Lucr. 1. 474 'Alexandri Phrygio
sub pectore'.
See O. Hey, *ALL* xiv, 105 ff.; Löfstedt, *Synt.* ii, 110;
W. Headlam, *CR* xvi (1902), 434 ff. (with many Greek
examples); HSz, 159 f.; Fraenkel on Aesch. *Ag.* 504; Pearson
on Soph. *frg.* 734; cf. 268, note.
  Cumarum : the landing is where Helenus had foretold
(3. 441). Cumae was the earliest Greek colony in Italy,
founded from Chalcis in Euboea about 750 B.C.; *Euboicis*
here is anachronistic. For its history and commerce see
Ogilvie on Livy 2. 14. 4, 2. 21. 5; C. G. Hardie, *PBSR* xxxvii
(1969), 17 f.; A. Maiuri, *The Phlegraean Fields*[4] (Rome,
1969), 106 ff. (with the archaeology of the region); cf. C.
Saunders, *Vergil's primitive Italy* (New York, 1930), R. V.
Schoder, *C.J.* lxvii (1971–2), 97 ff.
  adlabitur : Epic convention: cf. 3. 131 'antiquis Curetum
adlabimur oris', 3. 569 'Cyclopum adlabimur oris'.
  oris : the 'orae' of Cumae, the 'litora' (4) and 'litus' (6)
have generally been taken to be the sandy beach below and
to the west of the acropolis and lower city of Cumae, at the
southern end of the grand curve of the bay of Gaeta. But it
has been objected that the beach was, and is, open and ex-
posed to wind and wave. Strabo (5. 4. 4) mentions the view
that the name Cumae was derived by some from the waves,
κύματα, because the shore is ῥαχιώδης καὶ προσεχής. In antiquity
the sea washed the foot of the acropolis, as Agathias, *Hist.*
1. 8, mentions. The sea is now 200 m. from the west point
of the acropolis and 500 m. from where the acropolis and
lower city meet. This alteration is due in part to 'bradyseism',
the slow rise and fall of level, and also the accumulation of
sand on the beach, washed southwards by the current, as is
clear from Seneca, *Epp.* 55. 2: the 'narrow way' between the
sea and the Palus Acherusia, Lago Fusaro, is now 300–400 m.
wide. But there must have been south of the western spur
of the acropolis—the spur consists of lava, whereas all the
rest of Cumae is tufa—a protected bay, which the Cumaeans
later made into a regular harbour (according to R. F. Paget,

JRS lviii (1968), 152 ff., *Vergilius* xiv (1968), 4 ff.). So Virgil could imagine Aeneas' ships beached safely enough just under the Temple of Apollo and the 'Sibyl's Cave'.

3–8. The structure is planned to suggest swift, alert action. The pauses are effectively varied, and the movement is brought to rest in a full line without a pause. Alliteration is sharp, and the spondaic rhythm for the cumbrous work of beaching the ships contrasts with the dactyls as the men hurry out to their exploratory jobs.

3. obuertunt . . . proras : the ships' prows are turned seawards, ready for a launching when needed.

    dente : so of a ploughshare (*G.* 1. 262) and of a pruning-knife (*G.* 2. 406); cf. Livy 37. 30. 9 'ancora ictu ipso excussa e naue sua unco dente, uelut ferrea manu iniecta, adligauit alterius proram'.

    tenaci : cf. 12. 404 'prensatque tenaci forcipe ferrum' (of a surgeon probing a wound). Adjectives in -*ax* mark persistence, often excessive: a horse is *sternax* (12. 364), a dog *mordax* (Plaut. *Bacch.* 1146), an extravagant girl *emax* (Ovid, *ars* 1. 421), a slave abuses a *leno* as *procax, rapax, trahax,* and in return is called *edax, furax, fugax* (Plaut. *Persa* 410, 421). See S. De Nigris Mores, *Acme* xxv (1972), 263 ff., for a full list and discussion.

4. ancora : post-Homeric; Homer's ships used perforated anchor-stones (εὐναί), to which cables were attached (*Il.* 1. 436, etc.): see Morrison and Williams, *Greek Oared Ships* (Cambridge, 1968), 56 ff.

    fundabat : the tense marks the continuing process of making the ships fast, one after another. For *fundare* in this sense cf. Claudian 17. 113 'iam tibi compositam fundauerat ancora puppim' (a metaphorical ship); elsewhere it is used of laying the keel, as in Ovid, *ex Pont.* 4. 3. 5 'dum mea puppis erat ualida fundata carina' (again metaphorical). The arrangement with *ancora* as subject is partly for variety of construction, partly because only the nominative singular is possible in hexameters.

5. praetexunt : vivid; the ships form a decorative border to the shore; cf. Lucan 10. 537 'densae praetexunt litora classes', in a passage of high rhetoric; Ovid, *ars* 1. 255 'quid referam Baias praetextaque litora Baiis?'; Stat. *S.* 4. 4. 7 'suburbanisque uadum praetexitur hortis', where the decorative idea is clear.

    emicat : of quick, flashing movement, with *ardens* carefully chosen to suit the verb; cf. 5. 318 f. 'Nisus / emicat et uentis et fulminis ocior alis', 12. 325 ff. 'spe feruidus ardet; / poscit equos atque arma simul, saltuque superbus / emicat in currum' (of Turnus).

6. **Hesperium** : 'Hesperia', the Western Land, was the Greek name for Italy (see on 1. 530; Nisbet–Hubbard on Hor. *C.* 1. 28. 26), first used in Latin by Ennius (*Ann.* 23). The Trojans have reached their final goal, foretold by Creusa (2. 781 'terram Hesperiam uenies') and by the Penates (3. 163 'est locus, Hesperiam Grai cognomine dicunt').

    semina flammae : cf. *Od.* 5. 490, a countryman buries a smouldering torch in ashes σπέρμα πυρὸς σώζων: so Lucr. 6. 160 f. 'fulgit item, nubes ignis cum semina multa / excussere suo concursu'; Ovid, *Met.* 15. 347 f. 'habentem semina flammae / materiam iactant'.

    The search for basic necessities is described with Epic dressing; but it reflects also Virgil's feeling for what nature provides.

7. **abstrusa . . . silicis** : cf. *G.* 1. 135 'ut silicis uenis abstrusum excuderet ignem' (one of Iuppiter's plans for men's good). For the methodical and anxious process of fire-lighting see 1. 174 ff.; for kindling in general see L. A. Moritz, *OCD²*, s.v. *Fire*.

7 f. **densa . . . siluas** : the *ferarum tecta* are explained by *siluas* in apposition, an arrangement that Virgil likes (again, 10 f.): so 10. 601 'latebras animae pectus', *E.* 2. 11 'alia serpyllumque herbas', *G.* 2. 442 f. 'utile lignum / nauigiis pinus'. For a more complex appositional pattern see on 842 f. 'geminos, duo fulmina belli, / Scipiadas'.

    The Silva Gallinaria, a dense forest of pine, is mentioned by Cicero, *fam.* 9. 23, Strabo 5. 4. 4, Juvenal 3. 307, and Maiuri speaks of hunts in it until quite recently. Virgil seems to have thought of the whole region, uninhabited apart from the Sibyl, as densely wooded, like the crater of Avernus until Agrippa felled the trees in 37–36 B.C.

8. **rapit** : intentionally violent, to describe the raiding of the forest for wood, *lignatio* ('quae maxime necessaria est ad cibum coquendum', Vitruv. 5. 9. 8): Henry notes Silius 3. 189 f. 'iugis rapiens siluas ac robora uasto / contorta amplexu' (of a huge serpent), Stat. *Th.* 7. 627 'rapuit nemus et montes patefecit opacos' (of a wind). Others think that the woods are beaten for game; but *ferarum tecta* is only a picturesque detail to show the density of the trees (cf. 179 'itur in antiquam siluam, stabula alta ferarum').

    inuentaque . . . monstrat : for *inuenit et monstrat*, by the useful idiom in which the action of one verb is expressed participially as the object of another. The men dramatically point to their discovery of water (for cooking as well as for drinking; Virgil now describes *aquatio*).

    In the whole area of the Campi Phlegraei there is nothing

that could be described as a river, though it is bounded on
the north by the Clanius (*G*. 2. 225) and on the east by the
Sebethus (*A*. 7. 734). The Odyssean Nekyia had to encounter
this difficulty when transported to Avernus; Virgil has
wisely placed Homer's four rivers all in the Underworld.

9. **at pius Aeneas** : virtually a transition-formula (232, 1. 305,
4. 393¦ 7. 5, 12. 311); so 'tum pius Aeneas', 5. 26, 5. 685, 10.
783, 12. 175. Aeneas knows his duty; this was the bidding
of his father's ghost (5. 731 ff.), and what Helenus had fore-
told (3. 441 ff.); for some aspects of *pietas* see on 1. 10, 4. 393.

    arces : is this a plural of grandeur (as at 19, 26, 32, 41) or
a reference to the two sites of temples on the acropolis of
Cumae, as Norden takes it, although the temple of Apollo
is on the lower terrace to the south and the god does not seem
to preside over the whole? It is not known to whom the
temple on the summit or upper terrace was dedicated, but it
is usually presumed to be Zeus: Livy 27. 23. 2 says 'Cumis
. . . in aede Iouis', but without specifying the *arx*, as he does
when speaking of the temple of Apollo at 43. 13. 4. Servius
assumes one temple, Apollo's, on the summit: 'cum ubique
arx Ioui detur, apud Cumas in arce Apollinis templum est';
so Livy 43. 13. 4 'Cumis in arce Apollo . . . lacrimauit'. The
lower temple to the south is thought to have been Apollo's on
the evidence of a Samnite (Oscan) inscription found by
Maiuri in 1912, but never published and now lost. This temple
is near to what is now generally accepted to be the Cave of
the Sibyl, whereas the other is at a considerable distance,
about 300 m. from it. Virgil imagined his anachronistic
temple of Apollo as alone on the acropolis (as yet an un-
fortified hill) and to anyone approaching from the south
(there was no paved road from the north through the forest
until Domitian built his Via Domitiana) the temple of Apollo
would have been more prominent, half concealing the other
temple beyond it. But Statius (*S*. 3. 4. 114–15), approach-
ing from Rome, says 'fine uiae recentis imo / qua monstrat
ueteres Apollo Cumas'.

    The acropolis at Cumae is quite distinct from the lower
hill to the south on which the greater part of the Greek city
was sited, and Greek Cumae, with its upper and lower cities,
may well have served Virgil as a model for his Troy. The
acropolis is the remaining eastern fragment of a volcanic
crater, otherwise completely eroded by the sea, at the west
end of the elliptical hill, about 400 m. E.–W. and 200 m.
N.–S.; it is 80 m. high at its rounded top, with steep, even
sheer, sides, except on the SE. where a lower, 60 m. high,
triangular terrace projects southwards to a spur that over-

looks the Greek city to the south, and the Samnite–Roman city to the east on the plain. In Virgil's time both acropolis and lower city were ringed with curtain walls and towers at intervals.

A tower on the south spur of the acropolis guarded the only entrance to it, the so-called 'Via Sacra' that led from the lower city and the harbour below. The tower, ultimately Greek of the late sixth century, remains, but the gate to the west of it, and probably another, twin tower, perished in the siege of the Goths by Narses in A.D. 552.

altus : probably not conventional, but stressing the rocky height of Apollo's guardian shrine. Servius alternatively explains the epithet by reference to Apollo's outsize wooden statue: 'uel ad simulacri magnitudinem retulit, quod esse constat altissimum. (DServius) Caelius enim de Cumano Apolline ait ibi in fano signum Apollinis ligneum, altum non minus pedes xv; cuius meminisse putatur Vergilius'. This statue was notorious for its ominous sweating: Cicero, *diu.* 1. 98; Livy 43. 13. 4; Florus 1. 25. 3 (195 B.C.); Julius Obsequens 28, 54 (114 B.C.); Augustine, *CD* 3. 11.

10. **horrendae** : of religious awe ('uenerandae', Servius); cf. Livy 1. 16. 6 (Proculus narrating the apparition of Romulus) 'cum perfusus horrore uenerabundusque adstitissem petens precibus ut contra intueri fas esset'. On a lower plane, Camilla is *horrenda* (11. 507; '*horrenda* pro *admirabilis*', DServius): contrast the repulsion in 298 'portitor ... horrendus' (Charon); cf. Ovid, *Met.* 4. 782, 13. 760 (Medusa, Polyphemus). Lucretius (3. 28 f.) fuses this religious awe with a thrill of delight, 'his ibi me rebus quaedam diuina uoluptas / percipit atque horror'; a further stage is reached in Stat. *Th.* 1. 493 f. 'obtutu gelida ora premit, laetusque per artus / horror iit' (after an omen), Silius 8. 561 'gratusque inerat uisentibus horror' (of Scipio's demeanour).

procul : 'apart'; cf. 651, 10. 835 f. 'procul aerea ramis / dependet galea' (the wounded Mezentius has hung his helmet on a handy tree); Ovid, *Met.* 4. 357, 'ueste procul iacta mediis immittitur undis' (Salmacis, bathing, has tossed her clothes a little way from the water). Norden quotes *E.* 6. 16 'serta procul tantum capiti delapsa iacebant' (where the wreath cannot have fallen far from the drunken Silenus). Servius says that *procul* has a double meaning, 'near' and 'far', and gives an unacceptable double derivation ('prae oculis' and 'porro ab oculis'). This is a way of saying that 'at a distance', 'apart', is relative to the situation. It is not clear whether Servius' difficulty is based on any topographical knowledge. Obviously the Sibyl's *antrum* was not 'far off', whatever view is taken of its relation to the temple (see on 42 ff.). Conington suggested referring *procul* to the depth of the cavern, 'far-stretching' (but such a close conjunction with *secreta* is against the rhythm). Henry connected it with *petit*, referring it to Aeneas' separation from his men (ingenious, but too strained).

Norden accepted the Crypta Romana as the *secreta Sibyllae*, i.e. Cocceius' tunnel at ground level, below where the *arx* and lower city meet, some 46 m. below the stylobate of the temple. This seems too far, if Aeneas is to be imagined as reaching the Cave from inside the Temple. It is more natural if Maiuri's Antro be accepted as the Cave, but even then the descent would be some 28 m. vertically and 87 m. horizontally from the *cella* of the temple to below the surface of the lower city, presumably negotiated by means of a staircase cut in the tufa of the *arx*, the existence of which has been asserted and denied. For further discussion of the problem of the spatial relationship of the Temple to the Cave see below on 42 ff. *Procul* warns us of a transition to be imagined κατὰ τὸ σιωπώμενον (Servius on Achates, 34).

secreta : 'retreat'; a metrically convenient plural; cf. 8. 463 'hospitis Aeneae sedem et secreta petebat', *G.* 4. 403 'in secreta senis ducam'.

Sibyllae : 'the Sibyl' was originally a single prophetess, who became localized in various places, and the name gradually came to be generic: see K. F. Smith on Tib. 2. 5. 15, 67–80. Varro listed ten Sibyls (ap. Lactant. *Inst.* 1. 6. 8 ff.). The Sibyl of Cumae is first mentioned in Lycophron 1278 (from Timaeus; see Latte, *Röm. Religionsgesch.* 160 n. 1); it was from her that Tarquinius Superbus bought the original *libri Sibyllini*, which played such a significant part in Roman ritual. Virgil seems to have been the first to connect her with the legend of Aeneas. For the *libri* see on 71; for Virgil's handling of the Sibyl-theme see references in Hardie, *PBSR* xxxvii (1969), 24 n. 44.

11. **antrum immane :** for the apposition with *secreta* see on 7 f. Virgil introduced the noun, for the Greek ἄντρον (see Norden, and cf. G. Williams, *Tradition and Originality in Roman Poetry* [Oxford, 1968], 652 f.). For the *antrum* see on 42 ff.; *immane* marks not simply its huge size, but also its frightening awe.

cui : its placing at this point avoids a spondaic disyllable in the fourth foot (cf. 1. 602 'gentis Dardaniae, magnum quae sparsa per orbem'): see on 1. 1, with references.

mentem animumque : an abnormal line-ending, directly reminiscent of Lucretius, giving an archaic tone suited to the context. The collocation of *mens* ('understanding') and *animus* ('mind') occurs in Ennius, *Sc.* 237; it is especially Lucretian (Lucr. 1. 74, 3. 142, etc.): *mens* is intellectual only, *animus* includes the emotions (Kenney on Lucr. 3. 94).

12. **Delius . . . uates** : Apollo, who is Iuppiter's prophet: cf. 3. 251 f. 'quae Phoebo pater omnipotens, mihi Phoebus Apollo / praedixit, uobis Furiarum maxima pando', Aesch. *Eum.* 19 Διὸς προφήτης δ' ἐστὶ Λοξίας πατρός.

   inspirat : of actual afflatus (cf. 50); the Sibyl is 'breathed into' by Apollo: so Hesiod, *Th.* 31 f. (of the Muses) ἐνέπνευσαν δέ μοι αὐδὴν / θέσπιν, ἵνα κλείοιμι τά τ' ἐσσόμενα πρό τ' ἐόντα.

13. **iam subeunt** : 'presently they approach'; the change to the plural is Virgil's way of showing that Aeneas took companions with him, one of whom was Achates (34).

   Triuiae : Hecate τριοδῖτις, the chthonic form of Apollo's sister Diana, served likewise by the Sibyl (35). This association in the cult at Cumae seems to be a Virgilian innovation, preparing for the Sibyl's special function, granted her by Hecate, as priestess in charge of the Underworld and so guide to Aeneas (cf. 118).

   tecta : Virgil prefers the plural, which is metrically more flexible than the singular, especially with an epithet (with *aurea* here cf. *regia*, 1. 631; *frondea*, G. 4. 61; *daedala*, G. 4. 179), or in a prepositional phrase (e.g. 211).

   Aurea tecta, of which Servius says 'Apollinis scilicet', would not be appropriate to the Cave or the dwelling of the Sibyl—unless she lives at Avernus, as some infer from 211, *tecta Sibyllae*. The sacred groves of Hecate may in Virgil's fancy have surrounded both the Temple of Apollo and the Cave; Servius assumes the existence of a temple of Diana in her grove: 'congrue Apollini Dianae iuncta sunt templa'. But is the grove here the same as the *luci* at 118 and 564, and has Virgil simply made Cumae and Avernus (as well as Misenum) virtually contiguous? Such compression of space makes it the more plausible that the Sibyl should have a double office, as priestess of Apollo at Cumae and of Hecate at Avernus, perhaps in one continuous 'lucus Triviae'. The unity of the action is thus better secured. Bertha Tilly, *Gnomon* xlvii (1975), 362–8, reviewing F. della Corte, *La mappa dell'Eneide*, speaks of Virgil's habit of 'telescoping, even ignoring, distances'; 'the epic must move quickly, against a background of omissions'. For similar telescoping see notes on 42 ff., 201, 899.

   When the grove of Hecate was taken to be at Avernus, the temple of Apollo had to be there too, and it was identified . with what to us are obviously the remains of Thermae of imperial date on the eastern edge of the lake. Heyne rejected this identification and proposed instead the Arco Felice on the crater rim of Avernus, well to the east of even Samnite–Roman Cumae and now known to be Domitian's glorification of his new road. Likewise the cave at Cumae was popularly confused with that at Avernus, and already Servius (on 237) condemns this confusion, which is due to Virgil's invention of a double function for the Sibyl, as Norden saw in his second edition.

14–41. *The history of the temple, and a description of the sculptures on its doors: the Trojans are raptly contemplating them, until the Sibyl arrives and austerely recalls Aeneas to present needs.*

This is an artful piece of poetic construction. The action is suspended, while Virgil takes the reader into his confidence with a stage-setting: the purpose of the description is not apparent until line 34. He uses the technique of ἔκφρασις to develop the visual and dramatic possibilities of what is in itself an everyday experience, the engagement of eyes or mind during a period of waiting: so in Ter. *Eun.* 583 f. a girl, waiting for her bath to be prepared, 'in conclaui sedet / suspectans tabulam quandam pictam'. It is the technique of 1. 441 ff., where the Trojans gaze at the scenes on Iuno's temple before Dido arrives: but there the subjects are drawn from what to them was contemporary history, a deeply emotional experience; here, Aeneas is confronted with a dark and legendary past, scenes of murder and punishment and criminal passion. In this way, at the very outset of the Book, a sombre note is struck in preparation for the theme to come.

This form of ἔκφρασις, a description of a work of art, goes back to *Il.* 18. 478 ff. (Achilles' shield); in Hellenistic poetry cf. Theocr. 1. 29 ff. (a carved drinking-cup), Apoll. Rhod. 1. 721 ff. (Jason's cloak); Catullus used it for his embroidered quilt (64. 50 ff.); in Silver Epic cf. Silius 2. 406 ff. (armour given to Hannibal), Val. Flacc. 5. 410 ff. (Aeetes' palace). The classic list of ἐκφράσεις is in P. Friedländer's edition of *Johannes von Gaza und Paulus Silentiarius* (Berlin, 1912), 1–103.

14. Daedalus : artist and inventor, a mythical Leonardo: Ovid, *Met.* 8. 159 'ingenio fabrae celeberrimus artis'; Pausan. 2. 4. 5 Δαίδαλος δὲ ὁπόσα εἰργάσατο, ἀτοπώτερα μέν ἐστιν ἐς τὴν ὄψιν, ἐπιπρέπει δὲ ὅμως τι καὶ ἔνθεον τούτοις; for his works see Overbeck, *Die antiken Schriftquellen z. Gesch. d. bildenden Künste* (Leipzig, 1868), 11 ff.; with Icarus he was often represented on Roman and Italic vases and gems (Beazley, *JHS* xlvii [1927],

222 ff.; cf. Hollis on Ovid, *Met.* 8. 183 ff.), and the flight is the subject of Pompeian wall-paintings (see Maiuri, *Pompeian Wall Paintings* [Berne, 1960], pl. v, and cf. L. P. Wilkinson, *Ovid Recalled* [Cambridge, 1955], 170). His legendary connexion with Cumae may go back through Varro to Timaeus (see Norden); his name at once invests the temple with an aura of marvel and antique mystery.

ut fama est : cf. Silius 12. 89 ff. 'cum bella timeret / Dictaei regis (sic fama est), linquere terras / Daedalus inuenit'. Such expressions are sometimes parenthetic, as here and 4. 179 ('ut perhibent'), sometimes integrated with the construction (1. 532 f. 'fama minores / Italiam dixisse', *G.* 4. 507 ff. 'illum ... perhibent ... flesse'); similarly there is variation between *fertur* with a personal construction (1. 15 f.) and *ferunt* with infinitive (284, 7. 765 ff.). They indicate that the poet is reporting a traditional tale (cf. Nisbet–Hubbard on Hor. *C.* 1. 7. 23), sometimes implying a variant tradition (see Norden), not scepticism: Servius, however, comments here 'ostendit requirendam esse ueritatem', misunderstanding the manner (so on 3. 78 'bene se fabulosam rem dicturus excusat'; see H. Georgii, *Die antike Aeneiskritik* [Stuttgart, 1891], 179). Norden infers a variant tradition here; but see Leo, *Hermes* xlii (1907), 68 ff. (= *Ausg. kl. Schriften* ii, 103 ff.). Heinze discusses such expressions, 240 ff.; cf. Bömer on Ovid. *F.* 2. 203.

fugiens : he had been imprisoned by Minos for his services to Pasiphae over her passion for a bull (alternatively, for the help that he gave to Ariadne in devising Theseus' escape from the Labyrinth). He escaped and flew off on his newly invented wings to Sicily (or, according to Servius, to Sardinia), where he ingeniously killed Minos who had pursued him (see Pearson, *Fragments of Sophocles* ii, 3 f.), after which he reached Cumae.

Minoia regna : the adjective formed from the name is in Epic style, replacing the genitive of the name itself; see on 2. 543. For the plural *regna* see on 1. 206, and note on *aurea tecta* (13).

15. **praepetibus pennis :** cf. 3. 360 f. (of Helenus) 'qui sidera sentis / et uolucrum linguas et praepetis omina pennae', Cic. poet. fr. 7. 9 ff. 'hanc ubi praepetibus pinnis lapsuque uolantem / conspexit Marius, diuini numinis augur, / faustaque signa suae laudis reditusque notauit'. *Praepes* was originally an augural t.t., perhaps = 'flying ahead', but the precise meaning was disputed in antiquity: see Servius on 3. 361, and the discussion in Gellius 7. 6, where the critic Iulius Hyginus (freedman of Augustus, librarian of the Palatine

Library) is recorded as censuring Virgil's use of the word
here in a non-augural context ('quasi inproprie et inscite di-
ctum'). Gellius duly snubs Hyginus, quoting *praepes Victoria*
from Matius (fr. 3 Morel), *praepetibus locis* and *praepete portu*
from Ennius (*Ann*. 94, 488); he might have noted also *prae-
pete ferro* (*Ann*. 407).

In these passages there still lurks the idea of 'well-omened',
'successful', and something of it is present in *praepetibus
pennis* here, even though the meaning 'swift' is dominant
(cf. 5. 254 f. 'praepes ab Ida / sublimem pedibus rapuit
Iouis armiger uncis'). But however Virgil understood the
word, the relevant point here is that he has deliberately
chosen to use an ancient and evocative term to add to the
awe associated with Daedalus. See Nettleship, *Contr. Lat.
Lex*., s.v. *praepes*; M. Wigodsky, *Vergil and early Latin poetry*,
112 f. (*Hermes*, Einzelschr. 24, 1972).

16. **insuetum :** 'novel'; he was the first man to fly: cf. Silius 5.
12 'insueta tubae monstrauit murmura primus' (of the in-
ventor of the trumpet). So *E*. 5. 56 'candidus insuetum
miratur limen Olympi' (Daphnis has never been to heaven
before).

   enauit : 'floated out'; so Silius 12. 94 f. 'suspensum hic
librans media inter nubila corpus / enauit, superosque nouus
conterruit ales' (of Daedalus): for the metaphor cf. Ennius,
Ann. 21 (of Venus) 'transnauit cita per teneras caliginis
auras', Lucr. 3. 591 (of the soul) 'prolapsa foras enaret in
aëris auras'; it was deprecated by Quintilian (8. 6. 18) for
use in oratory 'licet hoc Vergilius in apibus [*G*. 4. 59] ac
Daedalo speciosissime sit usus'.

   Arctos: hyperbole, to show the great height at which he flew;
DServius' comment shows that some critics saw an allusion
to the need to keep the wax-fitted wings cool. Or Virgil may
mean simply that Daedalus' course was northward from
Crete: then there is a smile in *gelidas*, which no more suits
the climate of the Bay of Naples than the wintry scene of
G. 4. 135 f. suits the home of the old gardener of Tarentum.

17. **Chalcidica . . . arce :** the rocky height of Cumae (cf. 9); the
epithet is anachronistic, like *Euboicis* (2), a point which Vir-
gil's knowing critic Hyginus pounced upon (Gellius 10. 16. 7)
but forgave. For the characteristic arrangement of epithet
and noun framing the line see Norden, Anh. iii. A. 1; they
enclose a syntactical unit (see T. E. V. Pearce, *CQ* n.s. xvi
[1966], 144 ff.).

   leuis : the substitution of adjective for adverb is a usage of
poetic style from early times; cf. 1. 301 'Libyae citus astitit
oris': see K–S i, 234 ff., Löfstedt, *Synt*. ii, 368 ff.

super : probably the adverb. Norden sees a reminiscence of Pindar, fr. 30 OCT σκοπιαῖσιν ... ὀρέων ὕπερ ἔστα.

The lack of enjambment in the four lines 14–17 gives a curiously quiet, factual effect, each detail occupying a single line.

18. primum: cf. 3. 209 f. 'seruatum ex undis Strophadum me litora primum / excipiunt': Daedalus was brought safely back to earth (*redditus*), and it was this part of earth that first received him; Virgil writes as if there had been no intermediate stop.

tibi ... sacrauit : Daedalus' dedication of his wings to Apollo marks his gratitude for a safe landing and also his retirement from air-travel, in the manner of many Greek dedicatory epigrams: e.g. *A P* 6. 70. 1 f. νῆά σοι, ὦ πόντου βασιλεῦ καὶ κοίρανε γαίης, / ἀντίθεμαι Κράντας, μηκέτι τεγγομένην; 6. 90, where a retired fisherman dedicates his anchor, oars, and other gear to Poseidon, λήξας τῆς ἐπ᾽ ἠόνων ἄλης. The apostrophe is a marked feature of the style.

19. remigium alarum : 'the oarage of his wings'; so 1. 300 f. (of Mercury) 'uolat ille per aëra magnum / remigio alarum'; cf. Ovid, *Met.* 8. 228 'remigioque carens non ullas percipit auras' (of Icarus, losing height). The metaphor looks back to Lucr. 6. 743 'remigi oblitae pennarum uela remittunt' (of birds), and to Aesch. *Ag.* 52 (of vultures) πτερύγων ἐρετμοῖσιν ἐρεσσόμενοι; cf. Eur. *Ion* 161 f. ὅδε πρὸς θυμέλας ἄλλος ἐρέσσει / κύκνος, *A P* 9. 287. 3, where ταρσός is used of an eagle's wing: see Hollis on Ovid, *Met.* l.c.

posuitque ... templa : an extension of *sacrauit*; the dedication was the primary purpose for which the temple was built. The plural *templa* perhaps suggests grandeur (cf. 3. 84 'templa dei saxo uenerabar structa uetusto'); the singular of the epithet would not have been intractable (as a singular sometimes is; cf. 13, note). *Immania* again suggests awe.

It is natural to suppose that Virgil imagined his Temple of Apollo as occupying the site of the temple which he saw standing there. He may indeed have believed that it was the very same temple (but without the sculptured reliefs), just as Pausanias (5. 16. 1) believed that the Heraeum at Olympia, of *c.* 650 B.C., the first monumental peripteral temple known to us, was built by Oxylus *c.* 1100 B.C. Of the temple of the Graeco-Samnite period the podium in blocks of the local tufa, 34·60 m. by 18·30 m., with no fragments of columns or *cella*, alone survives. Its orientation is 40° E. of N. and the cult statue would have looked out towards Ischia and the channel by which ships from Greece would have approached. The temple was probably peripteral, like any large Greek temple, and presumably belonged to the Greek period, *c.* 500 B.C., if it was built in association with the Cave of the Sibyl (see on 42 ff.). But on the SE. side there are remains of an earlier, smaller temple, probably also Apollo's, unless his ecstatic prophecy was deliberately imposed to oust an oracle of Hera, attested for the seventh or early sixth century by the celebrated disc ('Hera does not allow supplementary questions'): L. H. Jeffery, *The Local Scripts of Archaic Greece*, 1961, no. 5, p. 238; M. Guarducci, *Epigrafia greca* i (1967), 229 f., who speaks of Hera as 'deposed' by Apollo.

For its date the Temple scarcely deserves its epithet 'immane', as it cannot compete with the great temples in Sicily nor with the Capitolium of Rome. But, if projected back into the past still further than the Heraeum, it would indeed be a portent and an anachronism, especially as regards its sculptures: the great frieze of the temple of Hera Argiva at Paestum belongs to the first half of the sixth century B.C. The temple at Cumae was almost entirely rebuilt some time in the Augustan period, and also reorientated to face SE. over the Roman city. The rather larger temple on the summit or upper terrace (39·60 m. × 24·60 m.), dated to the mid-fifth century by Maiuri, was also rebuilt at this time.

The main motif now begins, as Virgil describes the detail of the sculptured scenes on the doors of the temple: two Athenian subjects faced by two Cretan subjects (23), with the latter rather more fully developed. As yet there is no indication of the connexion of these lines with the action of the book.

20. in foribus : similarly Silius 3. 32 'in foribus labor Alcidae' (of the temple of Hercules at Gades). For other sculptured doors cf. *G.* 3. 26 f. 'in foribus pugnam ex auro solidoque elephanto / Gangaridum faciam', and the elaborate and wonderful description of the Sun's palace in Ovid, *Met.* 2. 1–18.

Androgeo : Greek genitive: so Servius and the grammarians, for *Androgei* of the manuscripts; in 2. 392 the Latin genitive (of a different Androgeos) is supported by DServius and Charisius, with the manuscripts. Minos' son Androgeos was murdered in Athens by rivals whom he had defeated at the Panathenaic games; another tradition had him sent to fight the bull of Marathon, which killed him: see Frazer on Apollod. *Bibl.* 3. 15. 7.

tum : a new scene, the punishment exacted by Minos for the murder, an annual human offering to the Minotaur; most versions speak of seven young men and seven girls (cf. Ellis on Cat. 64. 78). Virgil's economy of language has its own pathos; contrast Cat. 64. 76 ff. 'nam perhibent olim crudeli peste coactam / Androgeoneae poenas exsoluere caedis / electos iuuenes simul et decus innuptarum / Cecropiam solitam esse dapem dare Minotauro'.

21. **Cecropidae** : the Athenians, descendants of Cecrops, their mythical first king. The patronymic form (not recorded earlier) has obvious metrical advantage as well as its learned allusiveness; cf. Callim. *h.* 4. 314 f. (in allusion to the same legend) ἔνθεν ἀειζώοντα θεωρίδος ἱερὰ Φοίβῳ / Κεκροπίδαι πέμπουσι τοπήια νηὸς ἐκείνης.

   miserum : 'dolentis interiectio', Servius: the poet's comment, like *nefas* (8. 688, of Cleopatra), *infandum* (*G.* 1. 479); so Tib. 2. 3. 78 'heu miserum'.

22. **corpora natorum** : for the periphrasis cf. 2. 18 'delecta uirum sortiti corpora' (Greeks in the Horse), 9. 272 f. 'lectissima matrum / corpora', 12. 270 f. 'nouem pulcherrima fratrum / corpora'; Ennius, *Ann.* 93 f. 'cedunt de caelo ter quattuor corpora sancta / auium': similarly Soph. *Tr.* 908 εἴ του φίλων βλέψειεν οἰκετῶν δέμας, Eur. *Phoen.* 1507 Σφιγγὸς ἀοιδοῦ σῶμα φονεύσας. The implication here is that they were a living sacrifice; contrast the mannered 'funera Cecropiae nec funera' of Cat. 64. 83.

   stat . . . urna : 'the lots have been drawn, there stands the urn': a vivid and grim vignette, from which the spectator (and today's reader) might imagine the agony of those young people, and of their parents, waiting for the ghastly draw. The *sortes* were small wooden slips or tablets; cf. Plaut. *Cas.* 384 'num ista aut populna sors aut abiegnast tua?': they would be shown on the ground, so that the viewer would grasp the situation at a glance, just as in 1. 474 'fugiens amissis Troilus armis', where Troilus' arms, dropped in his flight from Achilles, are represented lying on the ground in a picture on Iuno's temple at Carthage (see note ad loc.).

23. **contra** : on the other half of the folding doors; cf. Ovid, *Met.* 2. 18 'signaque sex foribus dextris totidemque sinistris' (in the Sun's palace). Crete, 'rising high from the sea', is the counterpart (*respondet*) to the Athenian scenes.

24. **crudelis . . . tauri** : cf. *E.* 6. 45 f. 'fortunatam, si numquam armenta fuissent, / Pasiphaen niuei solatur amore iuuenci'. Pasiphae, wife of Minos, daughter of the Sun, formed a passion for a noble bull, caused by Poseidon as vengeance on Minos for breaking a promise to sacrifice the bull to him: see Apollod. *Bibl.* 3. 1. 3 f. A papyrus fragment of Euripides' *Cretes* (C. Austin, *Noua Fragmenta Euripidea* [Berlin, 1968],

fr. 82) contains a spirited speech by Pasiphae, attacking
Minos for his perfidy; Ovid (*ars* 1. 289 ff.) treats the theme
in his decorative way, with such bland charm that its horror
is almost unnoticed. It is the subject of a Pompeian painting:
Maiuri, *Pompeian Wall Paintings*, pl. XI.

suppostaque furto: 'mated by trickery'; but *furto* also
implies secrecy and a 'stolen' amour. Daedalus contrived a
wooden cow, covered with the hide of a real cow, into which
he smuggled Pasiphae (Apollod. l.c.; cf. Ovid, *ars* 1. 325 f.,
Prop. 4. 7. 58 'mentitae lignea monstra bouis'). With the
syncopated form *supposta* cf. *repostas* (59), *repostos* (655),
compostus (1. 249), *imposta* (9. 716), *exposta* (10. 694); they
often serve metrical need (cf. 59, note), and Virgil may have
liked them as archaic (cf. Ennius, *inc.* 23, *repostus*; Lucilius
84, *compostae*): see Norden for their use by various poets
(Lucretius is especially fond of them).

25. mixtumque ... biformis : 'a hybrid birth, a two-shape
progeny'. Virgil may reflect Eur. *Cretes* fr. 80 (Austin)
σύμμικτον εἶδος κἀποφώλιον βρέφος, 81. 29 ταύρου μέμικται καὶ βροτοῦ
διπλῇ φύσει (both from Plutarch, *Thes.* 15); cf. Ovid, *Met.*
8. 155 f. 'foedumque patebat / matris adulterium monstri
nouitate biformis', 169 'geminam tauri iuuenisque figuram'.
Biformis is not recorded before Virgil.

26. Minotaurus : the name comes with sharp impact at last
after a crescendo of detail, first the passion, then mating,
then the monstrous birth. For Ovid's famous conceit (*ars* 2.
24 'semibouemque uirum semiuirumque bouem') see Sen.
Contr. 2. 2. 12.

monimenta : 'a reminder', not only to Pasiphae but to all
who saw the sight; the sense of 'warning' lurks. The plural is
due to metrical needs (cf. Prop. 4. 6. 17 'Actia Iuleae pelagus
monumenta carinae'); contrast 4. 497 f. 'abolere nefandi /
cuncta uiri monimenta iuuat' (Dido will destroy everything
that reminds her of Aeneas).

27. hic ... error : 'here is that laboriously wrought dwelling,
the maze without a clue': more elaborately, 5. 588 ff. (to
illustrate the *lusus Troiae*) 'ut quondam Creta fertur Laby-
rinthus in alta / parietibus textum caecis iter ancipitemque /
mille uiis habuisse dolum, qua signa sequendi / frangeret
indeprensus et inremeabilis error'. Both passages look back
to Cat. 64. 114 f. 'ne labyrintheis e flexibus egredientem /
tecti frustraretur inobseruabilis error'. Ovid embroiders the
picture in his own inventive way, likening the maze to the
windings of the Maeander (was this in Coleridge's mind when
he wrote 'five miles meandering with a mazy motion'?): see
Met. 8. 157 ff., ending 'ita Daedalus implet /
innumeras

errore uias; uixque ipse reuerti / ad limen potuit, tanta est fallacia tecti'.

labor ille domus : cf. 1. 455 f. 'operumque laborem / miratur' (Aeneas at Carthage), G. 2. 155 'tot egregias urbes operumque laborem'; Aesch. fr. 357 ὑψηλὸν . . . τεκτόνων πόνον.

inextricabilis : first in poetry here; Pliny (NH 36. 91) quotes from Varro a description of the Etruscan tomb of Lars Porsena, enclosing 'labyrinthum inextricabile, quo si quis introierit sine glomere lini, exitum inuenire nequeat'. The word makes a good rhythmic pattern for this context, though the line lacks the pointed metrical art of 5. 591 or of Cat. 64. 115 (see above).

error : cf. Apollod. Bibl. 3. 1. 4 (clearly embedding a passage from some drama, perhaps by Sophocles) ἦν δὲ ὁ λαβύρινθος, ὃν Δαίδαλος κατεσκεύασεν, οἴκημα καμπαῖς πολυπλόκοις πλανῶν τὴν ἔξοδον; Callim. h. 4. 311 γναμπτὸν ἕδος σκολιοῦ λαβυρίνθου. Pliny (NH 36. 85 f.) holds that Daedalus modelled his Labyrinth on that at Heracleopolis in Egypt (see Hdt. 2. 148), 'centesimam tantum portionem eius imitatum, quae itinerum ambages occursusque ac recursus inexplicabiles continet . . . crebris foribus inditis ad fallendos occursus redeundumque in errores eosdem'.

A. B. Cook (Zeus i, 472 ff.) interprets the Labyrinth as an *orchestra*, constructed for a mimetic dance, in which a dancer imitating the Sun masqueraded as a bull; cf. Hollis on Ovid, *Met.* 8. 158 ff. For a wide range of anthropological speculation see W. F. J. Knight, *Cumaean Gates* (Blackwell, Oxford, 1936). The representation of the Labyrinth in Virgil's context has been seen as symbolic of Aeneas' journey through the Underworld: cf. M. Verrall, *CR* xxiv (1910), 43 ff.; R. D. Williams, *Aeneid* 1–6, p. 459. ·

28 ff. In a somewhat abrupt transition Virgil turns to the associated legend of Ariadne's love for Theseus, to whom she gave the 'clue' devised by Daedalus for his escape from the Labyrinth after killing the Minotaur (see Frazer on Apollod. *Epit.* 1. 9). Possibly he did not conceive the scene as formally shown on the *fores*: the passage could be regarded as an interpretation rather than a description (cf. Gow on Theocr. 1. 34). This would ease the transition, and would lead naturally to the scene that is left specifically to the viewers' imagination, Icarus' death and his father's anguish.

28. reginae : the Princess Ariadne, Minos' daughter (her name was always troublesome for hexameters): *regina* is used similarly of Numitor's daughter Rhea Silvia (1. 273), and of Medea (Val. Flacc. 5. 373). In the single word *magnum* Virgil expresses what Catullus describes in nineteen highly coloured lines (64. 86 ff.).

sed enim : a Virgilian archaism (Quintilian 9. 3. 14), *enim* having its original asseverative force (see on 1. 19) : the maze was *inextricabilis*, but in fact (*sed enim*) Daedalus, its creator (*ipse*, 29) unravelled its mystery out of compassion for Ariadne. The postponement of the connective is a neoteric mannerism, taken over from Hellenistic usage (see on 1. 333; Norden, Anh. iii. B. 3): so *aut* (663), *et* (449), *nam* (667), *namque* (72, 117, 860), *sed* (315); *sed enim* (cf. 1. 19, 2. 164) could not, of course, have begun a line.

29. ambages : 'winding ways', as in Ovid, *Met.* 8. 161 'ducit in errorem uariarum ambage uiarum'; cf. Löfstedt, *Synt.* ii. 427; but the transferred meaning 'puzzle' is hinted at: see Nettleship, *Contr. Lat. Lex.*, s.v.

30. Cf. Cat. 64. 113 'errabunda regens tenui uestigia filo' (of Theseus); Ovid, *Her.* 10. 71 f. (Ariadne speaking) 'cum tibi, ne uictor tecto morerere recuruo, / quae regerent passus, pro duce fila dedi'; Prop. 2. 14. 7 f. 'nec sic incolumem Minois Thesea uidit, / Daedalium lino cum duce rexit iter': these passages make it clear that the *uestigia* here are those of Theseus, guided by Daedalus' clue. With *caeca* cf. Soph. *OC* 182 ἔπε' ὧδ' ἀμαυρῷ κώλῳ, Eur. *Hec.* 1050 τυφλὸν τυφλῷ στείχοντα παραφόρῳ ποδί. The dramatic break after *uestigia* ('bucolic diaeresis') marks an emotional pause before the pathetic apostrophe (which vividly suggests the viewers' sad imaginings).

31. sineret : for the ellipse of *si* cf. Ovid, *Met.* 9. 490 'omnia, di facerent, essent communia nobis'. There would now be (so they think) a representation of Icarus too, if Daedalus' grief had not been too great for him to make it.

32. bis conatus erat : sc. *pater*, inferred from *patriae* below. For *bis* in anaphora cf. 134 f., 11. 629 f., *G.* 2. 410 f.; so *ter*, 4. 690 f., a good illustration (like the present passage) of the dramatic, emotional use of the figure; see on 1. 78 ff.

casus : Icarus' fall; the plural is due to the metre: contrast 2. 10 'si tantus amor casus cognoscere nostros', where *casus* = 'sufferings'. Virgil has quietly left it till now to tell us that the artist's work was done in gold.

33. patriae : for the genitive *patris*; cf. 2. 539 'patrios foedasti funere uultus', Ovid, *ars* 2. 70 (of Daedalus) 'nec patriae lacrimas continuere genae': see on 2. 543 for further discussion of the idiom.

cecidere manus : a subtle play on *casus*. Ovid tells the story of the disastrous flight marvellously; in *Met.* 8. 210 f. he ingeniously recalls Virgil, 'inter opus monitusque genae maduere seniles, / et patriae tremuere manus' (Daedalus starting Icarus off). Virgil breaks off emotionally at *manus*, with another pregnant pause.

quin : for *quin etiam*, in a climax ('yes, even . . .'); so *G.* 4. 481 f. 'quin ipsae stupuere domus atque intima Leti / Tartara'.

protinus : with *omnia*, 'successively'; perhaps hinting at the literal meaning 'moving forward', as in *E.* 1. 12 f. 'capellas / protinus aeger ago': their eyes move from detail to detail.

omnia : disyllabic, by synizesis (with consonantal *-i-*): a remarkable 'licence', for which R has *omne*; so in 7. 237 the line ends 'uerba precantia', with like scansion (*precantum*, R). Ovid once has a similar synizesis in the sixth foot, but with a name (*Met.* 15. 718, *Antium*, likewise 'emended' by scribes). Macrobius (*Sat.* 5. 14. 4) ignorantly took Virgil's line to be hypermetric.

34. perlegerent oculis : cf. Ovid, *F.* 1. 591 'perlege dispositas generosa per atria ceras', Stat. *Th.* 3. 500 'perlegere animis oculisque sequacibus auras' (of seers). Now at last the purpose of the ἔκφρασις is made plain: all this time, the Trojans have been looking at the sculptures.

Achates : see on 1. 174, 188; he is Aeneas' messenger in 1. 644 f. 'rapidum ad nauis praemittit Achaten, / Ascanio ferat haec ipsumque ad moenia ducat'. His mission here is also introduced with casual subtlety.

36. Deiphobe : only here as a Sibyl's name: see Lactantius 1. 6. 8 ff. for other names for the Cumaean Sibyl, on the authority of Varro in his list of Sibyls; cf. J. H. Waszink, *Mnemos.* ser. 4, i (1948), 54.

Glauci : sc. *filia*; cf. 3. 319 'Hectoris Andromache' (sc. *uxor*): see K–S i, 414. The sea-god Glaucus had prophetic powers (cf. Pausan. 9. 22. 6); see Rothstein on Ovid, *Met.* 13. 898 ff.: he came from Anthedon, opposite Chalcis in Euboea, a connexion which presumably explains Virgil's allusive choice of the Cumaean Sibyl's name (Norden, p. 118). Virgil does not name her mother: was it Circe or Scylla?

37 ff. The Sibyl speaks sternly and abruptly: Virgil succeeds in giving her a personality of her own (cf. 539, with her rebuke to Palinurus, 373 ff., and her masterly management of Charon, 399 ff.). The Trojans have been taking time off, experiencing the pure pleasure of the beautiful and poignant sculptures: the Sibyl tells them, almost contemptuously, that this is no time to stand and stare.

38. A ritual sacrifice must be made at once to Apollo and Trivia, with male and female offerings: the bullocks must be untouched by the yoke (cf. *G.* 4. 540 'intacta . . . ceruice iuuencas'), the sheep must be of a particular age.

intacto : cf. Macrob. *Sat.* 3. 5. 5 'in his ipsis hostiis . . . quaedam sunt quae iniuges uocantur, id est quae numquam

domitae aut iugo subditae sunt'. The elision of *de* is most
unusual; so Lucilius 497 (*de isto*), Lucr. 3. 853 (*de illis*): see
J. Soubiran, *L'Élision dans la poésie latine* (Paris, 1966),
404 n. 3, where Norden's curious theory that this is syn-
izesis, not elision, is well rebutted.

mactare : a ritual word ('uerbum sacrorum', Servius on 4.
57). Norden notes that the number seven had special associa-
tions with the cult of Apollo.

39. praestiterit : a toned-down assertion (like ἄν+optative,
Conington), = 'it would be much more to the point'.

lectas...bidentis : so 4. 57 'mactant lectas de more bidentis',
5. 96 'caedit binas de more bidentis', 8. 544 'mactat lectas de
more bidentis'; Mynors's preference for *ex more* (F) needs
justifying (so also Sabbadini and Geymonat; 'fortasse
praestantius', Ribbeck). Norden rightly connects the ad-
verbial phrase with *mactare*, not (as some prefer) with *lectas*.

bidentis : a ritual term for a sheep which in its first year
has lost the two central of its eight 'milk' teeth; these are
replaced by two permanent teeth, so much bigger than the
rest that at first sight they alone seem present: see Henry and
Pease on 4. 57. Gellius records (16: 6) a discussion of its
meaning with an impostor (light entertainment after a nasty
sea-crossing), and quotes Hyginus' definition with approval,
'quae bidens est hostia, oportet habeat dentes octo, sed ex
his duo ceteris altiores, per quos appareat ex minore aetate in
maiorem transcendisse'.

40. talibus : sc. *uerbis*; so 1. 370, 410, 559, etc. (following a
speech), 10. 860 (introducing a speech): useful and economi-
cal.

40 f. nec . . . uiri : the orders are *sacra* because they are given
by a priestess. The parenthesis resembles an aside: Virgil
likes the device, sometimes (as here) to avoid holding up the
narrative, sometimes for variety or liveliness (cf. 406, 848,
852, 860 ff.), often in geographical or historical 'footnotes'
(see on 1. 109, and cf. 9. 388, 12. 134 f.). Contrast the full
ritual detail of 243 ff., the performing of the sacrifice en-
joined in 153, a careful account such as the crucial context
needs.

42–76. *The Trojans come to the entrance of a vast cavern, from
which the oracles issue. The Sibyl, with the divine afflatus be-
ginning to work upon her, bids Aeneas pray, and he obeys.*

The effect of mystery and awe which Virgil has been creat-
ing is continued in the immediate ἔκφρασις of the *antrum*, in
which the poet has imaginatively blended with the mythical
tradition elements of contemporary reality.

The identification of Virgil's Cave of the Sibyl with specific parts of the complex archaeological substructure of Cumae has been a difficult and complicated process. Until 1932 the so-called 'Crypta Romana' was generally accepted as the Cave, even by Maiuri when he began to clear it in 1926. This is a cavernous passage rather than a cave, open at both ends and with no final *adytum*; it is 180 m. long, situated south of the acropolis, and slopes slightly S. of W. from the Samnite–Roman city, descending from about 8 m. above sea-level to about 3 m. at the site of the harbour. It can now be identified as one of the five tunnels which formed part of the vast naval base which M. Vipsanius Agrippa, with Cocceius as engineer, organized in 37–36 B.C. to build and train a new fleet for Octavian in his war against Sextus Pompeius. The centre of the base was Lake Avernus, transformed into the Portus Iulius by a canal to Lake Lucrinus, but the whole stretch of the Campi Phlegraei from Naples to Cumae was included by the improved communications that the construction of five tunnels through the tufa hills provided. Virgil celebrates the Portus Iulius in *G*. 2. 161–4 as one of the wonders of Italy, with no hint that any ancient sanctity was being violated at Avernus. All five tunnels were ascribed in the Middle Ages to Virgil the Magician: cf. D. Comparetti, *Virgilio nel Medio Evo*, 18, and G. Pasquali's edition, Florence 1943, xxii, for the learned, not popular Neapolitan, origin of these legends. Two of the tunnels, at the north and south ends of Posillipo, between Naples and Pozzuoli, do not concern us; but the remaining two are cut through the rim of the crater of Lake Avernus. One of these, running NW.–SE. for 1 km., points almost exactly to the east end of the Crypta Romana and thus reinforces its identification as Agrippa's work. The other, 200 m. long, runs due south from the shore of Lake Avernus (where extensive remains of Agrippa's dockyard may be seen) to Lake Lucrinus, ending in a circular vestibule, near which a corridor slopes west to a series of underground rooms, now owing to bradyseism under water. These until recently were shown, and perhaps still are, as the Grotto of the Sibyl. The western part of the Crypta Romana, below the bastion of the acropolis, is now roofless and its collapse, which carried with it the north end of the Cave of the Sibyl, can be assigned to Narses' siege of the Goths in the acropolis in A.D. 552.

The 'Antro' which Maiuri discovered in 1932 has come to be generally accepted as what Virgil must have seen and believed to be the Sibyl's cave. It corresponds closely enough to Virgil's description to warrant acceptance, and more

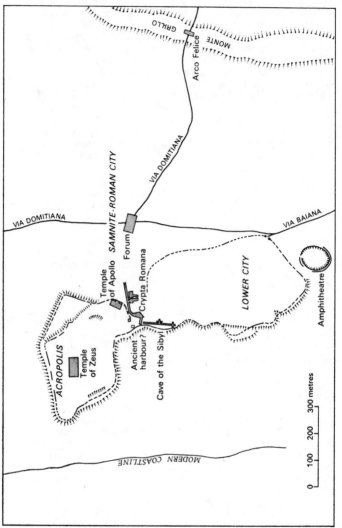

FIG. 2. Cumae

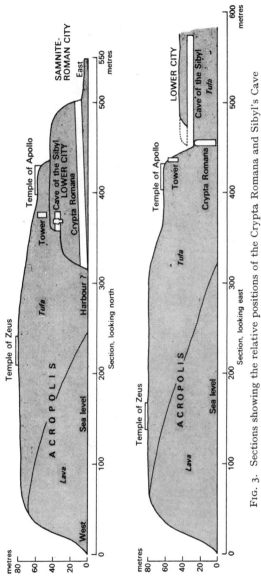

FIG. 3. Sections showing the relative positions of the Crypta Romana and Sibyl's Cave

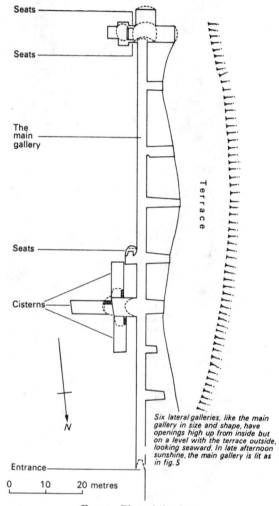

Seats

Seats

The
main
gallery

Seats

Cisterns

N

Terrace

Six lateral galleries, like the main
gallery in size and shape, have
openings high up from inside but
on a level with the terrace outside,
looking seaward. In late afternoon
sunshine, the main gallery is lit as
in fig. 5

Entrance

0   10   20 metres

Fig. 4. Plan of the Cave

closely than the Crypta Romana. The *limen* and *fores* have
perished, but there is no room for anything as elaborate as
the *aditus centum, ostia centum* of which Virgil speaks, a
piece of poetic heightening to convey Aeneas' feeling of awe

FIG. 5. A section of the Cave

and wonder. But what survives is unique and impressive in
its austere grandeur and ends in a recognizable *adyton*.

This subterranean structure, still not adequately published
with detailed plans and sections, is now 131·5 m. long (it
could have been some 7 m. longer), but roofless for its first
25 m. It is entirely man-made, cut in the yellow Neapolitan
tufa to a striking archaic section. It lies, where roofed, just
below the surface of the *lower* city, about 40 m. above sea-
level, under its western edge, where it sloped, or fell steeply,

to the site of the harbour. It runs southwards, precisely 5° W. of S.

On the west side of the main 'dromos' at regular intervals are eight lateral passages of the same section as the dromos (and also two other narrower passages), of which six have windows 0·6 m. square, about 3 m. above the present floor-level, and externally now on a level with the long terrace on which they give. This terrace, whether ancient or modern, is shaped like a willow leaf and extends the whole length of the dromos; it is 25 m. at its widest. Johannowski (971, 2) attributes the windows to the Roman period, but gives no reason. A passage as long as this without light or air seems unlikely; and the effect at sunset, when the section of the dromos is six times picked out by its rays, is impressive. On the east side of the dromos, opposite the third windowed lateral passage, is a round-vaulted passage with three trapezoidal offshoots, later and more probably in the Roman period converted into cisterns. Opposite the fourth window is a second, short, vaulted passage with a recess on its south side; opposite the last is a slightly larger chamber, with rock-cut benches on either side of the doorway and with two small lateral niches N. and S. The dromos ends in a rectangular vaulted room, a little wider and higher than the dromos itself, and markedly different in style; this is the so-called 'adyton'.

The shape of the dromos and lateral passages in section is the most remarkable and attractive feature of the Cave. The straight sides, 3·6 m. high, slope inward to each other at an angle of 15° from the vertical to a flat ceiling, 1·2 m. wide, about half the width of the floor. The inclined walls do not reach the floor, but 1·4 m. above it on both sides a vertical plinth projects 0·15 m. According to Maiuri, 132, and Johannowski, 971, 2, it was probably in the Hellenistic period, third century B.C., that the floor was lowered. The trapezoidal shape without plinth is found in the eastward lateral passages and is that of the Mycenaean tholos-tombs and of the casemate in the walls of Tiryns. But the section with plinth is found in Etruscan tombs, e.g. the Tomba Regolini-Galassi at Caere of the sixth century B.C., though with a different proportion of inclined to vertical sides, and at Volterra. Maiuri calls the section of the cave 'archaic', but ascribes it to the fifth century; the Etruscan parallels seem to point to the sixth rather than the fifth century B.C. The dromos may have been left unfinished without an adyton until the Hellenistic period; even without the adyton it is strikingly long in comparison with other dromoi.

This strange and unparalleled monument is now for the most

part accepted as the basis of Virgil's heightened poetic description that makes the verifiable facts even more impressive and numinous, though some doubts and difficulties remain. The 'flank of the cliff' in which the cave is cut (42 *excisum*; contrast the natural cave in *G*. 4. 418 f. 'specus . . . *exesi* latere in montis') is accurate, and *rupe sub ima* (3. 443) is acceptable if the *rupes* is that of the *arx*, not the lesser slope of the lower city to the harbour, since the Cave is just under the top surface of the lower city. Though there is only one *aditus*, with *limen* and *fores*, the lateral passages are too numerous to be counted at first sight along the dromos and have what look like sockets for door-hinges. Doors could have been roped together so as to open simultaneously (81 f.), though scarcely *sponte sua*, unless the opening of the *fores* let in a draught strong enough to swing them open. Such a draught, though no more than 'tenuis', is mentioned at 3. 448 f. ('uerso cardine uentus') as disturbing the Sibyl's written leaves.

The identification of Virgil's Cave with that discovered by Maiuri in 1932 has not removed one of the main difficulties which has faced commentators, namely the relationship of the Cave of the Sibyl to the Temple of Apollo. If we assume that the *templa* of 19 and 41 are the same, the Trojans are already in the temple when Virgil begins his description of the *antrum* (42 ff.). In the subsequent account Aeneas appears to follow the Sibyl through the temple to her cave. In 45 he has reached the *limen*; there, *ante fores* (47), the Sibyl's first symptoms of ecstasy come upon her. She leaves Aeneas as he prays; for in 77 she is *in antro*, where she suffers her full ecstasy and utters her prophecy (cf. *ex adyto*, 98); she then returns to the *limen*, where Aeneas has remained (151 'nostroque in limine pendes'), and on his plea she instructs him in his journeying to the Underworld. After learning her instructions Aeneas leaves the *antrum* (157) and returns with Achates (through the temple?) to the shore (162).

If Virgil's description of their movements is precise in its topography, then Aeneas and the Sibyl must have descended from the interior of the temple to the entrance of the cave by a subterranean staircase in the rock, perhaps destroyed in A.D. 552. Such a staircase was postulated by Voss and Beloch, and this was originally Norden's view. No traces survive of such a staircase, rising vertically and extending horizontally, from the cave to the temple, though there are two staircases near the north end of the dromos. One, on the west side of the dromos, leads up to join the Via Sacra some way along it at the foot of the tower. The other, on the east side, leads from

a low, roofed, vestibule on the same level as the *dromos* up
to the level of the temple, emerging 64 m. from its centre, on
the east side of the tower. If this existed in Virgil's time, it
might have suggested to him a staircase to the temple. Norden
later believed the *antrum* to be separate from the temple, set
in the rock at the base of the *arx* on which the temple stood;
he held that 42 ff. cover an action that we are led to infer,
Aeneas' departure from the temple and his descent to the
antrum. This is hard to defend: *uocat alta in templa sacerdos*
(41) must mean that the Sibyl summons the Trojans to the
place which is to be the scene of her prophecy: and why
should they have been summoned there at all if they were only
to leave immediately? Raymond J. Clark, in a forthcoming
article in *Latomus*, taking up the suggestion made by Heyne
(on 6. 40; cf. Excursus III, 1109), proposes that the *templa*
at 41 are not Apollo's but the Sibyl's *precinct*, τέμενος rather
than ναός, as it is used at 4. 484 to refer to the Garden of the
Hesperides. Others have argued in this sense, and Wagner in
Heyne[4] put a comma only at the end of 41.

It is part of the poetic mystery that the movements of the
Sibyl are not made explicit. We are not told how Achates
found her and brought her to Aeneas (35), and where the
sacrifices of 38–41 take place is likewise left in obscurity.

A religious purpose for the Cave seems certain, as with the
Cave of Initiation at Baiae, since it would have been useless
or unsuitable for defence, habitation, or storage. It was
shown in antiquity as the Cave of the Sibyl, and seems in fact
to have been built for her *c.* 500 B.C. She may have been
modelled on the Sibyl of Erythrae, which is the most ancient
and best attested seat of a Sibyl, and where there is also
a cave. If a Sibyl, or indeed the one and only Sibyl, was not
installed at Cumae until about 500 B.C. or later, we can
understand why only late legendary sources and poets (71 ff.)
make the Cumaean Sibyl the source of the *libri Sibyllini*, tra-
ditionally acquired by the last Tarquin: Dion. Hal. *ant. Rom.* 4.
62 speaks of γυνή τις οὐκ ἐπιχωρία (cf. Gell. 1. 19. 2. *anus hospita
atque incognita*), Pliny, *NH* 13. 88 of an undefined Sibyl, while
Livy ignores the story; according to Servius on 36 and 72 Varro
ascribed the *libri Sibyllini* to the Erythraean Sibyl. The annal-
istic poet Naevius, knowing, especially if he was a Campanian,
that there was no Sibyl at Cumae early enough to prophesy
to Aeneas, invents a Cimmerian; in Dion. Hal. 1. 55. 4 it is the
Erythraean whom Aeneas consults. There is also a crucial
difference between an ecstatic prophetess and a collection of
Greek hexameter verses prescribing the proper rituals to deal
with crises, prodigies, omens, dearths, and the like, concerned

with the present, not with the future. The Sibyl herself, unlike the books, played no part in Roman religion. One Sibyl is regularly referred to, e.g. Varro, *RR* i. 1. 3, though with a very long life (*longaeva* 321). It is not clear that there was any succession of incumbents, despite the multiplicity of names provided for the Sibyl, nor when the cult came to an end. Virgil has transported his Sibyl anachronistically back to the time of the original Erythraean prophetess of the Trojan war and put her, not in a crowded and prosperous city, but in total isolation, like Circe, whose mountain can be seen from Cumae on a clear day.

For the topography of the Phlegraean Fields and the Sibyl's Cave in particular see: J. Beloch, *Campanien, Topographie, Geschichte und Leben der Umgebung Neapels im Alterthum*, Berlin, 1897; E. Coccia, 'La Geografia nelle Metamorfosi d'Ovidio e l'Averno Virgiliano', *Atti R. Accad. Archeol. Napoli* xviii, pt. 1, no. 7, (1897), 31-48; H. Nissen, *Italische Landeskunde*, Bde. i, ii, Berlin 1883, 1902, especially i, 250-88 'Der Vulkanismus'; E. Gabrici, *Monumenti antichi* xxii (2 vols., 1913) 'Cuma'; A. Maiuri, *Boll. Assoc. Internaz. Studi Mediterranei* iii (1932), 321-9; *I Campi Flegrei (Dal sepolcro di Virgilio all'Antro di Cuma)*, Rome, 1934, 1958 (English version, rather poor, *The Phlegraean Fields*, 1969⁴); *Campania Romana* i (1938), 21-9; B. Rehm, *Das geographische Bild des alten Italien in Vergils Aeneis*, Philologus, Supplementband xxiv. 2, Leipzig, 1932; P. O'R. Smiley, 'Aeneas and the Cumaean Sibyl. A study in topography', *G & R* xvii (1948), 93-103; J. H. Waszink, 'Vergil and the Sibyl of Cumae', *Mnem.* i (1948), 43-58; *Bollettino del Servizio geologico d'Italia (= Boll. della Società geologica d'Italia)* lxix (1950), 115-360, 'I Campi Flegrei' (A. Rittmann, L. Vigli, F. Falini, U. Ventriglia, P. Nicotera), with a geological map opp. p. 362; J. H. Taylor, 'With Vergil at Cumae', *CB* xxix (1953), 37-40; J. D. Thomson, 'Geographia Vergiliana', Lecture to the Virgil Society, 1954; R. V. Schoder, 'Vergil's use of the Cumae area', *Virgil Society Lecture Summary* xl (1957), 6 ff.; 'Ancient Cumae. History, Topography and Monuments', *Scientific American* ccix (6. 12. 63), 109-18; 'Vergil's Poetic Use of the Cumae Area', *CJ* lxvii (1971-2), 97-105; A. J. Gossage, 'A Visit to Virgil's Country', *G & R* vi (1959), 86-9; W. Johannowski, *Enciclopedia dell'Arte Antica*, ii (Rome, 1959), 970-3 'Cuma'; *Napoli e dintorni*, Guida del Touring Club Italiano⁴, Milan 1960, 321-63 'I Campi Flegrei'; M. Napoli, 'La documentazione archeologica in Campania', *Atti IV Convegno di Studi sulla Magna Grecia*, 1965, 105-8; R. J. Clark, 'Christ's Resurrection at Avernus: a Vergilian

influence', *C & M* xxx (1969), 300–7; 'Vergil, *Aeneid* 6.
40 ff. and the Cumaean Sibyl's Cave' (*Latomus*, forthcoming);
A. G. McKay, *Vergil's Italy*, Bath, 1971, 194–248; H. D.
Reeker, *Die Landschaft in der Aeneis*, Hildesheim, 1971;
F. della Corte, *La mappa dell'Eneide*, Florence, 1972, 103–
20. For the, Cave of Initiation at Baiae cf. R. F. Paget
'The Antrum of Initiation at Baiae', *PBSR* xxxv (1967),
102–16; 'The Great Antrum at Baiae', *Vergilius* xiii (1967),
42–50; C. Hardie, 'The Great Antrum at Baiae', *PBSR*
xxxvii (1969), 14–33.

42. excisum . . . antrum : 'the flank of Cumae's rock is
scooped out to form a vast cavern'; the omission of *est* is
a frequent Virgilian usage (see on 125). The arrangement
is intricate, but the rhythm suggests that *ingens* should be
taken with *antrum*, not with *latus*.

excisum : cf. Cic. *Verr*. ii. 5. 68 'totum est ex saxo . . .
multorum operis penitus exciso' (the Syracusan quarries);
Petron. 120. 67 'est locus exciso penitus demersus hiatu' (the
entrance to the Underworld).

Euboicae . . . rupis : cf. 17; so *E*. 6. 29 'Parnasia rupes' (of
Parnassus), Cat. 68. 53 'Trinacria rupes' (of Etna). The
acropolis of Cumae rises abruptly from the shore.

in antrum : 'forming a cavern'; cf. 3. 533 'portus . . .
curuatus in arcum'; Livy 4. 39. 4 'in orbem se tutabantur'
(a circular defence-formation); so of lead sheets bent to
form a rounded pipe, Vitruv. 8. 6. 4 'antequam in rotunda-
tionem flectantur'.

43. lati : for this species of word-play involving prosody (*lāti*,
with *lătus* above) cf. 2. 606 f. 'părentis . . . pārere', 4. 238
'pārere părabat', 10. 191 f. 'cănit . . . cānentem', *G*. 2. 328
'āuia . . . ăuibus'.

aditus . . . ostia : a grandiose description. The *aditus* act
as voice-conductors for the oracles; they are closed by the
ostia, which open *sponte sua* (82) when the Sibyl is within the
adytum and ready to prophesy. It is a rhetorical picture,
reflecting the gallery-complex in general (see above); it is
easy to imagine the possibility of strange acoustic effects in
such a place (cf. the properties of a cathedral whispering-
gallery, e.g. at Gloucester or in the cupola of St. Peter's).

centum : for an indefinite number. Virgil likes the repeti-
tion with the metrical ictus falling differently at the second
occurrence: so 1. 634 f. 'magnorum horrentia centum / terga
suum, pinguis centum cum matribus agnos', 4. 199 f.
'templa Ioui centum latis immania regnis, / centum aras
posuit', *G*. 4. 383 'centum quae siluas, centum quae flumina
seruant'.

44. responsa : often of oracles or prophecies: so 7. 85 f. 'hinc Italae gentes omnisque Oenotria tellus / in dubiis responsa petunt', *G.* 3. 491 'nec responsa potest consultus reddere uates'.

These three lines are subtly suggestive of echoes: *antrum, centum ; ducunt, ruunt ; Euboicae, Sibyllae*: and the repeated *s* adds a rushing effect to the echoing sounds.

45. uentum erat : 'their steps had brought them'; for the impersonal use (marking the action rather than the agent) see on 1. 272, 2. 634; Fraenkel, *Horace*, 115 n. 1.

ad limen : sc. *antri*. This replaces the normal adverbial 'pick-up' after an ἔκφρασις-formula (cf. 243, where *hic* picks up 'spelunca alta fuit', 237); see on 1. 12, 2. 21.

fata : oracles, the 'utterances' of the god, as in 72, 7. 272 f. 'hunc illum poscere fata / et reor et . . . opto'; in the phrase *fata deum* (376, 2. 54, etc.) the idea of utterance merges into that of destiny (cf. Bailey, *Religion in Virgil*, 224 ff.).

46. deus ecce deus : the dramatic *ecce* marks the first sudden moment of afflatus; she feels the god near her, she seems to see him. Norden takes the repetition of *deus* as ritualistic in origin; he notes Ovid, *Met.* 15. 677 'en, deus est, deus est!', said by Aesculapius' priest to the worshippers, who 'uerba sacerdotis referunt geminata'; cf. *E.* 5. 64.

47 ff. Virgil's treatment of the Sibyl's frenzy is carefully restrained and controlled. There is no long continuous description, but the scene is broken up, by Aeneas' prayer (56–76) before the height of the frenzy (77–80), then the prophecy precedes the brief picture of the return to normal (98–102). In style and language the whole contrasts notably with Lucan 5. 169–224, Sen. *Agam.* 710 ff., where rhetoric has taken full charge.

47. non uultus . . . unus : her colour and expression are changed; *non unus = alius*: cf. Hor. *C.* 2. 11. 9 ff. 'non semper idem floribus est honor / uernis, neque uno Luna rubens nitet / uultu'; so of sick bees, *G.* 4. 254 'continuo est aegris alius color'.

48. non . . . comae : the triple anaphora of *non* is effective. Contrast Lucan 5. 169 ff. 'bacchatur demens aliena per antrum / colla ferens, uittasque dei Phoebeaque serta / erectis discussa comis per inania templi / ancipiti ceruice rotat'.

anhelum : cf. Sen. *Agam.* 713 'anhela corda murmure incluso fremunt' (of Cassandra). In classical Latin the word occurs only in poetry (first in Lucr. 4. 875).

49. maiorque uideri : sc. *erat*. This epexegetic infinitive after an adjective, a poetic use, is modelled on Greek; cf. Hor. *C.* 4. 2. 59 'niueus uideri', Stat. *S.* 2. 1. 168 'tune ille hilaris comisque uideri?'; Servius took *uideri* as historic infinitive, less likely. The Sibyl assumes a supernatural height: cf. Ovid, *F.* 6. 537 ff. (of the prophetess Carmentis) 'caelum uates ac numina sumit, / fitque sui toto pectore plena dei. / uix illam subito posses cognoscere, tanto / sanctior et tanto, quam modo, maior erat'.

50. nec . . . sonans : so 1. 327 f. 'haud tibi uultus / mortalis, nec uox hominem sonat'; Stat. *Th.* 4. 145 f. 'quis numerum ferri gentisque et robora dictu / aequarit mortale sonans?'

quando : causal. A conjunction ending a line is relatively rare (*quando* again, 10. 366, 11. 509): see on 2. 18; Norden, Anh. iii. B. 2.

50 f. adflata . . . dei : 'nondum deo plena, sed adflata uicinitate numinis' (Servius). The gloss suggests the anecdote in Sen. *Suas.* 3. 5 of Arellius Fuscus, who claimed that in a passage in a *suasoria* 'se imitatum esse Vergilianum *plena deo*', an expression which caught on among the wits for labelling the turgid style of certain declaimers, sometimes with amusing results. Seneca adds that, according to Gallio, Ovid (a student of Arellius, Sen. *Contr.* 2. 2. 8) borrowed it in his *Medea*, 'feror huc illuc, uae, plena deo', as an open take-over from Virgil ('non subripiendi causa, sed palam mutuandi, hoc animo ut uellet agnosci'). For similar phrases cf. Ovid, *F.* 6. 538 (above), Lucan 9. 564 'ille deo plenus tacita quem mente gerebat', Stat. *Th.* 10. 624 'plenum Phoebo uatem', Silius 5. 80 'plenus et ipse deum': cf. Leo, Sen. *Trag.* i. 167.

The phrase *plena deo* (= ἔνθεος, cf. Fraenkel, *Horace*, 199 n. 1) occurs nowhere in Virgil. Obviously it would fit the Sibyl, either in this context (with a negative, like Servius' *nondum*) or in that of 77 f. It is generally taken to be a remnant of an early draft; Norden (on 77–80) suggests, on very flimsy grounds, that the words were originally applied by the Sibyl to herself. Seneca's language (l.c. 7 'uersum Vergilii rettulit', of Gallio) seems to preclude the possibility of a misquotation (*if* it was this, it was a most ingenious one).

See E. K. Borthwick, *Mnemos.* ser. 4, xxv (1972), 408 ff., an important examination of the Senecan passage and its stylistic implications; he suggests tentatively that 'nondum plena deo' may have originally stood in place of 'iam propiore dei' (51). For a sceptical view of the phrase as Virgilian see F. della Corte, *Maia* xxiii (1971), 102 ff.

51. uota precesque : cf. 11. 157 f. 'nulli exaudita deorum / uota precesque meae'. The construction of *cessare* is unusual, but cf. Sen. *Medea* 406 'numquam meus cessabit in poenas furor'. The Sibyl makes a gentle rebuke: Trojan Aeneas should know his proper duty.

52. neque enim : again, 368. In this combination *enim* was probably once asseverative (cf. 28), with *neque* a true connective ('nor indeed'); then the connective force was weakened and *enim* became explanatory: a like development may be detected in *etenim*.

dehiscent : generally of the earth opening up (4. 24, *G*. 1. 479); here used like *hiscere*, of opening the mouth for speech.

53. attonitae ... domus : Servius explains *attonitae* as 'facientis attonitos, ut *mors pallida, tristis senecta*', not realising that the god's dwelling is personified. The *domus* is dumb with awe; prayer and worship are needed to unseal its lips; like the Sibyl herself, it is the mouthpiece of the god within. Lucan echoes Virgil, 2. 21 ff. 'sic funere primo / attonitae tacuere domus', of a household dazed and speechless in calamity.

talia fata : this balances *talia fanti* (46), with a framing effect for the description of the ecstasy.

54. conticuit : 'silence fell on her'; the intensity of the compound (see on 2. 1) is deepened by the strong pause that follows. It may have been at this point that the Sibyl mysteriously entered the *antrum*, leaving Aeneas to pray.

54 f. gelidus ... tremor : a conventional epic reaction; so 2. 120 f. 'obstipuere animi gelidusque per ima cucurrit / ossa tremor', 12. 447 f.: cf. [Quintil.] *decl. mai.* 9. 7 'obstipui, totumque corpus percurrit frigidus pauor'. *Dura* has some point: tough as the Trojans were, they were afraid.

55. pectore ab imo : a formula; so 1. 485, Lucr. 3. 57, Cat. 64. 198. Aeneas' prayer marks the divinity of Phoebus as supreme, and also recognizes the authority vested in the Sibyl: he vows to both a tangible sign of his gratitude when his prayer is granted.

57. Dardana ... tela : for the transference of the epithet see on 2. Hector, when dying, foretold the death of Achilles through the agency of Apollo and Paris (*Il.* 22. 359 f.); the story was told in the *Aethiopis* of Arctinus (OCT Homer, v, 106. 8; Kinkel, *EGF* 33); for various versions see Frazer on Apollod. *epit.* 5. 3. Ovid has a lively description, *Met.* 12. 600 ff. The significance of Achilles' death, both for Troy and as a consequence for Romans, is stressed by Horace in the opening of his hymn to Apollo, *C*. 4. 6. 3 f.

derexti : Virgil has a number of these syncopated forms of a perfect stem in *-si* (see on 1. 201), all in speeches and in emotional contexts; they reflect common pronunciation, and other poets avoid them in elevated style (see Norden, who suggests that for Virgil they had an archaic tone); they are often metrically useful.

58. Aeacidae : Achilles (again, 1. 99); but in 839 the patronymic
is used of Perseus, king of Macedon. For the postposition of
in cf. 7. 234 'fata per Aeneae', 9. 643 'gente sub Assaraci',
G. 3. 313 'usum in castrorum', Ovid, *Met.* 4. 507 'pectus in
amborum', Silius 5. 5 'effigiem in pelagi'; in midline, Lucr.
1. 170 'oras in luminis'.

   obeuntia : 'encircling' ('cingentia', Servius), a rare use,
only in poetry: so 8. 553 (of a lion's skin as a cloak), 10. 483 (of
a bull's hide on a shield), Silius 8. 523 (of a bearskin garment),
Ovid, *Met.* 5. 51 (of a gold border round a *chlamys*).
59. duce : apparently an allusion to the oracle given to
Aeneas and Anchises at Delos, 3. 94 ff.; Norden infers a refer-
ence to Apollo ἀρχηγέτης, the guide to a settlement and its
protector.

   repostas : see on *supposta*, 24; hexameters do not admit the
participle of this compound except in syncopated form.
60. Massylum gentis : the Numidians of North Africa; among
Dido's retinue at the hunt there are *Massyli equites* (4. 132),
and her pretended witch is 'Massylae gentis' (4. 483).

   praetentaque . . . arua : 'the lands fringed by the Syrtes':
not geographically exact, but Virgil is concerned to describe
a dangerous coast, just as *Massylum gentis* implies a dan-
gerous hinterland. Contemporary readers might have been
reminded of Cato's arduous march from Benghazi to Lepcis
in 47 B.C. (see Nisbet–Hubbard on Hor. *C.* 1. 22. 5).
61. Italiae : the first syllable is lengthened to make the word
possible in hexameters (so Callim. *h.* 3. 58); see on 1. 2. For
the emotional *tandem* cf. 2 'tandem Euboicis Cumarum ad-
labitur oris'.

   fugientis : accusative, with *oras*; rhythm and Virgilian
style forbid taking it as genitive with *Italiae*: cf. 5. 629
'Italiam sequimur fugientem'. I have changed the punctua-
tion of 60–2 from that of the OCT: after the address to
Phoebus (56 ff.), a statement of facts begins at *magnas* (58)
and continues to *oras* here; then the single line 62 contains
the request of the prayer, an apodosis as it were to what has
preceded.
62. hac . . . tenus : for the tmesis cf. 5. 603 'hac celebrata tenus
sancto certamina patri'; so Ovid, *Met.* 5. 642, *Tr.* 1. 10. 22,
Stat. *Th.* 11. 76. The force of *hactenus* is 'up to this point'
(and no more): *tenus* was originally a noun, connected with
tendere (Plaut. *Bacch.* 793, of a noose), but it early became
prepositional, denoting a 'stretch' of a distance in time or
place; see on 1. 737, 2. 553.

   Troiana . . . fortuna : the ill-luck of Troy (cf. Demosth. *fals.
leg.* 148 κακῶν Ἰλιὰς περιειστήκει Θηβαίους); the paired alliteration

(*Troiana tenus; fuerit fortuna*) is forceful. *Fuerit* is perfect subjunctive, of a wish.

63. Aeneas now invokes (but not by name) the divinities who were Troy's enemies; there can now be no divine sanction (*fas*) against sparing the Trojans from further sorrows: he is an optimist, for he does not say *fas sit*.

Pergameae : a useful variant adjective for *Troianus*: so 3. 109 f. 'nondum Ilium et arces / Pergameae steterant' (where it has point, since Pergamum was properly the citadel of Troy), 3. 476, 5. 744.

64. dique . . . omnes : cf. *G.* 1. 21 'dique deaeque omnes, studium quibus arua tueri' (summarizing, not quite as here); Virgil uses a high formal phrase in the elevated tone of the prayer. The correlating *que . . . que* (linking related concepts) is a feature of Epic style that looks back through Ennius to Homer: see on 1. 18, 4. 83.

64 f. Ilium . . . Dardaniae : a reminiscence of 2. 325 f. 'fuit Ilium et ingens / gloria Teucrorum'. Virgil never uses the forms *Ilion* or *Ilios* as other poets do; he deliberately chooses the Latin form (eight times), although it necessitates the rare elision of the final syllable in words of this shape. For an exhaustive and interesting discussion, with valuable tables, of this type of elision in Virgil and other poets see Soubiran, op. cit. 218 ff.; see also on 1. 599 (where it is wrongly stated that 10. 514 'ardens limitem agit' is unparalleled; see Silius 9. 379), 2. 625, 667, 4. 684.

64. ingens : Virgil delights in the word (see on 4. 89); Henry's note on it (at 5. 118) is itself a delight.

65. tuque . . . uates : a solemn address now to the Sibyl as the god's mouthpiece; the emotional *o* marks awe and respect (cf. 8. 72 'tuque, o Thybri tuo genitor cum flumine sancto').

66. praescia : the adjective (like *praesagus*, 10. 843 'praesaga mali mens') is not recorded before Virgil.

non indebita : the two negatives form a strong positive; cf. 1. 630 'non ignara mali miseris succurrere disco': see Wackernagel, *Vorlesungen über Syntax* (Basel, 1928), ii, 297 ff. *Indebitus* is not recorded before Virgil, who seems to have introduced a number of such negative forms (cf. A. Cordier, *Études sur le vocabulaire épique dans l'Énéide* [Paris, 1939], 144 f.). The parenthesis adds a certain nuance of modesty to Aeneas' claim.

67. considere : for the construction cf. 11. 794 f. 'uoti Phoebus succedere partem / mente dedit'; contrast 5. 689 'da flammam euadere classi', where the infinitive acts as direct object to *da*.

68. agitataque numina : a characteristic and powerful variation of *errantis deos*; Virgil means the Penates of Troy, vagrant and hounded by Iuno's enmity: cf. 12. 803 f. 'terris agitare uel undis / Troianos potuisti' (Iuppiter to Iuno). See 2. 293 ff. (Hector's ghost to Aeneas) 'sacra suosque tibi commendat Troia penatis; / hos cape fatorum comites, his moenia quaere / magna pererrato statues quae denique ponto'.

69. The suppliant must make a return to the god for granting his petition; cf. Silius 8. 229 f. (a prayer to a nymph for success in battle) 'ego te, compos pugnae, Carthaginis arce / marmoreis sistam templis'. Servius comments 'ut solet miscet historiam: nam hoc templum in Palatio ab Augusto factum est'; Aeneas' promise looks forward to Augustus' dedication, commemorating Actium, of a temple to Apollo on 9 October 28 B.C., celebrated by Horace (*C.* 1. 31) and Propertius (2. 31, 4. 6): see Nisbet–Hubbard on Hor. l.c. for literary and archaeological references. The statue of Apollo in the temple was flanked by that of Diana on one side and that of Latona on the other (Prop. 2. 31. 15 f. 'inter matrem deus ipse interque sororem / Pythius in longa carmina ueste sonat'); Virgil, in his special context, associates Diana (Triuia) with Apollo in the actual dedication.

de marmore : like Sychaeus' shrine (4. 457) and Virgil's fantasy-temple for Caesar at Mantua (*G.* 3. 13).

70. festoque dies: 'ludos Apollinares' (Servius): a further anticipation of historical fact. These games were established in 212 B.C., on the instruction of an oracle (Livy 25. 12. 9 ff.) delivered by a *uates Marcius* (cf. Macrob. *Sat.* 1. 17. 25): see Latte, *Römische Religionsgeschichte*, 223 f., 255 f., and Morel, *FPL* 64 (for the 'carmen Marcianum'). But Virgil's readers would think also of Augustus' revival of the *ludi saeculares* in 17 B.C., already at the planning stage in the poet's lifetime (see on 792 f.).

71. Aeneas turns again to the Sibyl, promising her a holy shrine for her prophecies; in *regnis nostris* he proudly assumes the granting of his prayer. The promise alludes to the history of the Sibylline Books, allegedly brought to Rome in the reign of Tarquinius Superbus (Gellius 1. 19) and kept under the temple of Iuppiter Capitolinus (Dion. Hal. *ant. Rom.* 4. 62): see above, pp. 56–7, Ogilvie on Livy 5. 13. 5. After this temple was burnt in 83 B.C. a fresh collection of Sibylline oracles was made and put in the rebuilt shrine on the Capitol. Augustus had them removed to his new temple of Apollo on the Palatine (for the date cf. K. F. Smith on Tib. 2. 5, a valuable introductory note), 'condiditque duobus forulis auratis sub Palatini Apollinis basi' (Sueton. *Aug.* 31. 1). Virgil characteristically hints at this in associating

Aeneas' vow to Apollo so closely with his promise of honour to the Sibyl.

72. namque : for its position see on 28 (*sed enim*); it introduces the specific way in which the Sibyl will be honoured, after the general statement in 71. *Hic* probably refers to the *penetralia* (so Sabbadini), not to *regnis* (so Conington, Butler).

sortis : the oracles of the Sibyl (cf. Tib. 2. 5. 19); her utterances are *arcana*, not revealed to the profane. For *fata* see on 45; in 1. 262 'uoluens fatorum arcana mouebo' the development from prophetic utterance to actual destiny is clear.

73. meae genti : again the air of assured royal power.

lectosque sacrabo : an anticipation of the 'quindecimuiri sacris faciundis', the custodians of the Sibylline Books: originally two (Livy 5. 13. 6), increased to ten in 367 B.C. (Livy 6. 37. 12), and to fifteen from (probably) Sulla's time; the first actual mention of *quindecimuiri* is in a letter from Caelius to Cicero (*ad fam.* 8. 4. 1) in 51 B.C. The name was retained even after later increases; Servius notes 'postea creuit numerus . . . sed remansit . . . quindecimuirorum uocabulum'. They formed one of the great priestly colleges, and their duties gradually widened to deal with varied foreign cults: see Latte, *Röm. Rel.* 397 f.

74. alma : primarily an epithet of divinities; it marks Aeneas' reverence for the Sibyl (again, 117).

ne . . . manda : the construction belongs to early Latin; cf. 544 'ne saeui', on which Servius comments 'antique dictum est, nam nunc *ne saeuias* dicimus'. It is very rare in prose: see on 2. 48, HSz 340. It has obvious metrical advantage.

Aeneas is obeying Helenus' instructions, 3. 456 f. 'adeas uatem precibusque oracula poscas / ipsa canat', after a warning that the Sibyl's written prophecies are put on leaves that scatter on the winds. Servius (on 3. 444) states that palm-leaves were used, on Varro's authority; magic papyri speak of bay-leaves (see Norden).

75. turbata : cf. 3. 448 ff. 'uerso tenuis cum cardine uentus / impulit et teneras turbauit ianua frondes, / numquam deinde cauo uolitantia prendere saxo / nec reuocare situs aut iungere carmina curat'.

rapidis . . . uentis : 'the plaything of winds that whirl them off'; cf. 1. 59 'ferant rapidi secum uerrantque per auras' (of the winds, if Aeolus did not curb them), 1. 116 f. 'illam ter fluctus ibidem / torquet agens circum et rapidus uorat aequore uertex': in such passages the force of *rapere* is clear in *rapidus*.

ludibria : cf. Hor. *C.* 1. 14. 15 f. 'tu, nisi uentis / debes
ludibrium, caue'; Lucan 8. 709 f. 'carpitur in scopulis hausto
per uolnera fluctu, / ludibrium pelagi'. The winds will make
a mockery of consulting the Sibyl if she does not speak in
person.

76. finem . . . loquendi : the words have a ring of early poetry
(for *ore*, 'aloud', see on 1. 614); cf. Ennius, *Ann.* 586 'pausam
facere ⟨ore⟩ fremendi' (see Vahlen), Lucilius 18 M 'haec ubi
dicta dedit, pausam ⟨dedit?⟩ ore loquendi'.

*77–97. The Sibyl, now within the cavern, struggles with the god
who possesses her. At last the entrances open mysteriously, and
she is heard in prophecy: war and bloodshed and misery await
the Trojans, but their first road to safety will be shown them by
a Greek city.*

In four powerful lines (77–80) Virgil describes the full
ecstasy of the Sibyl, of which the preliminary symptoms were
shown in 46 ff. In marked contrast to the extravagances of
Lucan and Seneca in similar contexts (see on 46), he uses
great economy of language: he envisages her like a Bacchant,
utterly possessed; he employs imagery from horse-breaking,
with Apollo taming the wild creature and forcing her to his
will. Her prophecy is fully in character with Sibylline tradi-
tion, allusive, obscure, alarming: it accords with the earliest
mention of a Sibyl, Heraclitus fr. 92 Diels (quoted by Plu-
tarch, *de Pyth. or.* 6) Σίβυλλα μαινομένῳ στόματι ἀγέλαστα καὶ
ἀκαλλώπιστα καὶ ἀμύριστα φθεγγομένη διὰ τὸν θεόν. Norden notes lin-
guistic parallels from extant Sibylline oracles in their earliest
stratum; the grammatical rhyming (84–6 *manent, uenient,
uolent*, emphasized by their placing at the caesurae; 93–4 *mali
tanti, externique . . . thalami*) is also a feature of these oracles
(cf. *CQ* xxi [1927], 102, xxiii [1929], 48 f.). On the whole sub-
ject of prophetic 'possession' see E. R. Dodds, *The Greeks
and the Irrational*, ch. iii.

77. nondum patiens : she is not yet submissive, not broken in
by the god; cf. Sueton. *Iul.* 61 'nec patientem sessoris al-
terius primus ascendit' (of Caesar's special horse with its
almost human feet). So Sen. *Agam.* 718 f. (of Cassandra) 'uerba
nunc clauso male / custodit ore maenas impatiens dei'; Stat.
Th. 10. 164 ff. (of the augur Thiodamas) 'uisu audituque tre-
mendus / impatiensque dei, fragili quem mente receptum /
non capit': for an opposite picture cf. Sen. *Oed.* 230 f. 'in-
cipit Letoa uates spargens horrentes comas / et pati commota
Phoebum'.

Norden, discussing *plena deo* (see on 50 f.), notes a possible sexual meaning in *patiens* and in *domans*, *premendo* (80), the Sibyl being considered as the 'bride' of Apollo (cf. Russell on 'Longinus' π. ὕψ. 13. 2, where the Pythia is described as ἐγκύμονα τῆς δαιμονίου καθισταμένην δυνάμεως): this is unnecessary (see Bömer on Ovid, *F.* 6. 538).

in antro : the Sibyl is now within the *adytum* (see on 42 ff.). *Immanis* is adverbial '(see on *leuis*, 17); it suggests the violence of her physical struggling, as well as her supernatural size (cf. 49): cf. Val. Flacc. 1. 207 ff. 'sacer totusque dei per litora Mopsus / immanis uisu uittamque comamque per auras / surgentem laurusque rotat'.

78. bacchatur : here the verb has the special significance of a religious experience, undergone by one who is ἔνθεος (see E. R. Dodds, Eur. *Bacch.* p. x): so Lucan 5. 169 f. (of the Delphic priestess) 'bacchatur demens aliena per antrum / colla ferens', and cf. Seneca's *maenas* of Cassandra, *Ag.* 719 (quoted above); the metaphor is more generally used in 4. 300 f., of Dido, 'saeuit inops animi totamque incensa per urbem / bacchatur'.

si : 'in case', 'in the hope that'; cf. 1. 181 f. 'prospectum late pelago petit, Anthea si quem / iactatum uento uideat', 4. 84 f. 'Ascanium . . . / detinet, infandum si fallere possit amorem'.

79. excussisse : the perfect infinitive looks forward to the act as if already completed. In early Latin this use is normal in prohibitions with *nolo*, *uolo*: e.g. Plaut. *Poen.* 872 'nolito edepol deuellisse', Cato, *R.R.* 5. 4 'nequid emisse uelit insciente domino, neuquid dominum celauisse uelit'. Its extension to positive wishes followed, e.g. Lucr. 3. 69 'effugisse uolunt longeque remosse', and later to other types of sentence (for *possum* there is already Plaut. *Aul.* 828 'non potes probasse nugas'). Augustan poets exploited it for its obvious metrical convenience, often without a genuine perfect sense but using the perfect timelessly as an equivalent of the present (cf. Kenney on Lucr. 3. 683). See HSz, 351 f., K–S i, 133 ff.; Bömer on Ovid, *F.* 2. 322, K. F. Smith on Tib. 1. 1. 29–32.

The metaphor is that of a horse throwing its rider; cf. Livy 8. 7. 10 'cum equus prioribus pedibus erectis magna ui caput quateret, excussit equitem' (so 11. 615, 640); Theognis 257 ff. ἵππος ἐγὼ καλὴ καὶ ἀεθλίη, ἀλλὰ κάκιστον / ἄνδρα φέρω . . . / πολλάκι δὴ 'μέλλησα διαρρήξασα χαλινὸν / φεύγειν ὠσαμένη τὸν κακὸν ἡνίοχον.

fatigat : again of horses, 1. 316 f. 'qualis equos Threissa fatigat / Harpalyce', 11. 714 'quadripedemque citum ferrata calce fatigat'; Silius 13. 142 'spumantis equi fera corda fatigans'.

80. rabidum : cf. 7. 451 'rabidoque haec addidit ore' (of Allecto). Virgil has ingeniously refashioned 'et rabie fera corda tument' (49).

domans : the metaphor continues; cf. Lucilius 1041 f. 'ante ego te uacuam atque animosam / Thessalam ut indomitam frenis subigamque domemque': so of the Pythia, Lucan 5. 193 'sonant domita iam uirgine uoces'.

fingitque premendo : the same metaphor; cf. Hor. *Epp.* 1. 2. 64 f. 'fingit equum tenera docilem ceruice magister / ire uiam qua monstret eques'. Apollo 'moulds her with his pressure'; cf. 1. 63 (of Aeolus controlling the winds) 'et premere et laxas sciret dare iussus habenas'. Virgil may have had in mind Varius fr. 3 Morel (quoted by Macrobius, *Sat.* 6. 2. 19 to illustrate *G.* 3. 115 ff.) 'quem non ille sinit lentae moderator habenae / qua uelit ire, sed angusto prius ore coercens / insultare docet campis fingitque morando'.

81. iamque : for the postponed connective see on 28; Norden, p. 404. Aeneas' prayer has been heard: the *ostia* (see on 43) fly open miraculously for the Sibyl to transmit Apollo's oracle.

patuere : perfect of instantaneous happening, as in *G.* 1. 330 'terra tremit, fugere ferae'. The mysterious opening increases the awe of the moment; it signals divine presence: so Callim. *h.* 2. 6 f. (to Apollo) αὐτοὶ νῦν κατοχῆες ἀνακλίνασθε πυλάων, / αὐταὶ δὲ κληῖδες· ὁ γὰρ θεὸς οὐκέτι μακρήν. Such automation of doors goes back to *Il.* 5. 749 (Hera passing through the gates of Olympus) αὐτόμαται δὲ πύλαι μύκον οὐρανοῦ; when Medea fled from her home, αὐτόματοι θυρέων ὑπόειξαν ὀχῆες, / ὠκείαις ἄψορροι ἀναθρώσκοντες ἀοιδαῖς (Apoll. Rhod. 4. 41 f.); when a girl's virginity was in question, she was enclosed in Pan's grotto, and if she was a virgin αὐτόμαται αἱ θύραι ἀνεῴχθησαν τοῦ σπηλαίου (Ach. Tat. 8. 6. 13); when St. Peter escaped from Herod's prison, through the agency of the Angel of the Lord (Acts 12. 10), ἦλθον ἐπὶ τὴν πύλην τὴν σιδηρᾶν τὴν φέρουσαν εἰς τὴν πόλιν, ἥτις αὐτομάτη ἠνοίχθη αὐτοῖς.

83 ff. Aeneas had already learned from Anchises in a vision (5. 729 f.) 'gens dura atque aspera cultu / debellanda tibi Latio est'. The Sibyl now develops the theme, with dark allusions whose meaning is as yet obscure: a dismal and daunting message. The prophecy ends with the most cryptic words of all, that a Greek city will bring the first glimmer of comfort, a strange and uneasy thought for the Trojans.

83. A fine sweeping address; cf. 1. 597 'o sola infandos Troiae miserata labores', 5. 870 'o nimium caelo et pelago confise sereno': it is in the Greek tragic manner, e.g. Aesch. *Pers.* 709 ὦ βροτῶν πάντων ὑπερσχὼν ὄλβον εὐτυχεῖ πότμῳ, Soph. *Phil.* 1380 ὦ δεινὸν αἶνον αἰνέσας, τί φής ποτε; Eur. *Tro.* 764 ὦ βάρβαρ' ἐξευρόντες

Ἕλληνες κακά. The staccato, breathless manner of the next two lines, with their parentheses, is quite in oracular style.

defuncte periclis : cf. Cael. ap. Cic. *ad fam*. 8. 1. 4 'si qua pericula tibi inpenderent, ut defungeremur optaui', Sen. *Contr*. 7. 3. 1 'iniqua fortuna nullo me periculo defungi semel passa est'. The syncopated form *periclis* is necessary in hexameters: cf. *gubernaclum*, 349; *oraclum*, 3. 143; *circlos* G. 3. 166.

84. terrae : parallel with *pelagi*; sc. *pericula*. The variant *terra* (R) may be due to misconstruing the genitive (Servius, reading *terra*, observes 'legitur et *terrae*; unum tamen est'). The force of *sed* is something like 'yes, but . . .': the Trojans would have thought the worst dangers over, and the Sibyl jolts their complacency.

Lăuini : the prosody of the first syllable varies, like that in the name *Lauinia* (see on 1. 2) ; contrast Ovid, *Met*. 15. 728 'Läuini sedes'. Aeneas had prayed *Latio considere Teucros* (67) ; the Sibyl specifies the precise place of his first settlement in Italy, the name of which he now hears for the first time. For the importance of Lavinium in the Trojan legend see on 1. 2, Ogilvie on Livy 1. 1. 10.

85. mitte . . . curam : this new, and comforting, parenthesis balances the previous grim one, neatly arranged to end the line in contrast with the placing of the other at a line-opening. *Hanc curam* = *curam de hac re*, a frequent idiomatic use of the demonstrative.

86. sed . . . uolent : for the perfect infinitive see on 78. They will reach their Lavinium, but they will also (*et*) rue their coming; cf. the Greek idiom as in, e.g., Soph. *O T* 363 ἀλλ' οὔ τι χαίρων δίς γε πημονὰς ἐρεῖς.

horrida bella : so 7. 41 f. 'dicam horrida bella, / dicam acies actosque animis in funera reges' (Virgil's own new theme).

87. Thybrim : the Greek name; Virgil has the Italian *Tiberis* twice only (7. 715, G. 1. 499), in specifically Roman and Italian contexts: see further on 2. 782. Blood-flooding rivers are part of oracular stock-in-trade, e.g. in the 'carmen Marcianum' (cf. 73, note) reported by Livy 25. 12. 6 (Morel, *FPL* 63) : Norden quotes examples from Greek oracles of the Flavian period.

spumantem sanguine : cf. 9. 456 'pleno spumantis sanguine riuos'; Ennius, *Sc*. 118 f. 'alia fluctus differt dissupat / uisceratim membra, maria salsa spumant sanguine'. The run of spondees with marked alliteration and assonance makes a notable line, needing slow and measured delivery.

cerno : so in prophecies, Sen. *Agam*. 730, Val. Flacc. 1. 226: the familiar clairvoyant technique.

88. Simois . . . Xanthus : the rivers of Troy, evocative names
(cf. the Somme). Servius sees an allusion to the Tiber and the
Numicus (where Aeneas was to die; see Ogilvie on Livy
1. 2. 6; Ovid, *Met.* 14. 598 ff.), rivers which Virgil couples
in 7. 150 f., 242, 797. The Sibyl's words suggest that Virgil
intends a Sibylline manner in *E.* 4. 34 ff. 'alter erit tum Tiphys
et altera quae uehat Argo / delectos heroas', etc.

Dorica castra : again evocative; 2. 27 f. 'iuuat ire et Dorica
castra / desertosque uidere locos', and see note there for
the collocation of syllables *-ca ca-*, criticized by Servius.

89. defuerint : the tense looks forward to a *fait accompli* (' you
will find that they are not lacking'); so *uidero* often (see on
Cic. *Cael.* 35): sometimes it is metrically useful (cf. 9. 297 f.
'erit ista mihi genetrix nomenque Creusae / solum defuerit').

alius . . . Achilles : Turnus, waiting already; cf. 2. 787 f.
'illic res laetae regnumque et regia coniunx / parta tibi' (the
phantom Creusa to Aeneas), where *illic* suggests that *Latio*
here is ablative, not dative.

90. natus . . . dea : Achilles' mother was the sea-nymph The-
tis; Turnus' mother was the nymph Venilia (10. 76; married
to Neptune, according to DServius there).

addita : 'dogging them'. Servius glosses it as *inimica*; but
the meaning comes from its context: contrast 528, 777,
2. 339 with this passage and with *G.* 1. 150 'mox et frumentis
labor additus', where the *labor* is hostile and implacable.

91. cum : with the force of *cum interea*, 'while all the time' (so
R. D. Williams); there is no need to take it as equivalent to
et tum (so Conington and others).

in rebus egenis : cf. 8. 365 'rebusque ueni non asper ege-
nis', 10. 367 'unum quod rebus restat egenis'; Silius 8. 55 f.
'quis rebus egenis / ferret opem?', Stat. *Th.* 11. 550 f. 'ex-
silio rebusque exercita egenis / membra uides'. Before Virgil
the adjective occurs only in Plaut. *Capt.* 406, *Poen.* 130, each
time with *res* and in a serious context; cf. Norden, Anh. i. 1,
p. 372.

92. quas . . . non : equivalent to *omnis*; cf. Ovid, *Her.* 11. 39 f.
'quas mihi non herbas, quae non medicamina nutrix /
attulit?', Juv. 3. 309 'qua fornace graues, qua non incude
catenae?'; the idiom is Greek, e.g. Soph. *OC* 1133 f. ἀνδρὸς ᾧ
τίς οὐκ ἔνι / κηλὶς κακῶν ξύνοικος; (cf. Jebb on Soph. *OT* 1526):
see Vahlen, *Opusc. acad.* i, 219 f.

Italum : with this form the original prosody is necessarily
kept ; see on 757. The archaic genitive plural form is especially
frequent in poetry for the names of peoples (cf. 60, 489, 503);
in formal usage it survived with certain words, e.g. *nummum,
sestertium, triumuirum, liberum, socium.*

oraueris : future perfect. The termination is short (cf.
3. 441 'Cumaeam accesseris urbem'), the original prosody;
in the perfect subjunctive forms the final syllable was
originally long: but the poets tend to blur the distinction,
using either prosody for either tense according to metrical
need, e.g. 1. 388 *adueneris* (subjunctive), Ovid, *Am.* 1. 4.
31 f. *reddideris, biberis* (future perfect). See S. G. Owen on
Ovid, *Tr.* 2. 323; Platnauer, *Latin Elegiac Verse*, 56; and on
514 below.

urbes : so MR: *urbis* P (so Norden, Sabbadini, Götte, Gey-
monat), which may be right, in view of the tendency to as-
sonance in Sibylline style; see Gellius 13. 21 for Probus'
ideas on the difference in sound-effect between the two ter-
minations. For a detailed study of these accusative forms,
with reference to the text of Virgil, see Bömer, *Emerita* xxi
(1953), 182 ff., xxii (1954), 175 ff.

93. coniunx : Lavinia (named as *causa mali tanti*, 11. 480) will
be a second Helen. There is Sibylline ambiguity in *hospita*:
she will be a 'foreign bride', but she will also, in a different
sense, be associated with the hospitality shown to Aeneas by
Latinus; cf. Hor. *C.* 1. 15. 1 f. 'pastor cum traheret per freta
nauibus / Idaeis Helenen perfidus hospitam'.

94. externique . . . thalami : the 'alien bridal' varies *coniunx
hospita*; cf. 7. 97 f. 'thalamis neu crede paratis; / externi
uenient generi' (an oracular response to Latinus).

This and line 835 are the only incomplete lines in the book:
in both, Virgil had not yet found what he wanted to finish his
train of thought. There is no valid reason for supposing that
such lines were a deliberate innovation in technique, al-
though they are sometimes accidentally effective in them-
selves: see on 1. 534, 2. 66, 4. 44. For a wise discussion see
W. A. Camps, *Introduction to Virgil's Aeneid* (Oxford, 1969),
128 ff.: for longer examination see F. W. Münscher, *Die
unvollständigen Verse in Virgils Aeneide* (progr. Jauer, 1879);
H. Belling, *Studien über die Compositionskunst Vergils in der
Aeneide* (Leipzig, 1899), 113 ff.; M. M. Crump, *The Growth of
the Aeneid* (Blackwell, Oxford, 1920), 8 ff.; F. W. Shipley,
Washington University Studies xii (1924, Humanistic Series),
122 ff.; J. Sparrow, *Half-Lines and Repetitions in Virgil*
(Oxford, 1931), 23 ff.; O. Walter, *Die Entstehung der Halb-
verse in der Aeneis* (diss. Giessen, 1933); K. Büchner, *P.
Vergilius Maro* (Stuttgart, 1955), col. 403; F. W. Lenz,
Vergiliana (ed. Bardon–Verdière, Leiden, 1971), 158 ff.

95. tu . . . ito : didactic technique: 12. 438 f. 'tu facito . . . / sis
memor'; *G.* 2. 408 f. 'primus humum fodito, primus deuecta
cremato / sarmenta, et uallos primus sub tecta referto'. The

line has a fine encouraging pomp; for the construction *ne cede* see on 74.

96. qua . . . sinet : a textual problem. The reading *qua* depends on a second hand in cod. Bernensis 165 (ninth century). The capital manuscripts read *quam*, which Servius evidently read also (he comments 'ne cedas, sed esto audentior quam tua te fortuna permittit'); Seneca quotes the line (to *sinet*) with *quam* (*epp.* 82. 18; the constant assertion by commentators, including Norden and Sabbadini, that he read *qua* is wrong: see Reynolds's app. crit. in OCT).

With *qua* there is no difficulty: cf. 2. 387 f. '"qua prima" inquit "Fortuna salutis / monstrat iter, quaque ostendit se dextra, sequamur"', 12. 147 f. 'qua uisa est Fortuna pati Parcaeque sinebant / cedere res Latio, Turnum et tua moenia texi'. It is well defended by Henry; see also G. Albini, *Atene e Roma* xi (1908), 327 ff., J. Svennung, *Eranos* liv (1956), 195 ff.

Servius' interpretation is quite unacceptable: a Sibyl has to be obscure, but need not be absurd; the 'parallels' quoted by Butler have no real relevance. Norden, accepting *quam*, assumes an ellipse of *uiam*, to be understood from the words that follow: but it is asking a lot of Aeneas (and the reader) to expect him to interpret *quam* from a sentence not yet spoken; and Norden conceals the fact that in 10. 49, which he quotes as decisive, although MR read *quamcumque* there is a variant *quacumque* in P (accepted by Ribbeck, Mynors, Geymonat).

In spite, therefore, of the weight of support for *quam*, the preference must go to *qua*. The early change to *quam* can be explained, as Henry notes, by a false connection with the comparative *audentior*; once so misunderstood (and Servius illustrates the misunderstanding), *quam* became accepted.

97. quod . . . reris : 'the last thing you expect'; another dramatic parenthesis: the idea of aid from a Greek city (i.e. Evander's Pallanteum) would seem incredible to Aeneas.

Graia : the normal form, not *Graecus*, in elevated style: see on 2. 148, and Housman on Lucan 9. 38.

98–123. *The Sibyl's ecstasy leaves her, and Aeneas entreats her to enable him to visit his father in the Underworld.*

We are not told specifically that the Sibyl leaves the *adytum* after her prophecy; but she presumably returns to the *limen* (cf. 45, 151) by the time Aeneas speaks. His tone is grave and anxious, dominated by his longing to fulfil his father's bidding (5. 731 ff.). He makes no attempt to speculate on the Sibyl's meaning.

98. ex adyto : this suggests that the Sibyl's *antrum* serves as the inner sanctuary of the temple (see on 42 ff.), the 'locus templi secretior, ad quem nulli est aditus nisi sacerdoti' (Servius on 2. 115).

99. ambages : the oracular pronouncement is a verbal labyrinth (cf. 29): so of the Sphinx, 'immemor ambagum uates' (Ovid, *Met.* 7. 761); Lucan 1. 637 f. 'flexa sic omina Tuscus / inuoluens multaque tegens ambage canebat' (of the seer Arruns); Sen. *Oed.* 214 f. 'ambage flexa Delphico mos est deo / arcana tegere'. For *horrendas* see on 10; cf. 9. 112 f. 'tum uox horrenda per auras / excidit'.

   remugit : cf. 3. 92 'mugire adytis cortina reclusis' (of the oracle at Delos). The Sibyl's voice reverberates through the *ostia* (43).

100. obscuris uera inuoluens : a succinct characterization of Sibylline style. The run of spondees into the fourth foot, with no third-foot caesura and a strong break after *inuoluens*, makes a subtle differentiation from the rhythm of 99, where there is also no third-foot caesura but a dactyl in the second foot.

   ea frena : for *ea* ('such') cf. 2. 17 'ea fama uagatur'. The horse-breaking metaphor is resumed; cf. Anacreon *PMG* 417. 3 (to a girl addressed as πῶλε) ἴσθι τοι, καλῶς μὲν ἄν τοι τὸν χαλινὸν ἐμβάλοιμι, / ἡνίας δ' ἔχων στρέφοιμί ⟨σ'⟩ ἀμφὶ τέρματα δρόμου.

   furenti : this, with *furor* (102) marks the Sibyl as μαινομένη. The alliterative effect with *frena* has much vigour; cf. Quintil. 12. 10. 29 (of the letter *f*) 'paene non humana uoce, uel omnino non uoce potius, inter discrimina dentium efflanda est'.

101. concutit : of charioteers, 5. 146 f. 'immissis aurigae undantia lora / concussere iugis pronique in uerbera pendent'.

   stimulos : cf. 9. 717 f. 'Mars . . . animum uirisque Latinis / addidit et stimulos acris sub pectore uertit'.

102. rabida . . . quierunt : there is a self-echo in 11. 300 'ut primum placati animi et trepida ora quierunt'. Lucan's Sibyl collapses in a faint after her prophecy (5. 219 ff.).

103. heros : *Aeneas heros* occurs here only; Aeneas is often *Troius heros* (cf. 451), once *Laomedontius heros* (8. 18), sometimes *heros* alone (4. 447, 5. 289). The word is seldom just a fill-in; the context usually, as here, suggests some special aspect of bravery, mental or physical.

104. mi : it is remarkable that this form of the dative occurs twice in this speech (cf. 123) and nowhere else in Virgil. Its frequent use in Comedy reflects common speech, and Cicero has it in his correspondence; Horace has it, but not in the *Odes*; Catullus has it, but not in his 'epyllion'. But Ennius'

fairly frequent use of it gave a precedent in elevated style
as an archaism, and Lucretius has it once (3. 105); yet why
did Virgil otherwise completely avoid it?

inopina : not recorded before Virgil; Tacitus brought it
into prose.

105. omnia . . . peregi : 'I have taken thought for all before-
hand, and worked it out in my inmost heart'. This is Stoic
language: see Sen. *epp.* 76. 33–4, where the lines are quoted and
interpreted in the Stoic manner: 'praecogitati mali mollis
ictus uenit. at stultis et fortunae credentibus omnis uidetur
noua rerum et inopinata facies . . .: sapiens scit sibi omnia
restare; quidquid factum est, dicit "sciebam"'.

praecepi : used like προλαμβάνειν; so Cic. *de off.* 1. 81 'illud . . .
ingenii magni est, praecipere cogitatione futura et aliquanto
ante constituere quid accidere possit in utramque partem,
et quid agendum sit cum quid euenerit, nec committere ut
aliquando dicendum sit "non putaram"'; cf. Cic. *Tusc.*
3. 29, 4. 37. Aeneas has come a long way from his earlier
fears and bewilderment (cf. Bowra, *From Virgil to Milton*
[London, 1945], 63): he can take the Sibyl's gloomy pre-
diction without flinching, and is prepared for the ordeal of
going to the Underworld if the Sibyl will be his guide.

106. unum oro : this is his special petition, that the Sibyl will
take him to his father, as his father had bidden him.

inferni : the adjective is a substitute for *inferus*, which
has only limited availability in hexameters (see Leo, *ALL* x,
436 f.); cf. Ovid, *Met.* 2. 261 'infernum terret cum coniuge
regem' (sc. *lumen*).

107. dicitur : sc. *esse*; the legendary place for the *ianua* is here
(see on *ut fama est*, 14).

tenebrosa . . . refuso : 'the murky swamp where Acheron
comes flooding up'. The *ianua* is lake Avernus, reputed to be
formed from an overflow of the underworld river Acheron;
the image in *refuso* seems to be of the river flooding up from be-
low and then pouring back, forming a perpetual vortex (cf. 1.
125 f. 'imis / stagna refusa uadis'). Virgil seems to have fused
Avernus and the Palus Acherusia. The adjective *tenebrosus* is
not recorded before Virgil. Strabo (5. 4. 5) describes the region
as originally covered by a vast forest, ἀγρίᾳ ὕλη μεγαλοδένδρῳ καὶ
ἀβάτῳ; this was cleared by Agrippa, and the area had become
built up (τῶν χωρίων κατοικοδομηθέντων).

108. ora : more precise than *conspectum* : Aeneas wants not only
to catch sight of Anchises, but to meet him face to face.

109. sacra : the entrance to the Underworld is sacred to the
chthonic powers.

110 ff. illum ego . . . ille meum : complementary aspects of *pietas*, neatly balanced, with some marked alliteration. The departure of Aeneas from Troy carrying Anchises is a frequent subject in art-forms, especially vase-paintings: see K. Schauenburg, *Gymnasium* lxvii (1960), 176 ff. (further on 2. 708).

111. eripui . . . recepi : a characteristic arrangement, with a verb at each end 'framing' the line: see Norden, Anh. iii. A. 2.

112. comitatus iter : Norden notes that *comitari* with a nonpersonal object is not pre-Virgilian (once again, 11. 61).

114. inualidus . . . senectae : Anchises is represented as a contemporary of Priam (2. 561), as *fessum aetate* (2. 596), *confectum aetate* (4. 599); in 2. 647 ff. he is crippled as a result of a thunderbolt, a detail that is hardly consistent with Virgil's picture of him elsewhere (see on 2. 649).

115. quin : 'yes, and . . .'; this emphatic use in statements developed from the original function of *quin* as a lively conversational interrogative (HSz, 676).

    peterem . . . adirem : there is no ὕστερον πρότερον here; *tua limina adirem* simply restates *te supplex peterem*, with *supplex* common to both verbs.

116. mandata : see 5. 731 ff. 'Ditis tamen ante / infernas accede domos et Auerna per alta / congressus pete, nate, meos', etc. *Dabat* may imply some further occasion also, as Conington suggests, possibly in some other vision: cf. 695 f. 'tua tristis imago / saepius occurrens haec limina tendere adegit'.

    gnatique patrisque : for *-que . . . -que* see on 64. The old form *gnati* is attested here by MP (*nati* R).

117. The metrical pattern of this line should be noted. Formally there is a 'strong' caesura in the fourth foot, compensating for the 'weak' caesura in the third; but the sensebreak after *miserere* cuts across the metre, and the 'weak' caesura dominates the line, so that the effect is that of a typically Greek hexameter rhythm, not of the normal Latin hexameter: contrast the previous line, or 136, with this or 131, 322; see Hardie, *Res Metrica*, 8 f.

    namque : for its position cf. 72, and see on 28. It is in formal prayer-style, explaining why the divinity addressed is appropriate to the occasion or marking the god's general power: so 366, 1. 65 f. 'Aeole (namque tibi diuum pater atque hominum rex / et mulcere dedit fluctus et tollere uento)', 1. 731 'Iuppiter, hospitibus nam te dare iura loquuntur'; Hor. *C.* 3. 11. 1 f. 'Mercuri, nam te docilis magistro / mouit Amphion lapides canendo'; *Il.* 24. 334 f. Ἑρμεία, σοὶ γάρ τε μάλιστά γε φίλτατόν ἐστιν / ἀνδρὶ ἑταιρίσσαι; Callim. *h.* 4. 226 ἀλλά, φίλη, δύνασαι γάρ, ἀμύνεο πότνια δούλους. See G. Williams, op. cit. 139 ff.; Norden ad loc. and *Agnostos Theos*, 154.

nec te : for the double monosyllable ending the line see
Norden, Anh. ix. 4. b. No rhythmic disturbance results such
as is caused by a single monosyllable at the line-end.

118. nequiquam : with the preceding negative, the sense is
strongly positive ('it was with very good reason'); cf. 66,
note. Virgil has a marked preference for *nequiquam* over
frustra (see on 2. 770): again with a negative, 8. 370 'haud
animo nequiquam exterrita mater' (but this is unusual; see
Wölfflin, *ALL* ii, 11).

lucis ... Auernis : cf. 564, and see on 13. Since the Sibyl
is to guide Aeneas in the Underworld, there is special appro-
priateness in mentioning her official status in the clause intro-
duced by *namque*.

119 ff. Aeneas ends his appeal with two pairs of *exempla* from
'history', in the approved manner of rhetoric: see Quintil.
5. 11. 6 (on 'ea quae ad probationem pertinent') 'poten-
tissimum autem est ... quod proprie uocamus exemplum,
id est rei gestae aut ut gestae utilis ad persuadendum id
quod intenderis commemoratio' (for the point see Volk-
mann, *Die Rhetorik der Griechen und Römer*[2], 233 ff.). The
first pair is carefully chosen to illustrate how *pietas* gained
admission to the Underworld: Orpheus made the descent to
recover Eurydice (his failure in his purpose is not relevant
here), Pollux took the place of his mortal brother Castor in
the Underworld on alternate days. The second pair, Theseus
and Hercules, has a different purpose: they are simply intro-
duced as heroes of semi-divine birth (like Aeneas) who went
down for other reasons than *pietas*.

The punctuation is disputed (see Conington), and some
editors take the two clauses with *si* as a protasis to *et mi genus
ab Ioue summo* (123), and *quid ... Alciden* as parenthetic.
But the difference in function between the two pairs of
exempla justifies the OCT arrangement: the balanced *si*-
clauses, with their bearing on *pietas*, have specific reference
to the central claim on which Aeneas bases his petition, so
that they are rightly attached to *gnatique patrisque ...
miserere*; the claim 'et mi genus ab Ioue summo' belongs
wholly to the precedent of Theseus and Hercules.

119. accersere : 'to summon'; the balance of testimony sup-
ports this form (cf. 5. 746) rather than *arcessere*: see Nettle-
ship here and in *Contr. Lat. Lex.* 17 ff. (he regards the two
as separate words). For the significance of the legend of
Orpheus and Eurydice see W. K. C. Guthrie, *Orpheus and
Greek Religion* (London, 1935), 29 ff., I. M. Linforth, *The
Arts of Orpheus* (Berkeley, 1941), 16 ff.

120. Threicia ... cithara : cf. the Orphic *Argonautica* 42,

where Orpheus speaks of his descent to Hades ἡμετέρη πίσυνος
κιθάρῃ, δι' ἔρωτ' ἀλόχοιο (Norden regards this as clear evidence
that Virgil used an Orphic κατάβασις); Eur. *Hypsipyle* fr. 1.
iii. 9 f. ἔλεγον ἰήιον | Θρῆσσ' ἐβόα κίθαρις 'Ορφέως (of Orpheus with
the Argonauts; cf. Linforth, op. cit. 6).

   fidibusque canoris : so Hor. *C.* 1. 12. 11 f. (of Orpheus)
'blandum et auritas fidibus canoris / ducere quercus'; Norden
suggests a common source, Nisbet–Hubbard that Virgil may
have borrowed from Horace. The alliteration-pattern of the
line is notable.

121. alterna morte : *Od.* 11. 303 f. ἄλλοτε μὲν ζώουσ' ἐτερήμενοι,
ἄλλοτε δ' αὖτε | τεθνᾶσιν; Pindar, *N.* 10. 87 f. ἥμισυ μέν κε πνέοις
γαίας ὑπένερθεν ἐών, | ἥμισυ δ' οὐρανοῦ ἐν χρυσέοις δόμοισιν (see Frazer
on Apollod. *Bibl.* 3. 11. 2); cf. [Quintil.] *decl. mai.* 9. 22
'inter fratres quoque illa maxime admirabilis, tamen alterna
mors est'.

   itque reditque : the first *-que* is connective, not correlative
with the second. The line has a curious rhythm, with its
dactylic run to the fourth foot and then an abrupt pause
that brings out prominently the anapaestic *totiens*. A metrical
picture of endless journeyings, to and fro?

122 f. quid Thesea ... Alciden : instead of a fresh pair of *si-*
clauses, the new *exempla* are introduced by the figure *praeter-
itio*, a rhetorical pretence. Servius comments (on *Thesea*)
'durum exemplum, unde nec immoratus est in eo': Theseus
behaved disreputably in the Underworld, attempting to
carry off Persephone (cf. 397); one legend represented him
as brought back safely by Hercules, another that he was
imprisoned there for ever, a version that Virgil adopts in
617 f., for which he was duly rebuked as inconsistent by the
knowing Hyginus (Gellius 10. 16. 11 ff.). But here Virgil is
simply concerned with the precedent of a descent (see on
119 ff.), and it is unlikely that he would have made any
change if he had been able to revise the poem (Gellius reports
of Hyginus 'correcturum fuisse Vergilium putat, nisi mors
occupasset').

   Hercules visited the Underworld on his last Labour, to
bring up Cerberus (for references see Frazer on Apollod.
Bibl. 2. 5. 12): both he and Theseus upset Charon's standards
of decorum for visitors (392 ff.).

   magnum : a punctuation-problem that goes back to Servius,
who preferred to punctuate as shown here, observing 'melius
sic distinguitur, licet quidam legant *quid Thesea magnum*, ut
epitheton ei dent qui per se non est magnus: nam Hercules
etiam sine epitheto magnum intelligimus. sed melius est
magnum dare Herculi quam sacrilego'. The point concerning

the appropriateness of *magnum* to the one or the other is silly
and irrelevant: the punctuation is a matter for the ear. Nor-
mally one would not expect a sense-break at the end of the
fifth foot if there were no clue to it other than punctuation:
see G. B. Townend, *CQ* n.s. xix (1969), 330 ff., *Proc. Virg. Soc.*
ix (1969–70), 81. But here *quid Thesea* can be read quite
naturally as a separate question, with a natural pause before
the more weighty clause containing the verb common to both
accusatives, and the arrangement causes no discomfort.
Modern editors are divided: Sabbadini, Goelzer, Götte also
punctuate as shown here; Ribbeck, Conington, Norden,
Geymonat punctuate after *magnum*.

123. **Alciden :** the hexameter will not admit the Latin name
Hercules. Norden notes the earliest occurrence of *Alcides*
at *E.* 7. 61, Hor. *C.* 1. 12. 25 (in Greek, Callim. *h.* 3. 145
καρτερὸν Ἀλκείδην). For *mi* see on 104.

124–55. *The Sibyl tells Aeneas that the descent to Avernus is easy,
the return hard. He must find the Golden Bough, and take it as
a ritual gift to Proserpina. But before he makes his journey he
must duly bury one of his companions who is even now lying
dead.*

The prophetess speaks solemnly and unambiguously: the
horrendae ambages have gone, her part as inspired seer is over,
and she begins to take on the character of guide. But her
instructions, so clear and direct, add a dimension to Aeneas'
immediate ordeal that her prophecy could not give. The
atmosphere of the passage is quite different from that of
Circe's instructions to Odysseus for his journey to the Shades
(*Od.* 10. 504 ff.): there, the reader is conscious of magic at
work; here, even the mystery of the Golden Bough does not
lessen the impression of a hard reality, a serious pilgrimage,
a journey that is no fairy-tale. Ovid, in his potted narrative
of the subject, lacks both the enchantment of Homer and
the *grauitas* of Virgil; he makes it all a press-button affair of
effortless ingenuity (*Met.* 14. 110 ff.):

> 'pone tamen, Troiane, metum! potiere petitis
> Elysiasque domos et regna nouissima mundi
> me duce cognosces simulacraque cara parentis:
> inuia uirtuti nulla est uia!' dixit, et auro
> fulgentem ramum in silua Iunonis Auernae
> monstrauit iussitque suo diuellere trunco.
> paruit Aeneas . . .

124. talibus . . . tenebat : cf. 4. 219 (Iarbas praying) 'talibus
orantem dictis arasque tenentem'. Grasping an altar was an

age-old ritual in supplications: so Nepos, *Hann.* 2. 4 (of the child Hannibal) 'simul me ad aram adduxit [sc. *pater*] . . . eamque ceteris remotis tenentem iurare iussit numquam me in amicitia cum Romanis fore'. The *limen* of the Sibyl's *adytum* would be a natural place for an altar. Virgil prefers the plural of *ara* (sometimes metrically useful, e.g. 1. 349, 2. 574), a use which developed on the analogy of *altaria*: see Löfstedt, *Synt.* i, 43; Landgraf, *ALL* xiv, 68; *Thes. L.L.* s.v. *ara*, 389. 3 ff.

125. orsa : finite (cf. 562, 1. 325, 12. 806). Virgil likes this omission of *est* with participles of deponent verbs, sometimes too with passives (so *excisum*, 42): see on 1. 72, 2. 2; Leo, *Sen. Trag.* i, 184 ff.

sate . . . diuum : cf. Ennius, *Ann.* 113 'o pater o genitor o sanguen dis oriundum'. The Sibyl now addresses Aeneas with high ceremony, picking up his own words in 123.

126. Anchisiade : the patronymic marks the mortal aspect of Aeneas' ancestry. Virgil likes it in contexts of special significance (e.g. 348, 10. 250, 822); in 8. 521 he has 'Aeneas Anchisiades', in the Homeric manner.

Auerno : v.l. *Auerni*, slightly less well attested; Servius' lemma has *Auerni*, but he comments 'legitur et *Auerno*, id est *ad Auernum*'. Norden, somewhat hesitantly, prefers the genitive (so too Butler); most editors accept the dative.

There is no parallel in Latin to a dative after *descensus*; the noun itself is quite rare in the classical period, and occurs in poetry only here, Prop. 4. 8. 5, and Manilius 5. 5. Virgil has used a construction with a verbal noun which is certainly possible with the related verb: cf. Stat. *Th.* 11. 463 f. 'luce relicta / descensuram Erebo', Silius 13. 708 'descendere nocti' (i.e. to the Underworld), 13. 759 'descendisse Erebo'. For a near illustration cf. Livy 44. 35. 17 'descensus ripae utriusque in alueum trecentorum ferme passuum erat', Mela 1. 73 'unus in eum [*sc.* specum] descensus est, angustus, asper'; Conington notes Hirtius, *Bell. Gall.* 8. 40. 4 'erat . . . oppidanis difficilis et praeruptus eo descensus' (i.e. to a river). Virgil's innovation has nothing impossible about it; but it was unusual enough to find no imitators, and to suggest *Auerni* as an improvement.

Servius, commenting on *Auerni*, notes 'inferorum significat et lacum pro inferis ponit'. This view that Avernus here means the lake (cf. 201) is defended by N. E. Collinge, *Phoenix* xiii (1959), 69 ff., reading *Auerni*. For the same view see K. Wellesley, *CR* n.s. xiv (1964), 235 ff.; he accepts *Auerno*, but interprets it as an ablative, 'by way of Avernus', an answer to Aeneas' request *doceas iter* (109). But Aeneas

knows that the entrance to the Underworld is at the lake
(106 f.), and does not need a signpost; his request is for
guidance in the Underworld, so that he may be led to his
father. The whole context makes it most unlikely that the
allusion is to the lake; and the assumption ignores the pointed
antithesis in 128 'superasque euadere ad auras': for *Auernus*
used of the Underworld cf. 5. 732 (quoted on 116), where
Auerna per alta is a variation on *infernas domos*, 7. 91 'imis
Acheronta adfatur Auernis' (of the priest of Faunus).

The famous words suffer from being remembered and
quoted in isolation from their context, as Fletcher observes:
the way down is easy, *but who may come up?* To interpret
Auerno of the lake is to miss a whole vision.

127. A marvellously slow, tolling line. The spondaic opening
disyllable, with no overspill from the first to the second foot,
and the further coincidence of words and feet in *patet atri
ianua Ditis*, combine with assonance and alliteration to
produce a memorable effect. There is a partly similar effect
in 2. 661 'patet isti ianua leto', 4. 384 'sequar atris ignibus
absens', but neither line has the opening slow movement
that this one has, nor the assonance.

noctes atque dies : so Lucr. 2. 12, 3. 62. For the initial
spondee, a relatively rare first-foot pattern in Virgil, see on
1. 30, and Norden, Anh. viii. The occurrence of *atque* without
elision of the second syllable is also infrequent; so 306
'matres atque uiri', 622 'fixit leges pretio atque refixit'
(these, like the present example, have the manner of a for-
mula): see on 1. 147; Platnauer, *Latin Elegiac Verse*, 78 ff.;
Axelson, *Unpoetische Wörter*, 84.

ianua Ditis : cf. Lucr. 6. 762 f. 'ianua ne pote eis Orci
regionibus esse / credatur'. Virgil's phrase is echoed by
Grattius 70, Manilius 2. 951 'nigri . . . Ditis ianua', Val.
Flacc. 6. 122 f.; Sen. *Apocol.* 13. 3 'momento temporis per-
uenit ad ianuam Ditis, ubi iacebat Cerberus' (of Claudius);
Carm. Lat. Epigr. 2075 'uiue deo dum fata sinunt, nam curua
senectus / te rapit et Ditis ianua nigra uocat'. In Val. Flacc.
3. 386 'patet ollis ianua Leti' the door ingeniously opens the
other way, for spirits to return to haunt the living.

128. **reuocare gradum :** contrast Sen. *HF* 675 ff. (on the same
theme) 'nec ire labor est; ipsa deducit uia: / . . . gradumque
retro flectere haud umquam sinunt / umbrae tenaces', etc.

superasque . . . ad auras : so *G.* 4. 486 'redditaque Eurydice
superas ueniebat ad auras'.

129. **hoc opus, hic labor est :** so Ovid, *ars* 1. 453 f. 'hoc opus, hic
labor est, primo sine munere iungi' (Ovid mocks his own
pretensions by the parody; see E. J. Kenney, *Ovidiana* [Paris,

1958], 201); Quintil. 6. 2. 7 'huc igitur incumbat orator, hoc
opus eius, hic labor est, sine quo cetera nuda ieiuna infirma
ingrata sunt' (of working on the emotions).

For the pronunciation of *hoc* before an initial vowel see
W. S. Allen, *Vox Latina* (Cambridge, 1965), 77.

quos ... amauit : cf. Pliny, *epp.* 1. 2. 2 (asking a friend
for candid criticism) 'temptaui enim imitari Demosthenen
semper tuum, Caluum nuper meum, dumtaxat figuris ora-
tionis; nam uim tantorum uirorum, "pauci quos aequus
..." adsequi possunt'.

aequus : 'impartial' (but the emphasis is on *amauit*); cf.
Stat. *Th.* 2. 181 f. 'utinam his manibus permittere gentis, /
Iuppiter aeque, uelis!': so 10. 112 'rex Iuppiter omnibus
idem'.

130. ardens ... uirtus : cf. Stat. *Th.* 2. 571 f. 'fulmineus Dory-
las, quem regibus ardens / aequabat uirtus': the Sibyl means
such beings as Hercules or Pollux: cf. Hor. *C.* 3. 3. 9 f. 'hac
arte Pollux et uagus Hercules / enisus arces attigit igneas'.

131. dis geniti : Aeneas might perhaps take this as encouraging
to some extent. It is difficult to fit Theseus into the Sibyl's
categories. The line is dominated by the 'weak' caesura in
the third foot, with a complete break in sense (see on 117).

media omnia : probably the 'whole heartland' of the
Underworld, surrounded by Cocytus. The usual interpreta-
tion is 'all the intervening space' between the upper and the
lower world.

132. Cocytus : the River of Lamentation; it is said (297) to
receive the sandy flood of Styx, but in *Od.* 10. 514 it is a
branch (ἀπορρώξ) of Styx. Virgil did not map out his Under-
world rivers with any great precision (see on 295): contrast
the splendid description in Plato, *Phaedo* 112 f.

sinu labens ... atro : the river coils round the Underworld
like a black serpent: cf. Cic. *Arat.* fr. 8 Tr. 'ueluti rapido cum
gurgite flumen / toruus Draco serpit ... / ... conficiensque
sinus e corpore flexos'.

133. tantus amor : Virgil likes the phrase; see on 2. 10 'si
tantus amor casus cognoscere nostros': the infinitive follows,
as if a verb of desiring had preceded (see references on 2. 10).
For the rhetorical *tantus ... tanta* cf. *G.* 3. 112 'tantus amor
laudum, tantae est uictoria curae'.

134. For the anaphora of *bis* see on 32. *Innare* is not recorded
in poetry before Virgil: for this transitive use ('float out
upon') cf. 369, 8. 651 'fluuium uinclis innaret Cloelia ruptis',
Silius 3. 363 f. 'bellis innare subactis / Eurotan patrium'.

135. Tartara : such neuter plurals are metrically useful (cf.
Pergama, Gargara); Virgil has *Tartarus* once only (577).

insano . . . labori : a self-echo, from 2. 776 'quid tantum insano iuuat indulgere labori?'; cf. Minucius Felix 5. 6 'indulgentes insano atque inepto labori ultra humilitatis nostrae terminos euagamur'. The Sibyl has returned for a moment to her more austere manner; *insano* suggests something wild and uncontrollable (of war, 7. 550; of love, *E.* 10. 44).

136. peragenda : for the omission of the verb (*sunt? sint?*) cf. 1. 362 f. 'nauis, quae forte paratae, / corripiunt' (sc. *sunt*), 1. 516 f. 'nube caua speculantur amicti / quae fortuna uiris' (sc. *sit*).

latet . . . opaca : a form of ἔκφρασις begins, picked up in 142 (*hoc . . . munus*). The juxtaposition of *opaca* with *aureus* (137) is striking; the epithet with *arbore* adds force to *latet*, and prepares for the fuller picture in 138 f.

137. aureus . . . ramus : the arrangement of epithet and noun is effective: the reader is suspended, as it were, until the crucial *ramus* is reached. That actual gold is meant becomes clear in 209.

lento : tough and bending: cf. 3. 31 f. 'rursus et alterius lentum conuellere uimen / insequor'; *uimen* can be used of the stem of any tree or shrub, not merely of varieties of willow (e.g. 11. 65 'uimine querno', *G.* 4. 123 'flexi . . . uimen acanthi').

138. Iunoni infernae : Epic style for Proserpina, and metrically useful; cf. Stat. *S.* 2. 1. 147 'infera Iuno', *Th.* 5. 156 'inferna Ceres': so *Ioui Stygio* (4. 638) means Pluto, Ζεὺς χθόνιος.

dictus : 'dicatus', Servius, i.e. 'set apart' ritually. But it need be no more than a variant on the type *fertur, dicitur* (see on 14), reporting a traditional legend. For the break at the fourth-foot diaeresis cf. 30; but here it is less dramatic, for the whole narrative is quieter.

hunc tegit omnis : not a frequent type of line-ending: see Norden, Anh. ix. 4(a), and references on 1. 199. All the examples in this book (cf. 30, 47, 278, 365, 434) of this pattern (two disyllabic words, the first being a pyrrhic) show a monosyllable preceding the disyllables (contrast, e.g., 10. 442 'soli mihi Pallas', a much rarer type): here the conflict of ictus and speech-accent is more marked than in 30, where *quoque* is enclitic, but far less so than in the pattern of 10. 442.

138 f. hunc . . . umbrae : assonance, alliteration, and language make a memorable picture of deep and enclosing darkness. It is here in this primeval forest, with its coombs and shadows, that Aeneas must seek the Golden Bough.

Virgil endows the Bough with attributes of solemn mystery. It is of actual gold (cf. 144, 209), gleaming on its tree like mistletoe in winter (205 ff.); when it is plucked, a new Bough grows to replace it (143 f.), but only those can pluck it who are called by destiny (147); its locality is only revealed after a sign from heaven (190 ff.). It has been established as her due gift by Proserpina (142); only when Aeneas has set it at her door (636) can he enter Elysium. Its authority is instantly respected by Charon, who has seen it before (406 ff.).

The Bough has no known literary ancestry. Within a century of Virgil's death Cornutus, freedman of Seneca, noted (on 4. 698 f.) 'adsueuit poetico more aliqua fingere ut de aureo ramo' (Macrob. *Sat.* 5. 19. 2). Servius' comment (on 136), in part allegorical, shows that no clearly informed opinion about the Bough had survived. Modern theories are equally speculative.

Servius offers two main possibilities. The first is that those 'qui de sacris Proserpinae scripsisse dicuntur' state that the Bough was *quiddam mysticum*: this cautious remark, se vaguely expressed, amounts to little more than a guess at the meaning of 'ferri munus instituit' (142 f.); however, Norden (pp. 171 ff.) thinks it probable that Virgil really had some knowledge of a rite used in the Mysteries of Proserpina. The second is that *publica opinio* connected the Bough with the tradition of the tree in Diana's grove at Aricia, from which a branch had to be plucked by a *fugitiuus* who sought the priesthood there, enabling him to kill the existing priest, himself a *fugitiuus*. The legend (which was Frazer's starting-point for his anthropological researches in *The Golden Bough*) has no definable relevance to Virgil: Servius does not identify the *aureus ramus* with the branch plucked from the tree at Aricia; he merely says that Virgil 'istum inde sumpsit colorem', and that the legend accounted for the poet's association of the death of Misenus (149 ff.) with the finding of the Bough.

Virgil's own simile of the mistletoe led inevitably to vast fields of folklore and magic (cf. 204, note), fascinatingly developed by Frazer in his famous work: another superadded growth has been provided by modern concern with symbolism. But the Bough remains an enigma. Some kind of tradition is suggested by *dictus* (138; see note), unless this is a device to make the legend authoritative. Yet even if Virgil did have some source in folk-lore, the imagination and beauty of his use of it is wholly Virgilian, a wonder of ancient poetry.

Norden discusses the Bough at length. Among recent papers see A. K. Michels, *A J P* lxvi (1945), 59 ff.; R. A. Brooks, *A J P* lxxiv (1953), 260 ff.; R. Merkelbach, *Mus. Helv.* xviii.

84 COMMENTARY

(1961), 86 ff.; C. P. Segal, *Arion* iv (1965), 617 ff., v (1966), 34 ff.; cf. R. S. Conway, *The Vergilian Age* (Harvard, 1928), 41 ff. Camps (op. cit. 93 f.) has a brief and wise summary of the various views.

140. telluris operta : cf. Stat. *Th.* 4. 502 f. 'telluris opertae / dissilit umbra capax'. The genitive is a true partitive ('the hidden places of earth'); contrast 633 (see note there). The line has the rare rhythm of a 'weak' caesura in both fourth and fifth feet (again, 167, 333): see on 1. 188, 2. 380, 4. 58.

141. auricomos : a Virgilian coinage, and a pretty one; cf. Val. Flacc. 4. 92 'auricomis . . . Horis', Silius 3. 608 'auricomo . . . Batauo': so χρυσοκόμας of Apollo, Eur. *Supp.* 975, and of "Ερως, Eur. *I.A.* 548 (both lyric passages): Lucretius (6. 152) has the remarkable *lauricomos . . . montis.* Virgil's discreet use of such compound epithets is in marked contrast with the practice of Lucretius and early poetry: see on 1. 224, 663, R. D. Williams on 3. 544, and Norden's important note here.

The metaphor of *coma* applied to leaves goes back to Homer (*Od.* 23. 195 κόμην τανυφύλλου ἐλαίης); cf. 7. 59 f. 'laurus erat . . . / sacra comam', *G.* 2. 368 (of vines), and Catullus' *comata silua* (4. 11). Here *auricomos fetus*, 'the gold-haired growth', is high Epic for *aureum ramum*; the branch is regarded as the 'fruit' of the tree (cf. *G.* 2. 69 'inseritur . . . fetu nucis arbutus'), but the phrase is a preparation for the *croceus fetus* of the mistletoe (207), where 'fetu' refers to the berries.

quis : so PR: *qui* M. The construction with either is impressionistic: with this text, *quis* (= *aliquis*) is put into the clause of *antequam* instead of *cuiquam* being used with *datur*; with *qui* there is a telescoping of 'non ante datur quam ⟨ei datur⟩ qui . . .'. The indefinite is neater, but *qui* is preferred by many editors.

142. pulchra : the epithet is strikingly placed: Proserpina in all her beauty ordains this gift as her due tribute. Cf. 4. 192 'cui se pulchra uiro dignetur iungere Dido' (where *pulchra* is stressed as a reproach).

144. aureus : emphatic, both in its position in the line and in its overspill from *alter*: a supply of *Golden* Boughs never fails.

frondescit : brilliantly conjoined with *metallo*, a verbal counterpart to the adjectival *auricomos* above: 'quam bene usus est *frondescit metallo*' (Macrob. *Sat.* 6. 6. 8); 'honeste locutus est dicens: habet frondes sui metalli' (Servius). The verb is Ennian (*Sc.* 151 'caelum nitescere, arbores frondescere'); cf. Lucr. 1. 1092 'arboribus summos frondescere ramos'.

metallo : cf. Claudian, *rapt. Proserp.* 2. 290 ff. (Pluto to Proserpina) 'est etiam lucis arbor praediues opacis / fulgentes uiridi ramos curuata metallo: / haec tibi sacra datur': a respectful echo. Silver Epic made no attempt to steal the Golden Bough.

145. alte : 'omni intentione' (Servius). Aeneas must search for it in the depths of the forest (cf. 139).

rite : this marks the essentially religious aspect of the quest. Servius took it with *carpe* ('non *rite repertum*'). But it belongs to both actions (*repertum carpe = reperi et carpe*): both finding and plucking must be done in due solemnity.

146. manu : pleonastic, as often: e.g. 12. 774 'uoluitque manu conuellere ferrum', 11. 332 'pacisque manu praetendere ramos'. There is no reason to assume, as some do, that *manu* emphasizes the hand as opposed to using a knife; the notion is ruled out by the implication of 147 f.

ipse : 'of itself', reinforced by *uolens* and *facilis*: the Bough will yield easily to a man chosen by destiny to pluck it.

149. praeterea : something else remains to be done: not, like the obtaining of the Bough, a universal requirement, but caused by a particular circumstance.

exanimum . . . corpus : cf. Lucr. 6. 705 f. 'corpus ut exanimum siquod procul ipse iacere / conspicias hominis'.

tibi : 'ethic' dative (a term coined by Buttmann; see Landgraf, *ALL* viii, 48), = 'I tell you': it marks the speaker's involvement with the feelings of the person addressed, corresponding to a tone or gesture of concern; naturally it shades off into the dative of 'person interested'.

150. heu nescis : an aside; cf. 97 'quod minime reris'. Virgil rather likes *heu* in this way; cf. 4. 541 'nescis heu, perdita', *G.* 4. 491 'immemor heu!'

incestat : the verb is not recorded in elevated poetry before Virgil; in Plaut. *Poen.* 1096 it = *stuprare*.

funere : for *funus* of a dead body cf. 510, 9. 490 f. 'artus auulsaque membra / et funus lacerum'; Varro, *R.R.* 1. 4. 5 'omnes domus repletae . . . aegrotis ac funeribus'; Prop. 1. 17. 8 'haecine parua meum funus harena teget?'

151. consulta : 'advice', 'decisions'; cf. Stat. *Th.* 10. 770 f. 'si non attonitis uatis consulta recepi / auribus'. Aeneas is like a client consulting on a point of law.

in limine : the entrance to the *antrum* (cf. 45, 115). *Pendes* combines the idea of mental suspense ('sollicitus es', Servius) with that of physical loitering (Conington notes Florus 1. 13 'sex mensibus barbari . . . circa montem unum pependerunt').

152. sedibus . . . suis : 'his due resting-place', explained by *sepulcro*: cf. 328, 7. 3 'seruat honos sedem tuus' (of Caieta's grave).

   conde sepulcro : cf. 3. 67 f. (of Polydorus) 'animamque sepulcro / condimus et magna supremum uoce ciemus'; so Ennius, *Ann.* 139 'heu quam crudeli condebat membra sepulcro'.

153. **duc nigras pecudes :** the Sibyl abruptly turns to a new injunction, not connected with the burial rites: appeasement offerings (*piacula*) must be made to the chthonic powers, to whom black victims were appropriate (see 243 ff.); this had already been foreshadowed by the ghostly Anchises, 5. 735 f. 'huc casta Sibylla / nigrarum multo pecudum te sanguine ducet'.

   sunto : formal and legalistic; cf. *ito*, 95.

154. **sic demum :** 'in this way, and in this only'; so 637 'his demum exactis' (when this had been done, and only then).

   inuia : Virgil first uses the word in poetry; in prose it occurs before him in Sall. *hist.* 1. 11 'Gallia . . . nisi qua paludibus inuia fuit, perdomita'.

155. **pressoque . . . ore :** 'she set her lips and a dumbness came upon her'; *presso ore* and *obmutuit* are complementary, each reinforcing the other. The verb *obmutesco* (the compound implies blockage or resistance) is very rare in poetry, and occurs only in this one form (again, 4. 279 'Aeneas aspectu obmutuit amens'; Ovid, *Met.* 13. 538; Stat. *Th.* 2. 628). Virgil introduced it to poetic style.

   The sudden silence is very Sibylline (cf. 54); Virgil likes to stress her brevity (321, 398, 538).

156–82. *Aeneas leaves the cave, and confers with Achates in perplexity. They come to the shore, and discover Misenus lying dead there. In much sorrow the Trojans cut down great trees to make a pyre.*

   The episode of Misenus is based on a tradition which may be derived from Varro (Norden, p. 179): see Dion. Hal. *ant. Rom.* 1. 53. 3 ἐκεῖθεν δὲ [sc. from Leucasia] κατάραντες εἰς λιμένα καλὸν καὶ βαθὺν ἐν Ὀπικοῖς, τελευτήσαντος καὶ αὐτόθι Μισήνου τῶν ἐπιφανῶν τινος, ἀπ᾽ ἐκείνου τὸν λιμένα ὠνόμασαν. In its aetiological motif and character it is paralleled by the episode of Palinurus (337 ff.), and both reflect the story of Elpenor in *Od.* 10. 552 ff. But the similarity lies in the aetiology only; the significance of the dead Misenus differs wholly from that of the ghostly Palinurus. With subtle art Virgil has interwoven this episode with the need to find the Golden Bough: the discovery of Misenus' body, and the preparations for his pyre, lead almost imperceptibly to the finding of the Bough, in the very forest where the trees are even now being felled. It is only when the

Bough has been plucked that the burning of the body is de-
scribed with ritual detail: so that death and burial encompass
and accentuate the miracle by which a living man can de-
scend to the Underworld. At the moment when Aeneas'
prayer is answered, the dead man's presence reminds him of
mortality. It has been argued by Sabbadini that the episode
of Misenus was not part of Virgil's original design for the
book; Mackail regards it as 'detachable'. But this is to ignore
the underlying unity and inner connexion of the whole pas-
sage 156–235, so highly characteristic of Virgil's thought.
Norden has a valuable discussion; cf. Butler on 149, and
R. S. Conway, *New Studies of a Great Inheritance* (London,
1921), 125 ff.

156. defixus lumina : the participle is used like a Greek middle,
with *lumina* as direct object (cf. 11. 507 'Turnus . . . oculos
horrenda in uirgine fixus'); see on 1. 228, and R. D. Williams
on 5. 135. The line is slow, with the maximum number of spon-
dees, and the effect continues in the next two lines, though
less markedly, with much assonance and alliteration; the
placing of *antrum* (157) and *secum* (158) at the same point in
the line is noteworthy, and the heavy sound-effect is accen-
tuated by the strong pause after *secum*.

157. ingreditur : 'walks forward' ('pro *graditur*', Servius); cf.
8. 308 f. 'comitem Aenean iuxta natumque tenebat / in-
grediens uarioque uiam sermone leuabat', Sen. *Oed.* 554
'squalente cultu maestus ingreditur senex'.
   uolutat : cf. 185, 10. 159 f. 'sedet Aeneas secumque uolutat /
euentus belli uarios'.

158. fidus : almost a 'perpetual epithet' for Achates (1. 188,
8. 521, 586, 10. 332, 12. 384).

159. it comes : again, 448; 8. 466 'illi comes ibat Achates',
11. 33 'comes . . . ibat alumno', 12. 881 'fratri comes ire per
umbras'.
   paribus . . . figit : a good picture of slow, worried pacing. Cf.
Lucr. 3. 3 f. 'inque tuis nunc / ficta pedum pono pressis
uestigia signis' (where *ficta* is the original form of *fixa*); for
another kind of measured walk cf. Prop. 2. 4. 5 'ibat et ex-
penso planta morata gradu'.

160. sermone serebant : a 'figura etymologica': 'hic proprie
dictus est sermo, qui inter utrumque seritur' (Servius); Varro,
LL 6. 64 'sermo . . . est a serie . . .; sermo enim non potest in
uno homine esse solo, sed ubi oratio cum altero coniuncta'.
With Virgil's construction cf. Livy. 3. 43. 2 'L. Siccium . . .
tribunorum creandorum secessionisque mentiones . . . ser-
monibus occultis serentem', 7. 39. 6 'haec qui in castris
erant occultis sermonibus serunt': contrast Plaut. *Curc.* 193

'seruus sermonem serat', *Mil.* 700 'me uxore prohibent, mihi quae huius similis sermones serat'.

161. quem socium . . . quod corpus : the indirect questions are loosely appended to *multa serebant*; cf. Stat. *Th.* 6. 942 f. 'multa duces errore serunt: hi nubila et altos / occurrisse Notos'. Such parallel questions are characteristic of Virgil's style: e.g. 198, 9. 525 ff. 'canenti / quas ibi tum ferro strages, quae funera Turnus / ediderit, quem quisque uirum demiserit Orco', 11. 249 f. 'nomen patriamque docemus, / qui bellum intulerint, quae causa attraxerit Arpos'.

exanimum : so PR; *exanimem* M, preferred by Norden on grounds of euphony (so Ribbeck, Conington, Sabbadini, Geymonat). But the assonance of *exanimum . . . humandum* reflects the heaviness of *antrum . . . secum* above, which justifies Mynors's preference (cf. 9. 444 'tum super exanimum sese proiecit amicum', where PR read *exanimem*: see Norden, p. 406).

Some commentators (e.g. Heyne, Conington) have been surprised that Aeneas and Achates were puzzled by the Sibyl's announcement, imagining that they would at once have thought of Palinurus. But they knew that Palinurus was dead; the Sibyl's *heu nescis* (150) makes it clear that here was something totally unexpected.

162. atque : introducing a dramatic moment, as in 494, 860 (see on 2. 796): so 4. 260 ff. 'Aenean fundantem arces ac tecta nouantem / conspicit. atque illi stellatus iaspide fulua / ensis erat', 10. 219 f. 'atque illi medio in spatio chorus, ecce, suarum / occurrit comitum'.

162. Misenum : mentioned 3. 239 f. 'dat signum specula Misenus ab alta / aere cauo' (for an attack on the Harpies). Misenus is not named in Homer; Strabo (1. 2. 18, cf. 5. 4. 6) knew a tradition that he was a companion of Odysseus. He appears on the *tabula Iliaca* (a first-century relief found at Bovillae, now in the Capitoline Museum) accompanying Aeneas on his departure from Troy: see F. Bömer, *Rom und Troia* (Baden-Baden, 1951), 17; K. Weitzmann, *Ancient Book Illumination* (Harvard, 1959), pl. 24. This relief purports to represent details from the *Iliupersis* of Stesichorus, but the actual Stesichorean element in it is problematic (see Bowra, *Greek Lyric Poetry*[2] [Oxford, 1961], 105 f.; Momigliano, *JRS* xxxv [1945], 100), and it is not safe to assume Stesichorus' authority for the presence of Misenus.

There are frequent allusions to the association of Misenus with Misenum (cf. 235): Mela 2. 4 'Misenum, id nunc loci, aliquando Phrygii militis nomen'; Prop. 3. 18. 3 'qua iacet et Troiae tubicen Misenus harena'; Silius 12. 155 f. 'Misenum

seruantem Idaea sepulcro / nomina'; Stat. *S.* 3. 1. 150 f.
'Phrygioque e uertice Graias / addisces, Misene, tubas',
4. 7. 17 ff. 'me natum propiore terra / non tamen portu
retinent amoeno / desides Baiae liticenue notus / Hectoris
armis', 5. 3. 167 f. 'lituo remoque notatus / collis'.

The Promunturium Misenum lies SSE. of Cumae, over
8 km. as the crow flies and 11 km. round the coast. If we did not
know this, we would think of Misenus' body as lying on the
beach below Cumae. But Triton drowns him *inter saxa* (174),
such as begin only at Torregaveta, over 4 km. to the south
beyond the Palus Acherusia. The promontory is 1 km. long
and 400 m. across, with a curiously flat top for the remains
of a crater, like a truncated pyramid, and high (167 m.) for
its size. The isolation emphasizes its height, greater than
any other hill between it and the Mons Gaurus, Monte Bar-
baro, 331 m. It can be seen in the background of Turner's
picture of Lake Avernus (Tate Gallery, 463) of *c.* 1798,
painted after a drawing by Sir Richard Colt Hoare, long
before Turner's first visit to Italy in 1820. In Virgil's time,
probably on the west side near to the shore, was the large
villa of Marius which passed to Lucullus and then to the
Imperial family; Tiberius died there in A.D. 37. There is now
a lighthouse at the south end.

It is not clear how Virgil conceived the tomb raised to
Misenus 'monte *sub* aerio' (234), which Servius interprets
as 'in aerio; nam supra est positus'. Virgil might have
imagined the tomb, if on top, as corresponding to the great
drum that Munatius Plancus built as his tomb on the hill
above Gaeta at the other end of the gulf of Cumae; but it is
clearly below, on the shore, *in litore sicco*, where the body
was cast up, as if by a storm. North of the promontory is
the harbour, formed in the eastern of two craters. It was used
by the Cumaeans, certainly as early as the sixth century,
and indeed by Aeneas, according to Dion. Hal. *ant. Rom.*
1. 53. 3. It declined in importance with the fortunes of
Cumae, but regained its position as Augustus' naval base
about the time of Actium, taking the place of the Portus
Iulius. If Virgil regarded the Portus Iulius as a remarkable
achievement, he must have been interested in the massive
development at Misenum.

in litore sicco : above high-water mark; cf. 3. 510 f. 'pas-
simque in litore sicco / corpora curamus'.

163. uident : 'Misenum *uident*, non audiunt, quo fortis sit
affectus' (Cerda).

indigna morte : so Aeneas and Achates felt; and so, no
doubt, did Virgil himself (cf. 173).

164. Aeoliden : Servius (on 3. 239) approves, 'quia constat
sonum omnem ex uento creari'; Aeolus' son did him credit.
There is a *Clytius Aeolides* in 9. 774, and a Trojan Aeolus in
12. 542: no reason to connect Misenus with either. Ovid,
either carelessly or following a different tradition about
Misenus, makes the aetiological legend anticipate Aeneas'
arrival, *Met.* 14. 102 ff. 'canori / Aeolidae tumulum et, loca
feta palustribus undis, / litora Cumarum uiuacisque antra
Sibyllae / intrat' (*sc.* Aeneas).

The rhetorical figure ('epanalepsis') in 'Misenum . . .
Misenum Aeoliden' is both ornamental and emotional: so
2. 318 f. 'ecce autem telis Panthus elapsus Achiuum, / Pan-
thus Othryades' (where, as here, the metrical ictus falls
differently in the repetition of the name), 10. 778 f. 'egregium
Antoren latus inter et ilia figit, / Herculis Antoren comitem'.
It is Homeric; see *Il.* 2. 671 ff. for a notable example which
drew interesting comment from Demetrius (π. ἑρμ. 62); in
Hellenistic poetry see Callim. *h.* 4. 118, 5. 40, Apoll. Rhod.
1. 957, *AP* 7. 476. 7 f.; before Virgil it occurs in Cicero
(*Prognost.* fr. 4. 5 f. 'matutinis acredula uocibus instat, /
uocibus instat et adsiduas iacit ore querellas'), Lucretius
(e.g. 5. 950 f.; Bailey, *proleg.* 156), and Catullus (e.g. 64. 61 f.,
285 f.; Fordyce, pp. 255, 275); for other Virgilian examples
see 495 f., 1. 108 f., 2. 405 f., 7. 586 f., 10. 821 f. See Norden
here; Wölfflin, *Ausg. Schr.,* 290.

quo . . . alter : so 1. 544 f. 'quo iustior alter / nec pietate
fuit, nec bello maior et armis', 7. 649 f. 'quo pulchrior alter /
non fuit', 9. 772 'quo non felicior alter', 12. 639 'quo non
superat mihi carior alter'.

The *uita Donati* records (34) that Virgil completed the line
(from *Aeoliden*) extempore during a recitation, and that he
added *Martemque accendere cantu* in 165 'simili calore iacta-
tum'; telling this, Virgil's freedman Eros claimed that he
was at once instructed to insert the additions in his copy.
Servius, much more probably, confines the story to 165 only;
in view of the other passages quoted above it is hardly likely
that 'quo non praestantior alter' was a sudden inspiration,
nor that (as Conington notes) 'aere ciere uiros' had nothing
before it to provide a construction.

165. A fine trumpeting line, with clanging assonances and
alliteration, suggesting pure joy in heralding battle.

aere . . . uiros : Norden notes Cat. 64. 262 'tereti tenuis
tinnitus aere ciebant' and 68. 88 'coeperat ad sese Troia
ciere uiros', lines which might well have been at the back
of Virgil's mind here.

accendere : cf. Silius 15. 594 'belliger is quondam scitusque accendere Martem'; Ammianus 27. 10. 12 'signoque erecto, quod solet ad pugnam hortari, tubarum minacium accendente clangore'.

166. Hectoris ... Hectora : the repetition is both a reminder of Trojan pride and sorrow, and marks the special status of Misenus.

167. lituo : strictly not synonymous with *tuba* (233), since it was curved while the *tuba* was straight (cf. Ovid, *Met.* 1. 98 'non tuba directi, non aeris cornua flexi'). On the *tabula Iliaca* Misenus carries a trumpet (according to some, an oar; see M. Paulcke, *de tabula Iliaca quaestiones Stesichoreae* [diss. Königsberg, 1897], 46 f.). For the caesura-pattern in the second half of the line see on 140; cf. 7. 45 'rex arua Latinus et urbes', 8. 229 'huc ora ferebat et illuc'.

168. uita uictor spoliauit : notable alliteration. Cf. 12. 935 'seu corpus spoliatum lumine mauis'.

170. non inferiora secutus : Aeneas is Hector's equal; so 11. 289 ff. 'Hectoris Aeneaeque manu uictoria Graium / haesit ... / ambo animis, ambo insignes praestantibus armis, / hic pietate prior'; *Il.* 5. 467 f. κεῖται ἀνὴρ ὃν ἶσον ἐτίομεν Ἕκτορι δίῳ, / Αἰνείας.

171. A sharp, vivid picture: Misenus casually blows a loud blast in sheer *joie de vivre*, proud of his skill and art.

　　personat : cf. 418. In 1. 741 the verb is used intransitively.

　　concha : Conington's idea that this is used for *lituus* or *tuba* spoils the drama: Misenus picks up a handy *concha* and tries it out. The whorled *concha* is Triton's special instrument: see the splendid picture of the ending of the Flood in Ovid, *Met.* 1. 333 ff., where Triton blows upon it and the waters retreat (the shell is his *bucina*, 'tortilis in latum quae turbine crescit ab imo'). For Lucan, Triton is 'deus quem toto litore pontus / audit uentosa perflantem marmora concha' (9. 348 f.); Silius (14. 373 f.) makes the noise of war-trumpets at a sea-battle so terrifying that 'excitus aequore Triton / expauit tortae certantia murmura conchae'; Apuleius (*Met.* 4. 31) pictures a whole bevy of Tritons in attendance on Venus, 'passim maria persultantes Tritonum cateruae hic concha sonaci leniter bucinat, ille serico tegmine flagrantiae solis obsistit inimici', etc.; Pliny reports (*NH* 9. 9) that a deputation from Lisbon waited on Tiberius to tell him that they had seen and heard a Triton in a certain cave, *concha canentem*. No wonder Wordsworth yearned to hear one too.

172. demens : Homer's νήπιος; for the first-foot spondee, with no overspill to the second foot, see on 127 (*noctes atque dies*).

　　uocat in certamina : like Marsyas (Ovid, *Met.* 6. 382 ff.; see Frazer on Apollod. *Bibl.* 1. 4. 2), or Arachne (Ovid, *Met.*

6. 5 ff.), or Thamyris (*Il.* 2. 594 ff.), or Orion (Apollod. *Bibl.* 1. 4. 5).

173. aemulus : 'jealous'; amusing, for the emulation was on Misenus' part.

    si credere dignum est : so *G.* 3. 391 (of the legend of Pan and the Moon), on which Macrobius comments (*Sat.* 5. 22. 10) 'quod sciens Vergilius adiecit *si credere dignum est*; adeo se fabuloso usum fatetur auctore' (the *auctor* being Nicander). For similar phrases cf. 3. 551 'si uera est fama' (again, *G.* 4. 42), 8. 140 'auditis si quicquam credimus'; they do not necessarily imply scepticism (cf. 14, note), only a disclaimer of personal responsibility: so Apoll. Rhod. 1. 154 εἰ ἐτεόν γε πέλει κλέος, 4. 985 οὐκ ἐθέλων ἐνέπω προτέρων ἔπος. Yet it is hard not to think that in telling the tale of this happy young trumpeter incurring such retribution from a petty-minded divinity Virgil is expressing his own feelings about human suffering (cf. 163).

174. inter saxa : it is noticeable that *inter* occurs often as a first-foot spondee (so too *intra*, *contra*, *circum*); the grammatical connexion with the following noun prevents the effect of isolation from the rest of the line, and there is no emphasis felt as there is in (e.g.) *demens* above.

    uirum : for *eum* (generally avoided; see on 4. 479); cf. 890, 1. 91 'praesentemque uiris intentant omnia mortem', etc.

175. A heavy line, with the maximum possible number of spondees, and strongly marked conflict of ictus and speech-accent. *Fremebant* suggests a noisy buzz of sound; Virgil likes the verb.

176. praecipue pius Aeneas : again, 1. 220 (in a similar context of mourning). The epithet marks Aeneas' devotion to his men and his sense of responsibility to them.

177. haud mora : in parenthesis, a Virgilian mannerism: so 5. 140, 11. 713; not formally parenthetic, 3. 207, 548, 7. 156, *G.* 4. 548.

    festinant : for the transitive use cf. 4. 575 'festinare fugam' (so Ennius, *Sc.* 426, Sall. *Iug.* 73. 1): contrast 7. 156 f. 'haud mora, festinant iussi rapidisque feruntur / passibus'.

    aramque sepulcri : the variant *sepulcro* (P) may be due to *conde sepulcro* in 152 (? 'for a tomb', which is scarcely intelligible). Silius borrowed from Virgil, 15. 387 f. 'alta sepulcri / protinus exstruitur caeloque educitur ara'. The 'tomb-altar' (*sepulcri* defines *aram*) is itself the *ingens pyra* of 215: Servius comments 'pyram dicit, quae in modum arae construi lignis solebat', adding 'Probus tamen et Donatus de hoc loco requirendum adhuc esse dixerunt', which shows that Virgil's remarkable phrase perplexed his critics.

The pyre is a tomb, in the sense that it consumes the body;
and it is also an *ara*, in the sense that it is heaped with ritual
offerings to the *Di Manes* of the dead man (224 f.). But the
phrase remains strange and solemn, a preparation for the
rich and elaborate detail that is to follow; it has no parallel
other than Silius' imitation, and the two passages from Ovid
adduced by commentators have no direct relevance (*Met*. 8.
480 'ante sepulcrales infelix adstitit aras', *Tr*. 3. 13. 2
'funeris ara mihi, ferali cincta cupresso'). Inscriptions, how-
ever, sometimes show *ara* as equivalent to *sepulcrum*, e.g.
Carm. Lat. Epigr. 461 'Suetrius Hermes hic situs est, cui
Tertia coniunx / aram constituit digno meritoque marito',
467 'aeternam tibi sedem Hermes aramque dicaui': see
R. Lattimore, *Themes in Greek and Roman Epitaphs* (Ur-
bana, 1962), 131 f., where a corresponding use of βωμός is
pointed out.

178. caeloque educere : a self-echo from 2. 185 f. 'hanc . . .
Calchas attollere molem / roboribus textis caeloque educere
iussit' (of the Wooden Horse). The infinitive with *certare* is
Ennian (*Ann*. 445 'indu mari magno fluctus extollere cer-
tant', 485 'currus cum sonitu magno permittere certant').
The line is noisy with alliteration.

179 ff. The description of the felling of the forest-trees, mag-
nificent in itself ('omnia grandia sunt, omnia magnifica',
Cerda) offers the rare opportunity of an extended comparison
with Ennius (*Ann*. 187 ff., quoted by Macrobius, *Sat*. 6. 2. 27):

> incedunt arbusta per alta, securibus caedunt,
> percellunt magnas quercus, exciditur ilex,
> fraxinus frangitur atque abies consternitur alta,
> pinus proceras peruortunt: omne sonabat
> arbustum fremitu siluai frondosai.

Macrobius' purpose in such quotations is to show (*Sat*. 6. 1. 6)
how Virgil 'et iudicio transferendi et modo imitandi con-
secutus est ut, quod apud illum legerimus alienum, aut
illius esse malimus aut melius hic quam ubi natum est sonare
miremur': it is seldom as easy as it is here to see the extent
and quality of Virgil's debt to a predecessor. Various points
may be noticed.

(1) Ennius uses far more spondees, producing a tremen-
dous effect of heavy blows, and culminating in the astonish-
ingly resonant final line with a spondee in the fourth and
fifth feet (Virgil has only three such lines, 3. 74 'Nereidum
matri et Neptuno Aegaeo', 7. 634 'aut leues ocreas lento
ducunt argento', *G*. 3. 276 'saxa per et scopulos et depressas
conuallis'). The effect of this final line is weighted by the two

archaic genitive forms in *ai*, frequent in Plautus and Lucretius (for Virgil's use of these see on 747).

(2) Ennius twice (*securibus*, *fraxinus*) has the archaic suppression of final *s* in a short syllable before a consonant, frequent in Comedy and in Lucretius (see Bailey, *proleg.* vi. 10), once in Catullus (116. 8): it was *subrusticum* by the time that Cicero wrote his *Orator* (46 B.C.; *Orat.* 161). Virgil has retained *securibus* at the same point in the line, but followed by a vowel, and for *fraxinus* he has substituted *fraxineaeque trabes*.

(3) Ennius' first line has a metrical pattern that is foreign to Virgil's practice: it has no 'strong' caesura in the third or fourth foot, and the sense-break at *alta* gives an effect of a line-ending in mid-line. In his third line, the two opening dactylic words, each occupying a foot with no overspill, provide a sledge-hammer rhythm which is most effective, but it is not a Virgilian technique.

(4) Ennius repeats *alta*, and *arbusta* is echoed by *arbustum*. Virgil has substituted the far more evocative *antiquam siluam* for Ennius' *arbusta alta*, and has transferred *alta* to his own variation *stabula alta ferarum*, giving his opening line a solemn tone that Ennius does not reach in his.

(5) Ennius has three successive passives, and four verbs with the woodcutters as subject (*incedunt, caedunt, percellunt, peruortunt*). Virgil varies his constructions: from the impersonal *itur* he passes to *procumbunt* with the trees as subject, and a tree is again the subject of *sonat* (cf. Ennius' *sonabat*), which with *icta* added gives a vivid personalization of the ilex, crying out at the blow; then *scinditur* is the solitary passive form, and in *aduoluunt* the subject is now the woodcutters.

(6) Ennius' use of alliteration and assonance is less sophisticated and more obtrusive than Virgil's: in Ennius the great smashing blows strike more vehemently on the ear, in Virgil the effect of noise is more distant.

(7) Ennius' trees are the oak, ilex, ash, fir, pine. Virgil keeps ilex and ash, puts *robur* for *quercus*, names the pitch-pine alone for Ennius' fir and pine, and adds the manna-ash.

The resulting impression is that Ennius' massive, rugged power does not suffer from the comparison, and Virgil's subtlety heightens our appreciation of the older poet. The whole passage is a remarkable illustration of the ancient way of acknowledging poetic greatness.

Both Virgil and Ennius look back to *Il.* 23. 114 ff. (the wood-gathering for Patroclus' pyre), especially 118 f. αὐτίκ' ἄρα δρῦς ὑψικόμους ταναήκεϊ χαλκῷ / τάμνον ἐπειγόμενοι· ταὶ δὲ μεγάλα κτυπέουσαι / πῖπτον. Virgil echoes himself (and Ennius), with interesting variations, in 11. 135 ff. (the burial of the dead, in a truce). After Virgil, the Silver poets develop the theme, each in his own manner: Lucan 3. 440 ff. (the felling of the Druids' grove), Silius 10. 527 ff. (funeral pyres after Cannae), Stat. *Th.* 6. 90 ff. (an expiatory pyre): each illustrates Virgil's strength. For an analysis cf. G. Williams, op. cit. 263 ff.

179. itur : 'their way led them': for the impersonal verb see on 45.

antiquam : 'venerable'; awe as well as age is implied (cf. 1. 12, note); for the forest see on 107.

stabula alta ferarum : probably *alta* = 'tall', stressing the great height of the trees rather than the depth of the coverts; in 10. 723 'stabula alta' presumably implies the 'high stalls' of a farm (again, 9. 388).

180. procumbunt piceae : cf. Lucan 3. 440 'procumbunt orni' (but in Stat. *Th.* 6. 100 Virgil is repeated). For the pitch-pine see J. Sargeaunt, *Trees, Shrubs, and Plants of Virgil* (Blackwell, Oxford, 1920), 99 f.; he comments 'Virgil must have forgotten that the tree did not grow near the sea-level'.

sonat icta : cf. Silius 10. 529 f. 'sonat acta bipenni / frondosis silua alta iugis'. Lucan has (3. 440) 'nodosa inpellitur ilex'.

181. fraxineaeque trabes : cf. Stat. *Th.* 6. 101 'ornique iliceaeque trabes'. Sargeaunt notes (op. cit. 48) 'the ash . . . out-towers the manna-ash, and is sometimes nearly a hundred feet high'.

cuneis : cf. 11. 137. The use of wedges preceded the invention of the saw (*G.* 1. 144); Virgil puts the Trojans' tools back to very primitive times. Probably *sonant* should be supplied with *trabes*, and *cuneis* taken with *scinditur*, the connective *et* being postponed (see on 28): Ti. Donatus evidently punctuated in this way.

182. aduoluunt . . . montibus ornos : cf. Silius 10. 533 'deuoluunt quercus'. The ablative ('from the mountains'; cf. Val. Flacc. 5. 253 'lapsus montibus anguis') is rather odd with *aduoluunt*: contrast *G.* 3. 377 f. 'congestaque robora totasque / aduoluere focis ulmos'. For the manna-ash see Sargeaunt, op. cit. 93: he notes that it is 'with some reason regarded by the Latin poets as the typical hillside tree of central and southern Italy'; it is the subject of a moving simile in 2. 626 ff.

183–211. *Aeneas prays for a glimpse of the Golden Bough, and is guided to it by the flight of two doves.*

Instead of the expected description of the funeral rites, the discovery of the Bough now follows (for the significance of

the interfusion see introductory note on 156 ff.). It is drama-
tic and subtle: Servius comments (on 183) 'bona oeconomia
uenitur ad ramum'.

183. nec non : an emphatic transition-formula, brought into
poetry by Virgil (see HSz, 778 f.). Aeneas takes the lead
(*primus*; cf. 176), working like his men and encouraging
them.

184. paribusque . . . armis : he fits himself out with tools like
theirs (cf. *G.* 1. 160 'quae sint duris agrestibus arma'). For
the 'middle' use of the verb cf. 2. 671 'ferro accingor rursus',
7. 640 'loricam induitur fidoque accingitur ense'.

185. haec . . . uolutat : cf. 157; here and in 8. 522 'multaque
dura suo tristi cum corde putabant' Virgil echoes Ennius,
Ann. 482 'haud temere est quod tu tristi cum corde guber-
nas'. *Haec* means his unspoken thoughts concerning Misenus
and the need to find the Bough, put presently into words (*sic*,
186). *Ipse* complements *suo*, as often, adding emphasis to
Aeneas' inner preoccupations while he was outwardly busy
among his men ('these were his musings in the deep privacy
of his grieving heart').

186. aspectans siluam immensam : the heavy rhythm expresses
his despondency: the spondees continue into the fourth foot
with no third-foot caesura, there are two elisions of -*am*, the
ictus and speech-accent clash strongly; even the fourth-foot
caesura is barely felt because of the close connexion of *et* with
sic. It seems that there is no chance of finding the Bough
in such immensity.

forte : Aeneas 'happens' to put his thoughts into the form
of a prayer, and this 'happens' (190) to be just at the moment
that guidance offered itself. Servius objects 'uacat *forte*, et est
uersus de his qui tibicines uocantur . . . nec enim possumus
intellegere eum fortuitu rogasse': there is nothing in this,
but some such idea may have caused the variant *uoce* for
forte in R. Page well remarks 'it is from two ordinary events
occurring thus, as it happened, together, that Aeneas infers
that the apparent accident is no accident, but a divine
intervention'.

187. The spondaic rhythm continues as Aeneas slowly prays,
and the next line labours (to *tanto*). The interlacing in *ille
aureus arbore ramus* is attractive: either *arbore* without
aureus, or *aureus* without *arbore* would have been enough:
the two words, so placed, suggest a special kind of bough on
a special kind of tree.

189 f. The Sibyl's words have been only too true, that he
would find a companion dead, and that companion has turned
out to be Misenus ('de te, Misene' is a compression): there-

fore Aeneas feels that there truly is a Golden Bough as she
has said, and that he may even yet find it.

190. uix ea fatus erat : a formula, equivalent to 'and im-
mediately'; cf. 1. 586, 2. 692, 3. 90, 8. 520, all in a context
of the supernatural. For the repetition of *forte* see on 186.

191. ipsa . . . uiri : 'directly within his view' (*uiri* = *eius*; see
on 174). Servius takes the words as a technical detail of
augury, 'perite, ne si longius uolarent non ad eum pertinere
uiderentur: nam moris erat ut captantes auguria certa sibi
spatia designarent, quibus uolebant uidenda ad se pertinere'.
The two doves were an *augurium oblatiuum*, sent without
man's request (see on 2. 691). Norden (pp. 173 ff.) has some
interesting parallels from bird-flight in myth and folklore.

   caelo : 'along the sky'; cf. *E*. 6. 86 'inuito processit Vesper
Olympo'.

   uenere uolantes : a reminiscence of Lucr. 6. 833 'cuius ubi
e regione loci uenere uolantes' (in the context of exhalations
from *Auerna loca*). The alliteration here and in the next line
adds pictorial emphasis.

193. maternas . . . auis : for the association of doves with Venus
see D'Arcy Thompson, *Glossary of Greek Birds* (Oxford,
1936), 244 ff., with much other dove-lore.

   laetusque precatur : Aeneas' mood changes at once: cf.
2. 687 f. 'at pater Anchises oculos ad sidera laetus / extulit',
where an *augurium oblatiuum* has occurred, followed pre-
sently by an *augurium impetratiuum* (just as happens here,
202 ff.; cf. Servius on 194).

194. o : with the imperatives; cf. 258, *G*. 2. 35 f. 'quare agite o
proprios generatim discite cultus, / agricolae': see Fraenkel,
Horace, 242 n. 1.

195 f. pinguem . . . humum : the careful chiastic arrangement
of juxtaposed epithets and nouns is notable: the richness of
the Bough enriches the ground beneath.

195. opacat : Norden wrongly states that the verb disappears
after Virgil: see G. B. A. Fletcher, *Hommages à Marcel
Renard* (Collection Latomus 101), 1969, 350.

196. o : with *ne defice* (cf. 194). For *ne* with imperative see on
74.

197. uestigia pressit : he stopped (cf. 331): Servius explains
'quia ad captanda auguria post preces immobiles uel sedere
uel stare consueuerant'. Henry interprets 'went more
slowly', possible (see his parallels, not all relevant), but less
likely: if Aeneas had continued moving he might have startled
the doves.

198. signa : i.e. directions for his search, explained in *quo ten-
dere pergant* (for the parallel indirect questions see on 161);

so 'signa tibi dicam', 3. 388, the 'signs' being the discovery
of the sow and her piglets.

199. After settling (192) the birds now fly forward from spot to
spot, feeding as they go (a good sign, Servius notes); the
spondaic rhythm marks a slow flight. Servius punctuated
after *pascentes*, not after *pergant*: an odd idea, for it upsets
the shapely line-structure and puts a wrong emphasis on
pascentes; what concerned Aeneas was the direction of their
flight, not primarily their feeding.

    prodire : the so-called 'historic' infinitive, for which see
HSz, 376 ff.

200. quantum . . . sequentum : cf. Silius 17. 55 ff. (of Scipio's
men, following the flight of eagles which point the way for
the fleet) 'secuti / tantum praegressos liquida sub nube
uolatus / quantum non frustra speculantum lumina seruant':
a clear imitation. The doves deliberately (*possent* is final sub-
junctive) keep within sight-range (*acie* = power of vision).

    sequentum : since Virgil has been at pains to imply that
Aeneas was quite alone at this supremely significant moment,
this must be a generalizing plural ('any who might follow').
Silius' imitation shows that following with the eye is meant.
The doves fly forward and Aeneas stays watching their
flight, until they soar (202) and reveal the Bough; then he
moves to the spot and plucks the Bough.

201. The line has an oddly jerky rhythm, perhaps meant to
suggest the movement of the birds.

    ubi uenere ad fauces . . . Auerni : the lake, not the Under-
world as at 126. As before (163 *ut uenere*) Aeneas quickly
reached Misenum from Cumae, so here he covers a similar
and more rugged distance from Misenum to Avernus, returns
to Misenum for the funeral, and then goes back again to the
cave. This is beside the lake, *tuta lacu nigro*, within the crater,
presumably on the south side of the lake. The *fauces* may be
the passage NNW. from Lake Lucrinus to Avernus, now a
road on the west side of the canal which runs from Avernus
into Lucrinus. It is scarcely a defile or pass, because on the
east the rim of the crater has virtually disappeared, though
it rises steeply on the west. But Virgil may be following the
exaggerated descriptions of the complete ring of steep slopes
enclosing the lake, true of Lake Nemi but not of Avernus: cf.
Pseudo-Aristotle, *Mir. Ausc.* 102, 839a; Tzetzes on Lyco-
phron 704; Antigonus, *Hist. Mir.* 152; Servius on *A.* 6, 107,
139. In antiquity Monte Nuovo did not exist. But the *fauces*
may rather mean the fissure in the ground from which the
mephitic fumes were supposed to have risen, making the
lake poisonous to birds; Virgil alludes to this in *grave olentis*

and explains it in 239–41, where he speaks of 'sese halitus atris / faucibus effundens'. For a similar use of *fauces* for a vertical fissure cf. 7. 570, *G.* 4. 467, Lucr. 6. 630; at *G.* 4. 428 it seems to mean a horizontal channel. The Golden Bough then grows on a tree at the entrance to the crater, before the lake is reached; the cave is within the crater, but all the countryside is wooded (188), and more densely within the crater (238).

The present Lacus Avernus is the product of a second eruption within and towards the SW. of the first and larger crater of 'Archiaverno'. It is a slightly elliptical sheet of water, 900 m. by 700 m., now 0·40 m. above sea-level. The depth is 34 m., so that the lake is not unbelievably deep, as the ancients averred: Diod. Sic. 4. 22; Pseudo-Aristotle, *Mir. Ausc.* 102, 839a; Lucan 2. 667 f. (deep enough to take the whole of Mons Gaurus, Monte Barbaro, 331 m.); Vibius Sequester, 182. On the south and west sides the crater rim is high (maximum 116 m.), steep and wooded. To the NE. the rim recedes, leaving a strip of alluvium by the lake and a gentler slope to the Masseria Marati. On the SE. from the Thermae to the canal the rim has since prehistoric times been levelled by the same marine erosion which has almost destroyed the Lacus Lucrinus and turned the Lacus Misenus into a lagoon. There is no reason to think that in antiquity the rim was complete, like those of the Lago Albano and the Lago di Nemi, despite the statements cited above; Avernus is much less strange than the Lago di Nemi, with its high (175 m.) and steep slopes on every side.

graue olentis : for the mythical exhalations of Lake Avernus see 240 f. (the doves do not fly over it; they go only *ad fauces*). For the epithet cf. *G.* 4. 270 'graue olentia centaurea'; Pliny has it (and the noun *graueolentia*) a number of times, mostly in medical contexts: contrast *E.* 2. 48 'florem . . . bene olentis anethi', Cat. 61. 6 f. 'floribus / suaue olentis amaraci'. Greek influence is obvious; Norden notes βαρύοδμος in Nicander (*Ther.* 51); Simonides 74 ἔαρος ἀδυόδμου.

202. tollunt se celeres : 'up they soar, swiftly'; the dactylic movement of the line contrasts markedly with the slow rhythms of 199 and 201. There is dramatic emphasis on *tollunt*; but its close sense-connexion with *se* prevents isolation from the rest of the line (cf. 174, note): so 1. 587 'scindit se nubes', 10. 892 'tollit se arrectum quadripes', *G.* 4. 432 'sternunt se somno'.

liquidumque per aera : a pretty contrast with *fauces graue olentis Auerni*. Virgil likes *liquidus* to describe bright, clear air: 7. 65 'liquidum trans aethera uectae', *G.* 4. 59 'nare per aestatem liquidam' (of bees); *G.* 1. 404 'apparet liquido sublimis in aëre Nisus'.

203. sedibus optatis : this surely means the place that Aeneas prayed that they would show him, with *unde* (204) explaining the nature of the *sedes*. Norden and Conington refer *optatis* to the doves ('the place of their choice'), which seems less natural.

    gemina : *geminae* R, a restatement of 190, marking the completion of the omen. But *gemina* is undoubtedly the true reading: the tree is 'double' because of the double character of its growth and leafage, explained by *discolor* below ('quae frondem duplicem materiamque portabat', Ti. Donatus). For an analogous use of *geminus* cf. Ovid, *Met.* 2. 630, 12. 449 (of Centaurs), *Met.* 8. 169 (of the Minotaur; also Manilius 4. 785), Stat. *S.* 3. 2. 35, *Th.* 5. 707 (of Triton); but in these passages there is an obvious clue, and Virgil's *gemina arbore* is far more striking and imaginative.

    super : the adverb ('high up'); cf. 17.

204. discolor . . . refulsit : 'from which a breathing of gold glinted in colour-contrast among the branches'.

    discolor : the gold contrasts with the dark-leaved ilex; cf. Claudian, *rapt. Pros.* 2. 192 f. 'rutilos obscurat anhelitus axes / discolor' (of the breath of Pluto's horses, darkening the brightness of the Sicilian sky).

    auri . . . aura : a Virgilian marvel; the gold is a shimmering airy wisp. Norden connects *aura* with *uento* in 209, taking the phrase to mean that the gold waves in the wind; but the gold is itself an *aura*. The ancient critics did not know what to make of the expression, and no wonder: 'splendor auri', Servius; Macrobius represents his young Servius as asking (*Sat.* 6. 6. 8) 'quid est enim aura auri, aut quem ad modum aura refulget? sed tamen pulchre usurpauit'. There is no real parallel to Virgil's phrase, with its impalpable *aura* as the substance of the tangible gold: but cf. Callim. *h.* 3. 117 f. φάεος δ' ἐνέηκας αὐτμὴν / ἀσβέστου (of Artemis, handling the lightning of Zeus); [Lactantius], *Phoenix* 44 'primi emicuit luminis aura leuis' (of sunrise).

205 ff. The appearance of the Bough (*species*, 208)—not the Bough itself—is likened to mistletoe, so mysteriously growing, so strangely in leaf at the winter solstice: the careful detail adds effectively to the solemn beauty of the whole episode of the Bough. We have no means of telling how much Virgil knew of primitive folklore in connexion with mistletoe (for speculations on the significance of the comparison see Norden, pp. 164 ff.); but it is likely that he knew something at least of the kind of legendary information reported by

Pliny from literary sources: see *NH* 16. 245 ff., 251 (the priest at a Gaulish Druid sacrifice 'candida ueste cultus arborem scandit, falce aurea demetit'), 24. 11 f. (medicinal uses; its efficacy *prima luna collectum e robore sine ferro*, without touching the ground).

205. brumali frigore : not simply 'winter's cold', but the cold at the winter solstice (*bruma*), which fell on 25 December ('a.d. viii kal. Ian. fere', Pliny, *NH* 18. 221).

206. quod . . . arbos : cf. *G.* 2. 82 'miraturque nouas frondes et non sua poma' (the grafted tree's surprise).

207. croceo : 'The colour of mistletoe is a yellowish green. Seen with the sun shining through it the leaves are edged and veined with gold and the stem seems powdered with gold dust' (Page).

208. auri frondentis : cf. 144: an arresting phrase, almost like something out of the *Metamorphoses*.

209. ilice : 'The leaves are much darker than those of the common oak . . . and the tree is evergreen' (Sargeaunt, op. cit. 62). It is characteristic of Virgil that he has delayed till now in naming the tree (cf. 32, note): Conington strangely thinks that the delay proves that Virgil 'attaches no importance to the specification'.

crepitabat : 'tinkled': not a point of the comparison; the Bough looked like that (*sic*) as it tinkled on the tree. The apple that tempted Atalanta grew on a tree that was 'fulua comas, fuluo ramis crepitantibus auro' (Ovid, *Met.* 10. 648).

brattea : gold foil, cobweb-thin (cf. Lucr. 4. 724 ff. 'rerum simulacra uagari / . . . tenuia, quae facile inter se iunguntur in auris, / obuia cum ueniunt, ut aranea bratteaque auri'); the golden apple at the judgment of Paris was *malum bratteis inauratum* (Apul. *Met.* 10. 30). The line is wonderfully onomatopoeic: its ingenious alliteration makes a fine climax to a markedly alliterative passage.

210. auidusque refringit : an amplification of *corripit*; Aeneas' eager alacrity is in sharp contrast with the gloom of 184.

211. cunctantem : the Bough took its time to be plucked; it was *lento uimine* (137), and 'gave' only gradually. There is no contradiction of 'ipse uolens facilisque sequetur' (146), and no ground for the cavillings of Conington and others: for some curious theories cf. G. Norwood, *CQ* xii (1918), 148 f.; J. D'Arms, *CJ* lix (1964), 265 ff.; W. T. Avery, *CJ* lxi (1966), 269 ff.; C. P. Segal, *Hermes*, xcvi (1968), 74 ff.

portat : the verb suggests carrying with some care. The meaning of *tecta Sibyllae* is not clear: it ought to be the *antrum* (cf. 10), and probably does mean this. Butler takes it of the *spelunca* at Lake Avernus (237), on the ground that

Aeneas did not return to Cumae; but his return is just the
sort of detail that Virgil leaves to the reader's common-
sense, and it is readily imagined if, as seems likely, Virgil
has telescoped the distances involved (see on 13).

212–35. *The Trojans make a great pyre for Misenus, and the
funeral rites are performed with faithful care: Aeneas raises
a tomb on the promontory, which keeps the name in perpetuity.*

The passage is a *locus classicus* for the most elaborate kind
of Roman funeral ceremony. It has some features in common
with *Il.* 23. 109 ff. (the funeral of Patroclus), but its ethos is
wholly Roman. The movement is deeply solemn, and all
Virgil's care for ancient ritual has been lavished on these
last acts of *pietas*. As the immediate prelude to Aeneas' de-
scent to the Underworld, its placing at this point has im-
mense poetic power.

For an authoritative account of Roman funerary rites
see J. M. C. Toynbee, *Death and Burial in the Roman World*
(London, 1971), 43 ff.; cf. C. Bailey, *Religion in Virgil* (Oxford,
1935), 287 ff. for a discussion of this passage. A comparison
with Stat. *Th.* 6. 54 ff. is instructive.

212. nec minus interea : a transition-formula (so 1. 633, 7. 572,
12. 107, *G.* 3. 311). Virgil returns to the scene of 177 ff.; in
Aeneas' absence the Trojan mourning continued unabated:
we are left to infer that he has now rejoined his men.

213. flebant . . . ferebant : the spondaic opening word, and the
grammatical rhyme of the two verbs 'framing' the line,
combine to give a melancholy effect. For the assonance cf.
2. 771 'quaerenti et tectis urbis sine fine ruenti', 4. 505 'erecta
ingenti taedis atque ilice secta' (but these 'rhymes' are less
downright).

cineri ingrato : 'the ash that gives no thanks'; the cremation
is anticipated. The phrase recurs in *Copa* 35 'quid cineri in-
grato seruas bene olentia serta?'; it is very striking: Servius
glosses *ingrato* by 'tristi', adding 'alii *ingrato* dicunt gratiam
non sentienti', certainly the true meaning. Cf. Cat. 96. 1 f.
'si quicquam mutis gratum acceptumue sepulcris / accidere
a nostro, Calue, dolore potest': far less explicit than Virgil.

214. taedis : pine-wood, very resinous: *pinguem* applies strictly
to *taedis* alone, but its force may be extended loosely to
robore secto; or (perhaps better) *pinguem taedis* can be re-
garded (as Norden implies) as a Virgilianism for *pinguibus
taedis*, balanced by *robore secto* in a variation of construction;
the whole description is then picked up and given further
colour in *ingentem* (215). An alternative is to take *robore*

secto with *ingentem* (cf. 4. 504 f. 'pyra . . . / ingenti taedis atque ilice secta') : this gives good sense (resinous pine-wood at the base, above it a great pile of oak logs), but it badly punctures the rhythm of *ingentem struxere pyram* and is therefore less attractive.

215. pyram : the Greek word, for Latin *rogus*; Norden notes that Virgil brought it into poetry. For cremation at Rome, a practice that goes back to very early times, see Toynbee, op. cit. 39 ff.

216. intexunt : cf. 2. 16 'sectaque intexunt abiete costas' (of the Horse); Virgil first uses the verb in poetry. So Stat. *Th.* 4. 460 f. (of an altar) 'frontis atque omne cupressus / intexit plorata latus'.

    cupressos : they form a facing for the pyre (*ante*). Servius quotes Varro for their use 'propter grauem ustrinae odorem, ne eo offendatur populi circumstantis corona'.

217. constituunt : in the same position as *intexunt* above and *expediunt* (219), *coniciunt* (222) : the heavy sound is accentuated in the two line-endings, *unguunt, reponunt* (219, 220).

    fulgentibus armis : perhaps Misenus' own; cf. 11. 196 'ipsorum clipeos et non felicia tela' (cast into the pyres of the dead in battle); *Il.* 6. 418, *Od.* 11. 74.

218. undantia : the bronze vessels bubble as they are heated; cf. 7. 462 ff. 'magno ueluti cum flamma sonore / uirgea suggeritur costis undantis aeni / exsultantque aestu latices' : the *latices* and the *aena* form a unit of thought, with the hot water having precedence over the means of heating.

219. lauant . . . unguunt : cf. Ennius, *Ann.* 155 'Tarquinium bona femina lauit et unxit' (see Vahlen). The washing and anointing of the body would normally be done after the *conclamatio* had been begun : this was the ritual calling of the dead man's name, continued at intervals until the obsequies were over; Virgil may allude to it in *fit gemitus* (220). Servius quotes Pliny as stating 'hanc esse causam ut mortui et calida abluantur et per interualla conclamentur, quod solet plerumque uitalis spiritus exclusus putari et homines fallere' : Toynbee suggests (op. cit. 288, n. 119) that the real purpose of the *conclamatio* may have been to ascertain that death had in fact occurred, and adds 'a relic of it survives to-day at a papal deathbed, when the dead pope is tapped three times on the brow and called three times by his baptismal name'. Pliny (*NH* 7. 173 ff.) reports several alleged cases where a man supposedly dead proved to be still alive.

220. toro : a funerary couch, placed on the bier, the *lectus funebris* (Toynbee, op. cit. 44).

    defleta : the mourners have taken their fill of weeping : so of

Evander's lament over Pallas' body, 11. 59 'haec ubi de-
fleuit' (the only other occurrence of the verb in Virgil); cf. the
memorable passage in Lucr. 3. 906 f. 'at nos horrifico cine-
factum te prope busto / insatiabiliter defleuimus', etc.

    reponunt : they 'duly place' the body on the *torus*, with
care and ritual observance.

221. nota : 'ipsi cara', Servius (cf. 11. 195 'munera nota', of the
armour cast upon a pyre); Norden notes Lucian, *Philops.* 27
(of a woman's cremation) τόν τε κόσμον ἅπαντα συγκατακαύσας καὶ
τὴν ἐσθῆτα ᾗ ζῶσα ἔχαιρεν. For noun-forms in *-amen* (found in-
creasingly useful by the poets, especially Ovid; cf. Hollis on
Met. 8. 729) see Norden, *Ennius und Vergilius*, 27 ff.: most
such forms in Virgil have the older type in *-entum* as a parallel
(see on 1. 649; cf. Sen. *Suas.* 2. 17 'omnia grandia probanti
inpositum est cognomen uel, ut Messala ait, cognomentum').

    An antiquarian reason for wrapping the dead in purple was
that the colour represented the blood of a sacrificial victim
(DServius on 3. 67, from Varro). Livy (34. 7. 3) represents the
tribune L. Valerius, attacking the sumptuary *lex Oppia*, as
listing among the uses of purple allowed to men but for-
bidden to women 'nec id ut uiui solum habeant insigne sed
etiam ut cum eo crementur mortui'.

222. feretro : the bier, with the *torus* set upon it, often very
elaborate (Toynbee, op. cit. 46). But *ingenti* here is designed
to give heroic quality to the dead man and to the ritual.

223. triste ministerium : often borrowed for grave-inscriptions:
see R. P. Hoogma, *Der Einfluss Vergils auf die Carmina
Latina Epigraphica* (Amsterdam, 1959), 281; the noun is not
recorded in poetry before Virgil. The phrase extends and ex-
plains the action of the sentence *pars . . . feretro*, as an in-
ternal accusative in apposition: in shouldering the bier they
ministered a sad *ministerium*. So 9. 52 f. 'iaculum attorquens
emittit in auras, / principium pugnae'; the construction
occurs first in Sallust, e.g. *H.* 4. 69. 8 'Eumenem . . . pro-
didere Antiocho, pacis mercedem'; stock examples in Greek
are *Il.* 24. 735 ῥίψει χειρὸς ἑλὼν ἀπὸ πύργου, λυγρὸν ὄλεθρον, Eur. *Or.*
1105 Ἑλένην κτάνωμεν, Μενέλεῳ λύπην πικράν (see Wedd's note). See
K–S i, 247; HSz, 429; W. R. Hardie (*Latin Prose Composition*,
7) is lucid and helpful.

    more parentum : cf. Cat. 101. 7 f. 'haec, prisco quae more
parentum / tradita sunt tristi munere ad inferias'; 11. 185 f.
'huc corpora quisque suorum / more tulere patrum'. Virgil
writes as if the Trojans were contemporary Romans (with
special reference in *auersi*).

224. auersi : so as not to see the dead man's spirit as it de-
parted. Similarly Ovid, *F.* 5. 436, the celebrant 'uertitur et

nigras accipit ante fabas / auersusque iacit': the ghosts must
not be seen (for other illustrations see Bömer on Ovid, *F.* 5.
439). The pause after *facem* is dramatic and solemn.

225. Offerings to the *manes* of the dead man: incense, a costly
meal (*dapes*), bowls of oil; cf. 3. 301 ff. 'sollemnis cum forte
dapes et tristia dona / . . . libabat cineri Andromache'.

   turea dona : cf. Lucan 8. 729 ff. 'non pretiosa petit cumu-
lato ture sepulchra / Pompeius, Fortuna, tuus, non pinguis
ad astra / ut ferat e membris Eoos fumus odores', Stat.
S. 2. 1. 160 ff. 'quod Cilicum flores, quod munera graminis
Indi, / quodque Arabes Phariique Palaestinique liquores /
arsuram lauere comam'.

   dapes : in the special sense of a meal prepared for a holy
rite: perhaps some form of cake.

   fuso . . . oliuo : the ablative describes the contents of the
bowls, as in 5. 77 f. 'duo rite mero libans carchesia Baccho /
fundit humi, duo lacte nouo, duo sanguine sacro'.

   crateres : the Greek form, with Greek prosody (-*ĕs*); so the
accusative *cratera*, 3. 525, 5. 536, etc., *crateras*, 1. 724, etc.;
ablative *cratere*, *G.* 2. 457. Virgil never has the feminine Latin
form *cratera*, partly because the Greek form is more pliable
metrically, partly because *crater* was felt to be choicer: see
W. V. Clausen, *CQ* n.s. xiii (1963), 85 ff.

226. conlapsi : for the omission of *sunt* cf. 1. 520 'postquam
introgressi et coram data copia fandi'. The line has a moving
simplicity, *quieuit* marking the hush as the great roaring pyre
sinks down; cf. *Il.* 9. 212 αὐτὰρ ἐπεὶ κατὰ πῦρ ἐκάη καὶ φλὸξ
ἐμαράνθη (in a very different context).

227. reliquias : for the lengthened first syllable, needed by the
metre, cf. Lucr. 1. 1109, 3. 656, 6. 825: see Bailey, Lucr.
proleg. 132; Leumann, *Kleine Schriften*, 146 n. 3. The word
is used specifically of the remains after cremation (Servius
on 2. 539); cf. Sen. *H.O.* 1828 f. 'Herculis cineres tenes; /
complectere ossa: reliquiae auxilium dabunt'; cf. Vahlen,
opusc. acad. ii, 494 f.

   uino : cf. Stat. *S.* 2. 6. 90, where Setian wine is used for the
purpose (a first-class wine, of which Augustus was fond; see
Pliny, *NH* 14. 61).

   bibulam . . . fauillam : explanatory of *reliquias*; *fauilla* is
used of the glowing ashes of the body, whereas *cineres* (226)
refers to the pyre in general; for the epithet cf. Soph. *Ant.* 429
χερσὶν εὐθὺς διψίαν φέρει κόνιν.

228. lecta : the t.t. was *ossilegium*; cf. Sueton. *Aug.* 100 're-
liquias legerunt primores equestris ordinis'.

   cado : for the varying kinds of receptacle for the ashes see
Toynbee, op. cit. 50. Characteristically, Virgil specifies the

man who had this duty; presumably Corynaeus had some close connexion with Misenus. For this detail (and others) cf. *Il.* 23. 250 ff.:

πρῶτον μὲν κατὰ πυρκαϊὴν σβέσαν αἴθοπι οἴνῳ,
ὅσσον ἐπὶ φλὸξ ἦλθε, βαθεῖα δὲ κάππεσε τέφρη·
κλαίοντες δ᾽ ἑτάροιο ἐνηέος ὀστέα λευκὰ
ἄλλεγον ἐς χρυσέην φιάλην καὶ δίπλακα δημόν

(see also *Il.* 24. 791 ff., *Od.* 24. 71 ff.).

The alliteration of 224–8 is notable, with *c*, *d*, *f*, *l* all woven into the sound-pattern; in the next three lines a new pattern begins, with *s*, *r*, *l*.

229. A lustration, to purify the Trojans from the pollution of death (cf. 150); it was performed three times, a ritual number (cf. 506, 11. 188 f., *G.* 4. 384 f., *E.* 8. 73 ff.), for which see Gow on Theocr. 2. 43, 17. 82 ff.

circumtulit : 'encircled', the construction being analogous to that of *circumdare* (so Conington). Servius comments 'purgauit. antiquum uerbum est', and quotes from Plautus 'pro laruato te circumferam' (not in an extant play, but cf. *Amph.* 775 f. 'quin tu istanc iubes / pro cerrita circumferri?'). This ancient technical use of the verb for a ritual act of purification is made explicit in *lustrauit* (231); cf. Tib. 1. 5. 11 'te circum lustraui sulfure puro'.

230. spargens : the isolated spondee gives a slow start to the line. Corynaeus sprinkles them with 'gentle drops from a branch of fruitful olive'; for the hendiadys *rore et ramo* cf. 11. 571 'equae mammis et lacte ferino'; sometimes the figure is useful metrically (e.g. 1. 648 'pallam signis auroque rigentem', *G.* 2. 192), but its main function is ornament and variety: see HSz, 782 f., with bibliography. For *ros* of water cf. 5. 854 'ramum Lethaeo rore madentem', *G.*1. 385 'largos umeris infundere rores'.

felicis : not only 'fruitful' (contrast *G.* 2. 314 'infelix . . . foliis oleaster amaris') but of good omen. Servius states that bay was usual, adding a story that Virgil made the innovation to please Augustus: 'nam nata erat laurus in Palatio eo die quo Augustus: unde triumphantes coronari consueuerant, propter quam rem noluit laurum dicere ad officium lugubre pertinere'.

231. lustrauitque uiros : the rite of lustration was essentially one of processional movement, the celebrant passing slowly from person to person or from point to point. From this basic implication other senses developed for *lustrare*, of ranging with the eye (cf. 681), or of traversing a region (cf. *E.* 10. 55 'mixtis lustrabo Maenala Nymphis'): see Warde Fowler

The Death of Turnus (Blackwell, Oxford, 1919), 96 ff., a fine discussion; also his *Religious Experience of the Roman People*, 209 ff., for *lustratio* in general as a religious cere-monial.

nouissima uerba : Servius interprets this as the formal *ilicet* ('quod ire licet significat', on 216), marking the end of the funeral rite (cf. S. Timpanaro, *Rivista di Filologia* xci [1963], 323). But it is simpler to take the phrase of the last farewell to the dead (cf. 11. 97 f. 'salue aeternum mihi, maxime Palla, / aeternumque uale'); so Dido speaks her own farewell to life, 4. 650 'incubuitque toro dixitque nouis-sima uerba'.

So the rite ends. The whole passage has great liturgical and emotional beauty; Virgil has himself mourned Misenus, and the reader mourns with him.

232. Another aspect of *pietas*: Aeneas ensures that his dead companion's memory shall live.

233. suaque arma uiro : 'the hero's own gear'. The reference of *sua* (= *propria*) is pegged by *uiro*, without which it could not have been used; cf. 5. 54 'strueremque suis altaria donis'.

arma : explained by *remumque tubamque* (for the correlat-ing *-que . . . -que* see on 64). So *arma* ('outfit', 'equipment') is used of a ship's tackle (353, 5. 15), of the farmer's imple-ments (*G.* 1. 160, Ovid, *Met.* 11. 35), of hunting gear (Ovid, *ex Ponto* 4. 16. 34). Servius, not realizing this sense, and as-suming that *fulgentibus armis* (217) must mean Misenus' own armour, imagined that Aeneas had a sculptured repre-sentation of those arms placed on the tomb. He has a fur-ther strange notion, that *remum* means a strap of some kind for holding the trumpet.

Virgil presumably had in mind *Od.* 12. 15 (of Elpenor's tomb) πήξαμεν ἀκροτάτῳ τύμβῳ εὐῆρες ἐρετμόν.

234. monte sub aerio : 'at the foot of the airy peak', the Punta di Miseno of today (see on 162); cf. Stat. *S.* 5. 3. 167 f. 'lituo remoque notatus / collis', a good example of the Silver manner.

235. Similarly 381 'aeternumque locus Palinuri nomen habe-bit'; for other aetiological explanations of place-names cf. 1. 367 (Byrsa), 7. 1 ff. (Caieta), 8. 338 f. (the *porta Carmen-talis*), 10. 145 (Capua). The manner is Alexandrian (cf. Callim. *h.* 5. 39 ff.; see on 1. 109): Propertius, the 'Roman Callimachus', has 'cognomina prisca locorum' (4. 1. 69) among his themes, e.g. 4. 4. 93 f. 'a duce Tarpeia mons est cognomen adeptus: / o uigil, iniustae praemia sortis habes'; for Ovid's use of aetiological legend see Bailey, *Fasti* 3 (Oxford, 1921), 20 ff. But Virgil does not use the manner as

a peg for learning; he took pleasure in such allusions partly
because of poetic tradition, partly from his own deep interest
in the antiquities of Italy (in which Varro's influence may
be seen), partly because in this way he could link past with
present in living history.

236–63. *Aeneas makes sacrifice to the powers of the Underworld;
the Sibyl bids him brace himself for the ordeal of descent, and
together they enter the depths.*

Aeneas now obeys the Sibyl's third instruction (153), and
the tension of the preliminaries to his descent reaches its
climax. The ritual of the sacrifice is described with solemn
precision of detail; there is the same kind of dark, uncanny
atmosphere as in 4. 478 ff. (Dido's recourse to black magic),
and it is in a moment of pregnant awe and apprehension that
the time comes, suddenly, for Aeneas to leave this world.

The passage owes something to *Od.* 10. 517 ff. (Circe's in-
structions to Odysseus, carried out in 11. 23 ff.), and to
Apoll. Rhod. 3. 1207 ff. (Jason's sacrifice to Hecate); Nor-
den explores the influence of magic literature. For a Silver
elaboration of the theme see Silius 12. 120 ff. (Hannibal's
conducted tour of the region near Baiae), 13. 400 ff. (Scipio
at Cumae).

236. his actis : cf. 12. 843 'his actis aliud genitor secum ipse
uolutat': the epic-historian manner. The rhythm suggests
Aeneas' speed, with its quick run to the fourth-foot caesura
(no caesura in the third foot), and the slurring elision in
propere exsequitur.

237 ff. An ἔκφρασις, picked up by *hic* (243). For the yawning
vowel-sounds in 237 cf. 576 'quinquaginta atris immanis
hiatibus Hydra'; in what follows there is much assonance
and alliteration.

No such *spelunca* has ever been found, despite careful
search, within the crater at Avernus. What was until 1932
shown as the Cave of the Sibyl at Avernus is now known to
be one of Agrippa's and Cocceius' tunnels (see on 42 ff.).
There is no reason to believe that a cave has been destroyed
by volcanic or human action. Cocceius' tunnels survive un-
damaged by natural decay, and the effects of the eruption of
Monte Nuovo in 1538 have been exaggerated. It was an
isolated and neatly confined explosion which did not alter
Avernus: cf. Orosius 4. 4. 4 for a similar one in 269 B.C. on
Rocca Monfina, otherwise extinct. By the time that fanatical
Christians were in a position to destroy pagan monuments,
the Sibyls had already been canonized as prophets of Christ.

The Sibyl's Cave at Cumae is intact apart from Narses' operation on its north end. R. V. Schoder, *CJ* lxvii (1971–2), 106, has rightly surmised that there never was any such cave at Avernus (see Appendix).

238. scrupea : jaggy, with small sharp stones, from the noun *scrupus* ('qui incedentibus impedimento est et pressus sollicitudinem creat', Servius): a word from early Latin (Ennius, *Sc.* 115; Pacuvius, fr. 310). It is clearly a natural cave.

tuta : 'protected'; for the participial force cf. 1. 571 'auxilio tutos dimittam'.

nemorumque tenebris : as it was until Agrippa's clearance (see on 107).

239 ff. Virgil has drawn on Lucr. 6. 740 f. 'principio, quod Auerna uocantur nomine, id ab re / impositumst, quia sunt auibus contraria cunctis', etc.; Lucretius explains the phenomenon, with others like it, as due to natural causes, 'ianua ne pote eis Orci regionibus esse / credatur, post hinc animas Acheruntis in oras / ducere forte deos manis inferne reamur' (6. 762 ff.).

Virgil has accepted the Greek derivation Avernus = Ἄορνος, as the ancients generally did, though there can be little doubt that it is a native Italic name, comparable with Liternum, Salernum, Falernus, Privernum, Lavernium, Lavernae (cf. *cauerna*, *cisterna*, etc.). Ironically the root *au-* would appear to that of *auis*, and, if the whole crater was sacred, uncut and uncultivated until the time of Agrippa, it would have been a bird-sanctuary! There is no geological evidence that Avernus was mephitic in antiquity, and it is inconceivable that so large an area could have been rendered dangerous to wild life. Our earliest notice, Ps.-Aristotle, *Mir. Ausc.* 102, 839a, from Timaeus, testifies to the quietness of the lake and to the presence of swans upon it. Near by in the Campi Phlegraei, at Solfatara and Agnano, there were poisonous exhalations which kept birds away from small areas: cf. Pliny, *NH* 2. 207, 208.

Virgil assumes, like Silius Italicus after him (12. 120 ff.), that, whatever Avernus was like in his day, it had been volcanically more active in the time of Aeneas. Modern commentators have made a similar assumption, that in antiquity, up to Virgil's time perhaps, Avernus teemed with hot water and mephitic fumes. On the time-scale of modern geology many millennia must be reckoned with, and there is no evidence that volcanic activity has generally declined since antiquity in the Campi Phlegraei; within the crater of Avernus the hot springs on the east edge of the lake, at the Thermae, remain.

239. Cf. Apoll. Rhod. 4. 601 f. (of the estuary of the Eridanus)
οὐδέ τις ὕδωρ κεῖνο διὰ πτερὰ κοῦφα τανύσσας / οἰωνὸς δύναται βαλέειν
ὕπερ. For the postponement of *super* cf. 602, 11. 526 (*hanc super*)
3. 260 (*quem super*); see HSz, 216, K–S i, 586. For postpone-
ment of monosyllabic prepositions (especially where at first
sight they would appear to relate to a different noun) see
Housman on Manilius 1. 245.

   uolantes : 'flying creatures', substantival, as in 728, Lucr.
2. 1083, etc.

240. tendere iter : cf. 1. 656 'iter ad nauis tendebat Achates',
7. 7 'tendit iter uelis', Lucr. 5. 631 'tendere cursum'; so *iter
intendere*, Cato, *Or.* fr. 83.

   talis ... atris : again the assonance of *ā*; cf. Silius 12. 137
'Stygios exhalat in aera flatus'.

241. supera ... conuexa : the vault of heaven, as in 750, 10. 251
(cf. 4. 451 'caeli conuexa'). The manuscripts are divided
between *supera* and *super*, as also in 750, 787, 7. 562, 10. 251;
but *conuexa* needs an adjective or a defining genitive like
caeli. Norden notes Sen. *Phaedra* 219 ff. 'non umquam am-
plius / conuexa tetigit supera qui mersus semel / adiit silen-
tem nocte perpetua domum', Stat. *Th.* 10. 916 f. 'uinctam
supera ad conuexa leuari / Inarimen Aetnamque putes'.

242. The line is agreed to be an interpolation. An etymological
note of this kind (*Aornum* = 'birdless') is alien to the tone
and tension of the passage. It is preserved by R alone of the
ancient manuscripts, and by two ninth-century codices (*b*,
γ) : it reads like some dutiful piece of school-learning.

   Heinsius noted the parallel in Priscian, *Periegesis* 1056
'unde locis Grai posuerunt nomen Aornis', a version of
Dionysius Periegetes 1151 τούνεκά μιν καὶ φῶτες ἐπικλείουσιν Ἄορνιν
(not in a context of Auernus); for Dionysius' work (a school
geography compiled under Hadrian) see J. O. Thomson,
History of Ancient Geography, 228. Norden took Priscian's
line to be the source of the interpolation here. But Fraenkel
argues cogently (*Mus. Helv.* xx [1963], 234 ff.) that Priscian's
text of Virgil must already have contained the interpolated
line, i.e. that the interpolation is earlier than the beginning
of the sixth century.

243. nigrantis terga : the Greek 'accusative of respect' de-
pendent on an adjective; see on 1. 320, R. D. Williams on
5. 97.

244. constituit : 'made to stand', a sacrificial term: cf. 5. 236 f.
'candentem in litore taurum / constituam ante aras uoti reus',
9. 627 'statuam ante aras aurata fronte iuuencum'. The vic-
tim must not struggle; if one escaped, it was a sinister omen
(see on 2. 223–4): cf. Macrob. *Sat.* 3. 5. 8 'obseruatum est a

sacrificantibus ut, si hostia quae ad aras duceretur fuisset
uehementius reluctata ... amoueretur quia inuito deo offerri
eam putabant. quae autem stetisset oblata, hanc uolenti
numini dari aestimabant'.

   inuergit uina : cf. Ovid, *Met.* 7. 246 f. (Medea about to boil
up Aeson) 'super inuergens liquidi carchesia uini / alteraque
inuergens tepidi carchesia lactis'. For the plural *uina* (Virgil
never uses the singular nominative or accusative) see on
1. 195, R. D. Williams on 5. 98. The *sacerdos* is the Sibyl,
Hecate's priestess (35), calling on the goddess whom she
serves (247).
245 f. So *Od.* 3. 445 f. πολλὰ δ' Ἀθήνῃ / εὔχετ' ἀπαρχόμενος, κεφαλῆς
τρίχας ἐν πυρὶ βάλλων (in an elaborately detailed account of a
sacrifice to Athene).
246. libamina prima : 'a first offering', ἀπαρχαί; cf. *Od.* l.c., Eur.
Or. 96 (of gifts at a tomb) κόμης ἀπαρχὰς καὶ χοὰς φέρουσ' ἐμάς.
Libamen is a Virgilian innovation for the older *libamentum*
(see on 221).
247. uoce uocans : 'calling aloud'; a formula in archaic tone
(a type of 'figura etymologica'); cf. 506, 3. 68, 12. 638. The
pleonasm goes back to Ennius (*Ann.* 44 'compellare pater
me uoce uidetur'), and has its counterpart in Homer (*Il.* 3.
161 Πρίαμος δ' Ἑλένην ἐκαλέσσατο φωνῇ: see Löfstedt, *Synt.* ii,
185 f.
   caeloque Ereboque : 'ut plenum numen ostenderet', Ser-
vius. She calls on Hecate in both her spheres of power,
according to the ritual in prayers by which a divinity was
addressed by his or her various titles, to ensure the desired
response to a proper and pleasing request: see Fraenkel on
Aesch. *Ag.* 160 ff.; Norden, *Agnostos Theos,* 144 ff.
248. supponunt : 'uerbum sacrorum', Servius; so *G.* 3. 492 (of
victims during the cattle-plague) 'uix suppositi tinguntur
sanguine cultri'. Cerda notes Dion. Hal. *ant. Rom.* 7. 72
(Roman ritual taken over from Greek) οἱ μὲν ἑστῶτος ἔτι τοῦ
θυμιάματος σκυτάλῃ τοὺς κροτάφους ἔπαιον, οἱ δὲ πίπτοντος ὑπετίθεσαν
τὰς σφαγίδας.
249. succipiunt : again a ritual word; they 'catch the blood
from below'; the form was originally distinct from *suscipere*
(cf. Nettleship on 4. 391; Housman, *JPh* xxi [1893], 143, =
Classical Papers, 263). Servius comments 'antique, nam
modo *suscipiunt* dicimus'.
   atri uelleris : so Circe bids Odysseus to offer up to Tiresias
a ram παμμέλαν', ὃς μήλοισι μεταπρέπει ὑμετέροισιν (*Od.* 10. 525);
cf. Silius 13. 404 ff. '"mactare repostis / mos umbris," in-
quit, "consueta piacula nigras / sub lucem pecudes"'.
250. matri Eumenidum : Night; cf. 7. 331 'uirgo sata Nocte'

(Allecto), 12. 845 ff. 'dicuntur geminae pestes cognomine Dirae, / quas et Tartaream Nox intempesta Megaeram / uno eodemque tulit partu'; Aesch. *Eum.* 416 ἡμεῖς γάρ ἐσμεν Νυκτὸς αἰανῆς τέκνα.

magnaeque sorori : Earth (Servius); so Medea invokes Tellus with Hecate (Ovid, *Met.* 7. 196). Virgil deliberately uses these grand, evocative periphrases to deepen the atmosphere of awe.

251. sterilemque . . . uaccam : so in *Od.* 10. 522 Circe instructs Odysseus to vow στεῖραν βοῦν, ἥτις ἀρίστη as an offering to the Shades on his return to Ithaca. The apostrophe gets round the metrically intractable dative *Proserpinae*; but it has the effect of a quotation from Aeneas' own dedicatory words (cf. 18).

252. Stygio regi : Dis; see on 138 'Iunoni infernae'.

nocturnas : this is Virgil's way of telling only now that the ritual is taking place at dead of night (cf. 32, note). Silius, describing Scipio's approach to the Underworld, pinpoints the time (13. 419 f.) 'ubi nox iussam procedens contigit horam / et spatia aequarunt tenebras transacta futuras'. With Virgil's phrase cf. Val. Flacc. 6. 440 'nocturnis qua nulla potentior aris' (of Medea).

incohat : 'improvises'; the verb implies something in rough outline, not a finished piece of work (for which Aeneas obviously had no time, as Henry notes). Servius glosses it as 'perficit', which is contrary to its normal sense; he adds that it is *uerbum sacrorum*.

253. solida . . . uiscera : 'the entire flesh', *uiscera* being 'quicquid inter ossa et cutem est' (Servius). For *solidus*, whole', 'complete', cf. Pliny, *NH* 8. 36 'Megasthenes scribit in India serpentes in tantam magnitudinem adolescere ut solidos hauriant ceruos taurosque'.

254. supēr : so some of the manuscripts later than the ninth century; *superque* FMPR, an attempt to 'heal' the metre (cf. 1. 668, with note), which Ribbeck retained, assuming a lacuna to follow. The final syllable is lengthened in arsis, bearing the metrical ictus; Norden (p. 452) suggests the influence of ὑπεὶρ ἅλα (*Od.* 3. 73, etc.). For 'irregular' lengthenings in Virgil see on 1. 308; some reflect archaic prosody, most occur at the caesura of the third or fourth foot, often before a marked pause or sense-break.

The line is modelled on *Il.* 11. 775 σπένδων αἴθοπα οἶνον ἐπ' αἰθομένοις ἱεροῖσι.

255. ecce autem : a formula that Virgil often uses to mark a sudden event affecting the development of the action (see on 2. 203; Köhler, *ALL* v, 18): 'ubicumque ponitur *ecce autem*

necesse est sequi quod metum adferat uel admirationem'
(Ti. Donatus). With dramatic suddenness, directly the ritual
has been duly completed, uncanny phenomena herald the
unseen presence of Hecate.

limina : so FM; *lumina* PR, Servius, Ti. Donatus, with
which cf. 8. 68 f. 'aetherii spectans orientia solis / lumina'.

With *lumina* there is no problem, but the addition *et ortus*
is then otiose after *primi lumina solis*. *Limina* is accepted by
Norden, Sabbadini, Götte, and Geymonat; its difficulty is
obvious. Virgil may have had in mind Cat. 64. 271 'Aurora
exoriente uagi sub limina Solis'. But there *sub limina* has its
proper local sense; here it has to be given a temporal sig-
nificance, for which there is no parallel (I am grateful to
Dr. H. Beikircher of *Thes.L.L.* for confirming this)—eased,
however, by the appended *et ortus*, which now gains real
point. The phrase is then a bold experiment, the place where
the sun first appears (*limina*) being fused with his rising
(*ortus*) to give a complex expression for 'dawn': perhaps
translate 'on the threshold of daylight, just at the first
moment of the sun's rising'. Conington condemned *limina*
as impossible, a somewhat too confident judgement.

ortus : normal poetic usage in the accusative; Ovid is in-
structive, *Met.* 14. 386 'bis ad occasum, bis se conuertit ad
ortus': see Maas, *ALL* xii, 487, 494; Landgraf, *ALL* xiv, 73;
there is a Greek analogy in ἀνατολαί.

256. mugire : 'historic' infinitive (cf. 199). A conventional
detail: cf. 4. 490 f. 'mugire uidebis / sub pedibus terram' (of
the witch's spells); Ovid, *Met.* 14. 409 f. 'lapides uisi mugitus
edere raucos / et latrare canes' (after a prayer to Hecate).

canes : cf. Sen. *Oed.* 569 'latrauit Hecates turba'; Theocr.
2. 35 f. (in the magic rite) ταὶ κύνες ἄμμιν ἀνὰ πτόλιν ὠρύονται· / ἁ
θεὸς ἐν τριόδοισι; Apoll. Rhod. 3. 1216 f. (Hecate answering
Jason's invocation) ἀμφὶ δὲ τήν γε / ὀξείῃ ὑλακῇ χθόνιοι κύνες ἐφθέγ-
γοντο. Lucian (*Philops.* 24) presents Hecate's hounds as more
gigantic than Indian elephants, black, with shaggy, grimy
coats.

The force of *uisae* (sc. *sunt*) is that they thought they heard
howling (a common use of *uideor*, e.g. Ter. *Eun.* 454 'audire
uocem uisa sum', 'I thought I heard a voice'): it serves to
emphasize the dark eeriness of the moment. Apart altogether
from this, the perception of sound is often expressed by
uidere, e.g. 4. 490 (see above), Prop. 2. 16. 49 'uidistis toto
sonitum percurrere caelo', and cf. Aesch. *Septem* 103 κτύπον
δέδορκα; so St. Aug. *Conf.*. 10. 35 'ad oculos enim uidere
proprie pertinet: utimur autem hoc uerbo etiam in ceteris
sensibus, cum eos ad cognoscendum intendimus. neque enim

dicimus *audi quid rutilet*, aut *olefac quam niteat*, aut *gusta quam splendeat*, aut *palpa quam fulgeat*: uidere enim dicuntur haec omnia. dicimus autem non solum *uide quid luceat*, quod soli oculi sentire possunt, sed etiam *uide quid sonet, uide quid oleat, uide quid sapiat, uide quam durum sit'*. See Norden here, Nisbet–Hubbard on Hor. *C.* 1. 14. 6; cf. Bailey on Lucr. 6. 778.

258. aduentante dea : cf. Theocr. 2. 36 (see on 257). They feel the near presence of the goddess; they do not see her.

procul . . . profani : a religious formula; cf. Callim. *h.* 2. 2 ἑκὰς ἑκὰς ὅστις ἀλιτρός: for *o* with the imperative see on 196. Aeneas is to witness a great mystery, and he has the right to do so, through his *uirtus* and through his possession of the Golden Bough: but those without the right must be warned away in solemn form.

profani : the uninitiate (cf. Kiessling–Heinze on Hor. *C.* 3. 1. 1): so Cat. 64. 260 'orgia quae frustra cupiunt audire profani', Calp. Sic. 2. 55. 'ite procul (sacer est locus) ite profani'; *Orphica* fr. 245 K φθέγξομαι οἷς θέμις ἐστί· θύρας δ' ἐπίθεσθε βέβηλοι (see I. M. Linforth, *The Arts of Orpheus* 124, 254).

259. absistite : before Virgil the verb is found in Caesar only: see Wölfflin, *ALL* v, 519.

260. tuque : the emphatic pronoun (cf. 95) marks Aeneas out as an initiate, in contrast to the *profani*; the force of *-que* is adversative ('but').

inuade uiam : 'go boldly forward on your road'; the verb has its counterpart in *se immisit* (262).

uaginaque . . . ferrum : for the phrase cf. 4. 579, 10. 475, 10. 896. So Circe bade Odysseus to have his sword drawn, to prevent the ghosts from drinking the sacrificial blood before he had speech with Teiresias (*Od.* 10. 535 f., closely followed by Silius, 13. 441 ff.). Odysseus used his sword (*Od.* 11. 48); Aeneas would have used his, confronted by the grisly apparitions *primis in faucibus Orci*, but the Sibyl prevented him (290 ff.). There is no real inconsistency between the present passage and the later one: the Homeric and the Virgilian situations are quite different, and the Sibyl's instruction here is simply to enable Aeneas to feel protected on his frightening journey, another way of expressing the exhortation that follows in the next line.

262. furens : her ecstasy returns: Servius comments 'deo plena, aut certe similis furenti' (cf. 50 f., note).

se immisit : this complements *furens*; a swift, impulsive plunge.

antro : the *spelunca* of 237. *Aperto* again shows Virgil's

quiet way of marking a significant fact: it is only now, after
the prescribed ritual and the solemn formula of 258 f., that
the way to the Underworld is open.

263. haud timidis : a strong assertion of Aeneas' boldness; he
keeps up with the Sibyl stoutly, step for step.

  aequat : cf. 3. 671 'nec potis Ionios fluctus aequare se-
quendo', 10. 248 'ocior et iaculo et uentos aequante sagitta':
with Aeneas here contrast the little Iulus, following him out
of Troy 'haud passibus aequis' (2. 724).

264-7. *An invocation by the poet to the gods of the spirit world,
praying for their sanction to unfold the secrets of darkness.*

  At this crucial moment of his narrative Virgil uses a tra-
ditional technique of Epic, an *ad hoc* prayer at a special point
within the poem: see *Il.* 2. 484 ff. (before the Catalogue),
14. 508 (before the exploits of Aias and others). The tech-
nique is used again in 7. 37 ff. (exordium to the second part
of the *Aeneid*), 7. 641 ff. (before the Italian Catalogue); see
Fraenkel, *JRS* xxxv (1945), 2 f., 9 f.: again, 9. 525 ff. (before
Turnus' *aristeia*), 10. 163 ff. (before the Catalogue of Aeneas'
ships), 12. 500 ff. (before the exploits of Turnus and Aeneas).

  But here it is not the Muses nor any Olympians that Virgil
calls upon for aid and sanction, but the gods who rule the
ghosts, and the silent ghosts themselves, and primeval Chaos,
and all the bleak world of everlasting darkness. The four lines
have a powerful beauty of language and sound, impressing
the reader both with the poet's consciousness of his task and
with the terror of Aeneas' ordeal. The pauses are carefully
varied: after *animarum*, with its final syllable fused by elision
with *umbrae*; at the third-foot caesura in 265, at the fourth-
foot caesura in 266, then an unbroken run to the end (with
a barely perceptible caesura after *alta*, 267). Heyne well ob-
served 'habet insignem uim ad animos excitandos et horrore
quodam sacro imbuendos subita haec deorum inferorum et
Manium appellatio'.

264. silentes : contrast 432, where *silentum* is substantival.

265. Chaos : 'inuocat . . . rerum primordia, quae in elemen-
torum fuerunt confusione' (Servius); so Dido invokes Chaos
with Erebus in her magic rites, together with *gemina Hecate*
(4. 510 f.).

  Phlegethon : representing the rivers of the Underworld
(cf. 551).

  loca . . . late : 'a world illimitably hushed under a pall of
night'; the appositional phrase adds further awe to the
names.

266. fas : what is allowable under divine law (cf. Latte, op. cit. 38; Warde Fowler, *Religious Experience of the Roman People*, 486 ff.; Hey, *ALL* xiii, 212 ff.). The poet must have sanction to tell what he has heard.

In invocations of this kind the poet makes it plain that his knowledge is derivative; he is the mouthpiece of the Muses, or of a divinity: so *audita* here, 7. 645 f. 'et meministis enim, diuae, et memorare potestis; / ad nos uix tenuis famae perlabitur aura'. The tradition goes back to Homer, *Il.* 2. 485 f. (to the Muses) ὑμεῖς γὰρ θεαί ἐστε, πάρεστέ τε, ἴστε τε πάντα, / ἡμεῖς δὲ κλέος οἷον ἀκούομεν, οὐδέ τι ἴδμεν; so Callim. *h.* 3. 186 (to Artemis) εἰπέ, θεή, σὺ μὲν ἄμμιν, ἐγὼ δ' ἑτέροισιν ἀείσω, Theocr. 22. 116 f. (to the Muse) εἰπὲ θεά, σὺ γὰρ οἶσθα, ἐγὼ δ' ἑτέρων ὑποφήτης / φθέγξομαι ὅσσ' ἐθέλεις σὺ καὶ ὅππως τοι φίλον αὐτῇ, Apoll. Rhod. 4. 1381 f. Μουσάων ὅδε μῦθος· ἐγὼ δ' ὑπακουὸς ἀείδω / Πιερίδων, καὶ τήνδε πανατρεκὲς ἔκλυον ὀμφήν.

sit numine uestro : either *sit = liceat*, or *fas* must be understood: preferably the former, as a variation (*fas* and *licet* are often parallel, e.g. Ovid, *F.* 1. 25 'si licet et fas est, uates rege uatis habenas', and see my note on Cic. *Cael.* 27).

267. pandere : cf. 3. 251 f. 'quae Phoebo pater omnipotens, mihi Phoebus Apollo / praedixit, uobis Furiarum maxima pando'. The poet enters upon an apocalypse.

res . . . mersas : parallel with *loca nocte tacentia late* above ('a world sunk in depth of earth and blackness'); cf. Pliny, *NH* 4. 88 'Pterophoros appellata regio, pars mundi damnata a rerum natura et densa mersa caligine'.

268–94. *Aeneas and the Sibyl travel through the darkness, and at the very doorway of the realm of Dis they are confronted by countless shapes of human misery. There is a great elm where dreams dwell; and horrible monsters cluster by the entrance.*

The transition to the Underworld is made in an imperceptible moment: and at once all the grisly fears that haunt men's imaginings in life seem to be coming true.

268 f. 'There they were, dim travellers in the loneliness of night, passing through the shadow, through the blank dwellings and flimsy domain of Dis'. The weight of 268 is in noteworthy contrast to the lightness of 269, a rhythmic sound-picture of the real and actual in a setting of insubstantiality. The intricate vowel-patterns, the alliteration, the disposition of the epithets, all contribute to the effectiveness of these two lines.

268. ibant obscuri : the opening spondaic disyllable sets the grave tone; the tense of *ibant* is significant, the only indication that the bound of the real world has been passed—*they* *were already on their way*. Robert Bridges chose the words to entitle his 'experiment in the classical hexameter' (*Ibant Obscuri*, Oxford, 1916), in which he offered a version in 'quantitive' English hexameters of *Aen.* 6. 268-751 and 893-8 (reprinted in the Oxford edition of his poems), with a 'cento of previous translations' and a fascinating introduction.

obscuri : the interchange of epithets is very striking: *obscura soli sub nocte* would have been effective, but *obscuri sola sub nocte* is memorable (for *obscurus* of persons cf. 453, 2. 135, *G.* 4. 424). Virgil's arrangement brings out, with great impact on the reader, the dim groping figures in a terrifying loneliness of night. For a somewhat similar double transference cf. Val. Flacc. 2. 288 'altae per opaca silentia noctis', Sen. *dial.* 6. 3. 2 'non licuerat matri ultima filii oscula gratumque extremi sermonem oris haurire': see 2, note, with references for the use of the figure, and cf. Leo, *Ausg. Kleine Schriften* ii, 174.

269. The *umbra* is further explained: they are in a world of phantom dwellings, homes of hollow men. The chiastic arrangement of *domos uacuas*)(*inania regna* is notable.

270 ff. quale . . . colorem : 'just as one journeys in a forest, when the moon is vague and her light is mean, and Jupiter has blanketed the sky in shadow, and black night has stolen all colour from the world': the simile is insistent on the insubstantiality of the Underworld.

270. incertam : the moon is so phantom-like that one cannot be sure that it is there at all; cf. Hor. *C.* 2. 16. 2 ff. 'simul atra nubes / condidit lunam neque certa fulgent / sidera nautis', Livy 41. 2. 4 'qua [sc. *nebula matutina*] dilabente ad primum teporem solis, perlucens iam aliquid incerta tamen ut solet lux speciem omnium multiplicem intuenti reddens tum quoque frustrata Romanos'.

sub luce maligna : this balances *sub nocte* (268), just as *per incertam lunam* is a counterpart to *per umbram*. The moon is stingy with her light ('non clara et non plena, et quae securos inuideat gressus', Ti. Donatus); cf. Lucan 9. 73 f. 'longe qui fulget luce maligna / ignis'; Pliny, *NH* 2. 172 'maligna ac pruina tantum albicans lux' (of the Arctic); Sen. *epp.* 65. 17 'quemadmodum artifices alicuius rei subtilioris quae intentione oculos defetigat, si malignum habent et precarium lumen, in publicum prodeunt et . . . oculos libera luce delectant'.

272. rebus . . . colorem : a fine summary of the effect of the conditions that Virgil has described. The simile reads like a personal experience by the poet in his country days. Its assonance and alliteration are deployed with much subtlety.

273 ff. They at once encounter a host of personified abstractions, shapes of human worries, such as Lucretius combats in his arguments against the terror of death (e.g. 3. 65 ff.). Such personifications (for which cf. 12. 335 f.) have a long ancestry and a long progeny, ranging from Homer (*Il.* 4. 440) and Hesiod (*Theog.* 211 ff.; see West, *proleg.* 33) to Spenser, Milton, Gray (cf. E. Nitchie, *Vergil and the English Poets* [New York, 1919], 95 f.). For Latin parallels see Cic. *de nat. deor.* 3. 44; Ovid, *Met.* 12. 59 ff. (cf. Hollis on *Met.* 8. 801 ff.); Stat. *Th.* 7. 47 ff.; Silius 13. 579 ff.; Sen. *Herc. Fur.* 689 ff.; Claudian, *in Ruf.* 1. 29 ff.

273. Virgil imaginatively represents Aeneas and the Sibyl as arriving at an actual 'house of Orcus', situated at the point where the road leads to Acheron (295) : see E. Wistrand, *Klio* xxxviii (1960), 146 ff. (= *Opera Selecta* [Stockholm, 1972], 352 ff.) for a reconstruction on the lines of Vitruvius' Greek house, with a peristyle court beyond the *uestibulum*; cf. the peristyle house described by R. Meiggs, *Ostia* (Oxford, 1960), 254.

uestibulum ante ipsum : defined by *primisque in faucibus*; so 2. 469 'uestibulum ante ipsum primoque in limine Pyrrhus'. These abstractions are 'in the very forefront of the entrance-way, in the opening of the jaws of Orcus'. The meaning of *ante* is clear from Ti. Donatus, 'in primo uestibulo'; cf. 9. 244 'sub uallibus', 11. 23 'Acheronte sub imo', where *sub* = 'in the depth of': see Rothstein on Prop. 1. 14. 12; E. Wistrand, *Eranos* lxviii (1970), 221 f.; A. Ollfors, *Textkritische und interpretatorische Beiträge zu Lucan* (Göteborg, 1967), 30 ff.

The *uestibulum* was properly a covered space or court projecting in front of the house-door (see Nettleship on 2. 469), with wings of the house extending on either side: see Gellius 16. 5. 12, Macrob. *Sat.* 6. 8. 14 ff., where the present passage is discussed (not very intelligibly); both take the *fauces* as different from the *uestibulum*, but Virgil's way of writing is quite against this (cf. Wistrand, *Eranos*, l.c.).

Orci : the name of the god (the Italian counterpart of Dis) is put for his realm, just as Ἀιδης is used both for the place and for its ruler; cf. Latte, op. cit. 156 n. 5.

274. posuere cubilia : as if they had looked over the 'house' and chosen their rooms here. Silius 'improves upon' Virgil, 13. 581 ff. 'Luctus edax Maciesque, malis comes addita morbis, / et Maeror pastus fletu et sine sanguine Pallor / Curaeque Insidiaeque atque hinc queribunda Senectus, / hinc angens utraque manu sua guttura Liuor', etc.—all for Scipio's benefit.

275. pallentesque ... Morbi : Quintilian quotes the line (8. 6. 27) to illustrate 'illud quoque et poetis et oratoribus frequens, quo id quod efficit ex eo quod efficitur ostendimus'. Wistrand (*Klio*, l.c. 148) takes *habitant* to mean that *Morbi*, *Senectus*, etc. 'live in the house', in *cellae* round the peristyle court; but the verb is surely just a variant on *posuere cubilia*, and there is nothing to imply a distinct and new grouping.

276. malesuada : only once in earlier Latin, Plaut. *Most.* 213 'illa hanc corrumpit mulierem malesuada'; after Virgil it occurs in Silius (14. 501, with *gloria*), Stat. *Th.* 11. 656 (with *amor*), but nowhere else in classical Latin.

277. terribiles ... formae : this ingeniously breaks up the catalogue of shapes. The archaic form *labos* occurs only here in Virgil, whereas he always uses *arbos* (cf. 206) and *honos*; see on 1. 253. The personified *Letum* recalls the remarkable phrase in Lucr. 1. 852 'ut mortem effugiat, leti sub dentibus ipsis'; cf. J. H. Waszink, *Mnemos.* ser. 4, xix (1966), 254.

278. consanguineus ... Sopor : the concept goes back to *Il.* 14. 231 Ὕπνῳ ... κασιγνήτῳ Θανάτοιο, 16. 672 Ὕπνῳ καὶ Θανάτῳ διδυμάοσιν, Hesiod, *Theog.* 756, etc. (see West); so Stat. *Th.* 5. 197 ff. 'cum consanguinei mixtus caligine Leti / . . . Somnus', Val. Flacc. 8. 74 (a prayer to Sleep) 'nunc age maior ades fratrique simillime Leto'. It has a distinguished English following: S. Daniel, *Sonnets to Delia* 54 'Care-charmer Sleep, son of the sable Night, Brother to Death'; Beaumont and Fletcher, *Valentinian* v. 2 'Care-charming Sleep, thou easer of all woes, Brother to Death'; Sir T. Browne, *On Dreams*, 'The brother of death exacteth a third part of our lives'; Tennyson, *In Memoriam* 68 'When in the down I sink my head, Sleep, Death's twin-brother, times my breath'.

278 f. mala mentis Gaudia : cf. Sen. *epp.* 59. 3 (quoting the words) 'diserte quidem dicit, sed parum proprie; nullum enim malum gaudium est. uoluptatibus hoc nomen inposuit et quod uoluit expressit; significauit enim homines malo suo laetos'.

279. mortiferumque ... Bellum : cf. Ennius, *Sc.* 314 'scibam me in mortiferum bellum, non in epulas mittere'. For the personification of *Bellum* cf. 1. 294, and notes ad loc.

aduerso in limine : 'in the doorway right confronting them' (cf. 636 'ramumque aduerso in limine figit'); this *limen* is at the far end of the *uestibulum*, barred by War, the most dread spectre of all the group.

280. ferreique ... thalami : i.e. the Furies in their iron chambers. They are associated, like Discordia, with war, and presumably are also *in limine*; Wistrand, however, in his arrangement (see on 275), puts Bellum, the Eumenides, and Discordia in 'the more distinguished rooms on the upper side of the court'. Elsewhere the Furies are in Tartarus (555, 570, 605); Virgil evidently uses a different tradition here (but see Conington's serious note): Servius gravely comments 'Furiae numquam nupserunt: unde thalamos accipiamus in quibus natae sunt: ... nam possunt hic natae esse, et alibi manere, et alibi officium exercere poenarum'.

   ferrei : a disyllable, by synizesis; so *aureā*, *aureis* (1. 698, 726), *aerei* (7. 609, 12. 541), *baltei* (10. 496). For the epithet cf. Ovid, *Met.* 4. 453, where the Furies 'carceris ante fores clausas adamante sedebant'; Claudian (*rapt. Proserp.* 3. 390) gives Megaera iron-shod feet.

   Discordia : so on the Shield, 8. 700 ff., 'saeuit medio in certamine Mauors / caelatus ferro, tristesque ex aethere Dirae, / et scissa gaudens uadit Discordia palla'. Here Discordia is given the attributes of a Fury.

281. uipereum : a Virgilian coinage; *uiperinus* will not fit a hexameter; cf. 7. 351, where Allecto's snake enters Amata's breast 'uiperiam inspirans animam'. For the construction of *crinem innexa* see on 156; Landgraf, *ALL* x, 220; cf. Hor. *Epod.* 5. 15 f. 'Canidia, breuibus illigata uiperis / crinis et incomptum caput'.

   uittis : woollen bands confining the hair; they would normally be white, but Discordia's grim work has stained them with blood: for their varied ritual uses see Smith's *Dictionary of Antiquities*, s.v.; cf. 2. 133, note, Bömer on Ovid, *F.* 3. 29. Similarly in 555 the Fury Tisiphone is 'palla succincta cruenta'.

   This ends the group of abstractions *uestibulum ante ipsum*. Cerda terrifyingly comments: 'finge, Lector, monstra haec uariis et formidandis figuris unguium, dentium, caudarum: formatis ad horrorem terrorem pauorem, plenis illuuie squalore sordibus: uel certe finge quicquid delitescere potest sub his formis ducta similitudine ab effectis, et uidebis quam taetra monstra concipi animo queant'.

282. in medio : this may mean the *uestibulum* (so Servius); but Ti. Donatus explains 'transiit a descriptione uestibuli, uenit ad interiorem partem quae non esset sub tecto', and Wistrand refers the words to his suggested peristyle-court.

   annosaque bracchia : a pictorial extension of *ramos*. For *bracchia* of a tree's branches cf. *G.* 2. 296, Cat. 64. 105: it is not 'poetic' as one might be tempted to think (cf. Cato, *agr.* 95. 2 'hoc uitem circum caput et sub bracchia unguito').

283. ulmus opaca, ingens : a Virgilian pattern: cf. 552, 3. 619 'intus opaca, ingens', 4. 181 'monstrum horrendum, ingens',

7. 170 'tectum augustum, ingens', 12. 697 'saxum antiquum, ingens'.

The elm, the dwelling-place of empty dreams, has no known literary source: like the Golden Bough, it bears witness to some unknown field of ancient lore. Silius, not to be outdone, tells of a great yew near Pluto's law-court, the home of *dirae uolucres* and Harpies (13. 595 f. 'dextra uasta comas nemorosaque bracchia fundit / taxus, Cocyti rigua frondosior unda'). Norden notes Lucian, *Ver. Hist.* 2. 33, the forest in the Island of Dreams, where only bats dwell.

uulgo : either 'all around', 'in swarms' (= *passim, cateruatim*, Servius), as in Ovid, *Met.* 11. 613 f. 'hunc circa passim uarias imitantia formas / somnia uana iacent' (in the Cave of Sleep), or 'commonly' (with *ferunt*, as DServius suggests). The first interpretation seems preferable; cf. 3. 643 f. 'haec habitant ad litora uulgo / infandi Cyclopes', *G.* 3. 494 'laetis uituli uulgo moriuntur in herbis'.

284. The line has a notable rhythm, fluttering lightly like the Dreams. Servius (on 282) appears to connect these *somnia uana* with the *falsa insomnia* of 896, locating the *porta eburna* (898) here in the *uestibulum Orci*.

ferunt : it is a traditional legend (see on 14); or at least Virgil wishes it to appear as such.

foliisque . . . haerent : a switch of construction, with *somnia* now as subject to *haerent*, as if *tenent* had preceded, not *tenere ferunt*; Conington notes 9. 592 ff. 'Numanum, / cui Remulo cognomen erat, Turnique minorem / germanam nuper thalamo sociatus habebat'. The Dreams roost in the Elm like birds; so some of Lucian's Dreams are πτερωτοί (*Ver. Hist.* 2. 34), and Earth is addressed as μελανοπτερύγων μῆτερ ὀνείρων (Eur. *Hec.* 71).

285 ff. A new grouping: goblinesque monsters from popular myth (cf. Cumont, op. cit. 221), such as Lucretius combats and mocks (4. 732 ff., 5. 890 ff.); they are stalled (*stabulant* is appropriate for the Centaurs) *in foribus*, which presumably means an outer doorway of the *uestibulum*, at the side of which the stables (*equilia*, Vitruv. 6. 7. 1) would be placed in a Greek house of the type that Wistrand postulates (see his diagram, *Klio*, l.c. 146). But it must be stressed that throughout this whole passage we are dealing with a poet's imagination, not with an architect's designs.

286. Centauri : cf. Lucr. 4. 732 f. (of the *simulacra* that men experience) 'Centauros itaque et Scyllarum membra uidemus / Cerbereasque canum facies'. They are not among the traditional monsters of the Underworld (but Statius follows Virgil, *Th.* 4. 533 f., *S.* 5. 3. 280 f.), and Virgil is presumably using some popular superstition. Norden notes that Theognis (542) terms them ὠμοφάγοι, in which they resemble other legends concerning the monsters of Hades: cf. Pausanias 10. 28. 7, a horrific detail in Polygnotus' painting of the Underworld (see Dieterich, *Nekyia*[2] [Berlin, 1913], 47 f.). The familiar image of kind old Chiron tends to obscure this other aspect of Centaurs, whose savage side is brought out by Ovid in his description of the Centaur–Lapith conflict (*Met.* 12. 210–535; there is a significant address in 219 'saeuorum saeuissime Centaurorum') and in the pediment at Olympia.

Scyllaeque biformes : again not traditional in chthonic myth; Virgil associates them with the Centaurs as Lucretius does (4. 732, 5. 891 ff.).

287. centumgeminus : a Virgilian coinage (cf. *tergeminus, septemgeminus*). Briareus was a hundred-headed giant, one of three sons of Gaea and Uranus: see West on Hesiod, *Th.* 149, 734 f.

belua Lernae : the Hydra; cf. Lucr. 5. 26 f. 'quid Cretae taurus Lernaeaque pestis / hydra uenenatis posset uallata colubris?' Its destruction was Hercules' second Labour (see Frazer on Apollod. *Bibl.* 2. 5. 2); it had the same mother (Echidna) as Cerberus (Hesiod, *Th.* 313 ff.), and may have borne the Chimaera (see West on *Th.* 319).

288. Chimaera : a tripartite monster: *Il.* 6. 181 πρόσθε λέων, ὄπιθεν δὲ δράκων, μέσση δὲ χίμαιρα; Hesiod, *Th.* 319 ff. ἡ δὲ Χίμαιραν ἔτικτε πνέουσαν ἀμαιμάκετον πῦρ, etc.; Apollod. *Bibl.* 2. 3. 1; Lucian, *dial. mort.* 30. 1 (where it rips apart the sacrilegious). For a mosaic Chimaera at Lullingstone, Kent, see J. M. C. Toynbee, *Art in Roman Britain* (London, 1962), 200 and pl. 228; for the splendid bronze Chimaera from Arretium see H. H. Scullard, *The Etruscan Cities and Rome* (London, 1967), 166 and pl. 81; for Bellerophon slaying the Chimaera see J. M. C. Toynbee, *JRS* liv (1964), pl. 1 (a mosaic from Hinton St. Mary, Dorset).

289. Gorgones : the final syllable is short, as in Greek. Of the three Gorgons, Medusa alone was mortal: see Apollod. *Bibl.* 2. 3. 1, where they are said to have serpents' scales coiled round their heads, huge tusks like swine, brazen hands, and golden wings. For Gorgons in Greek art see H. Payne, *Necrocorinthia* (Oxford, 1931), 79 ff., with impressive illustrations: the book contains also representations of the Hydra (127, fig. 45) and of the Chimaera (90, pls. 9. 4, 30. 8).

Harpyiaeque : 'tristius haud illis monstrum, nec saeuior ulla / pestis et ira deum Stygiis sese extulit undis' (3. 214 f.). In *Od.* 20. 77 f. they appear as death-spirits, handing their victims over to the Furies for guarding (cf. *Od.* 1. 241); see Dieterich, op. cit. 56 n. 1.

forma ... umbrae: the 'shape of the three-bodied phantom' is Geryon (Lucr. 5. 28 'tripectora tergemini uis Geryonai', Silius 13. 201 'monstrum Geryones immane tricorporis irae'). The fetching of his cattle from Erythia was Hercules' tenth labour (see Frazer on Apollod. *Bibl.* 2. 5. 10); cf. Hesiod, *Theog.* 289 ff. Virgil has coined the epithet *tricorpor*, on the analogy of *bicorpor* (Naevius, *Pun.* fr. 19. 2 Morel; Accius, fr. 307 R; Cic. poet. fr. 30. 38 Tr.).

DServius (on *Gorgones*) comments 'sane quidam dicunt uersus alios hos a poeta hoc loco relictos, qui ab eius emendatoribus sublati sint:

> Gorgonis in medio portentum inmane Medusae,
> uipereae circum ora comae, cui sibila torquent
> infamesque rigent oculi, mentoque sub imo
> serpentum extremis nodantur uincula caudis':

see Mynors, praef. p. xii; Ribbeck, *Proleg.* 91. There is no other witness to these four lines; Sabbadini holds that Virgil himself deleted them and substituted the present lines 282–9, not a very plausible theory: if Virgil ever wrote them, they could not have been intended for this context, where such a detailed description would have upset the balance and proportion of the whole passage. But their grotesqueness and awkward construction is wholly against Virgilian authorship.

This ends Virgil's vision of the crowding terrors that await Aeneas at the entrance to the Underworld, terrors in the heart of ordinary men: on the one hand haunting abstractions, on the other the horrid figures of ancient superstition, separated by the Elm Tree with its brood of Dreams (often the worst terrors of all).

290. hic: 'at this moment'; cf. (e.g.) 2. 533 f. 'hic Priamus, quamquam in media iam morte tenetur, / non tamen abstinuit'. The arrangement of *subita trepidus formidine* is very characteristic.

292. docta: the Sibyl in her wisdom knows everything, supernaturally instructed; so Silius' Sibyl is 'docta comes Triuiae' (13. 786): so *doctus* is used of Tiresias (Ovid, *Met.* 3. 322), and of Amphiaraus (Stat. *Th.* 1. 398), and Carmentis is *docta* (Ovid, *F.* 1. 499). She warns Aeneas that these monsters are 'flimsy, disembodied creatures, fluttering in hollow phantomshape'; the piling up of ghostly words vividly shows their utter insubstantiality.

293 f. admoneat ... inruat ... diuerberet: the present tenses (which are metrically useful) suggest vividly that Aeneas' action is still an open possibility: similarly 1. 58 f. 'ni faciat, maria ac terras ... / quippe ferant rapidi secum uerrantque

per auras', 5. 325 f. 'spatia et si plura supersint / transeat
elapsus prior ambiguumque relinquat', 11. 912 ff. 'ineant
pugnas et proelia temptent, / ni roseus fessos iam gurgite
Phoebus Hibero / tingat equos noctemque die labente re-
ducat': in these passages, as here, the apodosis has a like
pattern of two parallel verbs.

294. diuerberet: Aeneas would have slashed at them (for the
verb cf. Lucr. 1. 222, 2. 152), shadows as they were: the
position of *umbras* gives it special emphasis, summing up
the emptiness of 292–3. The passage reflects a detail of
the legendary *katabasis* of Hercules, Apollod. *Bibl.* 2. 5. 12 ἐπὶ
δὲ τὴν Γοργόνα τὸ ξίφος ὡς ζῶσαν ἕλκει, καὶ παρὰ Ἑρμοῦ μανθάνει ὅτι κενὸν
εἴδωλόν ἐστι: cf. Bacch., *Epin.* 5. 71 ff., Norden on 260.

295–336. *Here the road starts that leads to Acheron. Charon
guards the river, and Aeneas sees a throng of spirits, some
crossing, some turned away: the Sibyl explains the meaning of
what he sees.*

Virgil now leaves the 'house of Hades', a conception which
has served its purpose as a location of specific terrors, and
passes to the landscape beyond. Here Aeneas is at once con-
fronted with the problem that so deeply concerned the
ancient mind, the fate of the unburied dead: the recent
burial of Misenus takes on fresh meaning for him.

295. hinc: as if a road or drive led from the house to the river.
Virgil is not concerned with a precise plan of the rivers of the
Underworld (cf. 132, note): the significant waterway for him
is Styx, and he names the other streams indifferently to add
infernal colour to the whole: Cocytus receives the flood of
Acheron (297), then (323) Cocytus and Styx form a single
flood, and (385) Styx alone appears as the stream that Charon
serves.

296. hic: adverb, not pronoun; Aeneas goes down the road and
is now at the river-bank. He sees 'a boiling flood, aswirl with
a yawning maw of slime, spewing its load of sludge into
Cocytus': nouns, adjectives, and verbs alike are carefully
chosen to pile up the detail of a repulsive picture, aided by
effective assonance and alliteration.

    uoragine: cf. 7. 569 f. 'ruptoque ingens Acheronte uorago /
pestiferas aperit fauces', 9. 105, 10. 114 'per pice torrentis
atraque uoragine ripas' (of Iuppiter's oath by Styx).

    gurges: here of a whirling mass of water: for the many
aspects of the word see Henry on 1. 118 (122 in his number-
ing), a famous note. Possibly *uasta uoragine* is an ablative of
description, balancing *turbidus caeno*; or *caeno uastaque
uoragine* forms a kind of hendiadys, the whole being depen-
dent on *turbidus*.

297. eructat : cf. 3. 632 f. (of the Cyclops) 'saniem eructans et frusta cruento / per somnum commixta mero'. Possibly there is a reminiscence of Lucr. 3. 1012 'Tartarus horriferos eructans faucibus aestus'. Silius has his own improvement, 13. 571 ff. 'tristior his Acheron sanie crassoque ueneno / aestuat et gelidam eructans cum murmure harenam / descendit nigra lentus per stagna palude' (and from this *sanies* Cerberus drinks *non uno ore*).

298 ff. This memorable description of Charon is precise in its detail and has sharp colour and animation. It reads as if Virgil had an actual painting in mind, just as he certainly had in his picture of *Furor*, 1. 294 ff. (see note ad loc.). Augustan Rome abounded in Greek works of art, in both public and private collections (cf. Pliny, *NH* 35. 24 ff.); thus Apelles' painting of War was in the Forum of Augustus, and a painting of a warrior by Polygnotus was *in porticu Pompei*. Among these there might well have been a work inspired by Polygnotus' representation of Charon and his boat in the Lesche at Delphi, carefully described by Pausanias (10. 28).

Charon is post-Homeric. The earliest extant literary allusion to him seems to be in a fragment of a lost epic, the *Minyas*, which Pausanias quotes as a source for Polygnotus' painting: ἔνθ' ἤτοι νέα μὲν νεκνάμβατον, ἣν ὁ γεραιὸς / πορθμεὺς ἦγε Χάρων, οὐκ ἔλλαβον ἔνδοθεν ὅρμον (Kinkel, *EGF* 215). He is clearly a traditional figure in Eur. *Alc.* 253 f. νεκύων δὲ πορθμεὺς / ἔχων χέρ' ἐπὶ κοντῷ Χάρων, 361 οὑπὶ κώπῃ ψυχοπομπὸς . . . Χάρων; Dionysus is told by Heracles (Ar. *Ran.* 139 f.) ἐν πλοιαρίῳ τυννουτῳί σ' ἀνὴρ γέρων / ναύτης διάξει. He is shown on Greek white-ground funeral *lekythoi* from the fifth century; in Italy his boat is depicted on some of the tombs in the great cemetery of Isola Sacra (2nd–3rd c. A.D.; see Toynbee, op. cit. 138).

The Etruscans conceived him as a winged monster, Charun, 'beak-nosed, blue-fleshed, grasping or swinging a hammer or clutching a pair of menacing serpents' (Toynbee, op. cit. 13 and n. 14): see F. De Ruyt, *Charun, Demon étrusque de la mort* (Rome, 1934), with plates (the present passage is discussed, 246 ff.). Virgil's description (*horrendus*, and the staring eyes) perhaps suggests something of this grisly Etruscan element. He survives in medieval Greek folksongs as Charontas, a deadly wrestler (see P. Levi, *Pausanias' Guide to Greece* (Penguin Classics, 1971), i, 478, n. 170.

298. portitor : properly 'harbour-master', the collector of *portoria* (Plaut. *Asin.* 159 'ego pol istum portitorem priuabo portorio', *Trin.* 1107 'solutumst portitori iam portorium'); he could receive letters 'poste restante' (Ter. *Ph.* 149 f.

'epistulam ab eo adlatam esse audiui modo / et ad portitores esse delatam: hanc petam'). Ti. Donatus explains 'portitores dicuntur qui portus obseruant idcirco ut sine ipsorum iussu nullus transeat in alias regiones'; this function is clear in *seruat* here and in the discrimination of 315 f. But a transition to 'ferryman' (πορθμεύς), as if from *portare*, came easily; this sense is evident in 326 ff. (cf. Juv. 3. 265 f. 'iam sedet in ripa taetrumque nouicius horret / porthmea'). Later, *portitor* = simply 'carrier'; so the ram is 'portitor Helles', Lucan 4. 57, Columella 10. 155. Cf. O. J. Todd, *CP* xl (1945), 243 ff.

300. stant lumina flamma : 'his eyes stare flame-lit' (Ti. Donatus 'inflexibiles oculi eius et semper stantes quasi quasdam flammas emittebant'). *Stant* implies a fixed look, as in Ovid, *F*. 6. 133 'stantes oculi', of goggle-eyed vampire-birds; for the construction with *flamma* cf. 12. 407 f. 'iam puluere caelum / stare uident', of a sky 'stiff with dust'. The variant *flammae* has good manuscript support, and is defended by Henry; but the genitive would need an epithet (Fletcher's assumption that it is nominative plural is impossible). Dante saw Charon's eyes differently, *Inf*. 3. 99 'che 'ntorno a li occhi avea di fiamme rote'.

301. sordidus . . . amictus : 'a grimy cloak trails, knotted, from off his shoulders'. Charon is dressed like a working boatman, wearing an *exomis* secured by a rough knot, leaving the left shoulder bare (Virgil's *umeris* is presumably to avoid the collocation of *umero* with *nodo*): so Plaut. *Mil*. 1179 f. (of a sailor's get-up) 'palliolum habeas ferrugineum (nam is colos thalassicust), / id conexum in umero laeuo, exfafillato bracchio'.

The structure of this passage is a good example of Virgil's metrical control. The run of three consecutive lines (298–300) with 'weak' third-foot caesura is unusual (a point in which the Latin hexameter differs from the Greek); in 298 the pause after the fourth-foot caesura at *aquas* is quite slight, that after *Charon* (299) is much more marked, and in 300 there is a still stronger pause after *iacet*. The unbroken sense-unit *portitor . . . Charon* contrasts with the arrangement of *cui . . . flamma*, consisting of two shorter units with parallel juxtaposed verbs; and the description is closed by a single line (301) occupied by a single sense-unit.

Pictorially, the generalizing *horrendus* is developed in the details of *squalor* and staring eyes; the *squalor* is itself developed in *canities inculta* and *sordidus amictus*, and in the *nodus* that acts as a fastening. The lines contain some intricate assonance and alliteration (note *flumina* and *lumina*

in the same position). It is worth contrasting Sen. *HF* 763 ff.
'hunc seruat amnem cultu et aspectu horridus / pauidosque
manes squalidus uectat senex. / inpexa pendet barba, de-
formem sinum / nodus coercet, concauae squalent genae; /
regit ipse longo portitor conto ratem': conscientious, but
without Virgil's impact.

302. ipse : either 'unaided', or stressing Charon's authority as
master of the vessel.

conto subigit : he punts the boat out with a pole; cf. Eur.
Alc. 254 (see on 298), Sen. *Oed.* 166 ff. 'quique capaci turbida
cumba / flumina seruat durus senio / nauita crudo, uix
assiduo / bracchia conto lassata refert', Juv. 2. 150.

uelisque ministrat : when the boat is out of the shallows he
hoists sail: it is a wide river. The construction is uncertain:
uelis may be dative ('he attends to the sails'), or ablative ('he
runs the boat under sail'), balancing *conto* (so Norden); Ser-
vius gives both alternatives. Clear support for the dative is
given by 10. 218 'ipse sedens clauumque regit uelisque mini-
strat'. There is like uncertainty in two obvious imitations,
Val. Flacc. 3. 38 'ipse ratem uento stellisque ministrat' (prob-
ably ablative; dative, Langen), Stat. *Th.* 7. 752 'ipse sedens
telis pariterque ministrat habenis' (probably dative; abla-
tive, Langen).

303. ferruginea : a picturesque word for a dark colour: 'ferrugo
coloris genus est, qui uicinus est purpurae subnigrae' (Servius
on 9. 579). Dis has 'obscura tinctas ferrugine habenas' (Ovid,
Met. 5. 404); he wipes away Proserpina's tears *ferrugineo
amictu* (Claudian, *rapt. Pros.* 2. 275); there is a *ferrugineum
nemus* in the Underworld (Stat. *Th.* 2. 13). The sun in eclipse
'caput obscura nitidum ferrugine texit' (*G.* 1. 467); a stormy
sky is 'picea ferrugine caelum' (Tib. 1. 4. 43); a sailor's hat
and cloak are *ferruginea, ferrugineum* (Plaut. *Mil.* 1178 f.).
The predominant notion seems to be dark purple (cf. For-
dyce on Cat. 64. 227, K. F. Smith on Tib. l.c.); Munro suggests
(on Lucr. 4. 76) that the colour is 'a dark violet, like that of
steel after it has been heated in the fire and cooled'. See
J. André, *Étude sur les termes de couleur dans la langue latine*
(Paris, 1949), 105 ff., and cf. W. McLeod, *Phoenix* xxiv
(1907), 145 ff.

subuectat : odd in this context, for it suggests a heavy
load and considerable effort (cf. 11. 131, 473, of men carrying
building-material). But it suits *corpora*; it would hardly have
suited *umbras*.

cumba : virtually a t.t. for Charon's boat: so 413, *G.* 4. 506;
Hor. *C.* 2. 3. 28; Prop. 3. 18. 24 'torui publica cumba senis';
Stat. *S.* 2. 1. 186 'auidae trux nauita cumbae'; Silius 5. 267;

Petron. 121. 118; Juv. 2. 151 'una transire uadum tot milia cumba'.

304. senior : Charon is 'getting on'; *senior* is often metrically more convenient than *senex* (which Virgil uses four times only).

sed cruda ... senectus : 'but in his divinity he has a fresh and green old age'; Charon is no desiccated, feeble creature. The famous line has epigrammatic quality, and its original impact must have been remarkable: *senectus* is a surprise after *cruda* and *uiridis*; Tacitus stole the phrase, *Agric.* 29. 4 'adhuc adfluebat omnis iuuentus et quibus cruda ac uiridis senectus'.

cruda : the sense has passed from 'raw', 'unripe' to the idea of youthful vigour (Henry has a curious note); cf. *Il.* 23. 791 ὠμογέροντα δέ μίν φασ' ἔμμεναι (of Odysseus): so Silius 5. 569 ff. 'ille quidem cruda mente et uiridissimus irae / ibat, sed uani frigentem in Marte senectam / prodebant ictus' (of an old man mentally alert but physically feeble), 16. 331 f. 'sunt, cruda senectus / quos iuuet et longo sonipes spectatus in aeuo' (of a veteran race-horse, vigorous and experienced). But sometimes the notion of unripeness is uppermost, as in Stat. *Th.* 9. 391 f. 'tam cruda nepotis / funera' (of premature death): so *Od.* 15. 357 ἐν ὠμῷ γήραϊ (of premature old age), Lucian, *Katapl.* 5 ὀμφακίας ἡμῖν νεκροὺς ἥκεις ἄγων (of young people dead).

deo : for *ei*, explaining why he is so spry. There is no other literary allusion to Charon as a god; *Thes.L.L.* quote only *CIL* viii. 8992 (from Mauretania) 'deo Charoni Iulius Anabus uotum soluit'.

uiridisque senectus : the normal use of *uiridis* is seen in 5. 295 'Euryalus forma insignis uiridique iuuenta'; for the contrast with age cf. Sen. *Contr.* 4. pr. 3 'audiui ... illum et uiridem et postea iam senem', Stat. *S.* 1. 2. 276 f. 'longe uirides sic flore iuuentae / perdurent uultus, tardeque haec forma senescat', Val. Flacc. 1. 77 'Gloria, te uiridem uidet immunemque senectae'. Pliny (*epp.* 7. 24. 1) records the death of Ummidia Quadratilla at nearly eighty, 'usque ad nouissimam ualetudinem uiridis'. Greek uses χλωρός similarly; cf. Theocr. 14. 70 ποιεῖν τι δεῖ ἇς γόνυ χλωρόν (see Gow ad loc.).

305 ff. Virgil has drawn on *G.* 4. 471 ff., where Orpheus' song brings the ghosts to listen:

at cantu commotae Erebi de sedibus imis
umbrae ibant tenues simulacraque luce carentum,
quam multa in foliis auium se milia condunt,

Vesper ubi aut hibernus agit de montibus imber,
matres atque uiri defunctaque corpora uita
magnanimum heroum, pueri innuptaeque puellae,
impositique rogis iuuenes ante ora parentum,
quos circum limus niger et deformis harundo
Cocyti tardaque palus inamabilis unda
alligat et nouies Styx interfusa coercet.

There, the ghosts are those beyond the Styx; here they are
waiting to cross (and some are turned back, lacking burial).
There, the simile represents the birds as deep in the leaves,
either at bedtime or when sheltering from a storm; here, there
is a double simile, first the falling leaves in autumn woods,
then the gathering of migrant birds, both leaves and birds
affected by the cold. Each passage has its special pathos: in
the *Georgics*, the thrill of the ghosts as Orpheus' song sounds
in their silent world; in the *Aeneid*, the anguished anxiety
of the ghosts as they gather at the river.

The view that the Aristaeus–Orpheus episode of *G.* 4
replaced the original ending after Gallus' disgrace and death
in 26 B.C. (based on Servius' statement on *E.* 10. 1) could
imply that the passage in *G.* 4. 471 ff. was adapted from the
present passage. But that theory is now sufficiently dis-
credited; and in these particular lines everything points to
the priority of the passage in the *Georgics*: cf. B. Otis, *Virgil*
(Oxford, 1963), 411 f., a good exposition in spite of some
hazardous subjective statements.

305. huc : some take this as anticipatory to *ad ripas*, but *ad
ripas effusa* clearly forms a unit, for which reason Norden
refers *huc* to *cumba* (303): but the boat is only one detail of
the whole picture of Charon, and it is more likely that *huc* =
ad eum, picking up the ἔκφρασις (cf. Val. Flacc. 6. 579 f. 'con-
spicit Aesonium longe caput ac simul acres / huc oculos
sensusque refert'; *Thes.L.L.* s.v., 3068. 54 ff.).

  omnis turba : 'a whole throng', defined in the following
lines. Virgil looks back to *Od.* 11. 36 ff. αἱ δ' ἀγέροντο | ψυχαὶ
ὑπὲξ Ἐρέβευς νεκύων κατατεθνηώτων, | νύμφαι τ' ἠΐθεοί τε πολύτλητοί
τε γέροντες | παρθενικαί τ' ἀταλαὶ νεοπενθέα θυμὸν ἔχουσαι.

306. matres atque uiri : for *atque* not in elision see on 127. Virgil
substitutes *matres* for the metrically unmanageable *feminae*,
as in 2. 796 f. 'ingentem comitum adfluxisse nouorum /
inuenio admirans numerum, matresque uirosque' (see on
2. 501).

  defunctaque ... uita : their bodies had completed their
span of life; cf. Ovid, *H.* 14. 125 f. 'dede neci, defunctaque
uita / corpora furtiuis insuper adde rogis'. *Defunctus* alone
for 'dead' is post-Virgilian.

307. magnanimum : the archaic genitive plural form (cf. 92, note; Virgil otherwise uses it of nouns only); so. 3. 704 'magnanimum . . . generator equorum'. The word corresponds to the Homeric μεγάθυμος (see on 1. 260; F. Skutsch, *ALL* xii, 208 ff.).

pueri . . . puellae : so 2. 238 f. 'pueri circum innuptaeque puellae / sacra canunt'. The pathos is deepened by the extension in 308, envisaging the saddest of all family sorrows.

309 ff. The two parallel similes add special stylistic weight (see Fraenkel, *Horace*, 427 f.); cf. 2. 304 ff., 4. 469 ff., 12. 521 ff. They are carefully but not rigidly balanced. The first occupies 1½ lines, the second 2½; *quam multa* opens the first, *quam multae* is postponed in the second; the cause of the falling leaves precedes *cadunt*, the reason for the gathering of the birds follows *glomerantur* ; *frigore primo* and *frigidus annus* are emphasized by their parallel placing. The first begins with a slow spondaic movement, the second has dactylic speed. The first illustrates the withering of life, the second suggests the massing of the dead for their last journey.

The leaf-simile naturally recalls *Il.* 6. 146 ff. οἵη περ φύλλων γενεή, τοίη δὲ καὶ ἀνδρῶν. / φύλλα τὰ μέν τ' ἄνεμος χαμάδις χέει, etc. (cf. *Il.* 21. 464 ff.). In Apoll. Rhod. 4. 216 ff. the Colchians assemble ὅσα φύλλα χαμᾶζε περικλαδέος πέσεν ὕλης / φυλλοχόῳ ἐνὶ μηνί. In Bacchylides, *Epin.* 5. 63 ff. Heracles is in the Underworld (to fetch Cerberus), ἔνθα δυστάνων βροτῶν / ψυχὰς ἐδάη παρὰ Κωκυτοῦ ῥεέθροις / οἷά τε φύλλ' ἄνεμος / Ἴδας ἀνὰ μηλοβότους / πρῶνας ἀργηστὰς δονεῖ.

The bird-simile recalls *Il.* 3. 4 f., where the Trojan armies are as noisy as cranes, αἵ τ' ἐπεὶ οὖν χειμῶνα φύγον καὶ ἀθέσφατον ὄμβρον / κλαγγῇ ταί γε πέτονται ἐπ' Ὠκεανοῖο ῥοάων (cf. *Il.* 2. 459 ff.). In Soph. *OT* 174 ff. innumerable deaths are compared to bird-flight, ἄλλον δ' ἂν ἄλλῳ προσίδοις ἅπερ εὔπτερον ὄρνιν / . . . ἀκτὰν πρὸς ἑσπέρου θεοῦ.

Such were Virgil's 'models', if he needed them. Norden airily constructs a hypothetical origin for the conjunction of both his similes in a lost *Katabasis* of Heracles. Possible new evidence for this vanished epic is claimed by H. Lloyd-Jones, *Maia* xix (1967), 206 ff., from *P.Oxy.* 2622 ; he attributes the the fragment to Pindar, and infers that it contained a leaf-simile which Virgil knew. For discussion of this see R. J. Clark, *Phoenix* xxiv (1970), 244 ff.; G. Thaniel, *Phoenix* xxv (1971), 237 ff. (very sceptical).

These speculations can be tedious. What matters is Virgil's own art: the application of the two similes to their setting, and their treatment (especially in the bird-simile), bear all the marks of Virgilian thought and sensitivity. It may be

added that the bird-comparison has special point in view
of the ancient folk-belief that the soul is winged (Clark, l.c.
249 n. 14; Thaniel, l.c. 241 n. 20), or is itself a bird (Norden,
p. 165; Cumont, op. cit. 293 f.; cf. Dodds, op. cit. 141;
J. D. P. Bolton, *Aristeas* [Oxford, 1962], 126).

frigore primo : cf. *G.* 2. 321 'prima uel autumni sub frigora';
Virgil as a countryman knew what frosts can do.

310. lapsa cadunt : the leaves slip and fall; the elision of the
final syllable in *folia* is pictorially effective. Both *lapsa* and
cadunt give their separate detail, and there is no true pleo-
nasm: cf. Prop. 4. 4. 64 'ipsaque in Oceano sidera lapsa
cadunt', and see Vahlen, *opusc. acad.* i, 450. So Milton's
angel forms 'lay entranced, Thick as autumnal leaves that
strow the brooks In Vallombrosa' (*P.L.* 1. 302 f.); Dante
saw the spirits, hustled by Charon, 'come d'autunno si
levan le foglie / l'una appresso de l'altra, fin che 'l ramo /
vede a la terra tutte le sue spoglie' (*Inf.* 3. 112 ff.).

ad terram . . . alto : the birds gather 'landwards from the
deep tossing sea'; cf. 7. 703 ff. 'nec quisquam aeratas acies
examine tanto / misceri putet, aëriam sed gurgite ab alto /
urgeri uolucrum raucarum ad litora nubem'. They have
accomplished one stage of their journey in search of sunny
lands; the final stage lies before them. Warde Fowler sees the
picture as follows (*A Year with the Birds*[3] [London, 1902],
252 f.) : 'This must be a *northern* sea, and the coast on which
they collect must be the threshold of a more genial climate.
Where could Virgil have seen birds collecting on the shore
from the *North*, on their way to the South? . . . We must re-
call the fact (*uita Donati* 13) that he spent a great part of
his time in Campania and Sicily, where in an autumn walk
by the sea he might have seen what he here refers to. The
multitude of migrants from France, Holland, and England
take a south-easterly course in their autumn migration, and
alight on any resting-place they can find—ships, islands, or
wider sea-coasts like those of South Italy and Sicily. Here
Virgil, we may be fairly sure, had seen them, and the longing
of their hearts had entered into his, and borne fruit in a
noble simile that is his, and not another's': the concluding
words are significant. See also H. F. Macdonald, *Greece &
Rome* n.s. v (1958), 185, with an interesting quotation from
Axel Munthe.

311. annus : 'season', as in 3. 138 f. 'miserandaque uenit / ar-
boribusque satisque lues et letifer annus', *E.* 3. 57 'nunc
frondent siluae, nunc formosissimus annus'; Hor. *C.* 3. 23. 8
'pomifero graue tempus anno'.

312. terris . . . apricis : Egypt, perhaps: cf. Sen. *Oed.* 604 ff. 'nec

tanta gelidi Strymonis fugiens minas / permutat hiemes ales
et caelum secans / tepente Nilo pensat Arctoas niues'. The
sunshine with which the simile ends is unexpected: does it,
perhaps, hint at that Elysium in which 'solemque suum, sua
sidera norunt' (641)?

313. The pattern of this line is identical with that of 268, open-
ing with an emphatic spondaic disyllable, and with a like
slow rhythm.

    primi transmittere : 'figura Graeca est: ut primi transirent'
(Servius). Virgil introduced this infinitive construction with
oro (HSz, 346): so *E.* 2. 43 'a me illos abducere Thestylis
orat', 9. 230 f. 'Nisus et una / Euryalus confestim alacres
admittier orant'.

    cursum : internal accusative (cf. *ire uiam*), an innovation
with *transmittere*: contrast 4. 154 'transmittunt cursu cam-
pos', 3. 403 'transmissae . . . trans aequora classes'.

314. The slow movement of 313 is now quickened; the as-
sonance of *stabant orantes* is echoed in *tendebantque manus*
(with the ictus now falling on *-bant*). The elision in *ripae* and
the new echo in *ulterioris amore* magically suggest the elusive
distance of the shore and the pathetic longings of the ghosts.

315. tristis : 'sour', 'glum'. For the postponed connective see
on 28.

316. ast : archaic; normally, as here, it is followed by a vowel:
see on 1. 46, 2. 467; Nettleship, *Contr. Lat. Lex.*, s.v.; Leo,
Senecae tragoediae i, 214 ff.

    summotos : they are shoved aside unceremoniously; cf.
Livy 3. 48. 3 'i, inquit, lictor, submoue turbam et da uiam
domino'. For the construction *summotos arcet* cf. 8, note.

317. enim : asseverative ('indeed'); see on 28, and cf. 10. 874
'Aeneas agnouit enim laetusque precatur'. Servius took
miratus . . . tumultu as parenthetic, with *enim* in its usual
sense (and presumably regarding the participles as finite).

318. uult : 'means'; *sibi uelle* is more usual in this sense, e.g.
Ovid, *Met.* 9. 474 'tacitae quid uult sibi noctis imago?'.
The question is restated in Virgil's manner in two further
questions, the second of which develops and particularizes
the others.

319. discrimine : a parting, severance: English 'discrimination'
has lost much of the original Latin force.

320. linquunt : 'repulsae scilicet, non transeuntes' (Servius).
The disappointed ghosts turn away.

    remis . . . uerrunt : a vivid way of saying 'others make the
passage', in contrast to *linquunt*. The ghosts act as Charon's
crew: cf. Prop. 2. 27. 13 'licet et Stygia sedeat sub harundine
remex'; Ar. *Ran.* 197 κάθιζ' ἐπὶ κώπην (Charon's instruction

to Dionysus); Lucian, *dial. mort.* 22. 2 ἤντλησα καὶ τῆς κώπης συνεπελαβόμην (Menippus to Charon, trying to avoid paying his fare). Conington, however, interprets differently ('they are said to do what Charon does for them').

liuida : a graphic word for the murky water; cf. Cat. 17. 10 f. 'totius ut lacus putidaeque paludis / liuidissima maximeque est profunda uorago'.

uerrunt : so 3. 290, 5. 778 'aequora uerrunt'; Ennius, *Ann.* 384, Cat. 64. 7; Lucr. 1. 279 (of winds sweeping sea, land, and sky).

321. olli : archaic and solemn (so *ollis*, 730). For the effect of such archaic words cf. Quintil. 8. 3. 24 'et sanctiorem et magis admirabilem faciunt orationem, quibus non quilibet fuerit usurus, eoque ornamento acerrimi iudicii P. Vergilius unice est usus'. Ennius has *olli* (dative singular and nominative plural) and *ollis* (dative); Lucretius has *ollis* (both dative and ablative); Cicero quotes 'ancient laws' containing the forms *ollos, olla* (*de leg.* 2. 19 ff.). Such forms must have disappeared early from spoken Latin, for they do not occur in Plautus or Terence.

longaeua : not recorded before Virgil, who has it quite often; so *aequaeuus* (2. 561); *grandaeuus* (1. 121) and *primaeuus* (7. 162) occur in earlier poetry: see Norden, p. 177. So Stat. *S.* 5. 3. 270 'infernae uates longaeua Dianae'.

322 ff. Another run of lines with 'weak' third-foot caesura (cf. 301, note), which is dominant in 322 and 325 (see on 117), while 323–4 have the dominant break after *uides, timent* in the normal way.

322. Anchisa generate : the same kind of ceremonial address as in 125 f., but with the arrangement· of the doubled title in reverse.

323. For the Virgilian river-system see on 295; with *paludem* cf. 107.

324. iurare et fallere : 'utter a false oath', an ingenious solution for the unmanageable *peierare*: the oath by Styx was inviolable (*Il.* 14. 271, 15. 37, etc.; in 9. 104, 10. 113 Iuppiter swears 'Stygii per flumina fratris'). For the accusative after *iurare* (instead of *per*) cf. 351 'maria aspera iuro', 12. 197 (where Servius comments 'ornatior elocutio et crebra apud maiores, quam si uelis addere praepositionem'). The construction occurs first in Cic. *ad fam.* 7. 12. 2 'Iouem lapidem iurare' (*sanctissimum iusiurandum*, Gellius 1. 21. 4; see Latte, *Röm. Religionsgesch.* 123); cf. Callim. fr. 110. 40 Pf. σήν τε κάρην ὤμοσα σόν τε βίον, Tib. 3. 19. 15 'hoc tibi sancta tuae Iunonis numina iuro', Ovid, *Met.* 2. 101 'Stygias iurauimus undas', Stat. *S.* 3. 1. 186 'et Styga et aetherii iurauit fulmina Patris'.

325. haec omnis : those who *ripas linquunt*. The unburied are helpless; perhaps, as Butler suggests, there is an allusion to their lack of the fare for their passage, which would be provided to the buried (cf. Juv. 3. 266 f. 'nec sperat caenosi gurgitis alnum / infelix nec habet quem porrigat ore trientem').

327. nec . . . datur : Charon is not allowed to take the *inhumata turba* across.

   fluenta : first recorded in Lucr. 5. 949; Catullus coined the compound *fluentisonus* (64. 52).

328. transportare : for the construction cf. Caes. *B.G.* 4. 16 'orbant ut . . . exercitum modo Rhenum transportaret', *B.C.* 1. 54 'militesque his nauibus flumen transportat'; here the accusative of person must be supplied from the context. The addition of *ripas* to *fluenta* is unexpected: the sense is 'to carry from bank to bank over the grumbling river', a Virgilian compression.

   ossa quierunt : cf. *E.* 10. 33 'o mihi tum quam molliter ossa quiescant'; Ovid, *Am.* 3. 9. 67 'ossa quieta, precor, tuta requiescite in urna': for such formulae see J. E. Church, *ALL* xii, 226 ff.

329. centum errant annos : there is no definite source for this belief. Servius (on 325) explains the period 'quia hi sunt legitimi uitae humanae, quibus completis potest anima transire ripas, id est ad locum purgationis uenire ut redeat rursus in corpora'; Norden (p. 10) infers a Pythagorean origin, noting Plato, *Rp.* 10. 615AB, where (in a context of atonement) a hundred years are taken as a span of human life (ὡς βίου ὄντος τοσούτου τοῦ ἀνθρωπίνου).

   uolitant : 'hover'; the verb suggests their restlessness. *Circum* cannot be pressed too closely; they are *longe summoti* (316).

330. tum demum . . . reuisunt : 'then, and not till then, they are granted access, and come back to the waters of their longing': *admissi* refers to the shore from which they have been driven, *exoptata* to their longing for a passage.

331. Anchisa satus : this picks up the Sibyl's address (322; cf. 125).

   uestigia pressit : a restatement of *constitit* (cf. 197, note). For the two verbs framing the line see Norden, Anh. iii. A. 2.

332. putans : 'reputans, cum animo pertractans', Servius; so 8. 522 'multaque dura suo tristi cum corde putabant', the only other passage where Virgil has this use of *puto* (he does not use *reputo*).

   Putare is never synonymous with *cogitare*. Its literal meaning is 'to make clean' (e.g. Varro, *RR* 2. 2. 18 'ne lana inquinetur, quo minus uel infici recte possit uel lauari ac putari'); then it becomes used of trimming trees etc., making them neat (e.g. *G.* 2. 407 'persequitur uitem attondens fingitque putando'); then it is transferred to accounting, 'clearing up' accounts, making a tidy balance-sheet (*putare rationes*), and so in general 'to reckon' that something is so. Gellius has an interesting discussion of the verb (7. 5. 6 ff.).

Aeneas is here shown as clearing up in his mind what he has heard, working things out, *multa putans*. The use belongs to early Latin: cf. Plaut. *Amph.* 592 f. 'quo id, malum, pacto potest nam (mecum argumentis puta) / fieri . . . ?' ('clear it up by reasoning'), Ter. *Ph.* 718 'rem ipsam putasti' ('you've got the thing straight'), *Eun.* 629 ff. 'coepi egomet mecum inter uias / . . . aliam rem ex alia cogitare . . ./. . . dum haec puto, / praeterii inprudens uillam', where *dum haec puto* is exactly parallel to *multa putans* here and the distinction between *cogitare* and *putare* is clear.

animo : *animi* M[1], accepted by many editors; cf. 10. 686 'iuuenemque animi miserata repressit', where *animo* has much less authority. Probably *animo* belongs to *putans* as well as to *miseratus*.

333 ff. A dramatic moment: among the unburied, Aeneas sees some of his own lost men. Leucaspis is not named elsewhere, but Servius (on 1. 115) assumes that he was the helmsman, *magister*, of Orontes' ship, the loss of which is described vividly there.

333. mortis honore : the office due to the dead; cf. 11. 22 f. 'socios inhumataque corpora terrae / mandemus, qui solus honos Acheronte sub imo est'. For the double 'weak' caesura in the fourth and fifth foot see on 140.

335. uentosa . . . uectos : cf. 1. 376 'diuersa per aequora uectos', 7. 228 'tot uasta per aequora uecti', *G.* 1. 206 'in patriam uentosa per aequora uectis', with 692 below: a Virgilian association, reflecting Cat. 101. 1 'multas per gentes et multa per aequora uectus'.

336. Just as in 1. 115 f. (Orontes flung overboard), so here the rhythm is notable, depicting the tossing waves in the rough run-on to the fourth-foot caesura (none in the third foot), combined with the pictorial elision in *aqua inuoluens* (an unusual type; cf. Soubiran, op. cit. 440).

337–83. *The ghost of Aeneas' helmsman Palinurus meets them, and tells the tale of his death; he begs either for burial or that he may cross the Styx with Aeneas. The Sibyl sternly rebukes him, but comforts him with the knowledge that his name will be perpetuated.*

Leucaspis and Orontes are hardly more than mere names,

and their loss was now distant. Palinurus, so strangely lost at
sea, and so recently, comes with deeper impact upon Aeneas
and upon the reader, and Virgil develops his narrative of the
encounter in an emotional passage of high art. The story of
Palinurus' disappearance is told in 5. 827 ff., in such a way
that it seems significant of something yet to come, just as the
(much briefer) introduction of Camilla (7. 803 ff.) is so placed
and so drawn that the reader is expectant of a sequel; the
technique may also be seen in Virgil's treatment of Laocoon
in the second book. There are certain discrepancies between
this passage and that in book 5: see R. D. Williams on 5.
827–71, and his introduction to *Aen.* 5, xxv ff.

The encounter with Palinurus has a formal precedent in
Odysseus' meeting with the ghost of Elpenor (*Od.* 11. 51 ff.),
the wambling youth who got drunk and fell off the roof of
Circe's palace, breaking his neck. But in Virgil the motif is
developed and treated in an entirely different manner, owing
nothing to Homer. Like the story of Misenus (see on 156–82)
the legend of Palinurus is aetiological (cf. 381 ff. with 234 f.),
an explanation of the name of the headland (Capo di Pali-
nùro) on the Lucanian coast south-east of Elea (Velia), off
which a Roman fleet met disaster in the first Punic war (see
Walbank on Polyb. 1. 39. 6). Servius comments (on 378) that
when a plague struck the Lucanians 'respondit oraculum
manes Palinuri esse placandos: ob quam rem non longe a Velia
ei et lucum et cenotaphium dederunt'. Dionysius (*ant. Rom.*
1. 53. 2) represents the Trojans as making their first anchor-
age in Italy κατὰ λιμένα τὸν Παλίνουρον, ὃς ἀφ' ἑνὸς τῶν Αἰνείου
κυβερνητῶν τελευτήσαντος αὐτόθι ταύτης τυχεῖν λέγεται ὀνομασίας. Nor-
den suggests that the legend, like that of Misenus, goes back
to Timaeus.

In many sepulchral epigrams of the Greek Anthology the
dead man is made to tell the manner of his death, or the poet
describes it for him; sometimes the 'speaker' laments his
lack of burial (e.g. *AP* 7. 271–3). The theme of the ghost
relating his story is strikingly developed in Prop. 1. 21
(see G. Williams, op. cit. 172 ff.) and by Horace (*C.* 1. 28;
see Nisbet–Hubbard). But Virgil gives the theme his own
vividness and power, making the ghostly Palinurus tell his
tale in the world of ghosts, to a living man who had known
and honoured him. The narrative is simple and direct. It
brings out some of those problems of *pietas* that exercised
Virgil's mind: Aeneas must not think that Apollo had played
him false; Palinurus' uppermost concern as he fell was not
for himself but for Aeneas his lord; he beseeches Aeneas by
all that he holds dear to give him the rite of burial. And

Aeneas could do nothing to comfort him: *parumper* (382) has deep pathos.

337. ecce : dramatic (cf. 255); it reflects the frequent use in Comedy when a new character, or one not expected, suddenly enters.

sese . . . agebat : 'was moving towards him' (cf. 8. 465, 9. 696). This use of *se agere* for *ire* occurs often in Comedy in such expressions as 'quo agis te?' (Plaut. *Amph.* 450; cf. *Most.* 342, *Persa* 235, *Trin.* 1078). On Ter. *Andr.* 708 'quid tu? quo hinc te agis?' Donatus comments 'agere se . . . tardi et tristes dicuntur', an interpretation that Norden assumes here, unnecessarily. Servius oddly explains 'sine negotio incedere'.

338. Libyco . . . cursu : 'on the Libyan run'; in 5. 827 ff. Palinurus' loss occurred between Sicily and Cumae (for the discrepancy see R. D. Williams, *Aen.* 5, p. xxv); cf. Heinze, 146 n. 1.

339. mediis . . . in undis : 'pitched out in the depth of ocean'; for this intensive use of *medius* see Vahlen, *opusc. acad.* ii, 541, Fordyce on Cat. 64. 149. In 5. 858 ff. Somnus 'super incumbens cum puppis parte reuulsa / cumque gubernaclo liquidas proiecit in undas / praecipitem ac socios nequiquam saepe uocantem'.

340. Effective assonance and alliteration: *uix* well suggests the dim visibility of the Underworld (cf. 452 ff.).

341. sic . . . adloquitur : a formula: cf. 4. 8 'cum sic unanimam adloquitur male sana sororem', 4. 222 'tum sic Mercurium adloquitur', 10. 228 'tum sic ignarum adloquitur'.

342. medioque sub aequore : 'deep beneath the sea'; for the special horror of death by drowning see Nisbet–Hubbard on Hor. *C.* 1. 28. 23.

343. dic age : cf. 389, 531; 3. 169 'surge age', 4. 223 'uade age': *age* so used belongs to lively conversation, and is frequent in Comedy.

fallax . . . repertus : commentators quote Aesch. *Cho.* 559 ἄναξ Ἀπόλλων, μάντις ἀψευδὴς τὸ πρίν.

344. responso : there is no previous mention of this oracle; in 5. 814 Neptune tells Venus 'unus erit tantum amissum quem gurgite quaeres'.

345. finisque : for the accusative without preposition (cf. 542, 638, 696), a use which Virgil much extended, see on 1. 2; Landgraf, *ALL* x, 391 ff.; HSz, 49 f.

346. Ausonios : often in Virgil for 'Italian', both for variety and from antiquarian interest (the Ausones were the indigenous people of Campania). The oracle is typically oracular: Palinurus did reach the *fines* of Italy, in one sense of the word.

en . . . fides est : cf. 1. 253 (Venus to Iuppiter) 'hic pietatis honos?' The words could be regarded as an exclamation (like 4. 597 'en dextra fidesque'), and Norden takes them so; he quotes Donatus on Ter. *Ph.* 348 '*en* uim habet indignationis post enarratam iniuriam'. The monosyllabic ending, producing a vigorous clash of ictus and word-accent instead of the normal coincidence in the last two feet, emphasizes Aeneas' agitation. See on 1. 105, 4. 132.

347 f. neque te . . . nec me : a pointed balance; neither Aeneas nor Palinurus himself can reproach Apollo or any divinity. The reply gives a chiastic arrangement after Aeneas' questions, the second question being answered first.

347. cortina : properly, a vessel placed upon the sacred tripod, a convenient synonym here for 'oracle' (cf. 3. 92 'mugire adytis cortina reclusis'; Ovid, *Met.* 15. 635 f. 'cortinaque reddidit imo / hanc adyto uocem'). Lucilius (276) terms Apollo *cortinipotens*.

348. dux Anchisiade : cf. 126; Palinurus addresses Aeneas with the due ceremony of a subordinate to his commander.

nec me deus . . . mersit : Palinurus did not know that it was the god Somnus (5. 841 'puppique deus consedit in alta').

349. gubernaclum . . . reuulsum : cf. 5. 858 f. (see on 339). In the fifth book the sea is calm, and the wrenching off of the *gubernaclum* is supernatural; here the violence is due to a stormy sea (354 ff.), an 'accident' (*forte*).

multa ui : cf. 1. 271 'Longam multa ui muniet Albam', *G.* 3. 220 'illi alternantes multa ui proelia miscent', *G.* 1. 169 'in siluis magna ui flexa domatur' (sc. *ulmus*): such lines show Virgil's avoidance of a spondaic disyllable in the fourth foot; *ui multa* would have given coincidence of ictus and speech-accent, whereas *multa ui* gives clash and so emphasizes the violence. See on 1. 1 (*Troiae qui*), with references.

350. cui . . . custos : *cui* belongs to *haerebam* as well as to *datus*; for *haerere* with dative cf. 4. 73 'haeret lateri . . . harundo', Hor. *C.* 1. 32. 9 f. 'Veneremque et illi / semper haerentem puerum', Ovid, *Met.* 4. 34 f. 'aut stamina pollice uersant / aut haerent telae'. There is no need to supply *quo* with *regebam*, as some suggest; *cursusque regebam* restates *cui . . . custos*, extending the first clause ('to which I held fast as its appointed guardian, guiding the course').

351. praecipitans : probably intransitive ('as I hurtled down'), but it might be transitive with *gubernaclum* as object in common with *traxi* ('I dragged it down, pulling it with me'). The caesura after *traxi* is barely felt, and the rhythm sweeps on to the dramatic pause after *mecum*. For the accusative after *iurare* see on 324.

352. timorem : probably object of *cepisse*, with *me* to be supplied as subject, rather than the reverse arrangement. For the omission of the subject *me* cf. 2. 432 f. 'testor, in occasu uestro nec tela nec ullas / uitauisse uices'; this is not a Grecism but a normal Latin usage in conversational or otherwise informal style, when the necessary pronoun can be supplied without ambiguity and needs no stress (see on 2. 25).

353. armis : i.e. the *gubernaclum*, part of the ship's 'tackle'; Virgil is the first recorded writer to use *arma* of non-military equipment (like ὅπλα): cf. Stat. *Th.* 2. 106 f. 'iaceat sub nube magister / immemor armorum uersantisque aequora claui', 10. 185 f. 'stupet ipsa ratis tardeque sequuntur / arma' (of a ship without its proper helmsman). In 5. 15 *arma* seems used of sails (see R. D. Williams ad loc.); in Val. Flacc. 4. 647 'per arma uolans et per iuga summa carinae' it seems loosely equivalent to *iuga* ('thwarts'). For 'tackle' in general cf. Manilius 4. 275 f. 'puppes aut puppibus arma parabunt / quicquid et in proprios pelagus desiderat usus'.

   excussa magistro : an arresting inversion; the ship is 'knocked clean off its helmsman' ('noue dixit', Servius); contrast 1. 115 f. 'excutitur pronusque magister / uoluitur in caput'.

354. deficeret : 'might founder'; cf. *bell. Alex.* 13. 5 'Caesar Rhodias naues ix habebat (nam decem missis una ⟨sub⟩ litore Aegyptio defecerat)'.

   tantis . . . undis : but contrast 5. 870 'a nimium caelo et pelago confise sereno' (Aeneas' cry when he finds Palinurus lost).

355 ff. The narrative becomes even more graphic: the dramatic scene in 355–7 (divided between two elaborately balanced clauses) is followed by the brief and grim 'paulatim adnabam terrae', succeeded by a much longer line-group with no pauses and in mounting emotion; then one single line (362), eloquent of misery.

355. tris . . . hibernas : it is useless to attempt to find in this any indication of season or of chronology (cf. Butler's discussion): *hibernas* = 'wild' ('asperas', Servius).

   immensa per aequora : cf. 335. The alliteration with *s*-sounds is notable in the whole passage, from 351 onwards.

356. uexit : the verb gains great force from its position; its effectiveness is apparent if one were to substitute *me uexit*.

   aqua : 'over the water', with *uexit*; *uiolentus* is virtually adverbial (cf. *leuis*, 17).

   lumine quarto : cf. Ennius, *Sc.* 264 f. 'si te secundo lumine hic offendero, / moriere'.

357. summa . . . ab unda : 'perched high up on a breaker's crest'; cf. *Od.* 5. 392 f. ὁ δ' ἄρα σχεδὸν εἴσιδε γαῖαν / ὀξὺ μάλα προϊδών, μεγάλου ὑπὸ κύματος ἀρθείς.

358. paulatim ... terrae: 'stroke by stroke I kept swimming landwards'; his painful progress is marked by the spondees, with strong clash of ictus and speech-accent. *Adnare* with a dative is first recorded in Virgil (again, 1. 538, 4. 613). Servius thought it possible to punctuate either after *adnabam* or after *terrae*, and Conington and Butler think that either could stand; Norden accepts Servius' first method, putting a comma after *adnabam* and explaining *terrae* as ἀπὸ κοινοῦ with both the verb (as dative) and *tuta* (as genitive), an extraordinary notion. But *adnabam* needs a destination expressed; to understand *Italiae* from 357 is unsatisfactory: and with Norden's text a fine piece of rhythm is ruined. It is a pity that Servius dragged in his idea. Cf. G. B. Townend *Proc. Virg. Soc.* ix (1969–70), 83.

tuta tenebam: for *tuta* ('safety') cf. 9. 366 'excedunt castris et tuta capessunt', 11. 871 'tuta petunt'. The indicative is used vividly, with a suppressed apodosis to *inuasisset*, 361: Palinurus says 'I held safety in my grasp (and would have reached it) had not . . .'; cf. 8. 522 f. 'multaque dura suo tristi cum corde putabant, / ni signum caelo Cytherea dedisset aperto', *E.* 9. 45 'numeros memini, si uerba tenerem', Cic. *de leg.* 1. 52 'quin labebar longius, nisi me retinuissem'.

359. madida ... grauatum: 'clogged by wearing my soaking clothes'; cf. Plaut. *Rud.* 251 'sicine hic cum uuida ueste grassabimur?' Virgil has combined *madida cum ueste* and *madida ueste grauatum* (Conington): the first alone would not have stressed the weight, the second alone would not have emphasized the fact that he was still fully clothed.

360. capita aspera montis: 'jagged juts of cliff'. Ti. Donatus interprets 'aspera saxorum, quae ex radicibus montium quasi cum quibusdam capitibus in mare producta tenduntur', sharp points of rock projecting at the base of the cliff: Butler agrees, rightly; the idea that Palinurus had crawled to the top of a cliff and was clinging there (so Conington) seems most improbable.

361. praedamque ... putasset: characteristically, Virgil does not say outright that the *gens crudelis* killed Palinurus: *praedam* suffices. The clause explains and extends *ferro inuasisset*; the *gens* is *ignara*, because Palinurus was imagined to have something worth plundering. Cf. *A P* 7. 268 ναυηγόν με δέδορκας, ὃν οἰκτείρασα θάλασσα / γυμνῶσαι πυμάτου φάρεος ἠδέσατο, / ἄνθρωπος παλάμῃσιν ἀταρβήτοις μ' ἀπέδυσε, / τόσσον ἄγος τόσσου κέρδεος ἀράμενος.

362. The single line, a simple factual statement, has the pathos of epitaph; cf. *A P* 7. 273. 5 f. κἀγὼ μὲν πόντῳ δινεύμενος, ἰχθύσι κῦρμα, / οἴχημαι.

363. quod : a loose connective, as in *quod si*, equivalent to 'so', 'as to which', often used in adjurations: cf. 2. 141 ff. 'quod te per superos et conscia numina ueri, / per si qua est quae restet adhuc mortalibus usquam / intemerata fides, oro . . .', Ter. *Andr.* 289 ff. 'quod ego per hanc te dexteram et genium tuom, /. . . te obtestor', *Hec.* 338 'quod te, Aesculapi, et te, Salus, nequid sit huius oro'. See HSz, 571.

iucundum lumen : cf. Cat. 68. 93 'ei misero fratri iucundum lumen ademptum', *Carm. Lat. Epigr.* 963. 1 'o iucundum lumen superum, o uitae iucunda uoluptas'; Lattimore (op. cit. 162) quotes Kaibel, *Epigr. Gr.* 190. 4 λείπω τὸν γλυκὺν ἀέλιον.

This is the only occurrence of *iucundus* in Virgil; elsewhere in Epic it occurs only in Val. Flacc. 7. 336, Stat. *Th.* 8. 33; in poetry it is otherwise confined to Catullus and the Elegists. Its use here may then be deliberate, to suggest an elegiac tone: see M. Lossau, *Eranos* lxviii (1970), 109 ff., an interesting paper.

364. Palinurus appeals by all the dearest aspects of *pietas*; cf. *Od.* 11. 66 ff. (Elpenor to Odysseus) νῦν δέ σε τῶν ὄπιθεν γουνάζομαι, οὐ παρεόντων, / πρός τ' ἀλόχου καὶ πατρός, ὅ σ' ἔτρεφε τυτθὸν ἐόντα, etc.

spes . . . Iuli : cf. 4. 274 f. 'Ascanium surgentem et spes heredis Iuli / respice', 10. 524 f. 'per patrios manis et spes surgentis Iuli / te precor, hanc animam serues gnatoque patrique'; Callim. *epigr.* 19 Pf. δωδεκέτη τὸν παῖδα πατὴρ ἀπέθηκε Φίλιππος / ἐνθάδε, τὴν πολλὴν ἐλπίδα, Νικοτέλην.

365. inuicte : a heroic epithet: of Achilles, Hor. *epod.* 13. 12; of Ajax, Ovid, *Met.* 13. 386; of Scipio, Ennius, *Var.* 3.

tu mihi terram : for *tu* of solemn command cf. 95, 260; for the end-pattern of the line see on 138.

366. namque potes : formal prayer-style (see on 117).

portusque . . . Velinos : an explanatory extension of *terram inice*; the earth-casting is the primary thing, and so is given priority over the naming of the place where it must be done. For the plural *portus* cf. 7. 22, *G.* 4. 390, etc.; there seems no special reason for it here (Norden suggests euphony). Velia (Elea) in Lucania was founded in the sixth century by the Phocaeans: the anachronism was duly criticized by Iulius Hyginus (see Gellius, 10. 16. 1–10), and also by Servius (on 359).

367. diua creatrix : Venus (again, 8. 534). The line is noteworthy as containing eleven words (unless *si qua, si quam* are regarded

as units); a few in the *Aeneid* contain ten (cf. Mackail on
3. 155); in Stat. *Th.* 9. 70 there are eleven: cf. S. E. Bassett,
CP xiv (1919), 216 ff.

368. The parenthesis, almost an aside, serves to vary the tone.
For the casual-seeming *credo*, a realistic conversational
touch, cf. 1. 387 f. 'haud, credo, inuisus caelestibus auras /
uitalis carpis', 10. 865 f. 'neque enim, fortissime, credo, /
iussa aliena pati et dominos dignabere Teucros'.

    neque . . . sine numine diuum : i.e. 'with full divine assent';
cf. 2. 777 f. 'non haec sine numine diuum / eueniunt', 5. 56 f.
'haud equidem sine mente, reor, sine numine diuum / ad-
sumus'.

370. da dextram : both literally, and as a pledge; cf. 3. 610 f.
'dextram Anchises haud multa moratus / dat iuueni atque
animum praesenti pignore firmat'. The line has some
subtly arranged alliteration of *d, m, t*.

371. saltem : probably with *placidis*; after his restless flutter-
ings on the bank of Styx, unburied, it is final peace for which
he longs, a peace that so far death has not brought.

372. Palinurus has appealed to Aeneas, but it is the Sibyl who
replies, shocked at the notion that an unburied man might
presume to think of crossing Styx (even with an Aeneas to
help him). Somewhat similarly, Aeneas' reply to Deiphobus'
questionings (531 ff.) is not explicit; the Sibyl cuts him short.

    talia . . . talia : not 'awkward' (Conington, Butler), simply
blunt: *this* was his prayer, and *this* was the answer he got.

373. dira cupido : a Virgilian 'tag': again, 721, 9. 185, *G.* 1. 37.

374. tu : emphatic and rebuking. The 'stern river of the Furies'
is properly Cocytus, here merged in Styx (cf. 295, note); so
G. 3. 37 f. 'Inuidia infelix Furias amnemque seuerum /
Cocyti metuet'; Stat. *Th.* 1. 89 f. (of Tisiphone) 'inamoenum
forte sedebat / Cocyton iuxta'. There is the same association
in *AP* 7. 377. 7 f. ὑπὸ ζοφίαισιν Ἐρινύσιν ἀμμέσον ἧπται / Κωκυτοῦ
(an attack on a poet who called the Odyssey 'mud' and the
Iliad 'a dung-heap'; Gow–Page, *Garland of Philip*, p. 252).

376. A terrible line. Seneca quotes it with Stoic respect, *epp.* 77.
12 'quid fles? quid optas? perdis operam. *desine fata deum
flecti sperare precando*. rata et fixa sunt et magna atque
aeterna necessitate ducuntur: eo ibis quo omnia eunt'.

    fata deum : cf. 2. 54, 257, 7. 239. *Fata* (originally 'utter-
ances') = 'will'; 'quae dii loquuntur', Servius on 2. 54;
DServius on 4. 614 glosses *fata Iouis* as 'dicta, id est, Iouis
uoluntas'; see Bailey, *Religion in Virgil*, 224 ff.

377. cape dicta memor : cf. the Homeric ἄλλο δέ τοι ἐρέω, σὺ δ' ἐνὶ
φρεσὶ βάλλεο σῇσιν (*Il.* 1. 297, etc.).

    duri . . . casus : cf. Lucan 7. 657 f. 'sustinuit dignos etiam-

nunc credere uotis / caelicolas, uouitque, sui solacia casus'.
The Sibyl tempers her sternness with pity.

378. finitimi : the people of Lucania, who will raise a cenotaph;
for the allusion to *prodigia* see Servius, quoted in the intro-
ductory note on 337 ff. The opening *nam* is in the manner of
Greek 'Sibylline' prophecies, which is further suggested by
the run of three lines (379–81) each closed by a verb.

380. sollemnia mittent : they will dedicate ritual offerings
yearly. The repetition in *tumulum . . . tumulo* stresses the
significance of the cenotaph; cf. 10. 149 'regem adit et regi
memorat nomenque genusque', 11. 139 f. 'Fama . . . / Euan-
drum Euandrique domos et moenia replet'.

381. aeternumque . . . habebit : so 235 'aeternumque tenet per
saecula nomen', of Misenus. Servius comments on *Palinuri*
'plus est quam si *tuum* diceret'.

382. his . . . emotae : a slow, struggling rhythm, with clash of
ictus and speech-accent; *emotae* is striking, suggestive of the
force with which Palinurus' load of anxiety was lifted from
him at this comforting news.

   parumper : only here in Virgil; the tone is archaic; cf.
Ennius, *Ann.* 71 'passu permensa parumper', 455 'postquam
permensa parumper', Lucr. 4. 1116 'parua fit ardoris uiolenti
pausa parumper'. The pathos is very moving: just a moment
of present happiness—and then, how long still must he wait?

383. gaudet . . . terra : 'he takes delight in the land named after
him' (as if the thing had already happened). *Cognomine* is
from the rare adjective *cognominis* (cf. Plaut. *Bacch.* 39
'quid agunt duae germanae meretrices cognomines?'); the
ablative form in *-e*, for the normal *-i*, though remarkable, is
not impossible where the needs of metre are concerned: cf.
Ovid, *F.* 3. 654 'amne perenne latens Anna Perenna uocor',
with Bömer's note.

   The manuscripts all read *terrae*, with *cognomine* as sub-
stantive; *terra* is due to Servius alone, and is clearly more
pointed and preferable: Palinurus' pleasure is not 'in the
name of the land', but in the land itself that will bear his
own name. Henry's idea that *terra* is nominative involves
a very improbable switch of thought.

384–416. *They go to their path, and Charon sees their approach
with distaste; he calls roughly to them, saying that he cannot take
living passengers—disaster happened once when he broke the
rule. But the Sibyl mollifies him, and shows him the Golden
Bough; he relents, and takes them across the river.*

   It may now be seen how much is gained by Virgil's
separation of the description of Charon (298 ff.) from Aeneas'

actual encounter with him: his menacing presence through-
out the scene with Palinurus is vividly felt, adding to the
pathos of Palinurus' unburied state. Virgil now characterizes
the 'ferryman' with much subtle humour, giving him a
recognizable personality—rough, grumbling, reminiscent, a
character not unlike the Porter in *Macbeth*. The scene, to-
gether with the encounter with Cerberus that follows, gives
momentary relief from the tension of the preceding narrative,
before new tensions begin when the crossing has been safely
made. Virgil's treatment must have been influenced by tra-
ditional elements of a *Katabasis* (of Orpheus? of Heracles?):
see Norden here, and cf. the burlesque in Ar. *Ran.* 180 ff.

384. ergo : resumptive from 331 f.; but it sums up unspoken
thoughts in Aeneas' mind: Palinurus' misery remains, in
spite of the transitory comfort offered him by the Sibyl; but
nothing more can be done, the journey must be continued.

    peragunt : 'they go on with the journey'; cf. Hor. *Sat.* 2. 6.
99 'ambo propositum peragunt iter'.

385. iam inde : 'right from where he was', out on the stream
(*Stygia ab unda*). For elision of *iam* (again, 389; cf. *G.* 3. 74
'iam inde a teneris'), in which certain clear patterns of words
are discernible, see on 2. 254; Soubiran, op. cit. 414.

386. tacitum : cf. 265 'loca nocte tacentia': the footsteps sound
where no sound should be. The line has a notable rhythm,
markedly dactylic, with 'weak' caesura in the third foot
and a barely felt caesura in the fourth: the whole effect is
hurrying.

387. prior adgreditur ... increpat ultro : the variation is bal-
anced chiastically. Charon does not wait to be spoken to.
Servius comments on *adgreditur* 'hoc sermone ostendit
iratum'; but it is *increpat* ('scolds') that marks its tone: cf.
3. 358 'his uatem adgredior dictis', 4. 476 'maestam dictis
adgressa sororem'.

388. armatus : 'ac si diceret, nihil pium molitur armatus', Ser-
vius. Charon speaks peremptorily, like a policeman suspect-
ing criminal intent.

    nostra : the idiom of a slave in Comedy: cf. Plaut. *Truc.* 256
'quis illic est qui tam proterue nostras aedis arietat?'

389. quid uenias : cf. Plaut. *Amph.* 377 'loquere, quid uenisti?'
This use of *quid* (= *cur*) has its origin in familiar speech, e.g.
Plaut. l.c., Ter. *Eun.* 304 'quid tu's tristis? quidue's alacris?'
(so Livy 42. 36. 2 'mirari ... regem quid in Macedoniam
exercitus transportati essent'): see HSz, 458.

    iam istinc : with *fare* ('a loco in quo nunc es', Servius): he
is to speak right from where he stands, going no further; for
the elided *iam* see on 385.

istinc : a plain indication of lowered tone; cf. Plaut. *Capt.*
603 'istinc loquere, si quid uis, procul', *Rud.* 1148 f. 'tu,
puella, istinc procul / dicito quid insit': the word belongs
primarily to Comedy and to Cicero's letters, and its con-
versational colour is evident from Cat. 76. 11, Hor. *Sat.* 1. 4.
131, *Epp.* 1. 7. 32; it occurs only here in Epic, and a solitary
example in Ovid, *ex Pont.* 4. 10. 35 'qui ueniunt istinc, uix
uos ea credere dicunt', further illustrates its quality.

comprime gressum : cf. 197, 331: a restatement, in more
elevated language, of the implication in *iam istinc*.

390. The tone becomes grandiose and pompous, as Charon ex-
plains to his visitor where he is. *Soporus* is a Virgilian coinage
in high poetic style (only here in Virgil); cf. Lucan 2. 236
'nocte sopora', Stat. *Th.* 1. 403 'sub nocte sopora', Silius
11. 408 f. 'segnisque soporas / aut nostro uigiles ducat sub
numine noctes'.

391. corpora uiua : carefully placed to contrast with *umbrarum*
above. Perhaps a traditional motif; cf. Soph. fr. 224 P ἀλλ' οἱ
θανόντες ψυχαγωγοῦνται μόνοι (from the satyr-play *Heracles at
Taenarum*; see Pearson ad loc.). Charon's horror at the idea
is shown by the vigorous *nefas*.

uectare : cf. 303. The idea of a heavy load may be implied,
as in 11. 138 'nec plaustris cessant uectare gementibus
ornos'. Virgil brought the word into elevated poetry; it is
used of Charon both by Silius (13. 760 f.) and by Seneca
(*HF* 765, *Oed.* 170).

392. Charon now becomes reminiscent, just like an old man.
Servius comments 'lectum est et in Orpheo quod, quando
Hercules ad inferos descendit, Charon territus eum statim
suscepit: ob quam rem anno integro in compedibus fuit.
ideo ergo *non laetatus*, scilicet propter supplicium suum'.
The reference *in Orpheo* is not certainly known: Norden refers
it to a lost Ὀρφέως κατάβασις, others to Lucan's poem *Orpheus*
(for which cf. Stat. *S.* 2. 7. 57), mentioned by Servius on *G.* 4.
492 (naming Lucan); for a sceptical view of both theories
see Dieterich, *Nekyia*, 134 n. 1.

nec ... sum laetatus : Conington notes that this may re-
flect the Greek idiom with χαίρειν (see on 86): Charon 'rues
the day' when he let Hercules cross. Norden sees a possible
word-play on Charon's name; cf. Ar. *Ran.* 184 χαῖρ' ὦ Χάρων.
At least there is grim humour in the idea that this *nauita
tristis* (315) ever expected to be *laetus*.

393. Thesea Pirithoumque : for the legend see Frazer's refer-
ences on Apollod. *Bibl.* 2. 5. 12; for the polysyllabic ending,
with Greek proper name, cf. 444, 447, 483, 484 (see Norden,
Anh. ix. 1).

394. dis . . . geniti : a nasty knock at Aeneas (whom, however, Charon has not identified); cf. 123. Poseidon and Zeus are meant by *dis*.

inuicti uiribus : Aeneas too was *inuictus* (365).

essent : subjunctive of reported statement ('although, as they said . . .'); Charon had to take their word for it, yet their actions belied their august pedigree. The general poetic use of *quamquam* with subjunctive on the analogy of *quamuis* occurs first in Ovid (e.g. *Met.* 14. 465): see HSz, 602.

395. Tartareum . . . custodem : Cerberus; the periphrasis is in the high Epic manner: cf. 7. 1 'Aeneia nutrix' (Caieta), and see on 398. The adjective formed from the proper noun is often metrically convenient, to get round using the genitive of the noun itself; see on 2. 543. For *custodem* cf. Theocr. 29. 38 φύλακον νεκύων . . . Κέρβερον, Soph. *OC* 1572 f. ἀδάματον / φύλακα παρ' Ἄϊδᾳ. The capture of Cerberus was Hercules' final Labour (see the splendid burlesque in Ar. *Ran.* 465 ff.): the legend goes back to Homer (*Il.* 8. 366 ff., *Od.* 11. 623); for references see Frazer on Apollod. *Bibl.* 2. 5. 12.

manu : 'forcibly'; *manu* is often a fill-in word, implying personal effort of some kind: so 11. 116 'bellum finire manu', 12. 22 f. 'sunt oppida capta / multa manu', and such phrases as 'tela manu iaciens' (10. 886); see Vahlen, *opusc. acad.* i, 365, *Thes.L.L.* s.v. *manus*, 347. 27 ff.

in uincla : 'for imprisonment'; Cerda notes 'nam quae audacia facere, ut custos uinctorum sit ipse in uinclis; hoc ausus Hercules'.

396. ipsius . . . regis : Charon is making the most of his drama, as *trementem* ('poor frightened beast') shows. Servius, noting the inconsistency with Cerberus' official position as guard-dog at the entrance (cf. 417), sensibly suggests 'ad naturam canum referendum est, qui territi ad dominos confugiunt'. Norden takes *petiuit* of a demand by Hercules to Pluto that he might seize Cerberus, relying on Apollod. l.c., where Hercules is said to have asked Pluto's permission and then to have found the dog 'at the gates of Acheron'; he regards this as evidence that Virgil used a *Katabasis* of Hercules. But this interpretation makes *a solio regis* equivalent to *a rege*, and ignores the force of *ipsius* ('actually from the King's throne'). The natural meaning is perfectly reasonable, and the 'inconsistency' is unimportant. Charon's graphic detail may well have been traditional: a Middle-Corinthian kotyle depicts Pluto behind his throne, with Hercules making threatening gestures at a female figure standing protectively in front of it; Hercules is accompanied by Hermes, with an apparently retreating Cerberus; see Payne, *Necrocorinthia*, 127

(fig. 45c), 130 (he interprets the female figure as Athena);
Bowra, *Greek Lyric Poetry*[2], 94 (he takes the figure to repre-
sent Persephone).

397. dominam : 'The Mistress', whose servant Charon is.

  Ditis thalamo : just as Hercules abducted Cerberus 'ipsius
a solio regis', so these villains attempted to ravish Proserpina
from her very marriage-chamber.

  deducere : for the infinitive cf. Lucr. 3. 515 'commutare
animum quicumque adoritur'.

398. Amphrysia uates : the Sibyl; 'longe petitum epitheton',
Servius. The Sibyl served Apollo; Apollo had once been
herdsman to Admetus by the river Amphrysus in Thessaly
('pastor ab Amphryso', *G.* 3. 2). For a similar allusive-
ness cf. 2. 197 'Larisaeus Achilles' (Peleus, Achilles' father,
came from Thessaly, where Larisa was), *G.* 4. 287 'Pellaei
gens fortunata Canopi' (the Egyptians: Canopus was near
Alexandria, founded by Alexander, born at Pella in Mace-
donia).

  Sometimes this form of periphrasis (rather different from
that in 395, where *Tartareum* replaces a genitive) becomes
much more elaborate, in the Alexandrian manner: so. 4. 163
'Dardaniusque nepos Veneris' (Ascanius); Sen. *Tro.* 369
'Priami nepos Hectoreus' (Astyanax); Juv. 5. 45 'zelotypo
iuuenis praelatus Iarbae' (Aeneas); Cat. 64. 290 f. 'lentaque
sorore / flammati Phaethontis' (the poplar-tree): cf. Kroll,
Studien zum Verständnis der römischen Literatur, 266 f.

  Although Charon has addressed Aeneas, it is again the
Sibyl who replies (cf. 372), just as it is she who inquires of
Anchises' whereabouts from Musaeus (669): her role becomes
subordinate only when Aeneas meets his father.

399 f. The Sibyl deals with Charon's second complaint first,
then with the point in *armatus* (388): a chiastic arrangement
(cf. 347 f.).

399. absiste moueri : a polite way of telling Charon not to get
worked up. The parenthesis gives an illusion of lively talk,
with appropriate gesture and expression (again, 11. 408 f.
'numquam animam talem dextra hac (absiste moueri) /
amittes'): cf. 4. 116 'paucis (aduerte) docebo', 4. 478 'inueni,
germana, uiam (gratare sorori)', 11. 315 'paucis (animos ad-
hibete) docebo'.

400. ianitor : so 8. 296 'ianitor Orci'; Hor. *C.* 3. 11. 15 ff. 'cessit
immanis tibi blandienti / ianitor aulae / Cerberus'; Stat.
Th. 2. 53 f. 'Lethesque triformis / ianitor', *S.* 5. 3. 279 'nullo
sonet asper ianitor ore'; Silius 3. 35 f. 'Stygius saeuis terrens
latratibus umbras / ianitor'.

401. aeternum : adverbial (a usage not recorded before Virgil):

so 617, 11. 97 f. 'salue aeternum mihi, maxime Palla, /
aeternumque uale', G. 2. 400.

exsanguis : she mocks at the bold brave dog, doing his
duty.

402. casta : 'in chastity', predicative: there is further teasing
in the sardonic substitution of *patrui* for *Ditis*.

seruet . . . limen : cf. 8. 412 f. 'castum ut seruare cubile /
coniugis et possit paruos educere natos'. She can go on being
a good wife, with no fear of attack. So the Roman matron
Claudia 'domum seruauit, lanam fecit' (*Carm. Lat. Epigr.*
52. 9).

403. The Sibyl impresses Charon with Aeneas' full credentials:
cf. 1. 10 'insignem pietate uirum', 1. 544 f. 'rex erat Aeneas
nobis, quo iustior alter / nec pietate fuit, nec bello maior et
armis'.

405. nulla : 'not at all', emphatic; so 4. 272 'si te nulla mouet
tantarum gloria rerum'. The use is primarily colloquial,
e.g. Plaut. *Cas.* 305 'ecce me nullum senem', and the frequent
nullus uenit (Plaut. *Asin.* 408, etc.) : see Hofmann, *Lat. Um-
gangsspr.* 80, HSz, 205.

406. at : 'at any rate': often in an apodosis; cf. 1. 542 f. 'si
. . . mortalia temnitis arma, / at sperate deos memores',
Cat. 30. 11 'si tu oblitus es, at di meminerunt'. One must
imagine a pregnant pause after *imago*, and then *at ramum
hunc* follows slowly and dramatically. Here it is the Sibyl
who carries the Bough; in 636 it is Aeneas who has it.

aperit . . . latebat: an ingenious parenthesis, investing the
crucial moment with high drama. The repetition of *ramum*
adds to its significance, and the sound is adroitly varied,
with the final syllable of the word elided on the first occasion
but given its full syllabic value on the second. For a similar
but less striking parenthesis cf. 12. 206 f. '"ut sceptrum
hoc" (dextra sceptrum nam forte gerebat) / "numquam fronde
leui fundet uirgulta"'. It is a device much used by Ovid:
e.g. *Her.* 11. 95 f. '"Aeolus hunc ensem mittit tibi"—tra-
didit ensem— / "et iubet ex merito scire quid iste uelit"', *Ars*
2. 131 f. 'ille leui uirga—uirgam nam forte tenebat— / quod
rogat, in spisso litore pinguit opus', *Met.* 1. 590 f. '"pete" dixe-
rat "umbras / altorum nemorum" (et nemorum monstrauerat
umbras)', *F.* 4. 691 f. '"hoc" ait "in campo"—campumque
ostendit—"habebat / rus breue cum duro parca colona uiro"':
cf. M. von Albrecht, *Die Parenthese in Ovids Metamorphosen*
(Hildesheim, 1964), 93, 109.

407. tumida . . . residunt : Charon is immediately calmed (*ex
ira*, 'after his temper'), recognizing the authority of the
Bough. Norden puts the words in parenthesis, as a counter-

part to *aperit . . . latebat*, an arrangement that makes it plain that 'nec plura his' (408) refers to the Sibyl (sc. *dixit*).

408. The spondaic rhythm, continuing into 409, marks the gravity of the moment.

  donum : the *munus* of 142, defined in *fatalis uirgae* (cf. 146 f. 'sequetur, / si te fata uocant').

409. longo . . . uisum : a neat circumstantial invention by the poet (cf. Norden, p. 170); it is pointless to speculate on the existence of some earlier legendary occasion.

410. caeruleam . . . puppim : the *ferruginea cumba* of 303. For Servius' various comments on the meaning of *caeruleus* see on 2. 381; here it is a poeticism for 'dark', just as κυάνεος is used of Charon's boat in Theocr. 17. 48 f. πάροιθ' ἐπὶ νῆα κατελθεῖν / κυανέαν καὶ στυγνὸν ἀεὶ πορθμῆα καμόντων, *A P* 7. 67. 1 f. Ἀΐδεω λυπηρὲ διήκονε, τοῦτ' Ἀχέροντος / ὕδωρ ὃς πλώεις πορθμίδι κυανέῃ.

  propinquat : before Virgil the verb is recorded only in Sallust, *hist.* 4. 74 Maur. (Norden).

411. alias animas : 'his companions, the ghosts' (*alias* = other than himself). For the idiom cf. Lucr. 1. 116 'an pecudes alias diuinitus insinuet se' (sc. *anima*), Livy 4. 41. 8 'eo missa plaustra iumentaque alia': it is generally thought to be a Grecism, like *Od.* 8. 367 ff. 'Οδυσσεὺς / τέρπετ' ἐνὶ φρεσὶν ᾗσιν ἀκούων ἠδὲ καὶ ἄλλοι / Φαίηκες, Herod. 1. 216. 2 θύουσί μιν καὶ ἄλλα πρόβατα ἅμα αὐτῷ, Xen. *HG* 2. 4. 9 παρεκάλεσαν τοὺς . . . ὁπλίτας καὶ τοὺς ἄλλους ἱππέας. Löfstedt, however, doubts if Greek idiom completely explains the Latin instances (*Synt.* ii, 188 ff.), regarding them as examples of a natural linguistic usage in itself, influenced of course by Greek. See HSz, 208, and Ladewig–Jahn ad loc.; W. Barr, *Latomus* xxxii (1973), 856 ff.

  iuga : 'thwarts', a remarkable Grecism, noted by Servius ('ζυγά enim dicunt quae transtra nominamus'), elsewhere only in Val. Flacc. 4. 647 (see on 353); in Lucan 2. 695 it is obscurely used of a part of a ship's mast (see *Thes.L.L.*, s.v. 643. 20).

412. deturbat : he pitches them out; cf. 5. 175 'in mare praecipitem puppi deturbat ab alta', Lucr. 5. 401 'deturbauit equis in terram' (sc. *Phaethonta*): the picture is extended in *laxatque foros* ('clearing the gangways'). Statius, anxious for his father's ghost to have a pleasant crossing, prays 'umbramque senilem / inuitet ripis discussa plebe supremus / uector et in media componat molliter alga' (*S.* 5. 3. 281 ff.), a nice conceit.

  alueo : disyllabic, by synizesis (again, 7. 33, 7. 303, 9. 32).

413. ingentem Aenean : Virgil smiles at the thought of the big, solid man taken on board the flimsy craft, a most unghostly passenger. The pause after *Aenean* is artistic and satisfying.

gemuit . . . cumba : contrast Sen. *HF* 775 ff. (of Hercules, crossing Styx) 'cumba populorum capax / succubuit uni, sidit et grauior ratis / utrimque Lethen latere titubanti bibit' where Virgil's simple directness has given place to point and pomp.

414. sutilis : 'sewn'; the position of the epithet (not recorded before Virgil) gives it strong emphasis. The traditional view that a boat of stitched hides is meant (like an ancient British coracle) has been exploded by L. Casson, *CR* n.s. xiii (1963), 257 ff., who notes from Caes. *BC* 1. 54 that at this time (49 B.C.) the British method of hide-covered boats was an obvious novelty to Roman builders, so that this meaning for *sutilis* cannot have been traditional and would have been esoteric to many of Virgil's contemporary readers. He interprets Virgil as meaning that the boat was constructed of planks sewn together with twine, not mortised, a primitive method evident from Pacuvius, fr. 250 f. R (of Odysseus' raft) 'nec ulla subscus cohibet compagem aluei, / sed suta lino et sparteis serilibus' (contrast *Od.* 5. 244 ff., where Odysseus uses mortises). The 'sewn' construction is likewise implied in Agamemnon's words (*Il.* 2. 135) σπάρτα λέλυνται: 'the cording has loosened', and the ships' timbers have rotted: see Varro ap. Gell. 17. 3. 4, Pliny, *NH* 24. 65. So too Aeschylus (*Supp.* 134) speaks of a ship as λινορραφής. Casson has a clear case: see also J. S. Morrison and R. T. Williams, *Greek Oared Ships*, 50 (with further modern references), and J. O. Thomson, *History of Ancient Geography* (Cambridge, 1948), 274 (on the African mart called Rhapta).

Virgil's description reappears in Apul. *Met.* 6. 18, where Psyche is told 'ad flumen mortuum uenies, cui praefectus Charon, protinus expetens portorium, sic ad ripam ulteriorem sutili cumba deducit commeantes'.

rimosa : the twine was loosed with age, and so the boat leaked. So Hermes in Lucian, *dial. mort.* 4. 1, tells Charon that he has had to pay out for κηρὸν ὡς ἐπιπλάσαι τοῦ σκαφιδίου τὰ ἀνεῳγότα, and Charon observes to his passengers (ib. 10. 1) μικρὸν μὲν ἡμῖν . . . τὸ σκαφίδιον καὶ ὑποσαθρόν ἐστι καὶ διαρρεῖ τὰ πολλά.

415. tandem : it was a slow journey; if Virgil had written *trans fluuium tandem* the slowness would not have been so pointed. Servius engagingly speculates on the cause: 'aut propter pondus Aeneae, quod est melius; aut propter paludis magnitudinem; aut propter caeni densitatem'.

uatemque uirumque : the 'priestess and hero' have a special connexion with each other, so that the correlating *-que . . . -que* is in place; cf. 116 'gnatique patrisque', and note

on 64. Charon's whole animosity has been directed against
Aeneas alone; he drops it on finding that the suspected vil-
lain is covered by the Sibyl's supernatural powers.

416. An expressive line, with its stodgy, oozy sound. The mud
and slime are traditional (so Ar. *Ran.* 145, 273); cf. *G.* 4.
478 f. 'limus niger et deformis harundo / Cocyti'. *In* belongs
to *limo* as well as to *ulua* (see on 692).

The whole scene vividly shows the versatility of Virgil's
Epic art. For a modern picture cf. Fitzroy Maclean, *Eastern
Approaches*, Part III. ch. 4 (a wartime river-crossing in Jugo-
slavia): 'the raft was a minute, flimsy affair . . . on which
there was barely room for one passenger besides the aged
ferryman, who, grumbling to himself as he went, propelled
it across the rapid current with vigorous but erratic strokes
of his pole. Eventually, after a series of individual journeys,
each of which landed the passenger, soaked to the skin, at
a different point on the opposite bank, we were all across.
We bid farewell to the boatman, still grumbling to himself
in the darkness.'

417–25. *At once they encounter Cerberus, barking horribly. The
Sibyl flings him a drugged scrap, and he collapses unconscious.*

Homer does not name Cerberus, who is just 'the dog of
Hades' (*Il.* 8. 368). Hesiod names him, *Th.* 311 f. Κέρβερον
ὠμηστήν, Ἀΐδεω κύνα χαλκεόφωνον, / πεντηκοντακέφαλον (see West),
and tells how he fawns on new arrivals but eats those who
try to escape from the Underworld (*Th.* 771 ff.). Bacchylides
(*Epin.* 5. 60) terms him καρχαρόδοντα. For other references see
Frazer on Apollod. *Bibl.* 2. 5. 12; for representations in art
cf. *OCD*, s.v. *Cerberus*. Servius relationalizes (on 395), 'Cer-
berus terra est, id est consumptrix omnium corporum, unde
et Cerberus dictus est quasi κρεοβόρος, id est carnem uorans';
see Dieterich, *Nekyia*, 50.

Such horrors appear in 8. 296 f. (the hymn to Hercules) 'te
Stygii tremuere lacus, te ianitor Orci / ossa super recubans
antro semesa cruento'; cf. Lucan 6. 702 f. (the witch's spell)
'ianitor et sedis laxae, qui uiscera saeuo / spargis nostra cani'
(see Dieterich, *Nekyia*, 49 ff., 51 n. 1). No wonder that Lucre-
tius sought to dispel superstition and terror of chthonic bogies
(3. 1011 ff.); in the light of them there is special pathos in
Martial's prayer for his tiny slave-girl (5. 34. 3 f.) 'paruula ne
nigras horrescat Erotion umbras / oraque Tartarei prodigi-
osa canis'.

417. ingens : there is echoing assonance with *recubans . . .
uidens* below (the last two in the same position in the line).
Cerberus' huge bulk is stressed in the chiastic repetition of

ingens . . . immanis here by *immania . . . ingens* below (422 f.)
cf. Apul. *Met.* 6. 19 'canis namque praegrandis, teriugo et
satis amplo capite praeditus, immanis et formidabilis, tonan-
tibus oblatrans faucibus mortuos . . . frustra territando ante
ipsum limen et atra atria Proserpinae semper excubans ser-
uat uacuam Ditis domum'.

latratu . . . trifauci : the epithet is remarkable, applied as
it is to the abstract noun: contrast Silius 2. 551 f. 'formaque
trifauci / personat insomnis lacrimosae ianitor aulae', and cf.
Ovid, *Met.* 4. 450 f. 'tria Cerberus extulit ora / et tres latratus
simul edidit', a characteristic Ovidian conceit. *Trifaux* is
a Virgilian coinage (cf. Cic. *Tusc..* 1. 10 'triceps apud inferos
Cerberus'); the sound suggests a howl (cf. Lucr. 5. 1071, of
dogs left alone, 'deserti baubantur in aedibus', and the dog's
αὖ αὖ in Ar. *Vesp.* 903).

Cerberus has the proper qualities of a good watchdog: cf.
Columella 7. 3 'uillae custos eligendus est amplissimi corporis,
uasti latratus canorique, ut prius auditu maleficum deinde
etiam conspectu terreat, et tamen nonnunquam ne uisus
quidem horribili fremitu suo fuget insidiantem'.

419. colla : a true plural, since Cerberus had three heads (the
number varies according to poetic taste; see West on Hesiod,
Th. 312, Frazer on Apollod. *Bibl..* 2. 5. 12).

colubris : so Apollod. *Bibl..* 2. 5. 12 κατὰ δὲ τοῦ νώτου παντοίων
εἶχεν ὄφεων κεφαλάς, Hor. *C.* 3. 11. 15 ff. 'cessit immanis tibi
blandienti / . . . Cerberus, quamuis furiale centum / muniant
angues caput eius'.

420. melle . . . offam ; 'a titbit drowsed with honey and doctored
meal'. A muted line with gentle rhythm, in marked contrast
with the clatter of Cerberus' barking.

soporatam : not recorded before Virgil (again, 5. 854 f.
'ramum Lethaeo rore madentem / uique soporatum Stygia');
the striking application to a non-personal noun was imitated
by Val. Flacc. 5. 237 'rapta soporato fuerint cum uellera
luco' (the forest is made drowsy like the dragon who guarded
the Fleece). The finite verb occurs in Stat. *Th.* 6. 235 f. 'in-
stant flammis multoque soporant / imbre rogum' (of quench-
ing a pyre), 11. 94 'insuetos anguis nimia astra soporant'
(Tisiphone complains that her snakes are failing).

offam : a ball or faggot made up with some variety of grain
(*frugibus*). In Apul. *Met.* 6. 18 Psyche is to have ready for
Cerberus 'offas polentae mulso concretas'; Varro recom-
mends *offae* for the aviary, remarking (*RR* 3. 2. 4) 'eae
maxime glomerantur ex ficis et farre mixto'; cf. Cic. *diu.* 2. 73
(of the sacred chickens) 'inclusa in cauea et fame enecta si
in offam pultis inuadit'. For *puls* (a sort of porridge, made

from pounded *far*) and *polenta* (made from barley) see L. A. Moritz, *Grain-Mills and Flour in Classical Antiquity* (Oxford, 1958), 148 ff.

Henry has a lively note on the possible recipe for the *offa*. The scene is depicted in one of the miniatures in Vat. lat. 3225 (F); the Sibyl holds out an object (marked OFFA) to Cerberus, a grisly beast with three heads, on which snakes are discernible: see J. de Wit, *Die Miniaturen des Vergilius Vaticanus* (Amsterdam, 1959), 108 and fig. 34.

421. obicit : the dramatic moment is brought out by the placing of the verb, spilt over from the previous line and followed by a strong pause: so 2. 467 (*incidit*), 4. 23 (*impulit*), 4. 261 (*conspicit*), 11. 806 (*suscipiunt*); see Henry on 2. 246 f. (*Aeneidea* ii, p. 135). Cf. Sen. *dial.* 2. 14. 2 'sapiens non accedet ad fores quos durus ianitor obsidet? ille uero . . . illum . . . tamquam canem acrem obiecto cibo leniet'.

fame rabida : how like a dog. The prosody *famē* is regular (see *Thes. L.L.*, s.v., 228. 80 ff.).

422. corripit obiectam : he snaps it up instantly; the vivid follow-up of *obicit* by *obiectam* marks the simultaneous reaction. The elision in *obiectam* is expressive, as the *offa* vanishes.

immania . . . resoluit : cf. Apoll. Rhod. 4. 150 f. (of the serpent guarding the Fleece) οἴμῃ θελγόμενος δολιχὴν ἀνελύετ' ἄκανθαν / γηγενέος σπείρης, μήκυνε δὲ μυρία κύκλα. Virgil's economy of description is well seen by comparing this scene with the ornate technicolour of Apollonius, or (even more strikingly) with the corresponding scene in Val. Flacc. 8. 79 ff.

423. fusus humi : this, with the extended variation *totoque . . . antro*, graphically brings out the vast size of the beast (cf. 417, note), and consequently the Sibyl's anaesthetizing skill.

424. occupat : 'springs upon', like a commander seeing his enemy off guard.

sepulto : a remarkable compression. The idea goes back to Ennius, *Ann.* 292 'hostes uino domiti somnoque sepulti', echoed by Virgil in 2. 265 'inuadunt urbem somno uinoque sepultam' (see note ad loc.): here, the whole concept of a drugged or vinous sleep is telescoped into *sepulto* alone.

425. euaditque . . . ripam : he passes beyond the shore of Styx, into the hinterland of Hades. For the transitive *euadit* (before Virgil, only in Lucilius 313) cf. 2. 731 (*uiam*), 4. 685 (*gradus*).

inremeabilis : 'from which there is no returning': a Virgilian coinage (so of the Labyrinth, 5. 591 'indeprensus et inremeabilis error'); cf. *A P* 7. 467. 6 ἐς τὸν ἀνόστητον χῶρον ἔβης ἐνέρων, *Orph. hymn.* 57. 1 Κωκυτοῦ ναίων ἀνυπόστροφον οἶμον

ἀνάγκης. Both Statius (*Th.* 1. 96) and Seneca (*HF* 548) have
it in reference to the one-way traffic of the dead.

426–547. Virgil describes the dwellers in a region of the Under-
world which lies between Styx and the parting of the ways
(540 ff.) that lead to Elysium or Tartarus respectively; it is
neither a place of punishment nor one of blessedness, but
'neutral'. There are five groups of these spirits (for a similar
classification see Lucian, *Katapl.* 5 f.): babies (426–9), men
wrongfully condemned to die (430), suicides (434–9), the
victims of love (440–76), among them Dido, and those who
were *bello clari* (477–547), among them Deiphobus. Their
common characteristic is their premature death, and the last
four classes share the further bond of death by violence (βιαιο-
θάνατοι).

Commentators trace a doctrine that such souls must wait
and wander until their natural life-span is fulfilled: Tertul-
lian, *de anima* 56 'aiunt et immatura morte praeuentas eo
usque uagari istic donec reliquatio compleatur aetatum quas
tum peruixissent si non intempestiue obiissent'; Servius on
4. 386 'dicunt physici biothanatorum animas non recipi in
originem suam, nisi uagantes legitimum tempus fati com-
pleuerint'. But Virgil says no word of their destiny, nothing
to suggest that this region is not their abode for ever; and
in fact he includes some mythical figures whose natural life-
span must long since have been completed. Neither is it easy
to reconcile the *bello clari* of the region (478) with the 'manus
ob patrium pugnando uulnera passi' in Elysium (660); nor
possible to fit the fate of these grouped souls into any prospect
of reincarnation as expounded by Anchises (724 ff.). The pas-
sage shows that Virgil did not consider it his function as a poet
to provide a tidy, consistent eschatology. Its purpose is
apparent from the way in which the five categories of the
untimely dead are treated: the first three are quite briefly
touched on, while the other two are each developed with care
as a significant background for the dramatic encounters of
Aeneas with Dido and with Deiphobus, both (and especially
the first) of urgent and anguished personal concern to him.
The reader's 'logical instincts may not be satisfied, but more
than satisfaction is given to his imagination' (Nettleship,
Lectures and Essays [Oxford, 1885], 139).

See Norden, pp. 11 ff.; Dieterich, *Nekyia*, 150 ff.; Butler,
ad loc., and pp. 11 ff.; Camps, op. cit. 91 f., and *Proc. Virg.
Soc.* vii (1967–8), 25; F. Norwood, *CP* xlix (1954), 17. For
a wide-ranging examination of ancient lore see F. Cumont,
Lux Perpetua (Paris, 1949), ch. vii ('L'Astrologie et les morts
prématurées').

426-39. *The first three groups of the untimely dead.*

There is striking use of assonance in the opening lines: the repeated *-i-*; *auditae, animae, uitae* at the same point, with *uitae* dying away in elision; *uoces, flentes, dies*; *limine, ubere, funere, crimine*; *exsortis, mortis*, with *sorte* (431).

426. uoces : 'cries', not necessarily distinguishable words; cf. 4. 460 'hinc exaudiri uoces et uerba uocantis' (from Sychaeus' shrine). They are defined in *uagitus*; for the (slightly uncomfortable) postponement of *et* see on 27.

427. The punctuation is due to Wakefield in his London edition of 1796 (see also his note on Lucr. 2. 576): so Ribbeck, Norden, Sabbadini, Götte. Ancient scholarship clearly took the line as a unit, punctuating after *primo*; see Ti. Donatus, Servius (on 11. 59), Macrob. *Sat.* 4. 3. 2, Aelius Donatus on Ter. *Hec.* 517: so Conington, Geymonat. On the latter view, *in limine primo* must refer to this special region of the Underworld and imply the further bank of Styx just reached (cf. *continuo,* 426); Conington mistakenly refers it to Orcus, whose *limen* Aeneas has long since passed: thus it will be linked topographically with *hos iuxta* (430), *proxima loca* (434), *nec procul hinc* (440), *arua ultima* (478). This is possible, and agrees with natural rhythm: but *primo* is an odd extra in such a context, and indeed the concept of a *limen* for this vague region is unexpected.

Wakefield's punctuation (he in fact puts a semi-colon after *flentes*) links *in limine primo* with *uitae* (428): the infants have died 'on the edge of life's threshold'; there is still a satisfying sense-unit ending at *flentes*, giving a final definition of the sounds heard, and providing a typical 'growth' pattern in *uoces, uagitus ingens, infantumque animae flentes*. Servius' comment here suggests that this was his real interpretation ('quia de prima hi subrepti sunt uita'), and the phrasing is plainly supported by other passages: Lucr. 3. 681 'cum gignimur et uitae cum limen inimus'; Lucan 2. 105 f. 'non ... piguit ... / ... primo in limine uitae / infantis miseri nascentia rumpere fata'; Sen. *HF* 1131 ff. 'ite ad Stygios, umbrae, portus, / ite, innocuae, quas in primo / limine uitae scelus oppressit'; Stat. *Th.* 5. 260 f. 'semineces pueri trepidas in limine uitae / singultant animas'; Silius 13. 547 ff. 'infantum hinc gregibus uersasque ad funera taedas / passis uirginibus turbaeque in limine lucis / est iter exstinctae, et uagitu ianua nota'.

428. exsortis : first recorded in Virgil. These infants have 'lost their share' in life at its very start; *uitae* must be taken ἀπὸ κοινοῦ with *exsortis* and *in limine primo*.

429. This emotional line was echoed and adapted in many funerary inscriptions: see Hoogma, op. cit. 285 ff.; Lattimore, op. cit. 187. Virgil repeats it in 11. 28 (of Pallas' death).

atra dies : cf. Prop. 2. 11. 3 f. 'omnia, crede mihi, tecum uno munera lecto / auferet extremi funeris atra dies'. The feminine adjective is used for metrical convenience (so *longa dies*, 745); but where the feminine gives no such advantage Virgil has the masculine (e.g. *ille dies*, 2. 249; *festosque dies*, 70): see Fraenkel, *Glotta* viii (1917), 24 ff. (= *Kleine Beiträge* i, 27 ff.).

funere . . . acerbo: so Plaut. *Amph.* 190 'multa Thebano poplo acerba obiecit funera' (magniloquent), *Asin.* 595 'acerbum funus filiae faciet, si te carendum est' (pathetic): Virgil has promoted the expression to Epic. *Acerbus* in this sense of 'untimely' corresponds nearly to ἄωρος (see Lattimore, op. cit. 185 f.). The punctuation adopted here is Norden's, not as OCT (where there is a semi-colon after *acerbo* and a stop after *mortis*).

430. hos iuxta : the second group, those 'sentenced to death on a forged charge': for the genitive *mortis* cf. Hor. *C.* 2. 14. 19 f. 'damnatusque longi / Sisyphus Aeolides laboris'.

431 ff. The language is meant to suggest Roman court procedure: Heyne notes ps.-Asconius' *argumentum* of Cic. *Verr.* ii. 1 (p. 61, Klotz): 'ad hanc enim similitudinem poeta Vergilius Minoem iudicem apud inferos, tamquam si praetor sit rerum capitalium, quaesitorem appellat; dat ibi sortitionem, ubi urnam nominat, dat electionem iudicum, cum dicit *consilium uocat*, dat cognitionem facinorum, cum dicit *uitasque et crimina discit*'. Virgil plainly imagines a ghostly tribunal in formal session, to review the cases of those *falso damnati crimine mortis*. Their condemnation by an earthly court would presumably have destined them as sinners to Tartarus; now, instead, they are allocated to the 'neutral' region. This interpretation, linking these lines specifically to the single group named in 430, makes Norden's punctuation necessary (see on 429). It also provides a properly balanced account of this group, instead of its being left in the isolation of a single line, in contrast to the build-up given to the other groups. There is nothing to recommend the suggestion that the lines apply also to the three following categories (obviously such a tribunal could have no concern with the infants), or the view stressed by Butler that the passage is confused and lacking final revision.

431. sine sorte . . . sine iudice : a formal decision is made by a properly constituted court. Servius took *sors* as referring to the determination of the order of hearing ('non enim

audiebantur causae nisi per sortem ordinatae'); more prob-
ably it refers to the empanelling of a jury by lot (*sine iudice*
defines the meaning of *sine sorte*), and the process is then
described.

432. quaesitor : Minos is President of the court; cf. Sen. *Ag.*
23 f. 'quos ob infandas manus / quaesitor urna Cnosius uersat
reos '.

   urnam mouet : cf. Hor. *C.* 3. 1. 14 ff. 'aequa lege Necessitas /
sortitur insignis et imos; / omne capax mouet urna nomen ',
2. 3. 25 ff. 'omnium / uersatur urna serius ocius / sors exitura '.
   silentum : the dead: cf. Lucan 6. 513 ff. 'coetus audire
silentum / . . . non superi, non uita uetat' (of the witch
Erictho; a remarkable oxymoron); Stat. *S.* 2. 7. 121 f. 'unum,
quaeso, diem deos silentum / exores'; Sen. *Med.* 740 'com-
precor uulgus silentum uosque ferales deos'; Val. Flacc. 1.
750 'pia turba silentum '.

433. consiliumque uocat : Minos 'summons a panel' (of jurors);
so P, and ps.-Ascon. l.c.: the v.l. *concilium* (MR, Servius, Ti.
Donatus) would mean a general assemblage of the dead
whose cases need to be decided. The former, as a t.t., is cer-
tainly preferable in the context. But there is a slight awk-
wardness in the correlating *-que . . . -que*, since the members
of the *consilium* are not those whose *uitas et crimina* Minos
hears (cf. Wagner ad loc.): however, they are all ghosts to-
gether.

   crimina : 'charges' made against them in life (not 'crimes'),

434. The third group, suicides: but Virgil does not name Dido
among them. The introductory phrase is carefully varied (cf.
430, 440, 477). *Deinde* is disyllabic, by synizesis, the normal
prosody; Virgil avoids opening a clause with it (see on 1. 195).
For the pattern of the line-ending *qui sibi letum* see on 138.

435. insontes : clearly pitying. Does it represent Virgil's view
of suicide in general, or does it imply a special class of 'in-
nocents' who yet committed the act? In the later group of
those who died for love (445 ff.), three could have been
classed among the suicides: of these, Euadne and Laodamia
were clearly *insontes* on any count, but could Virgil have
thought of Phaedra as *insons*? Dido herself is in ambivalent
company there (see on 449): but Virgil's feeling about her
suicide is plain in 4. 696 'quia nec fato merita nec morte
peribat '.

   For an examination of ancient views on suicide see Cumont,
Lux Perpetua, 334 ff.; J. M. Rist, *Stoic Philosophy* (Cam-
bridge, 1969), ch. 13; cf. St. Augustine, *de ciu. Dei* 1. 17–27.
   manu : see on 395; they have used violence upon them-
selves.

perosi : the compound is not recorded before Virgil (cf. 9. 141); *exosus* occurs, 5. 687, 11. 436, 12. 517, 818): see Landgraf, *ALL* xii, 154 f. The phrasing suggests Lucr. 3. 79 ff. 'saepe usque adeo mortis formidine uitae / percipit humanos odium lucisque uidendae, / ut sibi consciscant maerenti pectore letum'; and it recalls Dido's misery, 4. 451 'taedet caeli conuexa tueri'. The alliterative effects with *p* are continued in the following lines, and there is grammatical 'rhyme' in *peperere . . . proiecere*.

436. proiecere : they have flung their lives away, 'quasi rem uilem' (Servius). From Servius onwards commentators recall the famous words of Achilles' ghost, *Od.* 11. 489 ff. βουλοίμην κ' ἐπάρουρος ἐὼν θητευέμεν ἄλλῳ / ἀνδρὶ παρ' ἀκλήρῳ, ᾧ μὴ βίοτος πολὺς εἴη, / ἢ πᾶσιν νεκύεσσι καταφθιμένοισιν ἀνάσσειν.

aethere in alto : the world above; cf. 11. 104 'aethere cassis', of the dead in battle.

438. fas obstat : the gods' law bars the way (cf. Charon's *nefas*, 391). The reading *fata obstant* (Servius and the ninth-century manuscripts) is imported from 4. 440.

tristisque . . . undae : 'the grisly swamp with its dismal waters'. Servius, not believing that *tristis* is genitive with *undae*, read *tristi . . . unda* (so too Ti. Donatus), from *G.* 4. 479 f. (in a passage drawn upon earlier, see on 305 ff.) 'tardaque palus inamabilis unda / alligat et nouies Styx interfusa coercet'. The change of construction is quite characteristic; but Conington and R. D. Williams follow Servius.

inamabilis : cf. Plaut. *Bacch.* 615 'incredibilis inposque animi inamabilis inlepidus uiuo'.

439. nouies : a 'magic' number, marking the power of the knotting stream (*alligat*).

interfusa : the verb is not recorded before Virgil and Horace (*C*. 1. 14. 19): cf. Stat. *Th.* 4. 524 'Styx discretis interflua manibus obstat'.

440–9. *The fourth group of the untimely dead: those who died of their love.*

In *Od.* 11. 235 ff. Odysseus meets the ghosts of many legendary women, among them the three named by Virgil in 445. But Virgil's 'heroines' have the single bond of unhappy love, a motif that reflects the psychological and emotional interests of Hellenistic poetry: he may well have been influenced by Parthenius, his Greek teacher (Macrob. *Sat.* 5. 17. 18), author of the ἐρωτικὰ παθήματα, a collection of love-stories. Victims of love may have been regarded as a particular category in myth: Lucian (*Katapl.* 6), after packing into Charon's boat babies and old men and those dead from wounds, has a group of those who δι' ἔρωτα αὑτοὺς ἀπέσφαξαν; and Hyginus, in a long list of women 'quae se ipsae interfecerunt' (*fab.* 243), includes many who died *ob amorem*. But Virgil has a deeper purpose than mythical convention or literary association, such as these lines might suggest: here, in the very heart of this book, he has planned for the confrontation of Aeneas with Dido's ghost. Aeneas has no escape from his personal sorrow and responsibility.

440. fusi : 'spreading' on every side. The application to space seems to have been introduced by Virgil: cf. Lucan 4. 670 f. 'non fusior ulli / terra fuit domino', Sen. *dial.* 6. 18. 4 'camporum in infinitum patentium fusa planities'.

monstrantur : the Grieving Fields are 'pointed out' by the Sibyl, acting as guide not just for Aeneas but for any travellers who come that way.

441. Lugentes campi : a striking phrase ('worthy of Bunyan', Page); contrast the *laeta arua* of Elysium (744). The personification could be Virgil's own, in spite of the formal disclaimer: it accords so clearly with the sentient Nature that is so apparent in the *Georgics*; cf. *E.* 5. 62 f. 'ipsi laetitia uoces ad sidera iactant / intonsi montes', *E.* 10. 13 'illum etiam lauri, etiam fleuere myricae'. Conington notes [Plato], *Axiochus* 371C, where the dead are judged in a place ὃ κλήζεται πεδίον ἀληθείας.

sic . . . dicunt : cf. 7. 607 'sunt geminae Belli portae (sic nomine dicunt)', *G.* 3. 280 f. 'hippomanes uero quod nomine dicunt / pastores'. For the phrase, implying a received tradition, see on 14; but one would prefer not to accept the implication.

442. quos : a generalizing masculine, though in fact Virgil names women only. Servius (on 444) thought that Sychaeus' presence in the Fields (474) accounts for the gender; but Sychaeus was not a victim of *durus amor*, and his presence with Dido is itself a problem.

crudeli . . . peredit : they are consumed by a wasting sickness; cf. Ovid, *H.* 21. 59 f. 'tibi iam nulla est speratae cura puellae, / quam ferus indigna tabe perire sinis', *Met.* 4. 259 'tabuit ex illo dementer amoribus usa'.

peredit : cf. 4. 66 'est mollis flamma medullas' (of Dido); Cat. 58. 9 'multis languoribus peresus', 66. 23 'quam penitus maestas exedit cura medullas!'

443. calles : 'walks' (Fairclough), forest 'rides'; cf. 9. 383 'rara per occultos ducebat semita calles': the forest itself is *myrtea* because the myrtle was Venus' tree (cf. 5. 72, *G.* 2. 64, *E.* 7. 62). It is a romantic picture, but there is no happiness in it; cf. Ausonius, *Cupido cruciatur* (Peiper, p. 110), 2 'myrteus amentes ubi lucus opacat amantes'.

444. curae : the 'cares' of love. The gulf between Virgil and Lucretius in their view of death is very clear.

445 ff. Virgil's choice of heroines in this context is remarkable (see on 449). He begins with a line that recalls two lines of Homer, *Od.* 11. 321 Φαίδρην τε Πρόκριν τε ἴδον καλήν τ' Ἀριάδνην and *Od.* 11. 326 Μαῖράν τε Κλυμένην τε ἴδον στυγερήν τ' Ἐριφύλην.

445. Phaedram : wife of Theseus, daughter of Minos. For the legend of her passion for her stepson Hippolytus see W. S. Barrett's introduction to Euripides' play (Oxford, 1964); for Sophocles' play on the theme see Pearson, *Fragments of Sophocles* ii, 294 ff.; for other references see Frazer on Apollod. *epit.* 1. 19. Pausanias says (1. 22. 1) that her story was known to all, even to ὅστις βαρβάρων γλῶσσαν ἔμαθεν Ἑλλήνων. Phaedra hanged herself: was she *insons* (cf. 435) ?

Procrim : daughter of Erechtheus; her husband Cephalus killed her by mistake: for the story, which has many variations, see Pearson, op. cit. ii, 170 f., Frazer on Apollod. *Bibl.* 3. 15. 1; Ovid has an accomplished and charming version (*Met.* 7. 690 ff.). Like Phaedra and Eriphyle, Procris was depicted by Polygnotus in his painting on the Lesche at Delphi (Pausanias 10. 29. 6).

Eriphylen : wife of Amphiaraus; she was bribed by the gift of a necklace to betray her husband, and was killed by her son Alcmaeon (see Pearson, op. cit. i, 130, Frazer on Apollod. *Bibl.* 3. 6. 2). She was an arch-traitress of Greek mythology, and Virgil's *maestam*, applied to her especially, is significant of his compassion: Servius records that Virgil was attacked for it, on the ground that he had taken Homer's στυγερήν as if it were στυγνήν (a pedantic criticism, for the meaning of both words developed from 'hateful' to 'unhappy'; cf. Jebb on Soph. *Ant.* 144, 1226).

446. monstrantem uulnera : cf. 450, 494 ff., 2. 278; so Odysseus saw many ghosts with wounds and bloodstained armour (*Od.* 11. 40 f.); similarly Silius 13. 824 f. 'Verginia iuxta, / cerne, cruentato uulnus sub pectore seruat' (in the world of ghosts); Tib. 2. 6. 39 f. (a nightmare vision of a dead girl) 'qualis ab excelsa praeceps delapsa fenestra / uenit ad infernos sanguinolenta lacus'.

447. Euadnen : wife of Capaneus, so devoted that she threw herself on his funeral pyre and was burned with him: see the moving treatment in Eur. *Suppl.* 990 ff.; Prop. 1. 15. 21 f. 'coniugis Euadne miseros delata per ignis / occidit, Argiuae fama pudicitiae' (for other references see Frazer on Apollod. *Bibl.* 3. 7. 1; C. Robert, *Die griechische Heldensage* iii, 923 n. 6).

Pasiphaen : see on 24; Propertius, in his list of fabled beauties claimed by death, includes 'nec proba Pasiphae' (2. 28. 52). Virgil's source for a tradition of her death by violence, implied in the context, is not known.

Laodamia : 'Ah, judge her gently who so deeply loved! / Her, who, in reason's spite, yet without crime, / Was in a trance of passion thus removed' (Wordsworth, *Laodamia*). Servius neatly summarizes her story: 'uxor Protesilai fuit. quae cum maritum in bello Troiano primum perisse cognouisset, optauit ut eius umbram uideret: qua re concessa non deserens eam, in eius amplexibus periit.' There was a tradition that she had only one day of married life before her husband went off to the war: see Palmer's introduction to Ovid, *H.* 13, with a valuable collection of references. A few fragments remain of Euripides' play *Protesilaus*; for the fragments of Laevius' poem *Protesilaudamia* see Morel, *FPL* 58 f.; cf. Frazer on Apollod. *Epit.* 3. 30. The legend made a deep impression on Catullus (68. 73 ff., 105 ff.; see Fordyce on 68. 74 for the spelling of her name).

448. Caeneus : once Caenis, daughter of the King of the Lapiths; Poseidon seduced her, and then at her request changed her to a man, Caeneus, to whom he granted invulnerability. Caeneus fought against the Centaurs; he is shown on the Phigalia frieze depicting the battle, and on the François vase: after a brilliant *aristeia* he was crushed by trees and hammered into the ground; see Ovid, *Met.* 12. 189 ff., 459 ff., where a novel version makes him metamorphosed into a bird (Ovid amusingly represents the Centaurs as jeering at his sex-change). The legend was treated by Hesiod (see Merkelbach–West, *Fragmenta Hesiodea* [Oxford, 1967], fr. 87), Pindar (fr. 150. 5 OCT), and by the Alexandrians (Apoll. Rhod. 1. 57 ff.; cf. Callim. fr. 577 Pf.). Gellius (9. 4. 14) quotes Pliny (*NH* 7. 36, on Roman and other cases of sex-change) 'ut neque respuenda neque ridenda sit notissima illa ueterum poetarum de Caenide et Caeneo cantilena'; cf. Gow–Page, *Garland of Philip* ii, p. 292 (on *A.P.* 9. 602). Virgil alone represents Caeneus as becoming a woman again in the Underworld; inclusion here among victims of *durus amor* is remarkable.

For a collection of references see Frazer on Apollod. *Epit.* 1. 22; cf. J. T. Kakridis, *CR* lxi (1947), 77 ff.; M. Delcourt, *Rev. de l'histoire des religions* cxliv (1953), 129 ff.; and see below.

449. reuoluta : as if Caenis, not Caeneus, had preceded; cf. the changes of gender in Cat. 63 (see Fordyce on 63. 8).

The group of 'heroines', now completed, is strange and

disturbing: an incestuous woman, a notorious traitress, a woman of unnatural lust, a bizarre man-woman; Procris, a jealous and suspicious wife (and, in Apollodorus' version, immoral); the devoted Euadne, the loving Laodamia—such, we find, are Dido's companions. The common factor is Virgil's pity for those who dwell (for ever?) in these *Lugentes campi*, all in their several ways equal victims of *durus amor*. It would deny him both imagination and understanding if the list were thought to be casually or mechanically compiled, merely to suit an Epic convention. But his choice of just this company deepens the enigma of his attitude to Dido. Does he think of her here as the girl-wife who had devotedly loved her husband (1. 344, 350)? Or of her guilty self-deception (4. 172 'coniugium uocat, hoc praetexit nomine culpam') in her passion for Aeneas, brought about by the heartless plotting of Iuno and Venus?

For a sensitive discussion of the passage as a clue to Virgil's judgment of Dido see J. Perret, *RÉL* xlii (1964), 247 ff., a most interesting paper. He suggests that the elusive figure of Caeneus, now once more a woman, symbolizes Dido's own changes from young bride to warrior-ruler, now again united with Sychaeus in wifely affection (474). For a like conclusion, differently argued, see E. Kraggerud, *Symb. Osl.* xl (1965), 66 ff.

450–5. Among them Aeneas sees the ghostly figure of Dido. She comes with intense dramatic impact: even for Aeneas, those other women were from a legendary past; Dido he had himself known, and loved. It is a measure of Virgil's creative power that her presence still comes as a shock: the rest are myth, Dido is real.

450. recens : as if her death had happened yesterday; she is as pitiful a sight as Eriphyle. The rhythm is dominated by the 'weak' caesura after *Phoenissa*, with *recens a uulnere* forming a unit (for the construction cf. Varro, *RR* 2. 8. 2 'pullum . . . a partu recentem').

451. errabat . . . magna : her painful restlessness is marked by the laboured spondees, with their strong clash of ictus and speech-accent.

Troius : an emotional confrontation with *Phoenissa* above.

452. agnouitque per umbras : Dido, whom Aeneas last saw (4. 387) vivid and fierce, storming at him in bitter rage, is now a phantom, glimmering so faintly that he can scarcely be sure that he sees her at all.

453. obscuram : emphatically placed; she is a misty vision. The following simile is borrowed from Apoll. Rhod. 4. 1479 f., where Lynceus sees Heracles in the distance ὥς τίς τε νέῳ ἐνὶ ἤματι μήνην | ἢ ἴδεν ἢ ἐδόκησεν ἐπαχλύουσαν ἰδέσθαι; but in this poignant context it is a whole world away from the original. The postponement of *lunam* to the last word is a subtle piece of suspense.

454. aut uidet ... putat : cf. Ovid, *Met.* 8. 513 'aut dedit aut uisus gemitus est ille dedisse'.

455. demisit lacrimas : cf. *Od.* 16. 191 δάκρυον ἧκε χαμᾶζε; Ovid, *Tr.* 1. 8. 19 f. 'inque meos si non lacrimam demittere casus, / pauca tamen ficto uerba dolore pati', Sen. *dial.* 7. 17. 1 'lacrimas audita coniugis aut amici morte demittis'.

adfatus : affectionate; cf. 2. 775 'tum sic adfari et curas his demere dictis', *G.* 4. 530 'ultro adfata timentem'. But his *dulcis amor* meets stony silence (470).

456–76. *Aeneas entreats Dido to believe that he left her in obedience to the gods, against his own will. But she keeps stony silence, then flings herself from him, running to Sychaeus for comfort.*

A formal 'model' for this confrontation, as Servius noted (on 468) is Odysseus' attempt to placate the angry ghost of Ajax (*Od.* 11. 541 ff.). But it is no more than formal: situation and sensitive perception have made this passage one of the great moments of literature. T. S. Eliot found it 'not only one of the most poignant, but one of the most civilized passages in poetry . . . complex in meaning and economical in expression, for it not only tells us about the attitude of Dido —what is still more important is what it tells about the attitude of Aeneas. Dido's behaviour appears almost as a projection of Aeneas' own conscience: this, we feel, is the way in which Aeneas' conscience would *expect* Dido to behave to him' (*What is a Classic?* [London, 1945], 20 f.).

The speech, like those of the Fourth Book, is in the manner of Greek Tragedy, transmuted into high Roman Epic. Ti. Donatus (in an unexpectedly perceptive comment) observes of its opening 'dictio ista mira arte concepta est et pro personarum et causarum ratione composita'. Both in language and situation the Fourth Book is constantly recalled: Virgil will not let Aeneas escape the past, which has caught him up at last in the world of ghosts.

456. infelix Dido : a constant vignette of her misery, already anticipated in 1. 712 'infelix, pesti deuota futurae', 1. 748 f. 'uario noctem sermone trahebat / infelix Dido longumque bibebat amorem', and repeated in 4. 68, 450, 529, 596.

ergo : 'so, then', like ἄρα, of something only just realized (Denniston, *Greek Particles*, 36; Nisbet–Hubbard on Hor. *C.* 1. 24. 5): till now Aeneas has been smothering his conscience. It is unprofitable and unnecessary to speculate on the occasion or manner of this *nuntius* (which cannot simply refer to the forebodings of 5. 4 ff.) : its existence is a piece of poetic economy (cf. the allusion to the Bough in 409).

457. exstinctam . . . secutam : for the construction cf. Caes. *BG* 7. 48. 1 'crebris nuntiis incitati, oppidum ab Romanis teneri'. For *extrema* of death cf. 1. 219 'extrema pati', Tac. *H.* 4. 59. 3 'aliter nihil spei ; famem ferrumque et extrema passuros'.

458. funeris : this is the emphatic word: 'was it *death* that I brought you?' For a suggestion that the clause is exclamatory, not a question, see M. von Albrecht, *Hermes* xciii (1965), 58.

   per sidera : earnest and solemn; cf. 3. 599 f. (of Achaemenides) 'per sidera testor, / per superos atque hoc caeli spirabile lumen', 4. 519 f. (Dido, preparing her magic rites) 'testatur moritura deos et conscia fati / sidera'.

459. Cf. 2. 141 ff. (Sinon's plea) 'quod te per superos et conscia numina ueri, / per si qua est quae restet adhuc mortalibus usquam / intemerata fides, oro, miserere laborum'; Soph. *Phil.* 469 πρός τ' εἴ τί σοι κατ' οἰκόν ἐστι προσφιλές.

460. A restatement of Aeneas' words in 4. 361 'Italiam non sponte sequor'; cf. Quint. Smyrn. 10. 284 ff. (the dying Paris to Oenone) ὦ γύναι αἰδοίη, μὴ δή νύ με τειρόμενόν περ / ἐχθήρῃς, ἐπεὶ ἄρ σε πάρος λίπον ἐν μεγάροισι / χήρην, οὐκ ἐθέλων περ· ἄγον δέ με Κῆρες ἄφυκτοι / εἰς Ἑλένην.

   The line is a famous example of poetic transference. In his translation of Callimachus' *Coma Berenices*, Catullus (66. 39) makes the lock protest 'inuita, o regina, tuo de uertice cessi' (the Greek line is not extant)—a clever and sophisticated mock-heroic conceit. With minimal change, Virgil has applied the frivolity to an anguished moment of high Epic: anyone ignorant of chronology might be excused for thinking that Catullus was parodying Virgil, somewhat like Ovid's use of *hoc opus, hic labor est* (see on 130). It is scarcely possible that the borrowing was not conscious. Modern susceptibilities are pained by Virgil's presumed indifference to the incongruity so produced, and suggest that his line is an unconscious reminiscence: this is mere wishful thinking. He knew what he was about, and this means that for him no violation of literary taste existed in his ennoblement of a piece of fun.

   Poets are their own accountants. Here is Wordsworth, *The Prelude* 10. 85 ff., 'And in this way I wrought upon myself, / Until I seemed to hear a voice that cried / To the whole city, "Sleep no more".'

461. iussa deum : cf. 4. 345 f. 'Italiam magnam Gryneus Apollo, /

Italiam Lyciae iussere capessere sortes', which Dido hurls back, 4. 376 ff. 'nunc augur Apollo, / nunc Lyciae sortes, nunc et Ioue missus ab ipso / interpres diuum fert horrida iussa per auras'.

462. senta situ : 'drear with desolation'. The epithet is archaic ('squalida', Servius); its meaning is brought out in *situ*, the mouldering decay resulting from long neglect, Homer's Ἀΐδεω δόμον εὐρώεντα (*Od.* 10. 512); cf. West on Hesiod, *Th.* 731, Richardson on *Hom. h. Dem.* 482: so of a grimy, ragged old man, Ter. *Eun.* 236 'uideo sentum squalidum aegrum, pannis annisque obsitum'; cf. Ovid, *Met.* 4. 436 'pallor hiemsque tenent late loca senta' (of the Underworld), Val. Flacc. 3. 583 f. 'tali se concitat ardens / in iuga senta fuga' (of Hercules).

noctemque profundam : cf. 4. 25 ff. (Dido's prayer) 'pater omnipotens adigat me fulmine ad umbras, / pallentis umbras Erebo noctemque profundam, / ante, pudor, quam te uiolo'.

463. imperiis egere suis : as if *dei*, not *iussa deum*, had preceded.

quiui : the verb belongs largely to Comedy, Horace's Satires and Epistles, and is frequent in Lucretius; Virgil has it once again, 10. 19 'namque aliud quid sit quod iam implorare queamus?'

464. Cf. 4. 419 f. (Dido to Anna) 'hunc ego si potui tantum sperare dolorem, / et perferre, soror, potero'. Aeneas still thinks of the *nuntius*; yet he had had his misgivings (5. 4 ff.), and there is deep self-questioning behind what seem to us strangely insensitive words.

465. aspectu : dative; cf. *curru* (1. 156), *metu* (1. 257), *uenatu* (9. 605), and see Gellius 4. 16. 7: metrical need accounts for most such forms: examples occur in prose (e.g. Caes. *BC* 1. 1. 2, *senatu*; Cic. *ad Fam.* 16. 4. 2, *sumptu*; Tac. *H.* 2. 71, *luxu*), but their manuscript authority often varies.

At this point Dido begins to move away (cf. 472); till now she has listened motionless (cf. 469 ff.).

466. quem fugis? : cf. Dido's 'mene fugis?' (4. 314): but now it is Aeneas who speaks, and Dido who shrinks away.

extremum . . . hoc est : 'this is the last word that Fate lets me speak to you'; cf. 4. 429 'extremum hoc miserae det munus amanti' (Dido's appeal to Aeneas through Anna): Servius comments 'quia post mortem tenebo alterum circulum, uiris fortibus scilicet, non amantibus datum'.

467. torua tuentem : cf. 9. 794 'asper, acerba tuens' (from Lucr. 5. 33), Cic. *Arat.* fr. 25. 2 Tr. 'truculenta tuetur'; so Hesiod, *Sc.* 236 ἄγρια δερκομένω. See HSz, 40; Löfstedt, *Synt.* ii, 420 f. The application to *animum* is remarkable; Dido's

mind comes to the window of her eyes. Norden notes Aesch.
Cho. 854 οὔτοι φρέν' ἂν κλέψειεν ὠμματωμένην, Soph. *Ai.* 955
κελαινώπαν θυμόν; cf. Soph. *Phil.* 1013 f. ἡ κακὴ σὴ διὰ μυχῶν
βλέπουσ' ἀεὶ / ψυχή.

468. lenibat : for the form cf. *insignibat*, 7. 790; *uestibat*, 8. 160;
nutribat 11. 572: all from metrical necessity. The imperfect is
obviously conative: Aeneas 'kept trying to soften her heart'.

lacrimasque ciebat : one would expect the imperfect to be
conative also, so that the tears would be Dido's. In that case,
there is a reversed situation from 4. 369 f. 'num fletu inge-
muit nostro? num lumina flexit? / num lacrimas uictus dedit
aut miseratus amantem est?' (Dido reproaching Aeneas). But
Servius must be right in his comment 'sibi, non Didoni', in
spite of the lack of coordination between the two imperfects;
for *ciere* in such phrases is normally used of the emotions of
the subject, not of an emotion stirred in another person; cf.
3. 344 f. 'talia fundebat lacrimans longosque ciebat / incas-
sum fletus', *G.* 3. 516 f. 'mixtum spumis uomit ore cruorem /
extremosque ciet gemitus'. Virgil is in fact restating the
situation as Aeneas was speaking: this line looks back to 455,
with *lenibat* here corresponding to *dulci adfatus amore* there,
demisit lacrimas there picked up in *lacrimas ciebat* here,
a chiastic arrangement. Similarly, what follows describes first
Dido's reaction to the opening of Aeneas' speech (*incepto
sermone*, 470), then her convulsive movement (472) at the
point where Aeneas cries *siste gradum* (465). For an argument
that *ciebat* is conative, and that the tears are Dido's, see
O. Seel, *Hommages à M. Renard* (Coll. Latomus, 1969),
677 ff.

469. Again a reversal of situation: cf. 4. 331 f. 'ille Iouis moni-
tis immota tenebat / lumina' (Aeneas after Dido's imploring
speech); but also a parallel to 4. 362 'talia dicentem iam-
dudum auersa tuetur' (Dido listening to Aeneas' excuses).
Cf. *Od.* 11. 563 (Odysseus and Ajax) ὣς ἐφάμην, ὁ δέ μ' οὐδὲν
ἀμείβετο.

tenebat : for the grammatical rhyme with *ciebat* cf. 4. 331 f.
(*tenebat ... premebat*; a rather odd coincidence): see on 1.
626, 4. 55. With this and the next line cf. Eur. *Med.* 27 ff. οὔτ'
ὄμμ' ἐπαίρουσ' οὔτ' ἀπαλλάσσουσα γῆς / πρόσωπον· ὡς δὲ πέτρος ἢ
θαλάσσιος / κλύδων· ἀκούει νουθετουμένη φίλων.

470. uultum ... mouetur : for the construction see on 156 (cf.
Sen. *Med.* 800 f. 'tibi mota caput / flexa uoces ceruice dedi');
but this 'middle' use of the passive with direct object is
much less frequent when the verb is finite (cf. 2. 510 f.
'inutile ferrum / cingitur') than with a participle.

471. dura silex : cf. 4. 366 f. 'duris genuit te cautibus horrens /

Caucasus' (Dido to Aeneas). *Stet* is common to both *silex* and *cautes*; for examples of this type of ἀπὸ κοινοῦ arrangement see E. J. Kenney, *CQ* n.s. viii (1958), 55: the monosyllabic verb sounds as rock-like as its meaning (cf. Prop. 4. 11. 4 'non exorato stant adamante uiae').

Marpesia : 'learned' but apposite; Marpessus was a mountain in Paros, and Parian marble had a luminous quality of surface (D. E. Eichholz on Pliny, *NH* 36. 14, Loeb); cf. Nisbet–Hubbard on Hor. *C.* 1. 19. 6. Dido's ghost glimmers in the darkness.

472. tandem : cf. 415 for its position (Virgil could have written *corripuit sese tandem*).

corripuit sese : so of Turnus, 11. 461 f. 'nec plura locutus / corripuit sese et tectis citus extulit altis'. It is a phrase from drama: cf. Plaut. *Merc.* 661 'ut corripuit se repente atque abiit!', Ter. *Hec.* 376 f. 'corripui ilico / me inde lacrumans', 518 'ita corripuit derepente tacitu' sese ad filiam'.

inimica refugit : cf. Matthew Arnold, *The Scholar Gypsy*, 'Still fly, plunge deeper in the bowering wood, / Averse, as Dido did with gesture stern / From her false friend's approach in Hades turn'.

473. umbriferum : 'providing shade'; cf. Varro, *RR* 2. 2. 11 (of sheep) 'circiter meridianos aestus, dum deferuescant, sub umbriferas rupes et arbores patulas subigunt'; Virgil does not use the adjective again. Statius has it in the curious sense of 'ghost-carrying', *Th.* 1. 57 'umbrifero Styx liuida fundo', *Th.* 8. 18 (of Charon!) 'umbriferaeque fremit sulcator pallidus undae'. For this type of compound in *-fer* or *-ger* see J. C. Arens, *Mnemos.* 4th ser., iii (1950), 240 ff.; H. Tränkle, *Die Sprachkunst des Properz* (1960, *Hermes*, Einzelschr. 15), 58 f.

pristinus : 'of long ago'; perhaps there is a hint of the simple happiness of her early married life, before trouble came.

474. Sychaeus 'answer'd all her cares and equall'd all her love' (Dryden, memorably); *respondet curis* is restated and developed in *aequat amorem*. For the caesura-pattern in the fourth and fifth feet cf. 140, note.

Formally, Sychaeus has no place in the *Lugentes campi*; his presence here is a supremely imaginative touch, and a warning against rigid attempts to systematize Virgil's Underworld. His death by murder (1. 349 ff.) explains why he is in the general region of the untimely dead; but Virgil has chosen to put him specifically just where Dido needs him most, to protect and tend her. She has finally rejected Aeneas, who had come between her and her loyalty to Sychaeus' memory, and now husband and wife are together in mutual care and trust; Sychaeus has not thought her false. Nothing could better express Virgil's belief in a continuance of feeling beyond the grave.

475. nec minus : cf. 212, note. In spite of her rejection, Aeneas still loves and pities her.

iniquo : formally the *casus* is Dido's, and the epithet shows the unease of Aeneas' conscience. But his own *casus* was *iniquus* also, and no-one could bring him comfort. Conington, Norden, and Sabbadini prefer the variant *concussus* (cf. 5. 700 'casu concussus acerbo').

476. prosequitur lacrimis : cf. 12. 72 f. 'ne me lacrimis neue omine tanto / prosequere in duri certamina Martis euntem'; Sueton. *Tib.* 7. 3 'Agrippinam . . . semel omnino ex occursu uisam adeo contentis et umentibus oculis prosecutus est ut custoditum sit ne umquam in conspectum ei posthac ueniret', a moving passage. For an echo of the line cf. Val. Flacc. 8. 55 (Jason with Medea) 'ille haeret comes et miseratur euntem'. Dido's name is mentioned twice again: 9. 266, where Ascanius promises among his rewards to Nisus and Euryalus 'cratera antiquum quem dat Sidonia Dido'; 11. 72 ff., where Aeneas gives as coverings for Pallas' body two *uestes*, 'quas illi laeta laborum / ipsa suis quondam manibus Sidonia Dido / fecerat et tenui telas discreuerat auro', a pathetic glimpse of a vanished happiness.

477–93. *They move on, and Aeneas meets the ghosts of dead soldiers, some from the Theban war, some from Troy; but the Greek ghosts are frightened when they see him.*

A transitional passage, linking the scene with Dido and the scene with Deiphobus (494 ff.): just as Dido is singled out from the grouped women (445 ff.), so now the grouped war-heroes lead to Deiphobus alone.

477. inde . . . iter : the emotional moment is past, and there must be a return to routine; somewhat similarly 4. 396 'iussa tamen diuum exsequitur classemque reuisit' (Aeneas, longing to comfort Dido). *Molitur* suggests the effort needed; cf. Sen. *Oed.* 995 ff. (of the blinded Oedipus) 'ipse suum / duce non ullo luminis orbus / molitur iter'; *datum*, either allotted by destiny, or indicated by the Sibyl, cf. 537.

iamque arua tenebant : an odd 'echo' of 2. 209, where the phrase is used of the serpents coming to devour Laocoon.

478. ultima : the last and furthest place in this region, set apart (*secreta*) for heroes of war, the fifth group of the untimely dead. *Frequentant* suggests their vast numbers.

479 ff. First come three of the Seven against Thebes: 'ancient history', as it were, to Aeneas, representing the most famous war before the Trojan War.

479. Tydeus : king of Calydon, father of Diomede, son-in-law of Adrastus; *Il.* 5. 801 Τυδεύς τοι μικρὸς μὲν ἔην δέμας, ἀλλὰ μαχητής : see Robert, *Griechische Heldensage*, 924 ff.

inclutus armis : rather like a Homeric epithet. The adjective is old-fashioned (Ennius, Lucretius), a stately word (cf. 562, 781).

480. Parthenopaeus : see the elaborate picture of him in Stat. *Th.* 4. 246 ff., where he is an Arcadian, son of Atalanta (cf. Aesch. *Septem* 547, Eur. *Phoen.* 1153); an earlier tradition made him an Argive, brother of Adrastus: see Robert, op. cit. 914 f.

Adrasti . . . imago : Virgil likes to diversify his name-catalogues by differing arrangement or construction (cf. 1. 220, note); here he names Tydeus with no epithet, Parthenopaeus with one, and gives this periphrasis for Adrastus.

For Adrastus see Robert, op. cit. 911 ff. He was the leader of the Seven, which presumably explains his inclusion here, for he alone of them survived, being saved by his miraculous horse Arion, a gift from Hercules (Pausanias 8. 25. 10; cf. *Il.* 23. 346 f.). One tradition held that he died in old age, through grief at the loss of his son Aegialeus in the successful attack on Thebes by the Epigoni (Pausanias 1. 43. 1); another, that he threw himself on a pyre with his son Hipponous (Hyginus, *fab.* 242). But Virgil puts him with his companions, where he ought to be.

481. The Trojan heroes now appear. *Ad superos = apud superos* (so Servius), i.e. in the world above ('magnum uiuis reliquerant luctum', Ti. Donatus); cf. Silius 13. 606 f. 'insultant duro imperio non digna nec aequa / ad superos passi manes'.

caduci : the only example of the word being used of persons in this sense; but cf. Ovid, *ex Pont.* 2. 8. 47 f. 'sic, quem dira tibi rapuit Germania Drusum, / pars fuerit partus sola caduca tui'. Ti. Donatus (on 10. 622) sees an implication of premature death: 'translatum est ut caduci dicantur homines qui in pueritia aut iuuenta moriuntur'.

482. longo ordine : a favourite phrase, e.g. 754, 2. 766 'pauidae longo ordine matres', 8. 722 'incedunt uictae longo ordine gentes', etc.

483. ingemuit : 'he gave a deep sigh'; another favourite expression (10. 789 'ingemuit cari grauiter genitoris amore', etc.). The names are taken from *Il.* 17. 216 Γλαῦκόν τε Μέδοντά τε Θερσίλοχόν τε; the Homeric rhythm is kept, with 'weak' caesura in the third foot and no caesura in the fourth; so too

the Greek accusative *Medonta* and the Greek polysyllabic
ending.

484. tris Antenoridas : from *Il.* 11. 59 τρεῖς τ' Ἀντηνορίδας (ac-
companying Hector and Aeneas); Homer adds their names.
For their father Antenor see on 1. 242 ff.

　　Polyboeten : not in Homer; Norden suggests a Cyclic
origin. Priests as fighting men are posthomeric; cf. 11. 768
'sacer Cybelo Chloreus olimque sacerdos'.

485. Idaeum : a herald (*Il.* 3. 248, etc.), and Priam's charioteer
(*Il.* 24. 325, 470). Here he is armour-bearer also (like Auto-
medon, Achilles' charioteer, 2. 477).

　　etiam ... tenentem : primarily a description of Idaeus'
special function (like *Cereri sacrum* above); but in its pathos
it resembles the picture of the blest in Elysium, 653 ff. 'quae
gratia currum / armorumque fuit uiuis ... / ... eadem sequi-
tur tellure repostos'.

486 ff. The pathetic eagerness of these Trojan ghosts to walk
and talk with Aeneas, their unwillingness to let him go, adds
vividness and a subtle contrast with the behaviour of the
Greeks that follows.

488. conferre gradum : 'to walk with him', side by side; cf.
Plaut. *Men.* 554 'propera, Menaechme, fer pedem, confer
gradum'.

489 ff. In pointed contrast now, the Greek ghosts are not
named. It is a superb little scene: the opening line, so swiftly
and noisily dactylic, makes one forget that these are no
tramping soldiers but phantoms; but immediately they
break their ranks in scuttling terror, and when some try to
shout defiance their feeble ghostliness betrays them.

490. uirum : not a mere substitute for *eum* : it marks the hero
in all his living strength among enemy ghosts.

491. trepidare ... uertere : 'historic' infinitives, an effective
technique in animated description. This and the next line
are exactly parallel in pattern and rhythm, with a spondaic
start, then a quick movement to the main pause in the fourth
foot. The alliteration with *t* is noteworthy.

492. ceu ... rates : an allusion to 2. 399 ff. 'diffugiunt alii ad
nauis et litora cursu / fida petunt; pars ingentem formidine
turpi / scandunt rursus equum et nota conduntur in aluo' (the
rout of the Greeks by Trojans in Greek *insignia*). Cf. *Il.* 8.
75 ff., 15. 320 ff.

493. exiguam : 'a wispy cry', with no body to it; cf. the bat-
like squeakings of the suitors' ghosts, *Od.* 24. 9 ὡς αἱ τετριγυῖαι
ἄμ' ἤϊσαν. The position of the epithet gives it great emphasis,
and the elision of the final syllable is masterly: as the cry
fades off, so does the word, left in the air at the pause that

follows. When Nero sang, he was 'exiguae uocis et fuscae'
(Sueton. *Nero* 20. 1).

inceptus . . . hiantis : 'the shout that they start belies their
gaping jaws'; they are discomfited by the thin piping sound,
when they thought to roar defiantly.

494–534. *Among the Trojan ghosts Aeneas sees Deiphobus,
horribly mutilated; Deiphobus tells of his betrayal by his wife,
Helen.*

Deiphobus was Hector's dearest brother (*Il.* 22. 233); for
his exploits see *Il.* 13 *passim*; it was to his house that Odys-
seus and Menelaus went on leaving the Wooden Horse (*Od.*
8. 517 ff.), and there some of the fiercest fighting took place.
Homer does not mention the legend that he married Helen
after the death of Paris; but it may perhaps be an inference
from *Od.* 4. 276, where he is said to have crept round the
Horse with Helen, as she called to the Greeks within it. The
earliest record of the marriage is in the summary of Lesches'
Ilias Parua (Kinkel, *EGF* 36; OCT Homer v, 106; cf. Frazer
on Apollod. *Epit.* 5. 9). The tradition that Deiphobus was
killed by Menelaus is also posthomeric; it occurs in Arctinus'
Iliupersis (*EGF* 49; OCT Homer v, 108); cf. Sen. *Agam.*
748 f., Quint. Smyrn. 13. 354 ff., Tryphiodorus 626 ff. (with
horrid details). Hyginus (*fab.* 240) makes Helen commit the
murder.

Virgil's choice of Deiphobus for this encounter enabled him
to tell a particularly ghastly story in the high Epic manner,
with an evocative memory of the Wooden Horse. The meet-
ing with Dido had brought to Aeneas the misery of a per-
sonal past: now the public calamity of Troy is recalled by
Deiphobus.

494. Priamiden : the first syllable is lengthened, *metri gratia*, as
in *Il.* 13. 157. Deiphobus' appearance is even more ghastly
than that of Hector in 2. 272 ff.; Virgil piles up the horror
ruthlessly, with a certain complexity of style. For similar
mutilations cf. *Od.* 18. 86 f., 22. 475 f., and see Jebb on
Soph. *El.* 444 ff.

Poggio used the lines (*lacerum . . . naris*) in a letter to
Guarino of Verona (1417), to describe the mutilated state of
existing texts of Quintilian before his discovery of a complete
text at St. Gallen in 1416: see Lemaire's *Quintilian* (Paris,
1825), vii. 2, 5.

495. uidet et : the manuscripts show *uidit et, uidit* (so too Ser-
vius, Ti. Donatus), *uidet*. Mynors has accepted the reading
of N. Heinsius, approved by Wagner. The general consensus
of editors (including Geymonat) is for *uidit*, which seems

preferable on balance: *laniatum corpore toto* gives the general
picture, which is then particularized in *lacerum . . . naris*;
a linking *et* is unnecessary and uncomfortable; further, with
uidet et the rhythm becomes upset since there is then no real
pause before *lacerum*, a pause that is needed because *lacerum
crudeliter ora, ora manusque ambas* forms a single long unit of
expression.

    lacerum . . . ora : for the Greek accusative of respect cf.
243, note. Before Virgil the adjective occurs in Sallust and
Lucretius.

496. ora manusque ambas : for the emotional repetition of *ora*
see on 164; cf. 2. 405 f. 'ad caelum tendens ardentia lumina
frustra, / lumina, nam teneras arcebant uincula palmas' (of
Cassandra).

    populataque tempora : probably also dependent on *lacerum*
(so too *naris* below). *Populata* is very strong (almost 'looted'),
a Virgilian innovation in such a context; it is explained, in
Virgil's manner, in *raptis auribus*: cf. Ovid, *Met.* 2. 319
'Phaethon rutilos flamma populante capillos' (much less
gruesome). Dictys Cretensis drew on Virgil for the murder,
5. 12 'Menelaus Deiphobum . . . exsectis primo auribus brac-
chiisque ablatis deinde naribus ad postremum truncatum
omni ex parte foedatumque summo cruciatu necat'.

497. truncas : 'lopped'; cf. Cat. 64. 370 'proiciet truncum sub-
misso poplite corpus' (of Polyxena). *Inhonesto* suggests some-
thing morally disgraceful, such as no decent enemy would
stoop to ('foedo, deformi, turpi', Servius); so, from a dif-
ferent angle, Ovid, *F*. 2. 211 f. 'diffugiunt hostes inhonestaque
uulnera tergo / accipiunt'.

498. adeo : underlining *uix*; Aeneas *really* hardly knew him; cf.
2. 567 'iamque adeo' ('at this very moment'), 4. 533 'sic
adeo' ('*this* is the way'), *G*. 1. 94 'multum adeo' ('a very
great deal'), *E*. 4. 11 'teque adeo . . . te consule' ('in *your*
consulship, yes, yours'): see *Thes. L.L.* s.v., 614. 43 ff.

499. notis : pathetic; cf. 11. 195 'munera nota', offerings that
the dead would recognize and so be comforted.

    compellat uocibus ultro : again, 4. 304, and cf. 2. 372, 10.
606; Ennius, *Ann.* 44 'exim compellare pater me uoce uide-
tur': see on 2. 280. Aeneas takes the initiative in speaking
(*ultro*).

500 ff. Cf. 2. 285 f. (Aeneas to Hector, in a dream) 'quae causa
indigna serenos / foedauit uultus? aut cur haec uulnera
cerno?'; Ennius, *Sc*. 72 ff. 'o lux Troiae, germane Hector, /
quid ita cum tuo lacerato corpore / miser es, aut qui te sic
respectantibus / tractauere nobis?'

500. armipotens : a fine compound from early poetry (Accius, fr. 127, of Minerva); so of Achilles, 839; of Mars, Lucr. 1. 33. The ringing, elevated address is in marked contrast with Deiphobus' cringing, pathetic state: not merely Epic courtesy, but a means of comfort to the poor ghost, giving him his due dignity.

genus . . . Teucri : again, 4. 230; cf. 648, 5. 45 'Dardanidae magni, genus alto a sanguine diuum'. For *genus* ('son', 'descendant') cf. 792, 839, 7. 213, Cat. 61. 1 f. 'collis o Heliconii / cultor, Uraniae genus'.

501. optauit: a strong word, suggesting deliberate choice: 'who chose to?'

502. de te : this properly belongs to the idea in *sumere poenas*, the meaning of which is restated in *tantum*.

suprema : with *nocte* (cf. 513); Aeneas means Troy's last night.

503. Pelasgum : for the genitive form see on 92 (*Italum*). In Homer the Pelasgi are a tribe from Larissa, in alliance with the Trojans (*Il.* 2. 840); later, the name became used for 'Greeks' in general, and for autochthonous Greeks in particular. Aeneas refers to the fierce fighting at Deiphobus' house (*Od.* 8. 519 f.).

504. procubuisse : 'had fallen dead'; cf. 2. 426 (of Coroebus).

505. egomet : for such forms in poetry see G. B. A. Fletcher, *Hermes* xciv (1966), 254 ff.; Norden wrongly states that they disappear after Virgil.

Rhoeteo in litore : Rhoeteum was a place on the shore north of Ilium (cf. 3. 108); here Catullus' brother was buried (65. 7 f. 'Troia Rhoeteo quem subter litore tellus / ereptum nostris obterit ex oculis'). There is a valid variant *Rhoeteo litore*, preferred by Norden, Sabbadini, Geymonat.

506. magna . . . uocaui : the ritual phrase is given added solemnity by the double initial alliteration. The purpose of this triple call was to invite the soul to enter its new home in the cenotaph: see Toynbee, op. cit. 54. For *uoce uocaui* see on 247; the words must be clear and loud (cf. 3. 67 f. 'animamque sepulcro / condimus et magna supremum uoce ciemus').

507. nomen . . . seruant : cf. 233 ff., of Misenus. Here *nomen* has no aetiological background, and the *arma* would be represented only ('depicta scilicet', Servius; see Norden).

tĕ, amice : the monosyllable (unaccented) *tē* is shortened in hiatus. This is not an imitation of Greek Epic prosody, like 3. 211 'insulāe Ionio in magno': it reflects the pronunciation of ordinary Latin speech (as in Comedy), giving a tone of conversational informality to Aeneas' words which in this context has a pathetic realism. This is the only example in Epic, but Virgil has it in *E.* 8. 108 'credimus? an, quĭ amant, ipsi sibi somnia fingunt?', *E.* 2. 65 'te Corydon, ŏ Alexi'.

For Plautine illustrations see Lindsay, *Early Latin Verse* (Oxford, 1922), 226 ff. For other examples cf. Lucr. 2. 404 'at contra quāē amara . . . uidentur', 2. 617 'uiuam progeniem quĭ in oras luminis edant', 6. 730 'tempore eo fiant, quŏ etesia flabra aquilonum', 6. 796 'tempore eo sĭ odoratast quo menstrua soluit' (see Bailey, *proleg.* 128); Cat. 55. 4 'te in circo, tĕ in omnibus libellis', 97. 1 'non (ita me dĭ ament) quicquam referre putaui'; in Hor. *Sat.* 1. 9. 38 'si mĕ amas': see W. R. Hardie, *Res Metrica* (Oxford, 1920), 46; Soubiran op. cit. 374.

508. conspicere : 'catch sight of', after searching among the heaps of slain.

509. amice : Deiphobus' opening repetition of Aeneas' closing endearment adds to the illusion of a normal meeting between close friends. The separation of *o* from the vocative increases its emotional effect; *tibi* is dative of agent, 'undone by you'.

510. omnia : in balanced contrast with *nihil* above.

Deiphobo : an emotional use of the speaker's own name instead of a personal pronoun. The technique has various nuances, depending on the context: here it may suggest Deiphobus' shame and despair; in 2. 79 *Sinonem* brings out Sinon's bogus uprightness; in 7. 261 *Latino* marks Latinus' sense of honour; in 11. 537, 582 Diana's use of her own name marks her pride in Camilla's affection (in 566 *donum Triuiae*, over which commentators stumble, is clearly spoken from Metabus' point of view). See J. Kvíčala, *Vergil-Studien* (Prague, 1878), 17 ff., for an interesting list of such passages from Virgil, Homer, and Sophocles; Norden has a useful note.

funeris umbris : 'the shade of his dead body'; for *funus* so used see on 150; for the plural *umbris* cf. 5. 81 'animaeque umbraeque paternae' (of Anchises), Livy 40. 56. 9 'species et umbrae insontis interempti filii'.

511. exitiale : cf. 2. 31 'donum exitiale Mineruae' (nowhere else in Virgil).

Lacaenae : Helen, contemptuously: 'the Spartan woman' could mean no-one else, cf. Prop. 2. 15. 13, Ovid, *H.* 5. 99, Sen. *Ag.* 704, Eur. *Androm.* 486 ἡ Λάκαινα; 2. 601 'Tyndaridis facies inuisa Lacaenae', Eur. *Tro.* 34 f. ἡ Λάκαινα Τυνδαρὶς / 'Ἑλένη; Hor. *C.* 3. 3. 25 f. (of Paris) 'iam nec Lacaenae splendet adulterae / famosus hospes'.

512. monimenta : his wounds are 'souvenirs' of Helen; cf. 26, note, 12. 945 f. 'oculis postquam saeui monimenta doloris / exuuiasque hausit' (Aeneas sees Turnus wearing Pallas' belt).

513. falsa . . . gaudia : the unsuspecting celebrations of the Horse's entry into Troy (2. 238 ff.); cf. Eur. *Tro.* 527 ff. τίς οὐκ ἔβα νεανίδων, / τίς οὐ γεραιὸς ἐκ δόμων; / κεχαρμένοι δ᾽ ἀοιδαῖς / δόλιον ἔσχον ἄταν.

514. egerimus : Norden notes this as the earliest certain example of this prosody in this perfect subjunctive form, in which -*i*- was originally long. In contrast, Catullus (5. 10; see Fordyce ad loc.) has *fecerimus* in the future perfect indicative, where -*i*- was originally short. See on 92 (*oraueris*).

515. fatalis equus : 2. 237 f. 'scandit fatalis machina muros / feta armis'. For the traditions of the Wooden Horse see on 2. 15, and *JRS* xlix (1959). 16 ff.; for some discussion of the Horse in art see M. Scherer, *The Legends of Troy in Art and Literature* (New York–London, Phaidon, 1963), 114 ff.

saltu . . . uenit : Ennius, *Sc.* 76 f. 'nam maximo saltu superabit grauidus armatis equus, / qui suo partu ardua perdat Pergama'; Aesch. *Ag.* 825 ff. ἵππου νεοσσός, ἀσπιδηφόρος λεώς, / πήδημ᾽ ὀρούσας ἀμφὶ Πλειάδων δύσιν· / ὑπερθορὼν δὲ πύργον ὠμηστὴς λέων / ἅδην ἔλειξεν αἵματος τυραννικοῦ.

516. armatum peditem : cf. 2. 20 'uterumque armato milite complent'. For the names of the Greeks inside the Horse see on 2. 260 ff.

grauis . . . aluo : cf. Ennius, l.c. (above), 2. 238 (above); Eur. *Tro.* 11 ἐγκύμον᾽ ἵππον τευχέων.

517. euhantis : cf. Cat. 64. 391 'Thyiadas effusis euantis crinibus egit', Prop. 2. 3. 18 'egit ut euhantes dux Ariadna choros'. The women cry *euhoe* (Cat. 64. 255 'euhoe bacchantes, euhoe capita inflectentes'); cf. 7. 389 'euhoe Bacche fremens', of the maddened Amata.

orgia : the 'secret rites' especially associated with Bacchic revellings; cf. Cat. 64. 259 'pars obscura cauis celebrabant orgia cistis', with Fordyce's note. Here Virgil startlingly makes it an internal accusative after *euhantis* ('shrieking the *euhoe*-ritual'); cf. Sopater ap. Athen. iv. 175D ἐγρέτου δέ τις / τὸν ἡδονῆς μελῳδὸν εὐάζων χορόν.

circum : with *ducebat* below, by tmesis; cf. *G.* 4. 274 f. 'in foliis, quae plurima circum / funduntur'.

518. flammam . . . tenebat : so of Amata, 7. 397 f. 'ipsa inter medias flagrantem feruida pinum / sustinet'. This was part of Helen's pretended ritual, really intended as a signal to the Greeks.

The tradition of a fire-signal on the night of Troy's fall is constant, but versions vary. In 2. 256 the signal comes from the Greek flagship to Sinon (see note), for him to open the Horse at the right time. Others make Sinon send up a flare for the Greeks to sail, either from outside Troy (Apollod.

Epit. 5. 19) or from inside (Arctinus; see OCT Homer v, 107, 26 f.; so too Quint. Smyrn. 13. 23 ff.). Another version made the traitor Antenor responsible (schol. Lycophr. 340). According to Tryphiodorus (510 ff.) there were two flares, one from Sinon (outside) and one from Helen (inside), παννυχίη δ' ἑτάροι- σιν ὑπὲρ θαλάμοιο καὶ αὐτὴ / εὐειδὴς ῾Ελένη χρυσέην ἐπεδείκνυτο πεύκην. This last version might perhaps help to reconcile the present passage with 2. 256, i.e. that two signals were sent, one to Sinon from the Greek ships (or, alternatively, from him to the Greeks), another from Helen to guide the Greeks after they had landed. But the relationship of Tryphiodorus to Virgil is itself a problem: see Heinze, 63 ff.; F. Vian, *Recherches sur les Posthomerica de Quintus de Smyrne* (Paris, 1959), 95 ff.

The present passage is inconsistent with 2. 567 ff. (the opening of the debatable 'Helen-episode'), where Helen is said to have taken refuge at the shrine of Vesta, in fear of reprisals. Servius noted this on 2. 592, and it has been stressed by those who reject the authenticity of the 'episode' (cf. *CQ* n.s. xi [1961], 186), but its importance has been exaggerated.

To the bibliography of the 'episode' (my commentary on *Aen.* 2, p. 219) add: R. T. Bruère, *CP* lix (1964), 267 ff.; H. T. Rowell, in *The Classical Tradition*, ed. L. Wallach (New York, 1966), 211 ff.; G. P. Goold, *HSCP* lxxiv (1970), 101 ff., a vigorous and penetrating argument against Virgilian authorship of the passage.

520. confectum curis : this worried Servius, who comments 'atqui uacauerat gaudiis'; Schrader in 1776 conjectured *choreis*! But it is a perfectly natural statement in Deiphobus' circumstances, as Norden notes, and preserves his dignity. In Quint. Smyrn. 13. 355 Menelaus came on Deiphobus καρη- βαρέοντα, which suggests that he was drunk.

522. Sound and rhythm combine to make this a gentle, slumbrous line; commentators quote *Od.* 13. 79 f. καὶ τῷ νήδυμος ὕπνος ἐπὶ βλεφάροισιν ἔπιπτε / νήγρετος ἥδιστος, θανάτῳ ἄγχιστα ἐοικώς.

523. egregia : 'that splendid wife of mine': for the sneer cf. 4. 93 f. 'egregiam uero laudem et spolia ampla refertis / tuque puerque tuus' (Iuno to Venus), 7. 556 'egregium Veneris genus' (Iuno to Allecto, a gibe at Aeneas).

524. emouet : the well-attested variant *amouet* is preferred by Sabbadini and Geymonat, providing the only instance of the verb in Virgil.

    fidum : so 7. 640 'fidoque accingitur ense'; cf. 9. 707 'lorica fidelis', Silius 12. 384 'enses, fidissima tela'. The 'trusty sword' would lie by Deiphobus' head, ready for in-stant use; cf. Tac. *H.* 2. 49 'adlatis pugionibus duobus, cum utrumque pertemptasset, alterum capiti subdidit' (of Otho, on the night before he killed himself). Helen's first precaution was to remove the sword, which explains the tense of *subduxerat*.

526. scilicet : 'naturally'; the bitter sarcasm is continued in the spiteful *amanti*, the onetime husband who was to receive such a 'present'.

527. Helen hopes to save her face after her desertion of Menelaus, first for Paris, then for Deiphobus.

528. quid moror? : 'to cut my story short'; a rhetorical summing-up; cf. 2. 102.

529. hortator ... Aeolides : so Ovid terms Ulysses 'hortator scelerum' (*Met.* 13. 45). *Aeolides* has venom, for it alludes to the legend that Ulysses was a bastard, son of Aeolus' son Sisyphus: see Servius here, and cf. Soph. *Ajax* 190, *Phil.* 417, Ovid, *Met.* 13. 31 f. For posthomeric vilification of Ulysses cf. W. B. Stanford, *The Ulysses Theme* (Blackwell, Oxford, 1954), ch. 10.

530. instaurate : properly a religious word, of renewing a sacrifice or other solemn rite (4. 63, 145, 5. 94, 8. 283), then extended to other kinds of 'renewal', as in 2. 669 f. 'sinite instaurata reuisam / proelia'. Here, in a difficult turn of language (helped by *poenas* in the context) that has no precise parallel, Deiphobus prays that his sufferings may be 'renewed' in reprisal upon the Greeks. With Virgil's characteristic reticence, *talia* alone represents the actual murder.

pio ... reposco : the emphasis is on *pio*; *si* implies protestation, not doubt (= 'as sure as'), a feature of prayers, e.g. Cat. 76. 19 f. 'si uitam puriter egi, / eripite hanc pestem perniciemque mihi'.

531. sed : he breaks off, to ask Aeneas what brings him, a living man, to the Underworld; cf. 1. 369 'sed uos qui tandem? quibus aut uenistis ab oris?'

age fare : cf. 389, an impatient questioning. For the use of *uicissim* see Thielmann, *ALL* vii, 371 f. An adverb at the end of a line is fairly rare in Virgil, but *uicissim* could stand nowhere else with any metrical comfort or grace: see Norden, Anh. iii B. 2, and cf. note on 2. 18.

532. pelagine ... erroribus : i.e. by being driven off course on your voyage; cf. 7. 199 'siue errore uiae seu tempestatibus acti'. The (to us) curious question reflects *Od.* 11. 13 ff., where Odysseus reached the Underworld by a sea-voyage to the land of the Cimmerians (but cf. pp. 279 f., below) on the bounds of Ocean.

533. fatigat : the 'wearying' is not yet over, but it began long

ago, an implication of past time which accounts for *adires* below; cf. Cat. 101. 2 f. 'aduenio . . . / ut te postremo donarem munere mortis'.

534. sine sole : 'sunless'; cf. Eur. *Alc.* 851 f. εἶμι τῶν κάτω | Κόρης Ἄνακτός τ' εἰς ἀνηλίους δόμους. For this use of *sine* to express a negative adjectival notion cf. Ovid, *Met.* 1. 20 'sine pondere' ('weightless', ἀβαρῆ), *Met.* 8. 518 'sine sanguine leto' ('a bloodless death', i.e. not by fighting): see HSz, 428.

turbida : cf. Silius 13. 421 f. 'pergitque ad turbida portae / ostia Tartareae'. Probably the meaning is 'this region of cloud'; Ti. Donatus interprets 'quae nihil aliud praeter caligines habeant' (cf. 265 'loca nocte tacentia late'): for the contrast with sunshine cf. Lucr. 4. 168 ff. 'modo cum fuerit liquidissima caeli / tempestas, perquam subito fit turbida foede, / undique uti tenebras omnis Acherunta rearis / liquisse et magnas caeli complesse cauernas'.

535–47. *The Sibyl warns Aeneas that his time is short: he is now at the parting of the ways, one leading to Elysium, the other to the place of the damned. Deiphobus apologizes and turns away.*

The passage is both a colophon to the whole scene that began in 426 ff., and a transition from the 'neutral' region to the abodes of punishment and bliss, whose occupants have been allotted their due place.

535. hac uice sermonum : cf. Ovid, *Tr.* 4. 4. 79 'cum uice sermonis fratrem cognouit'. Virgil leaves us to infer that Aeneas replied to Deiphobus.

roseis . . . quadrigis : cf. 7. 26 'Aurora in roseis fulgebat lutea bigis'. Aurora accompanies the Sun in his chariot, and it is now past midday. The ornate indication of time is in the tradition of Epic (cf. *Il.* 8. 68 ἦμος δ' Ἥλιος μέσον οὐρανὸν ἀμφιβεβήκει); it seems bizarre in this context, but for Aeneas the ordered brightness of the upper world continues.

Such descriptions are more commonly of dawn (cf. 4. 584 f.), or of night (cf. 10. 215 f.). They could easily become hackneyed: cf. Sen. *Epp.* 122. 11 ff., a cautionary tale of the poet Iulius Montanus, who 'ortus et occasus libentissime inserebat'. Horace has fun with the technique, striking an attitude, *Sat.* 1. 5. 9 f. (the journey to Brundisium) 'iam nox inducere terris / umbras et caelo diffundere signa parabat', 2. 6. 100 f. (the town and country mice) 'iamque tenebat / nox medium caeli spatium'. Seneca uses it wittily, to pinpoint the month, day, and hour of Claudius' death, *Apocol.* 2: after some grandiloquent verses, ending 'iam medium curru Phoebus diuiserat orbem / et propior nocti fessas quatiebat habenas / obliquo flexam deducens tramite lucem', he adds 'cum omnes poetae, non contenti ortus et occasus describere, etiam medium diem inquietent'. Perhaps some Romans were tickled by the present passage.

537. fors : 'very likely'; this adverbial use is a Virgilian innovation, perhaps an archaism (so Norden): see on 2. 139, Nisbet–Hubbard on Hor. *C.* 1. 28. 31.

traherent : the protasis is expressed paratactically in *sed comes admonuit* (contrast 292 ff. 'ni docta comes . . . / admoneat . . . inruat').

539. nox ruit : 'night is coming up fast': an exaggeration, but the Sibyl wants to get on. Cf. 2. 250 'uertitur interea caelum et ruit Oceano nox' (see note), 8. 369 'nox ruit et fuscis tellurem amplectitur alis'. The Sibyl cuts their conversation short (cf. 373, note).

540. partis . . . in ambas : 'where the path splits into the two ways'; *ambas* suggests that the division was expected, or had been already mentioned. Virgil uses Orphic–Pythagorean tradition; cf. Plato, *Grg.* 524A, where Zeus explains that Minos, Rhadamanthus, and Aeacus shall judge the dead ἐν τῷ λειμῶνι, ἐν τῇ τριόδῳ ἐξ ἧς φέρετον τὼ ὁδώ, ἡ μὲν εἰς μακάρων νήσους, ἡ δ' εἰς Τάρταρον: cf. Dieterich, *Nekyia*, 192; Cumont, *Lux Perpetua*, 278 ff.

542. Elysium : for the simple accusative after *iter* ⟨*est*⟩ cf. 3. 507 'unde iter Italiam', and see on 345.

543. exercet poenas : 'keeps punishments busy' (contrast 739 'exercentur poenis'); the variation of construction from the ablative (*hac*) to a nominative is characteristic. The road is vividly personified; the punishment of the wicked starts while they are still on their way to Tartarus. For the phrase cf. Stat. *Th.* 3. 4 f. 'inuigilant animo scelerisque parati / supplicium exercent curae'; Tac. *Ann.* 1. 44 'iudicium et poenas de singulis in hunc modum exercuit'. Virgil likes using *exercere* in various ways: cf. 4. 623 'exercete odiis', *G.* 3. 152 'exercuit iras', and the strange 'pacem . . . pactosque hymenaeos / exercemus' (4. 99 f., where see note). For a valuable examination of some aspects of the verb see Shackleton Bailey, *Propertiana*, 7 f.

impia Tartara : the place shares in the evil of its inhabitants.

544. ne saeui : for the construction see on 74. The ghost pathetically takes the blame on himself, as if it was he whom the Sibyl had rebuked.

545. explebo numerum : 'I will complete the count', explained in *reddarque tenebris*: he will return to his place among the ghosts, the group of the *bello clari* (478), 'quem abeundo minuerat' (Ti. Donatus). Both Servius and Macrobius

(*Somn.* 1. 13. 11) invent strange interpretations for *explebo numerum*; but for the idea of a tally being kept of the dead cf. Stat. *Th.* 4. 528 f. 'in speculis Mors atra sedet dominisque silentis / adnumerat populos', Sen. *Phaedr.* 1153 'constat inferno numerus tyranno'. Lucian guys the notion, *Katapl.* 4 (Hermes speaking) ἐμοῦ τοὺς νεκρούς, ὡς ἔθος, ἀπαριθμοῦντος τῷ Αἰακῷ κἀκείνου λογιζομένου αὐτοὺς . . . λαθὼν οὐκ οἶδ' ὅπως ὁ τρισκατάρατος ἀπιὼν ᾤχετο. ἐνέδει οὖν νεκρὸς εἰς τῷ λογισμῷ.

546. The high-sounding address to Aeneas rounds off the encounter that had begun with Aeneas' own ceremonious address to Deiphobus (500); it adds further pathos to Deiphobus' miserable condition.

    melioribus . . . fatis : 'Aeneae felicia optauit et prospera, sed magna breuitate sermonis, ne loquendo plurimis moras necteret, quas reprehenderat Sibylla' (Ti. Donatus). Presumably Deiphobus means 'a better destiny than mine', rather an odd encouragement in the circumstances.

547. **tantum effatus, et . . . torsit :** words and action are simultaneous: cf. 10. 877 'tantum effatus et infesta subit obuius hasta'; so 2. 376 f. 'dixit, et extemplo . . . / . . . sensit . . . delapsus in hostis', 2. 692 f. 'uix ea fatus erat senior, subitoque fragore / intonuit laeuum'.

    in uerbo . . . torsit : 'turned on his heel as he spoke'; cf. 4. 76 'incipit effari mediaque in uoce resistit'; 3. 669 'sensit, et ad sonitum uocis uestigia torsit'.

548–61. *Aeneas sees a great walled bastion on his left, surrounded by a flaming river: from it come ghastly sounds of torment. He asks the Sibyl the meaning of it.*

    This powerful ἔκφρασις is the setting for the account of Tartarus that follows, told by the Sibyl from what she had herself seen: Aeneas himself does not enter this region. It reads almost as if it was based on a painting: however, the battlemented and walled castle, the river, the grisly Fury guarding the gate, are of universal imagination. The scene is illustrated in Vat. lat. 3225: see de Wit, op. cit. fig. 35, with his discussion of the detail (112), some of which he thinks shows affinity with Pompeian wall-painting.

548. **respicit :** they had presumably already moved a little way from the parting of the roads, on the right-hand path to Elysium.

549. **moenia :** the buildings that form a city; cf. 2. 234 'diuidimus muros et moenia pandimus urbis'. For *triplici muro* cf. Hesiod, *Th.* 726 f. (of Tartarus, the prison of the Titans) τὸν πέρι χάλκεον ἕρκος ἐλήλαται· ἀμφὶ δέ μιν νὺξ / τριστοιχὶ κέχυται περὶ δειρήν.

550. The river of fire is Homer's Πυριφλεγέθων (*Od.* 10. 513): see Plato, *Phaedo* 113A τρίτος δὲ ποταμὸς ... ἐκπίπτει εἰς τόπον μέγαν πυρὶ πολλῷ καόμενον, καὶ λίμνην ποιεῖ ... ζέουσαν ὕδατος καὶ πηλοῦ· ... περιελιχθεὶς δὲ πολλάκις ὑπὸ γῆς ἐμβάλλει κατωτέρω τοῦ Ταρτάρου· οὗτος δ' ἐστὶν ὃν ἐπονομάζουσιν Πυριφλεγέθοντα.

551. torquetque ... saxa : an extension of *ambit*, with a slight switch of construction; cf. *G.* 2. 207 f. 'unde iratus siluam deuexit arator / et nemora euertit', where *unde* is disregarded in the extension just as *quae* is here. For the phrase cf. Pindar, *P.* 1. 23 f. (of Etna) πέτρας / φοίνισσα κυλινδομένα φλὸξ ἐς βαθεῖαν φέρει πόντου πλάκα σὺν πατάγῳ.

552. porta aduersa ingens : see on 283. The spondees suggest the heaviness and grimness of the gate (contrast the dactyls of 551).

adamante : so Ovid, *Met.* 4. 453 'carceris ante fores clausas adamante sedebant' (of the Furies in Tartarus), Prop. 4. 11. 3 f. 'cum semel infernas intrarunt funere leges, / non exorato stant adamante uiae'.

Adamas was originally a legendary metal of extreme hardness; it is first mentioned in Hesiod (*Th.* 161), and West (ad loc.) thinks it was perhaps a pre-Iron Age word for iron. Later it became used for the diamond: Pliny notes (*NH* 37. 57) 'duritia est inenarrabilis, simulque ignium uictrix natura et nunquam incalescens, unde et nomen—interpretatione Graeca indomita uis—accepit'. Augustus once termed Maecenas *adamas Supernas* (Macrob. *Sat.* 2. 4. 12).

553. exscindere : not recorded in poetry before Virgil.

554. ferrea turris : Norden compares Pindar, *O.* 2. 70, where the souls of the righteous ἔτειλαν Διὸς ὁδὸν παρὰ Κρόνου τύρσιν, in the Isles of the Blest.

ad auras : as if a verb of rising had preceded. Servius records an absurdity of Pollio's, that the *aurae* were 'Aeneae et Sibyllae, quas illi secum traxerant' (surely a joke?).

555. Tisiphone : a different tradition from that in 280. The reason for her *palla cruenta* is apparent from 570 f.; she is *succincta* like a huntress, for greater nimbleness in action; cf. Hor. *Sat.* 1. 8. 23 f. 'uidi egomet nigra succinctam uadere palla / Canidiam'.

556. exsomnis : a Virgilian innovation, which he does not use again; cf. Hor. *C.* 3. 25. 9, Silius 9. 5, its only other occurrences in poetry.

noctesque diesque : so Ennius, *Ann.* 334 'sollicitari te Tite sic noctesque diesque'; contrast 127, 5. 766 'complexi inter se noctemque diemque morantur', 9. 488 f. 'ueste tegens tibi quam noctes festina diesque / urgebam'. For the correlating *-que ... -que* see on 64.

557. hinc exaudiri : again, 4. 460, 7. 15, in gruesome contexts. The notable sound-effects of this and the next line make an impressive finale to the rich ἔκφρασις (which is picked up by *hinc*, in the usual manner).

    gemitus : cf. Dante, *Inf.* 3. 22 ff. 'quivi sospiri, pianti e alti guai / risonavan per l'aere senza stelle, / . . . diverse lingue, orribili favelle, / parole di dolore, accenti d'ira', etc.

558. stridor . . . catenae : 'clanging of iron and clanking of chains'; cf. Pliny's ghost-story, *Epp.* 7. 27. 5 'per silentium noctis sonus ferri, et si attenderes acrius, strepitus uinculorum'. For like traditional terrors see Norden, p. 275.

559. strepitumque . . . hausit : there is good manuscript support for *strepitu . . . haesit*, which Norden prefers (cf. 3. 597 'aspectu conterritus haesit', 11. 699 'subitoque aspectu territus haesit'): a good illustration of the dilemmas that sometimes face an editor of Virgil's text. It does not seem conclusive that *hausit* would need an ablative to complete its sense (so *animo*, 10. 648, 12. 26; *auribus*, 4. 359; *oculis*, 4. 661, 12. 945): cf. 10. 898 f. 'ut auras / suspiciens hausit caelum', *G.* 2. 340 'cum primae lucem pecudes hausere', Sen. *Ag.* 31 'non pauidus hausi dicta', Val. Flacc. 1. 262 f. 'stupet in ducibus magnumque sonantes / haurit'.

560. The staccato questions, and the use of *o*, mark Aeneas' agitation, and the effect is continued by the unusual sense-break in the fifth foot and by the emphasis put on *quibusue* at the end (a rare type of end-word; see Norden, Anh. iii B. 2).

561. plangor ad auras : *plangor* picks up *gemitus* (557), just as the preceding *quibus poenis* picks up *uerbera*, etc. (558), a chiastic arrangement (Norden). The variant *clangor* (P, Servius) *ad auris* (P) was preferred by Ribbeck; but *clangor* could refer only to *stridor ferri*, etc. (558), and the arrangement becomes less artistic, while the change from *auras* to *auris* was probably due to the idea that the former was inappropriate to the Underworld (see on 554). The repetition of *ad auras* so near 554 is no objection (see on 2. 505, with references).

562–627. *The Sibyl tells Aeneas of the sinners in Tartarus, their sins and their punishments: she has been shown it all by Hecate herself.*

    After a general picture of Tartarus, with its ruler Rhadamanthus in judgment over the wicked (some of which is explanatory of 552 ff.), the Sibyl lists various sinners, most by name, some in categories of wrongdoers (608 ff., 621 ff.);

for such categories see on 663. Some of this goes back to Homer (*Od.* 11. 576 ff.); for the conception of Tartarus as a place of punishment cf. Plato, *Rp.* 616A, *Phaedo* 113E, *Grg.* 523B. Norden (p. 276) suggests that Virgil made use also of a *katabasis* of Orpheus.

The whole passage develops and intensifies the visual impact of 548 ff., as the Sibyl's narrative gradually creates the illusion that these horrors are present to the reader's eye. Virgil has carefully avoided giving the impression of a mere catalogue, partly by varying his introductions of the persons named, partly by the way in which he passes from sinner to sin and from individuals to categories. He sometimes diverges from tradition in his assignment of particular punishments, and there are some matters of order that have made some scholars suspect lack of revision: but it is not likely that such revision (if it is really needed) would have been extensive.

562. dux inclute Teucrum : a ceremonious address (cf. 125); for *inclutus* see on 479.

563. nulli fas casto : the slow measured rhythm continues in the opening of the next line.

sceleratum . . . limen : cf. 543 'impia Tartara'; the place itself is criminal. Virgil may reflect a traditional phrase; cf. Tib. 1. 3. 67 f. 'scelerata iacet sedes in nocte profunda / abdita, quam circum flumina nigra sonant' (perhaps written soon after Actium; see K. F. Smith on the poem); Ovid, *Met.* 4. 456 'Sedes Scelerata uocatur' (of the home of the Furies in Tartarus).

564. The Sibyl, *casta* though she was, had Hecate's authority and protection in being allowed to enter Tartarus, to learn all that she should know for her solemn charge (cf. 118). It is an ingenious solution of two problems, the source of the Sibyl's knowledge and its transmission to Aeneas.

566. Rhadamanthus : brother of Minos. Plato (*Grg.* 524A) represents him as judge of the dead from Asia, with Aeacus judging those from Europe, while Minos is present to make a decision ἐὰν ἀπορῆτόν τι τὼ ἑτέρω. See Lucian, *Katapl.* 23 ff., for a lively judgment-scene.

durissima : perhaps with a side-glance at the adamant of 552.

567. The summary nature of Rhadamanthus' court is emphasized by the arrangement of the line, with the repeated *-que* linking the actions so closely that they seem virtually simultaneous. The meaning of *castigat* is disputed. It could mean 'punishes' (Norden's point has little force, that it is Tisiphone who carried out the actual punishment): then the sentence becomes an elaborate example of so-called ὕστερον πρότερον, with the most significant action brought forward for emphasis and terror (cf. A. S. McDevitt, *CQ* n.s. xvii [1967], 316 ff.). But there is no need for this. It is more natural to take *castigat* as 'reproves' (see A. Platt, *CR* v [1891], 337): the judge first reads them a lecture, then hears what they have done, then forces confession of the allegations. This interpretation gains support from Stat. *Th.* 4. 530 ff. 'arbiter hos dura uersat Gortynius urna / uera minis poscens adigitque expromere uitas / usque retro et tandem poenarum lucra fateri' (where *uera minis poscens* = *castigat* here).

subigitque fateri : cf. Plaut. *Truc.* 783 'uis subigit uerum fateri, ita lora laedunt bracchia'.

568. apud superos : 'in the world above'; cf. 481, note.

furto . . . inani : 'gloating over a hollow piece of trickery'; *inane*, because their crimes had not escaped notice.

569. Rhadamanthus forces confession of 'sins committed and left without expiation until death has made it too late'.

This interpretation of a notoriously difficult line (passed over in silence by Norden) is due to W. B. Anderson, *CR* xlv (1931), 13. He notes that *piaculum* in the sense of 'a sin that needs expiation' appears in Livy 5. 52. 12 'nonne in mentem uenit quantum piaculi committatur?' (of the proposal to move the capital from Rome to Veii), Livy 29. 18. 9 'ne quod piaculi commiserunt non suo solum sanguine sed etiam publica clade luant' (a warning to the Roman senate to make atonement to the Locrians for a temple-robbery committed by Roman soldiers): so Gellius 19. 13. 5 (a mock apology by a *grammaticus* for venturing to speak in learned company) 'si piaculum . . . non committitur praesente Apollinare quid de uoce ulla Graeca Latinaue sentiam dicere'. For *distulit* in the sense of 'putting off attention' to something, Anderson notes Ovid, *Rem. Am.* 101 f. 'uidi ego, quod fuerat primo sanabile, uulnus / dilatum longae damna tulisse morae', with Tac. *H.* 1. 47 'omisisset offensas an distulisset breuitate imperii in incerto fuit' (of Otho).

For other views see A. I. Wagner and T. J. Haarhoff, *CR* xliv (1930), 170 f., W. F. Witton, ibid. 171 ff.; cf. E. W. Cornwall, *CR* xxvii (1913), 229 f. The line well illustrates Virgil's power to use linguistic economy for a complex and memorable phrase, which probably caused some of his contemporary critics to raise their eyebrows.

570. continuo : cf. 426; not a moment is lost before punishment begins.

ultrix : perhaps with a word-play on the name (Servius on 4. 609 '*ultrix* uero, hoc est Tisiphone; nam Graece τίσις

ultio dicitur'). For other examples see on 1. 298, with refer-
ences; and Norden here.

   accincta : 'armed'; cf. 4. 493 'magicas inuitam accingier
artis'. Servius suggests, as an alternative to this meaning,
'hoc dicit quod uidemus, quia qui longo flagello utitur ut id
post ictum in se reuoluat necesse est'!

571. quatit insultans : 'makes them writhe as she leaps upon
them': cf. 12. 337 ff. 'talis equos alacer media inter proelia
Turnus / fumantis sudore quatit, miserabile caesis / hostibus
insultans'. There is noteworthy alliteration of -*t*- and -*s*- in
these lines, with *insultans* picked up in *intentans* below.

572. agmina . . . sororum : her Sister Furies: cf. 4. 469
'Eumenidum ueluti demens uidet agmina Pentheus'; Val.
Flacc. 2. 227 f. 'tantum oculos pressere manu, uelut agmina
cernant / Eumenidum'; Sen. *Thy.* 250 'dira Furiarum cohors',
Med. 958 ff. 'quonam ista tendit turba Furiarum impotens? /
. . . aut cui cruentas agmen infernum faces / intentat?' For
a discussion of *agmina* in such a context see J. H. Waszink,
Harvard Theological Review lvi (1963), 7 ff.

573. The judgment and the scourging have taken place at the
gate guarded by Tisiphone (552 ff.) : not till then (*tum demum*)
is the gate opened to receive the damned into their pit of
punishment.

   horrisono : again, 9. 55; Lucr. 5. 109 'horrisono . . .
fragore', Cic. *Arat.* 13 'horrisonis . . . alis' (quoted in *de nat.
deor.* 2. 111 with *horriferis* substituted, an interesting change):
for analogous compounds cf. *altisonus* (Ennius, *Sc.* 93), *clari-
sonus* (Cic. *Arat.* 280, Cat. 64. 125, 320) *fluentisonus* (Cat.
64. 52), *raucisonus* (Lucr. 5. 1084, Cat. 64. 263). Cf. note on
auricomos, 141.

   cardine : not our 'hinge', but the combined socket and pin
at top and bottom of the *postes*, attaching them to the archi-
trave and sill of the door (see Page on 2. 493): there is a use-
ful illustration in Smith's *Dictionary of Antiquities*.

   sacrae : cf. 109 'sacra ostia'; the *portae* are sacred to the
chthonic powers ('exsecrabiles', Servius).

574. custodia : here of a single 'watch', Tisiphone (cf. 556); the
line has a fine clattering alliteration. For *custodia* so used cf.
Tib. 1. 2. 5 'posita est nostrae custodia saeua puellae', Ovid,
Met. 8. 684 'unicus anser erat, minimae custodia uillae' (of
the goose that Baucis and Philemon wanted to kill for their
exalted visitors).

   The sentence is traditionally made a question, as in OCT
(some insert a question-mark after *sedeat* also). But Aeneas
has seen Tisiphone on guard, so that a question here is un-
necessary: the point is a distinction between what he has

seen and what he cannot see, i.e. the Hydra on the other side
of the gate; 575 and 576 f. are in adversative asyndeton. This
is Norden's punctuation; it goes back at least to Brunck's
text (Strasbourg, 1789): cf. 9. 188 (but there what follows
is not an antithesis).

576. A magnificently onomatopoeic line (cf. 237): the Hydra
with its fifty inky yawning jaws is clearly not the *belua
Lernae* (287) but a relative.

577. Tartarus ipse : a fathomless oubliette, just on the inner
side of the gate. For its depth cf. *Il.* 8. 16 τόσσον ἔνερθ᾽ Ἀΐδεω
ὅσον οὐρανός ἐστ᾽ ἀπὸ γαίης; Hesiod, *Th.* 720 (of the Titans'
prison) τόσσον ἔνερθ᾽ ὑπὸ γῆς ὅσον οὐρανός ἐστ᾽ ἀπὸ γαίης; Apollod.
Bibl. 1. 1. 3 τόπος . . . ἐρεβώδης ἐστὶν ἐν Ἅιδου, τοσοῦτον ἀπὸ γῆς ἔχων
διάστημα ὅσον ἀπ᾽ οὐρανοῦ γῆ. Possibly, as Conington suggests
(following Cerda), Virgil had in his memory Lucr. 4. 414 ff.
(of a puddle) 'collectus aquae digitum non altior unum / . . .
despectum praebet sub terras impete tanto / a terris quantum
caeli patet altus hiatus'.

579. caeli suspectus : 'the view upward to the sky from be-
neath': *caeli* (objective genitive) is amplified in *ad aetherium
Olympum*, just as in 578 *in praeceps* is extended by *sub
umbras*. The Sibyl means the view heavenward of one who
is in the upper world. Norden notes that *suspectus* is not
recorded before Virgil.

580. The list of sinners now begins, each varyingly introduced:
uoluuntur (581), *Aloidas . . . uidi* (582), *uidi . . . Salmonea*
(585), *Tityon . . . cernere erat* (595 f.), *quid memorem Lapi-
thas?* (601). For a study of the passage see L. Radermacher,
Rh. Mus. n.f. lxiii (1908), 534 ff.

    genus antiquum: the Titans, sons of Sky and Earth, the 'old
gods' (Hesiod, *Th.* 424, 486; see West on *Th.* 133, 617 ff.); Zeus
defeated them in their war against him, and they were flung
into Tartarus (cf. *Il.* 14. 279 τοὺς ὑποταρταρίους, οἳ Τιτῆνες καλέονται).
For the 'Orphic' myth of their punishment for dismembering
Dionysus see W. K. C. Guthrie, *Orpheus and Greek Religion*
(London, 1935), 107 ff.; I. M. Linforth, *The Arts of Orpheus*,
324 ff.; E. R. Dodds, *The Greeks and the Irrational*, 155 f.
With *Titania pubes* ('the Titan folk'; for *pubes* see on 2. 798)
cf. 5. 450 'Trinacria pubes', 7. 105 'Laomedontia pubes',
7. 219 'Dardana pubes', etc.

581. fulmine deiecti : cf. Varro Atacinus, fr. 10 Morel 'tum te
flagranti deiectum fulmine, Phaethon'.

582. Aloidas : Otus and Ephialtes, sons of Aloeus (*Il.* 5. 386) or
of Poseidon by Aloeus' wife (*Od.* 11. 306 ff.); when aged nine
they were nine cubits broad and nine fathoms tall (*Od.* l.c.,
Apollod. *Bibl.* 1. 7. 4). For the apposition *immania corpora*

cf. 10. 430 'o Grais imperdita corpora, Teucri'; but here the arrangement is more striking, with the adjective and noun separated by *uidi* and in different lines, so that *corpora* is highly emphatic.

583. rescindere caelum : so *G.* 1. 280 'coniuratos caelum rescindere fratres', *Od.* 11. 315 f.

584. adgressi : finite (see on 125).

585. Salmonea : his sin is first summarized (586) and then both sin and punishment are described in detail, adding vividness and variety to the list. See Frazer on Apollod. *Bibl.* 1. 9. 7, where some kind of weather-magic is suggested for the myth; for Sophocles' satyric play *Salmoneus* see Pearson, *Fragments* ii, 177 ff.; for some papyrus fragments from the *Eoiae* of Hesiod, where the subject was treated, see Merkelbach–West, *Fragmenta Hesiodea*, fr. 30.

585 f. The connexion in *dantem poenas dum . . . imitatur* is a problem. It is really not credible that Virgil means to represent Salmoneus as mechanically continuing his impious mimicry in Tartarus, as a punishment: Butler, supporting this idea, notes *AP* 16. 30, an epigram (first century A.D.) on a painting by Polygnotus showing Salmoneus in Hades, assaulted by the thunderbolts of Zeus; but the scene probably represents his actual killing (see Gow–Page, *Garland of Philip* ii, p. 297). Norden, convincingly rejecting both this explanation and Ribbeck's deletion of 586 as a dittograph of 590 ff., takes *dum* as causal (Cerda's view; so *Thes. L.L.* s.v., 2211. 14): but this is only possible because of the temporal connexion, which cannot be evaded (cf. HSz, 614).

Some editors punctuate with a full stop after *poenas* and a comma after *Olympi*, linking the *dum*-clause to what follows (so Sabbadini): this leaves 585 as an abruptly isolated statement, with *dum* as a flat opening to the following description: such a punctuation virtually necessitates an arbitrary transposition of 586-7 (so Goelzer, following Havet and Cartault).

It is simpler and preferable, though still not easy, to assume a Virgilian compression of thought, with *quas dedit* (or *quas meruit*, Wagner) to be understood before *dum*: the Sibyl saw Salmoneus paying the penalty which came upon him in the very moment of his impiety. Virgil did not mind making demands on his readers.

587. quattuor . . . equis : similarly Manil. 5. 91 ff. 'qui caelum imitatus in orbe, / pontibus inpositis missisque per aera quadrigis / expressisse sonum mundi sibi uisus et ipsum / admouisse Iouem terris, dum fulmina fingit / sensit, et inmissos ignes super ipse secutus / morte Iouem didicit': a passage with Virgil clearly in mind.

588. Graium : cf. *Pelasgum*, 503, and see on 92. The added clause pinpoints the city that Salmoneus founded, Salmone or Salmonia in Pisatis, 'the heart of Elis' (Apollod. *Bibl.* 1. 9. 7, Diodorus 4. 68, Strabo 356). Servius comments 'hinc est indignatio, quod in ea ciuitate Iouem imitabatur in qua specialiter Iuppiter colitur' (an allusion to Olympia in Elis, the chief sanctuary of Zeus).

589. ouans : as if he had won a victory. The word might suggest a further enormity to a Roman, for a general who celebrated an *ouatio* did not ride in a chariot, but entered his city on foot.

590. demens : like Misenus (172); but Salmoneus' impiety was very different from the casual moment of euphoria that made Misenus challenge Triton. 'Nimbos . . . fulmen' reverses the order of 586; for *nimbi* of thunderclouds cf. 2. 113 'toto sonuerunt aethere nimbi'.

591. aere : a brazen bridge (Manilius: see on 587); or brazen vessels (Apollod. *Bibl.* 1. 9. 7 βύρσας μὲν ἐξηραμμένας ἐξ ἄρματος μετὰ λεβήτων χαλκῶν σύρων ἔλεγε βροντᾶν, βάλλων δὲ εἰς οὐρανὸν αἰθομένας λαμπάδας ἔλεγεν ἀστράπτειν; or was the chariot itself of bronze?

    cornipedum . . . equorum : 'with the tramping of horn-hoofed horses'; *cornipes* is not recorded before Virgil (again, 7. 779; cf. *aeripes*, 802); Silver poets, especially Silius, use it as a noun (see Rittweger, *ALL* vii, 328 f.). The subjunctive *simularet* is causal, explaining *demens*.

592. Cf. Lucr. 5. 399 ff. 'at pater omnipotens ira tum percitus acri / magnanimum Phaethonta repenti fulminis ictu / deturbauit equis in terram'. For *omnipotens* (Ennius, *Ann.* 458, *Sc.* 177) see Fraenkel, *Plautinisches im Plautus*, 207 ff., and on Aesch. *Ag.* 1648.

593. contorsit : a forceful compound; cf. 2. 51 f. (Laocoon with his spear) 'in latus inque feri curuam compagibus aluum / contorsit' (with a dramatic pause to follow).

    non ille : a pleonastic use of *ille*, like ὅ γε, picking up the subject and marking a new aspect of it (see on 1. 3): so 5. 334 'non tamen Euryali, non ille oblitus amorum', 9. 478 ff. 'agmina cursu / prima petit, non illa uirum, non illa pericli / telorumque memor'.

    fumea : first recorded here (Virgil does not use it again); in classical Latin it recurs only in Val. Flacc. 4. 596 (of Acheron): contrast 7. 76 'fumida lumine fuluo', 9. 75 f. 'piceum fert fumida lumen / taeda'. Servius comments 'id est terrena; nam aetherius ignis caret fumo, solo enim splendore uiget'.

594. praecipitemque . . . adegit : 'and pitched him spinning down with savage blast'; *praecipitem* suggests that Salmoneus was flung straight into Tartarus. For *turbo* of the

wind-force cf. 1. 45 'turbine corripuit scopuloque infixit
acuto' (of Ajax, struck by a thunder-bolt by Pallas).

595. nec non et : a connecting formula, found first in Virgil and
not used in prose until the Silver period. But *nec non etiam*
(*G.* 2. 413) occurs in Varro (*RR* 1. 1. 6, etc.), so that the
type did not originally belong to elevated style: see HSz, 524;
Kübler, *ALL* viii, 181; Lease, *ALL* x, 390; Löfstedt, *Per.
Aeth.* 95 ff.

Tityon : a giant who assaulted Leto; his punishment re-
sembles the traditional torment of Prometheus (see West on
Hesiod, *Th.* 523–33): for collected references see Frazer on
Apollod. *Bibl.* 1. 4. 1. Virgil's description of his sufferings
reflects *Od.* 11. 576 ff. καὶ Τιτυὸν εἶδον, Γαίης ἐρικυδέος υἱόν, /
κείμενον ἐν δαπέδῳ· ὁ δ' ἐπ' ἐννέα κεῖτο πέλεθρα, / γῦπε δέ μιν ἑκάτερθε
παρημένω ἧπαρ ἔκειρον, / δέρτρον ἔσω δύνοντες· ὁ δ' οὐκ ἀπαμύνετο χερσί.
The difference in standpoint between him and Lucretius is
strikingly shown in Lucr. 3. 984 ff., where the legend is part
of the indictment of the reality of Hell and its punishments:

> nec Tityon uolucres ineunt Acherunte iacentem
> nec quod sub magno scrutentur pectore quicquam
> perpetuam aetatem possunt reperire profecto:
> quamlibet immani proiectu corporis exstet,
> qui non sola nouem dispessis iugera membris
> obtineat, sed qui terrai totius orbem,
> non tamen aeternum poterit perferre dolorem
> nec praebere cibum proprio de corpore semper.
> sed Tityos nobis hic est, in amore iacentem
> quem uolucres lacerant atque exest anxius angor
> aut alia quauis scindunt cuppedine curae.

Terrae . . . alumnum : in Apollod. *Bibl.* l.c. Tityos was born
of an amour of Zeus with a girl Elare; Zeus hid her under
the earth, and there she bore her monstrous son: cf. Apoll.
Rhod. 1. 761 f. Τιτυὸν μέγαν, ὅν ῥ' ἔτεκέν γε / δῖ' Ἐλάρη, θρέψεν
δὲ καὶ ἂψ ἐλοχεύσατο Γαῖα.

omniparentis : so of the Earth, Lucr. 2. 706, 5. 259; cf.
Hom. h. 30. 1 Γαῖαν παμμήτειραν ἀείσομαι.

alumnum : either 'son' or 'foster-son', according to which
version of the legend Virgil followed ('elegit sermonem quo
utrumque significaret', Servius); but probably 'son', as in
Od. l.c.

596. cernere erat : like ἦν ἰδεῖν; so 8. 676 ('Graeca figura',
Servius), Stat. *S.* 3. 1. 15; cf. Silius 6. 10 f. 'nec cernere
deerat / frustra seminecum quaerentia lumina caelum';
similarly with *uidere*, Hor. *Sat.* 1. 2. 101, Tac. *Germ.* 5, etc.:
see HSz, 349; Wölfflin, *ALL* ii, 135 f.

tota nouem . . . iugera : cf. Ter. *Ad.* 396 'sex totis mensibus', Ovid, *Tr.* 5. 2. 13 'paene decem totis aluit Poeantius annis'. For the 'iugera' (not really 'acres', cf. Kenney on Lucr. 3. 988) cf. *Od.* l.c., Lucr. l.c., Tib. 1. 3. 75 'porrectusque nouem Tityos per iugera terrae', Prop. 3. 5. 44 'Tityo iugera pauca nouem', Ovid, *Met.* 4. 457 f. 'uiscera praebebat Tityos lanianda nouemque / iugeribus distractus erat'.

Pausanias reports (10. 4. 4) a tomb of Tityos at Panopeus in Phocis (significantly, together with a statue said to be that of Prometheus): the locals, he adds, say that Homer's line has no reference to Tityos' size, ἀλλ' ἔνθα ὁ Τιτυὸς ἐτέθη, πλέθρα ἐννέα εἶναι τῷ χωρίῳ.

597. uultur : contrast Homer's *two* vultures; perhaps the Tityos-legend and the Prometheus-legend are contaminated (cf. K. F. Smith on Tib. 1. 3. 76). The series of paratactic clauses here, with a four-fold *-que*, gives a rather breathless effect, perhaps meant to suggest the never-resting character of Tityos' punishment (cf. 600).

obunco : curving inwards. The compound is rare, and not found before Virgil: again, 11. 755 (of an eagle's *rostrum*); Ovid, *Met.* 6. 516 (of an eagle's talons); see A. Müller, *ALL* iii, 246.

598. immortale iecur : so of Prometheus, Hesiod, *Th.* 523 f. αὐτὰρ ὅ γ' ἧπαρ / ἤσθιεν ἀθάνατον; cf. Hor. *C.* 3. 4. 77 ff. 'incontinentis nec Tityi iecur / reliquit ales, nequitiae additus / custos': for the liver as the seat of lust see West on Hesiod, *Th.* 523–33; the rapist is fitly punished. The monstrous hook-beaked vulture slices away the liver that never dies; with *tondens* cf. Homer's ἔκειρον (*Od.* l.c.).

poenis : dative ('in poenam', Servius): the *uiscera* are 'fertile for punishing', as they never cease to yield a good harvest for the vulture; cf. Manil. 4. 666 f. 'saeuosque leones / in poenas fecunda suas parit horrida tellus'.

599. rimaturque epulis : correlative with *habitatque*; the vulture rummages for a rich meal (*epulis*, dative of purpose), and is 'resident' deep down in Tityos' breast. For the expressive *rimatur* cf. *G.* 1. 383 f. 'quae Asia circum / dulcibus in stagnis rimantur prata Caystri' (of cranes, geese, etc.); for *habitat* cf. Manil. 4. 664 'horrendos angues habitataque membra ueneno'; for the force of *sub* see on 273. Maecenas borrowed from Virgil Sen. *epp.* 114. 5 (examples of his curious style) 'inremediabilis factio rimantur epulis lagonaque temptant domos et spe mortem exigunt'.

600. nec . . . renatis : the filaments of the liver grow again to give the vulture a constant meal. In Polygnotus' painting in the Lesche at Delphi (Pausanias 10. 29. 3) Tityos was

shown as a mere wraith, ὑπὸ τοῦ συνεχοῦς τῆς τιμωρίας ἐς ἅπαν
ἐξαναλωμένος, ἀμυδρὸν καὶ οὐδὲ ὁλόκληρον εἴδωλον.

601. quid memorem : a rhetorical transition-formula ('praeter-
itio'); so 123, 8. 483; *G.* 2. 158, 161 'an memorem?'

Ixion attempted to violate Hera, but Zeus tricked him by
substituting a cloud, from which Centaurus was born, the
progenitor of the Centaurs (Pindar, *P.* 2. 21 ff., Apollod.
Epit. 1. 20). Pirithous was son of Ixion's wife by Zeus (*Il.* 14.
317 f.), sometimes termed Ixion's own son (Ovid, *Met.* 12.
210, Apollod. *Bibl.* 1. 8. 2). He became king of the Lapiths
in Thessaly, and invited his relatives the Centaurs to his
marriage-feast; their hooligan behaviour caused the great
Lapith–Centaur battle, described with relish by Ovid (*Met.*
12. 210–535) and depicted on the temple of Zeus at Olympia
and on the Parthenon metopes (cf. Nisbet–Hubbard on Hor.
C. 1. 18. 8), also on the François vase.

Both are classic inhabitants of the ancient Underworld:
Pirithous was imprisoned for his attempt (with Theseus) to
seize Proserpina (cf. 393, 397), Ixion whirled for ever on
a wheel (set, however, in the upper air by Pindar, l.c., and
others; see K. F. Smith on Tib. 1. 3. 73–4, and cf. Housman,
CR xlii [1928], 9, = *Classical Papers*, 1147).

Unexpectedly, however, Virgil proceeds to describe two
torments traditionally associated neither with Ixion nor
with Pirithous, but with Tantalus—the overhanging rock
and the feast that he may never taste (see K. F. Smith on
Tib. 1. 3. 77 f., a useful collection of references; Kenney on
Lucr. 3. 980–3). Many attempts, therefore, have been made
to 'heal' the text, all arbitrary and unconvincing. Ribbeck
deleted 601, assuming a lacuna in which Tantalus was
named, and reading *quo* (so R) in 602 (so Nettleship, but
retaining 601). Madvig (*Adu. crit.* ii, 38) proposed the oddity
Pirithoumque et (601), with *quo* to follow (Mackail accepts
this, incredibly). Others resort to transposition: thus Havet
(*RPh.* xii [1888], 145) transposed 616–20 to follow 601, with
quo in 602, and referring 602–7 to Phlegyas (so Goelzer);
on this and similar games see Jahn–Ladewig–Schaper–
Deuticke (Berlin, 1912), p. 337, and cf. Geymonat's app. crit.
In fact there is no positive evidence of any text-dislocation:
and *quos* (602) has the consensus of the capital manuscripts
apart from R, and is attested by Servius (on 616), Ti. Dona-
tus, Macrob. *Sat.* 4. 4. 15, and ps.-Probus on *G.* 3. 37.

The necessary inference is that Virgil has chosen to be
original, regarding this Underworld Rogues' Gallery as pro-
viding a common stock of punishments, without a parti-
cular torment being the exclusive copyright of one particular

villain. It is relevant that in Stat. *Th.* 1. 712 ff. the torture of
the feast is assigned to Phlegyas, and in Val. Flacc. 2. 193 ff.
to Phlegyas and Theseus, not to Tantalus. Havet took these
passages as decisive support for his theory of transposition,
but they clearly point to a non-rigid application of traditions
as being within the rules. An alternative is to assume a new
question at 602, punctuating accordingly, with an ellipse of
the 'praeteritio' formula, *quos* being a generalized plural like
alii in 616: this is Jahn's view, and it may be right, but it is
less simple.

602. **iam iam lapsura** : 'just on the point of slipping'; cf. 12.
754 f. 'haeret hians, iam iamque tenet, similisque tenenti /
increpuit malis' (the hound hunting a stag), Ovid, *Met.* 1.
535 f. 'alter inhaesuro similis iam iamque tenere / sperat'
(a similar context), Tib. 1. 3. 78 'iam iam poturi deserit unda
sitim' (of Tantalus). For this emotional repetition of *iam*
see *Thes. L.L.* s.v., 119. 16 ff.; Wölfflin, *Ausg. Schriften*, 314.

   The line is hypermetric, with *cadentique* in elision with the
vowel beginning the next line; *cadenti adsimilis* is even more
dramatic than *iam iam lapsura*, the rock now being 'just
as if it is actually falling', and the hypermetre is clearly
pictorial.

   There are no hypermetric lines in Homer. The archaic ac-
cusative Ζῆν ends a line at *Il.* 8. 206, 14. 265, 24. 331, and in
Hesiod, *Th.* 884 (see West ad loc.); in all these passages the
following line begins with a vowel, which might suggest that
the archaic form was taken to be an elided form of Ζῆνα. In
Callim. *ep.* 41. 1 Pf. elision occurs between hexameter and
pentameter (as if the couplet was a unit; see West, l.c.).
Ennius presumably first experimented with the device in
Latin: see Sen. ap. Gell. 12. 2. 10 (= Sen. *Epp.* p. 541,
OCT) 'Vergilius . . . non ex alia causa duros quosdam uersus
et enormes et aliquid supra mensuram trahentis interposuit
quam ut Ennianus populus adgnosceret in nouo carmine
aliquid antiquitatis'. Virgil alone uses it with any freedom,
normally with *-que* as the elided syllable (exceptions are
7. 160, *G.* 1. 295, *G.* 2. 69, *G.* 3. 449, out of twenty-one
examples): other poets (for references see on 1. 332) also
show elided *-que* as the norm, the only exceptions being
Lucr. 5. 849, Hor. *Sat.* 1. 6. 102. Some of Virgil's examples
plainly intend some special effect, as here or in 5. 422 (see
R. D. Williams ad loc.), *G.* 1. 295 (where the final syllable of
umorem spills into the next line); in 4. 629 'pugnent ipsique
nepotesque' Dido's savage speech ends with the redundant
-que dying away in the following pause before 'haec ait', a
remarkable effect. But most do not suggest anything other

than a technique that Virgil liked to explore, and in this he set no fashion. For discussion see Soubiran, op. cit. 466 ff.

603. At *lucent* a developed picture of the feast-torment begins. *Genialibus* belongs so closely to *toris* that the two words form a single concept, with *altis* as epithet (cf. 2. 2 'toro pater Aeneas sic orsus ab alto'). Strictly, *genialis* is used of the bridal bed, but here it has the wider sense of 'festal' (cf. *G.* 1. 302 'inuitat genialis hiems', the party-season).

604. toris : dative (cf. Cat. 64. 45 'candet ebur soliis'); 'tall festal couches glitter with golden supports'. Virgil thinks of the elaborately decorated *fulcra* of contemporary Rome; cf. Prop. 2. 13. 21 'nec mihi tunc fulcro sternatur lectus eburno': Juvenal speaks of tortoiseshell, 'clarum Troiugenis factura et nobile fulcrum' (11. 95, where *fulcrum* = *lectus*; see Mayor's references). For a discussion of *fulcrum* see W. C. F. Anderson, *CR* iii (1889), 322 ff.

paratae : finite (see on 125).

605. regifico : Virgil does not use the compound again (contrast 1. 637 'domus interior regali splendida luxu'); *regifice* occurs in Ennius, *Sc.* 96 (see Jocelyn, p. 250). Val. Flacc. 2. 651 f. imitates Virgil, 'stant gemmis auroque tori mensaeque paratu / regifico'; cf. Silius 11. 270 f. 'instituunt de more epulas festamque per urbem / regifice exstructis celebrant conuiuia mensis'.

Furiarum maxima : unidentifiable; in 3. 252 the phrase is used of the Harpy Celaeno; Statius, with equal vagueness, compares Iocasta to *Eumenidum antiquissima* (*Th.* 7. 477).

606. accubat : cf. Stat. *Th.* 1. 712 ff. 'torua Megaera / ieiunum Phlegyan subter caua saxa iacentem / aeterno premit accubitu dapibusque profanis / instimulat', where the feast-torment is assigned to Phlegyas, and Megaera may be the 'eldest of the Furies'.

607. facem : a traditional attribute; cf. Sueton. *Nero* 34. 4 'confessus exagitari se materna specie uerberibusque Furiarum ac taedis ardentibus', Stat. *S.* 2. 7. 118 f. 'pallidumque uisa / matris lampade respicis Neronem'.

intonat ore : so *Culex* 179 (of a serpent). The Fury thunders out a prohibition; *intonat* is followed by direct speech in Stat. *Th.* 12. 771, Sen. *Phaedr.* 1065.

608 ff. Virgil now turns from myth to real life, from individuals to categories, in three pairs of parallel sins with a common basis, the violation of the laws of *pietas*. The background is largely Greek (cf. Dieterich, op. cit. 163 ff.); but its application is to aspects of contemporary Rome.

608. quibus inuisi fratres : cf. *G.* 2. 496 'infidos agitans discordia fratres'; Ovid enlarges the guilt-complex in his picture

of the Age of Iron, *Met.* 1. 144 ff. 'non hospes ab hospite
tutus, / non socer a genero, fratrum quoque gratia rara est.
. . . filius ante diem patrios inquirit in annos; / uicta iacet
pietas'.

    dum uita manebat : cf. 661, 5. 724; the words became a
cliché in grave-inscriptions (see Hoogma, op. cit. 275): so
apud superos, 568.

609. pulsatusue parens : in Plato, *Phaedo* 114A, dwellers in
Tartarus include those who have sinned πρὸς πατέρα ἢ μητέρα
ὑπ' ὀργῆς βίαιόν τι πράξαντες (cf. *Rp.* 615C); in Ar. *Ran.* 147 ff.
Heracles similarly lists εἴ που . . . τις / . . . ἢ μητέρ' ἠλοίησεν, ἢ
πατρὸς γνάθον / ἐπάταξεν. Commentators quote an ancient law
of Servius Tullius (Festus 260 L), enacting that a son who
beats his father 'deiuois parentom sakros estod'; cf. Sen.
Contr. 9. 4, a declamation on the 'law' *qui patrem pulsauerit,
manus ei praecidantur,* and similarly [Quintil.] *decl. min.*
358, 362, 372 (see S. F. Bonner, *Roman Declamation* [Liver-
pool, 1949], 96 f.).

    et : 'virtually disjunctive' (Conington); see Fordyce on Cat.
45. 6 f.

    fraus . . . clienti : Servius quotes from the *leges XII
tabularum* 'patronus si clienti fraudem fecerit, sacer esto',
adding 'si enim clientes quasi colentes sunt, patroni quasi
patres, tantundem est clientem quantum filium fallere':
another aspect of Roman *pietas.*

    innexa : as we speak of a web of deceit. Virgil first uses
innectere in poetry; there is no precise parallel for his use of
it here (in Lucan 4. 448 *fraudes innectere* = 'to construct
a trap'), but cf. Manil. 2. 487 'Lanigero qui fraudem nectit'
(of Taurus), 2. 500 'Sagittifero conatur nectere fraudem'
(of Erigone).

610. incubuere : cf. *G.* 2. 507 'condit opes alius defossoque in-
cubat auro'; Hor. *Sat.* 1. 1. 70 f. 'congestis undique saccis /
indormis inhians'. For the 'locus de diuitiis' in rhetoric see
J. De Decker, *Juvenalis declamans* (Ghent, 1913), 44 ff.

611. posuere : 'set aside' (for *deposuere*), 'assigned'; or there
may be an idea of investment, as in Hor. *Epod.* 2. 69 f.
'omnem redegit Idibus pecuniam, / quaerit Kalendis ponere',
AP 421 'diues positis in faenore nummis'.

    suis : 'cognatis, adfinibus', Servius; for *sui* of family,
close friends, etc., see on Cic. *Cael.* 5. Norden notes Gellius
5. 13. 2 'constabatque ex moribus populi Romani primum
iuxta parentes locum tenere pupillos debere . . . secundum
eos proximum locum clientes habere [cf. 609] . . . tum in
tertio loco esse hospites; postea esse cognatos adfinesque'.

    quae maxima turba est : *maxima* is 'very great', rather than 'greatest'; contemporary Rome would provide plenty of examples for Virgil's mind: cf. 3. 56 f. 'quid non mortalia pectora cogis, / auri sacra fames!' So Manil. 1. 777 'Romanique uiri, quorum iam maxima turba est'.

612. ob adulterium caesi : in early times the husband of a woman taken in adultery had the right to kill her: cf. Cato ap. Gell. 10. 23. 5 'in adulterio uxorem tuam si prehendisses, sine iudicio inpune necares'. It is clear also from Hor. *Sat.* 1. 2. 41 ff. that the adulterer could be killed also, or horribly punished (cf. Val. Max. 6. 1. 13, where cases of scourging or castration are recorded). But adultery was not brought within the scope of criminal law until the passing of the *lex Iulia de adulteriis coercendis* in 18 B.C., which enacted that the father of an adulteress might kill both her and her paramour. In Sen. *Contr.* 1. 4 the declamation turns on a law 'adulterum cum adultera qui deprehenderit, dum utrumque corpus interficiat, sine fraude sit' (cf. [Quintil.] *decl. min.* 347). See S. F. Bonner, op. cit. 119 ff. for discussion of these passages, and of the legal position in general.

The *lex Iulia* had been preceded by an earlier attempt by Augustus (28 B.C.) to curb sexual licence, but without success (see G. Williams, op. cit. 532 n. 2): it is unlikely that Virgil did not have in mind the contemporary scene and its moral climate (cf. Hor. *C.* 3. 6. 21 ff., an outspoken passage), and the prospect of some intended reform.

612 f. quique arma . . . dextras : *arma impia* (the epithet is strongly stressed by its position) alludes to civil war in general, but it is so closely linked to *dominorum fallere dextras* that the particular reference is almost certainly to the war with Sextus Pompeius, as Servius notes ('occiso patre Siciliam tenuit et collectis inde seruitiis uastauit sex annis ultro citroque Siciliam, postea uictus est ab Augusto et Agrippa'), quoting Hor. *Epod.* 9. 9 f. 'minatus urbi uincla, quae detraxerat / seruis amicus perfidis': cf. Velleius 2. 73. 3 'occupata Sicilia seruitia fugitiuosque in numerum exercitus sui recipiens magnum modum legionum effecerat'; *Mon. Anc.* 25. 1 'mare pacaui a praedonibus. eo bello seruorum, qui fugerant a dominis suis et arma contra rem publicam ceperant, triginta fere millia capta dominis ad supplicium sumendum tradidi'.

613. dextras : i.e. the trust put in them by their masters; so *dextra* is coupled with *fides*, 4. 597, Livy 1. 58. 7; cf. Val. Flacc. 7. 344 'cur tibi fallaces placuit coniungere dextras?'

614. inclusi . . . exspectant : after sentence they are waiting for the torments to begin; the grimness is stressed in the solemn

spondees and by the heavy following pause. For *ne quaere*
see on 74.

615. quam poenam : sc. *exspectant*, parallel with *mersit* below.

forma . . . fortunaue : 'fashion or fortune' (of punish-
ment); for *fortuna* of ill fortune cf. 533; Ovid, *Tr.* 3. 8. 35 f.
'ante oculos . . . / astat fortunae forma legenda meae'. Ser-
vius interpreted *forma* as *regula*, the 'rule' or formula legally
applicable to individual punishments (Norden and Nettle-
ship approve); but this hardly suits its linking with *fortuna*.

uiros : a good instance of this use, replacing *eos*.

mersit : generally regarded as an example of the indicative
in a dependent question (so Norden). But Conington rightly
took *quae* as relative, not interrogative, with the clause
equivalent to 'doceri formam fortunamue quae mersit': this
is often the true explanation of other alleged examples of
a dependent indicative, especially with *cur* (see Housman,
CR xlviii [1934], 137, = *Classical Papers*, 1235).

But the dependent indicative does occur in classical Latin,
a legacy from early Latin, where it is frequent in certain types
of phrasing that reflect a paratactic origin (e.g. *uiden ut*; see
on 779): most such examples conform to these types, e.g.
Cic. *Lael.* 96 'meministis . . . quam popularis lex de sacer-
dotiis . . . uidebatur' (see Seyffert–Müller on *Lael.* 37),
Lucan 9. 563 'quaere quid est uirtus'; for more free examples
cf. Cat. 69. 10 'admirari desine cur fugiunt', Tib. 2. 4. 17 f.
'nec refero . . . qualis, ubi orbem / compleuit, uersis Luna
recurrit equis' (see K. F. Smith ad loc.), Ovid, *H.* 7. 53 'quid
si nescires insana quid aequora possunt?', *Met.* 10. 637 'quid
facit ignorans amat et non sensit amorem' (but Ehwald's
illustrations in his note are sometimes misleading). Some-
times indicative and subjunctive appear in parallel dependent
clauses, e.g. Prop. 2. 16. 29 f. 'aspice quid donis Eriphyla
inuenit amaris, / arserit et quantis nupta Creusa malis';
in Prop. 3. 5. 25 ff. there is a long run of lines with the moods
alternating as if by a deliberate pattern (but some at least of
the dependent clauses are relative, not interrogative); cf.
Val. Flacc. 1. 277 ff., 7. 119 f.

See HSz, 537 ff.; Leo, *Sen. Trag.* i, 92 ff. (but in both
caution is needed, for some examples quoted are based on
faulty texts or on uncertain readings).

616. alii : 'some', with *alii* implied in the following clause. The
punishment suggests Sisyphus as a pattern; Odysseus saw
him (*Od.* 11. 593 ff.) in the Underworld λᾶαν βαστάζοντα πελώριον ;
when the stone was just about to roll over the top of the hill
up which he had pushed it, αὖτις ἔπειτα πέδονδε κυλίνδετο λᾶας
ἀναιδής.

radiisque rotarum : *-que* is disjunctive (cf. *et*, 609). This punishment is on the Ixion-pattern. Virgil is still generalizing.

617 ff. Virgil returns to mythical sinners, using for Theseus a different tradition from that of 122 (see note). Pausanias (10. 29. 4) notes that Polygnotus painted Theseus and Pirithous in the Underworld, seated on thrones, adding that according to the epic poet Panyassis they were not bound by chains, but their bodies had become fused with the rock on which they sat.

618. Phlegyas : father of Ixion; Apollo raped his daughter Coronis, and in revenge Phlegyas set fire to the god's temple, for which he was duly punished (Servius ad loc.; cf. Frazer on Apollod. *Bibl.* 3. 10. 3). Virgil is the first to assign him to Tartarus (cf. Norden, p. 276), followed by Stat. *Th.* 1. 712 ff., Val. Flacc. 2. 193 ff. (see on 601). Dante represents him as the ferryman of Styx (*Inf.* 8. 19; Charon is ferryman of Acheron, ib. 3. 82 ff.). Hesiod (*Scut.* 134) applies an epithet φλεγύας to an eagle or vulture (cf. J. Martha, *RPh.* xiii [1889], 112).

619. admonet : the concept goes back to Pindar, *P.* 2. 21 ff. (of Ixion) θεῶν δ' ἐφετμαῖς 'Ιξίονα φαντὶ ταῦτα βροτοῖς | λέγειν ἐν πτερόεντι τροχῷ | παντᾷ κυλινδόμενον· | τὸν εὐεργέταν ἀγαναῖς ἀμοιβαῖς ἐποιχομένους τίνεσθαι; in Plato, *Grg.* 525c, certain hardened criminals suffer eternally, ἀτεχνῶς παραδείγματα ἀνηρτημένους ἐκεῖ ἐν Ἅιδου ἐν τῷ δεσμωτηρίῳ τοῖς ἀεὶ τῶν ἀδίκων ἀφικνουμένοις θεάματα καὶ νουθετήματα.

620. A startling line, austere and dreadful: it is as if Virgil had himself heard the echoing cry in some ghastly vision. Norden (p. 275) detects Orphic influence.

temnere : a solemn word, used by Virgil in speeches only (1. 542, 665, 7. 236, 10. 737): see on 1. 542 (where it is wrongly said to occur in later Epic in Statius only; see Val. Flacc. 4. 154, 5. 127 'monitus non temnere Phinei', 6. 124; add Sen. *HF* 90).

621 ff. A fresh group of categories begins, treason paired with incest. Here Macrobius (*Sat.* 6. 1. 39) notes a borrowing from Varius, *de morte* (fr. 1 Morel), 'uendidit hic Latium populis agrosque Quiritum / eripuit: fixit leges pretio atque refixit': the context is unknown, and the nature of the poem is disputed (see Schanz–Hosius ii, 163), but it has been thought that the lines refer to Antony; if so, Virgil's readers could draw their own conclusions from his generalizing here. For Virgil's use of Varius cf. M. Wigodsky, op. cit. 103.

621. uendidit . . . patriam : Servius, observing 'licet generaliter dicantur', saw an allusion to Curio, tr. pl. in 50 B.C., bribed by Caesar to join his side; he quotes Lucan 4. 820 'Gallorum captus spoliis et Caesaris auro' (cf. id. 4. 824 'emere omnes, hic uendidit urbem', 1. 269 'audax uenali comitatur Curio lingua'). This, however, would imply a nasty insinuation against Caesar in *dominum potentem*, such as Virgil himself could not have countenanced. In fact, there is no ground for separating the subject of *uendidit* from that of *fixit . . . refixit*, which Servius himself refers to Antony (he does not mention the borrowing from Varius).

   dominumque potentem : Norden notes Livy, *Per.* 117 'M. Antonius consul cum impotenter dominaretur', Velleius 2. 61. 1 'torpebat oppressa dominatione Antoni ciuitas'.

622. fixit . . . refixit : cf. Cic. *Phil.* 2. 92; 'toto Capitolio tabulae figebantur, neque solum singulis uenibant immunitates sed etiam populis uniuersis', 12. 12 'num figentur rursus eae tabulae quas uos decretis uestris refixistis?', 13. 5 'acta M. Antoni rescidistis; leges refixistis', passages that add clear point to Virgil's (and Varius') words. For *atque* without involving elision see on 127.

   Laws were engraved on bronze tablets (cf. Ovid, *Met.* 1. 91 f. 'nec uerba minantia fixo / aere ligabantur', of the Golden Age). A provision of the *S.C. de Bacchanalibus* of 186 B.C. (on a brazen tablet, now in Vienna) runs 'utei hoce in tabolam ahenam inceideretis, ita senatus aequom censuit, uteique eam figier ioubeatis, ubi facilumed gnoscier potisit' (see Warmington, *Remains of Old Latin* iv, 258).

   The grammatical 'rhyme' (*fixit . . . refixit*) between mid-line (at the third-foot caesura) and the line-ending makes this line a 'leonine'; for better examples see 3. 36 'secundarent . . . leuarent', 10. 756 'caedebant . . . ruebant', Lucr. 1. 318 'salutantum . . . meantum', Ovid, *Ars* 1. 59 'stellas . . . puellas', *Met.* 6. 247 'uersarunt . . . exhalarunt'. Such internal rhyming is a feature of much medieval Latin hexameter poetry; see F. J. E. Raby, *Christian Latin Poetry* (Oxford, 1927), 26 f., *Secular Latin Poetry* (Oxford, 1934) i, 228, ii, 1. For the term 'leonine' see C. Erdmann in *Festgabe Karl Strecker* (Leipzig, 1941), 15 ff.: he notes that the term *uersus leoninus* occurs first in verse manuals of the twelfth century; the epithet, however, was originally applied to prose rhythm ('cursus leoninus', 'leonitas') in connexion with papal letters, suggesting a derivation from the epistolary style of Leo I (Pope 440–61); during the twelfth century 'leonitas' gradually lost the meaning 'rhythm' and its original prose connexion, and became used only of 'rhyme' in poetry, and then settled down as a t.t. for the internally rhymed line.

623. The subject of incest obviously attracted Alexandrian writers. Among the ἐρωτικὰ παθήματα of Parthenius (cf. introductory note, 440 ff.) are several such tales, e.g. the story of Leucippus (from Hermesianax), and that of Harpalyce (from Euphorion); see Gaselee (Loeb ed.), 269, 297: the work was dedicated to Gallus, Virgil's friend, devotee of Euphorion (*E*. 10. 50). Ovid tells the story of Byblis (*Met*. 9. 454 ff.; summarized by Parthenius, Gaselee 293), and of Myrrha (*Met*. 10. 300 ff.), often very movingly in spite of the rhetorical elaboration. See Hyginus, *fab*. 253, Frazer on Apollod. *Bibl*. 3. 14. 4 (Myrrha).

Obviously here no identifiable allusiveness could be latent; but we may remember the common allegations against Clodius (e.g. Cic. *Cael*. 36). The theme became a topic of the declamation-schools: see Quintil. 5. 10. 19, 7. 8. 3, [Quintil.] *decl. mai*. 18, 19, Tac. *Dial*. 35. 5. For some actual cases see Tac. *Ann*. 6. 19, 12. 8; Syme, *Tacitus* (Oxford, 1958), 301, 315, 543: on the subject see P. E. Corbett, *The Roman Law of Marriage* (Oxford, 1930), 50 f.; R. Turcan, *Rev. de l'histoire des religions* cl (1956), 155 f.

hymenaeos : the Greek word allows the quadrisyllabic ending; among the quite numerous examples of the word in Virgil (all in this position, except *hymenaeus*, 4. 127) there is sometimes abnormal prosody in the line (see on 1. 651).

624. immane nefas : 'a monstrous abomination'; cf. Silius 13. 841 f. 'hostibus arcem / uirgo, immane nefas, adamato prodidit urbem' (of Tarpeia), Ovid, *Met*. 10. 351 f. 'at tu, dum corpore non es / passa nefas, animo ne concipe' (of Myrrha). Although the language of the line is especially appropriate to the sexual crime (see Norden), it sums up all the enormities that receive punishment in Tartarus.

ausoque potiti : cf. Ovid, *Met*. 11. 241 f. 'quod nisi uenisses uariatis saepe figuris / ad solitas artes, auso foret ille potitus '. The substantival use of *ausum* is not recorded before Virgil; cf. DServius on 12. 351 'quaeritur quis ante hunc *ausis* dixerit ', and see on 2. 535.

625 ff. The Sibyl ends with a rhetorical flourish (cf. *G*. 2. 43 f.) which has its ancestor in *Il*. 2. 488 ff. πληθὺν δ' οὐκ ἂν ἐγὼ μυθήσομαι οὐδ' ὀνομήνω, / οὐδ' εἴ μοι δέκα μὲν γλῶσσαι, δέκα δὲ στόματ' εἶεν, / φωνὴ δ' ἄρρηκτος, χάλκεον δέ μοι ἦτορ ἐνείη. Ennius took it over, *Ann*. 561 f. 'non si, lingua loqui saperet quibus, ora decem sint, / innumerum, ferro cor sit pectusque reuinctum '; Macrobius (*Sat*. 6. 3. 6) quotes a line of Hostius (late second century B.C.; cf. M. Wigodsky, op. cit. 98) 'non si mihi linguae / centum atque ora sient totidem uocesque liquatae' (fr. 3 Morel); Servius states that Virgil's line is from Lucretius, who wrote *aerea uox* (similarly on *G*. 2. 42, but with *aenea*); this has no relation to our texts of Lucretius (cf. H. D.

Jocelyn, *CQ* n.s. xv [1965], 140 f.). For variations on the
theme see Ovid, *Met.* 8. 533 f., *F.* 2. 119 f., *Tr.* 1. 5. 53 f.,
Silius 4. 525 f., Val. Flacc. 6. 36 f. (see Langen ad loc.),
Apuleius, *Met.* 11. 25. Virgil would have been surprised at
Dracontius' embroidery, *de deo* 3. 354 ff. 'non si mihi ferrea
uox sit, / ora tot exsurgant quot dentes ossibus albent, / aut
mihi sint linguae quantos caput omne capillos / pectinet . . .'.
Persius mocks the cliché, 5. 1 f. 'uatibus hic mos est, centum
sibi poscere uoces, / centum ora et linguas optare in carmina
centum'. See Wölfflin, *ALL* ix, 185 f.; P. Courcelle, *RÉL*
xxxiii (1955), 231 ff. (with many examples from Christian
writers); A. Cameron, *Philologus* cxi (1967), 308 f.

626. comprendere : cf. *G.* 2. 103 f. 'neque quam multae species
nec nomina quae sint / est numerus, neque enim numero com-
prendere refert' (ending the list of vines).

627. The long emotional passage ends in a quiet line, with only
one clash of ictus and speech-accent (*poenarum*).

628–36. *The Sibyl tells Aeneas that it is time to go on their way,
and to set the Bough duly at Proserpina's gateway.*

All this time the Sibyl and Aeneas have been standing
near the road-junction for Tartarus and Elysium (540 ff.).
These lines form a transition, from what Aeneas is told but
does not see to what he does see personally; and we now learn
what happens to the Golden Bough, last mentioned in 406.

628. longaeua : see on 321 (of which this line is a variation).

629. sed iam age : for elided *iam* see on 385; but Virgil elides it
before a short syllable only here and in 12. 582 ('bis iam
Italos hostis'). The majority of examples have a mono-
syllable preceding *iam* (see on 2. 254).

carpe uiam : 'step out on your road'. The basic sense of
carpere (a versatile verb) is to lessen by taking something
away; here the road is 'lessened' by hurrying (cf. 'ac-
celeremus', 630). The usage occurs first in Hor. *Sat.* 1. 5. 94 f.
'inde Rubos fessi peruenimus, utpote longum / carpentes iter
et factum corruptius imbri', which shows that speed is not
necessarily implied (cf. *G.* 3. 346 f. 'acer Romanus in armis /
iniusto sub fasce uiam cum carpit', where the context implies
unexpected speed). The idea is extended to cover other things
traversed: so *G.* 3. 191 (*gyrum*), *G.* 4. 311 (*aëra*; Ovid, *Ars*
2. 43 f. 'quis crederet umquam / aerias hominem carpere
posse uias?'), Prop. 1. 6. 33 (*pontum*), Ovid, *Met.* 12. 196
(*litora*), *Tr.* 1. 10. 23 (*campos*), Stat. *Th.* 3. 109 (*Elysias
plagas*), Silius 10. 62 (*fugam*).

susceptum . . . munus : 'complete the duty that you have
undertaken'; the 'duty' is the bringing of the Bough as a

gift (*munus*) to Proserpina (142), and so in 637 we find 'perfecto munere diuae' when the duty is done.

630. educta : 'built up high'; cf. 178, 2. 460 f. 'turrim in praecipiti stantem summisque sub astra / eductam tectis', Tac. *Ann.* 2. 61 'instar montium eductae pyramides'. The Cyclopes would use bronze or iron in their forges; cf. Callim. *h.* 3. 60 f. ἢ χαλκὸν ζείοντα καμινόθεν ἠὲ σίδηρον / ἀμβολαδὶς τετύποντες.

631. aduerso . . . portas : 'arched gateways confronting us'; *aduerso fornice* is descriptive ablative, functioning like a compound epithet. For *aduerso* cf. 279, 418, 636, 1. 166 'fronte sub aduersa scopulis pendentibus antrum'.

632. praecepta : of the gods, and of Proserpina in particular (cf. *instituit*, 143).

633. pariter gressi : they march in step, like soldiers; cf. Plaut. *Pseud.* 859 'si quo hic gradietur, pariter progredimino', *Truc.* 124 'fer contra manum et pariter gradere'. The participle *gressus* is found here only (*Thes. L.L.* s.v. *gradior*, 2137. 54).

opaca uiarum : cf. 2. 725 'ferimur per opaca locorum'. The genitive is formally partitive, but often (as here; contrast 140) the partitive notion has faded. The type goes back to Ennius (*Ann.* 89 'recessit in infera noctis') and Accius (*tr.* 336 'terrarum anfracta reuisam'): see on 1. 422, 2. 332.

634. corripiunt spatium : they 'seize upon' the intervening distance: a climax after *carpe uiam* and *acceleremus*. For this use of the verb (not recorded before Virgil) cf. 1. 418 (*uiam*), 5. 316 (*spatia*), G. 3. 104 (*campum*); Hor. *C.* 1. 3. 33, Stat. *Th.* 2. 143 (*gradum*); Pliny, *Epp.* 4. 1. 6 'subsistemus fortasse . . . sed tanto magis uiam ipsam corripiemus'. The extension in *foribusque propinquant* is characteristic; cf. 384, 410, 5. 185, 8. 101.

The line has a notable rhythm. Besides having the maximum possible number of dactyls, it shows a remarkable group of three anapaestic words in midline, *spatium medium foribus*: this, with the obtrusive assonance in *spatium medium* (a type of collocation that Virgil tends to avoid; see Norden, Anh. iv), results in a thudding effect, as of quick running.

635. occupat . . . aditum : repeated from 424.

recenti : 'fresh' ('semper fluenti', Servius); cf. G. 3. 301 'fluuios praebere recentis'. Servius thinks that the lustration was needed because of pollution 'uel aspectu Tartari uel auditu scelerum atque poenarum'. But it would be a natural action at the entrance to Proserpina's dwelling, and especially at such a moment: cf. Macrob. *Sat.* 3. 1. 6 (where this passage is quoted) 'constat dis superis sacra facturum corporis ablutione purgari, cum uero inferis litandum est, satis

actum uidetur si aspersio sola contingat'. See in general
Pease on 4. 635, Bömer on Ovid, *F.* 2. 35.

636. aduerso in limine : 'at the doorway facing him'; cf. 631.
The whole passage 633–6 is a good example of Virgil's
paratactic method; the effect resembles that of 597 ff. (see
on 597), with the series of clauses linked by *-que*.

637–78. *They reach Elysium, and see the blessed souls in radiant
light. Musaeus shows them where to go in order to find Anchises.*

From a tunnel of darkness Virgil's narrative passes into
a dwelling of light, in an apocalyptic vision of bliss and
rewarded virtue. Again, some individuals are named, some
are generalizing categories (see on 663); happy pleasures
contrast with the torments of Tartarus.

The concept of an Elysium is first found in *Od.* 4. 561 ff.,
Proteus' prophecy that Menelaus would not die in Argos,
but that the immortals would send him to the plain of Ely-
sium at the bounds of Earth τῇ περ ῥηΐστη βιοτὴ πέλει ἀνθρώποισιν· |
οὐ νιφετός, οὔτ' ἄρ χειμὼν πολὺς οὔτε ποτ' ὄμβρος, | ἀλλ' αἰεὶ Ζεφύροιο
λιγὺ πνείοντος ἀήτας | Ὠκεανὸς ἀνίησιν ἀναψύχειν ἀνθρώπους. In
Hesiod, this paradise is also at the bounds of Earth, but set
in the Islands of the Blessed, where certain heroes of the
generation before Hesiod's own have been granted a dwelling
of happiness by Zeus (*Op.* 170 ff.). For other versions of the
theme see K. F. Smith on Tib. 1. 3. 57–66.

Virgil conceives Elysium as a special region of the Under-
world, but the *fortunata nemora* of 639 hint at the island-
tradition that he could not use, as Servius notes. He is
clearly indebted to Pindar, *O.* 2. 56 ff. (an ode composed for
a Sicilian audience with Orphic–Pythagorean tendencies; see
W. K. C. Guthrie, *Orpheus and Greek Religion*, 236), and to
the lovely θρῆνος (fr. 114, OCT) preserved by [Plutarch], *Con-
solatio ad Apollonium*, 35: both passages convey, as Virgil
does, a sense of light and colour and serenity; there are the
same innocent pleasures, the same just reward to the just.
Platonic influence appears also: see *Grg.* 526c, where Rhada-
manthus sends those who have lived in holiness and truth
to the Isles of the Blest; *Phaedo* 114c, where those who have
been purified by philosophy reach a final dwelling-place of
special loveliness, living there without bodies; *Axiochus*
(pseudo-Platonic) 371c–d, where the good dwell in a region
of clear streams and gay flowery meadows, with no winter
cold or excessive heat. The presence of Orpheus (645) and
Musaeus (667) is a pointer, if any were needed, to Virgil's
thought; his indebtedness to Orphic–Pythagorean doctrine

becomes unmistakable in Anchises' exposition of reincarnation (724 ff.). See also note on *aëris in campis* (887).

637. his demum exactis : cf. *sic demum*, 154. The action is restated in 'perfecto munere diuae', which looks back to 629; for *perficere* of the completion of a ritual cf. 4. 638 f. 'sacra Ioui Stygio, quae rite incepta paraui, / perficere est animus'.

638. deuenere locos : so, in a very different context, 1. 365; for the accusative without preposition see on 345. Here and in the next line there is a remarkable group of four nouns with adjacent epithets, bringing out the happiness and beauty of the place; but there is a chiastic order in both lines, with the substantives enclosing the juxtaposed epithets in 638, the epithets enclosing the juxtaposed substantives in 639; while *locos laetos* and the synonymous *sedes beatas* are kept apart by the unit *amoena uirecta fortunatorum nemorum.*

amoena : of lovely natural scenery; cf. Cic. *de nat. deor.* 2. 100 'quanta maris est pulchritudo! quae species uniuersi! quae multitudo et uarietas insularum! quae amoenitates orarum ac litorum!' For the *locus amoenus* as a motif in poetry over many centuries see E. Curtius, *European Literature and the Latin Middle Ages* (London, 1953), 192, 195 ff.; in an interesting note (200 n. 31) he quotes from the *Commendatio Mortuorum* in the Roman Ritual 'constituat te Christus inter paradisi sui semper amoena uirentia'.

uirecta : a Virgilian coinage ('greeneries'); so *Dirae* 27 'optima siluarum, formosis densa uirectis': neither Ovid nor Silver Epic uses it, but Prudentius borrowed it for Paradise, *Cath.* 3. 101 f. 'tunc per amoena uirecta iubet / frondicomis habitare locis' (cf. Curtius, l.c.). Norden notes Ennius, *Ann.* 39 'amoena salicta'.

639. fortunatorum nemorum : a substitute for the μακάρων νῆσοι; cf. Plaut. *Trin.* 549 ff. 'sicut fortunatorum memorant insulas, / quo cuncti qui aetatem egerint caste suam / conueniant'. Ancient geographers took the Isles to be Madeira (Plutarch, *Sertorius* 8), or the Canaries (cf. Pliny, *NH* 6. 202 ff., with fascinating reports from Juba): see J. O. Thomson, *History of Ancient Geography*, 184, 262. The line makes a fine finale to a miniature ἔκφρασις (picked up by *hic*, 640), with its single impressive spondaic word stretching to the third-foot caesura.

640. largior : 'more generous' (than the *aether* of the mortal world). The construction is uncertain: either *uestit* does double duty ('a more generous aether clothes the plains, covering them with lustrous light'), or *lumine purpureo* is a descriptive ablative, linked to *largior* by *et* ('an aether more generous and of lustrous light clothes the plains'): the former perhaps preferable. It might have been simpler if Virgil had written 'largior hic aether, campos et lumine uestit . . .', with *et* as a postponed connective.

Possibly, as commentators suggest, Virgil may have had in mind Lucr. 3. 21 f., of the *sedes quietae* of the gods, where there is no wind or cloud, 'semperque innubilus aether / integit et large diffuso lumine ridet', which in turn reflects *Od.* 6. 44 f. (of Olympus) ἀλλὰ μάλ' αἴθρη / πέπταται ἀνέφελος, λευκὴ δ' ἐπιδέδρομεν αἴγλη ('all around stretches the cloudless firmament, and a white glory of sunlight is diffused about its walls', T. E. Lawrence, quoted by Kenney on Lucr. l.c.).

uestit : cf. Lucr. 2. 147 f. 'quam subito soleat sol ortus tempore tali / conuestire sua perfundens omnia luce'; Cicero rather overworks the metaphor in his *Aratea* (fr. 34. 60 Tr., 262, 332, 473; 205, 440, with *umbra*; 479, with *caligine*).

641. purpureo : not the English 'purple', but lustrous, dazzling; so in 1. 590 f. Venus endows Aeneas with *lumen iuuentae purpureum*, the bright glow of youth. It is used of varying objects that sparkle, such as salt (Val. Flacc. 3. 422) or swans (Hor. *C.* 4. 1. 10) or light on waves (Cat. 64. 275) or perhaps snow (*Eleg. in Maecen.* 1. 62; but see Kenney's app. cit.): see Fordyce on Cat. 45. 12, J. André, op. cit. 93 ff. Elysium has the delight of a bright sparkling day in spring, full of colour and animation ('uer purpureum', *E.* 9. 40); cf. Pindar, *O.* 2. 72 f. ἄνθεμα δὲ χρυσοῦ φλέγει, τὰ μὲν χερσόθεν ἀπ' ἀγλαῶν δενδρέων; Lucian, *Ver. Hist.* 2. 12 (of the City of the Blessed) αἰεὶ γὰρ παρ' αὐτοῖς ἔαρ ἐστὶ καὶ εἷς ἄνεμος πνεῖ παρ' αὐτοῖς ὁ ζέφυρος : so Pope, *Pastorals, Spring* 1. 28 'And lavish Nature paints the Purple Year' (see D. Davie on Thomas Hardy's Virgilian Purples, *Agenda* x [1972], 138 ff.).

solemque suum : somewhat similarly Manil. 1. 760 f. (of the *fortes animae*) 'huc migrant ex orbe suumque habitantia caelum / aetherios uiuunt annos'. For the perpetual sunshine of the blessed cf. Pindar, *O.* 2. 61 f., where the good live a life free from toil, ἴσαις δὲ νύκτεσσιν αἰεί, / ἴσαις δ' ἐν ἀμέραις ἄλιον ἔχοντες, fr. 114. 1 τοῖσι λάμπει μὲν μένος ἀελίου τὰν ἐνθάδε νύκτα κάτω : so Val. Flacc. 1. 842 ff. (of Elysium) 'lucet uia late / igne dei, donec siluas et amoena piorum / deueniant camposque, ubi sol totumque per annum / durat aprica dies', Claudian, *rapt. Pros.* 2. 282 ff. (Pluto, showing Proserpina the amenities of his kingdom) 'amissum ne crede diem: sunt altera nobis / sidera, sunt orbes alii, lumenque uidebis / purius Elysiumque magis mirabere solem', etc.

642 f. For the athletic scene cf. Pindar, fr. 114. 4 f. τοὶ μὲν ἵπποισί ⟨τε⟩ γυμνασίαις ⟨τε⟩, τοὶ δὲ πεσσοῖς, / τοὶ δὲ φορμίγγεσσι τέρπονται. Athletics are among the many pleasures of the dead shown in

Etruscan tomb-paintings of the sixth and fifth centuries B.C.:
see Toynbee, *Death and Burial*, 12; Scullard, *The Etruscan
Cities and Rome*, 89, 154.

643. ludo : sport of any kind, here specifically of wrestling; cf.
9. 606 'flectere ludus equos et spicula tendere cornu'. It
could include board-games (cf. *G.* 3. 379), like Pindar's πεσσοί
(for πεττεία, a battle-game, see H. J. R. Murray, *A History of
Board-Games* [Oxford, 1952], 25 ff.). A tomb-scene from Tar-
quinia shows two men playing kottabos (Toynbee, op. cit.
14; cf. Scullard, op. cit. 154).

644. pars . . . choreas : they 'stamp the beat of the dance'
(*choreas* is an internal accusative); cf. *Od.* 8. 264 πέπληγον δὲ
χορὸν θεῖον ποσί, where χορόν is the dancing-floor. For dancing
and song (and bird-song) in Elysium cf. Tib. 1. 3. 59 f. 'hic
choreae cantusque uigent, passimque uagantes / dulce
sonant tenui gutture carmen aues'; so in Ar. *Ran.* 155 ff.
Heracles tells Dionysus ὄψει τε φῶς κάλλιστον, ὥσπερ ἐνθάδε /
καὶ μυρρινῶνας, καὶ θιάσους εὐδαίμονας / ἀνδρῶν γυναικῶν, καὶ κρότον
χειρῶν πολύν (of the initiates). With the pictorial alliteration cf.
Lucr. 5. 1402 'duro terram pede pellere matrem', Cat. 61. 14
'pelle humum pedibus'. For the prosody *chorĕas* cf. Tib. l.c.,
Prop. 2. 19. 15; but *chorēa* is more frequent (9. 615, 10. 224;
Lucr. 2. 635, Cat. 64. 287, Tib. 1. 7. 49, Prop. 2. 10. 1).

645. nec non . . . sacerdos : Virgil means Orpheus. For *nec non*
see on 183. The *longa uestis* is the traditional dress of a
citharoedus; cf. Prop. 2. 31. 16 'Pythius in longa carmina
ueste sonat' (of a statue of Apollo); *cum* is regular in the
sense of 'wearing' (cf. 359; Cic. *Rab. Post.* 27 'L. uero Sci-
pionis . . . non solum cum chlamyde sed etiam cum crepidis
in Capitolio statuam uidetis').

Orpheus is shown here primarily as the magically skilled
musician, on which see Guthrie, op. cit. 39 ff., Linforth, op.
cit. 165 f., 293. But in adding *sacerdos* Virgil ingeniously con-
trives to mark the other great aspect of the Orpheus-legend,
its association with religion and the mysteries. On the vast,
controversial, and fascinating problem of 'Orphism' in
general, Guthrie and Linforth provide essential treatment
each in his own way; Dodds (*The Greeks and the Irrational*,
147 ff.) has a ruefully cautious brief discussion, of great value;
and there is a crisp, useful, summarizing note by W. S.
Barrett on Eur. *Hipp.* 952-5 (Oxford, 1964). See also
Cumont, op. cit. 243 ff.

646. 'In accompaniment to the rhythm he sounds the seven
separate notes': seven strings very early became the canonical
number for the lyre; see *OCD*[2] s.v. *Music*, 710. *Numeris* is
dative, referring to the dancers' songs, not to Orpheus' own

singing as some assume; a solo turn by him is hardly in
place. Henry, less probably, takes it as ablative, referring
the line to singing only, with the playing described in the
next line. Orpheus was shown with his lyre in Polygnotus'
painting of the Underworld in the Lesche at Delphi (Pausanias
10. 30. 2).

obloquitur : the normal meaning is to interrupt or contra-
dict; here, remarkably, it is used with an internal accusative
(*discrimina*) explaining the form of a 'reply' in harmony, not
in opposition. St. Ambrose borrowed Virgil's phrase, *Hexam.*
5. 14. 49 (of birds) 'quaedam ex natura, aliae ex institutione,
diuersarum uocum obloquuntur discrimina, ut hominem
putes locutum cum locuta sit auis' (in contrast to mere
chirping or aimless song); cf. Ovid, *ex Pont.* 3. 1. 21 'non auis
obloquitur' (in his desolate place of exile, where no bird
answers bird in melody).

647. Orpheus strikes the notes (*eadem*, i.e. *discrimina uocum*)
now with his fingers, now with a plectrum; for the former
action he would use his left hand, for the latter his right
(*OCD*[2], l.c.); Cerda quotes the younger Philostratus, *Imag.* 6
(of Orpheus) ἡ μὲν δεξιὰ ξυνέχουσα ἀπρὶξ τὸ πλῆκτρον ἐπιτέταται
τοῖς φθόγγοις . . . ἡ λαιὰ δὲ ὀρθοῖς πλήττει τοῖς δακτύλοις τοὺς μίτους (ed.
Loeb, p. 312): see Guthrie, pl. 6 (a red-figured Attic vase
from Gela, mid fifth century).

iamque . . . iam : Virgil introduced this use of *iam . . . iam*
for *modo . . . modo* (Wölfflin, *ALL* ii, 244 f.; *Thes.L.L.* s.v.
iam, 118. 60).

pectine : Virgil does not use *plectrum*; he has introduced
this transference of *pecten* from weaving (cf. *G.* 1. 294) to lyre-
playing: so Juv. 6. 382 'crispo numerantur pectine chordae'.

648. The line is carefully parallel with 580 'hic genus antiquum
Terrae, Titania pubes', opening the list of sinners in Tar-
tarus. First among the blessed are the legendary figures of
Troy: Teucer (cf. 500) was the traditional ancestor of the
Trojan race, but a variant legend made Dardanus (cf. 650)
already in Troy when Teucer arrived there from Crete: see
R. D. Williams on 3. 107. *Pulcherrima* = 'glorious', 'noble';
cf. *G.* 2. 534 'rerum facta est pulcherrima Roma'.

649. magnanimi heroes : see on 307. The line may reflect Cat.
64. 22 f. 'o nimis optato saeclorum tempore nati / heroes'.
Virgil conjures up a picture of a golden age of heroes in a
golden past.

650. Ilus was Priam's grandfather; his brother Assaracus was
grandfather of Anchises; cf. *Il.* 20. 232 Ἴλός τ' Ἀσσάρακός τε
καὶ ἀντίθεος Γανυμήδης.

651. procul : 'a little way off' (see on 10); their arms and

chariots would not be 'far away' from the heroes. Fair-
clough takes it with *miratur*, against the run of the line (and
from 666 it is clear that they were all gathered closely
round Aeneas).

    inanis : 'empty' of their owners (cf. 1. 476), matching the
picture of the spears out of use and the horses grazing free
(652 f.). Servius appears to interpret it as 'ghostly'.

652. stant . . . hastae : the heroes are relaxed and have no need
of their spears any more: cf. *Il.* 3. 134 f. οἱ δὴ νῦν ἕαται σιγῇ,
πόλεμος δὲ πέπαυται, / ἀσπίσι κεκλιμένοι, παρὰ δ' ἔγχεα μακρὰ πέπηγεν.

652 f. passimque . . . equi : sound and rhythm present a pretty
scene, as the horses, unyoked, graze quietly in little groups
over the meadow. The following lines have a special serenity
and happiness, a comforting reassurance: very different from
the blankness of Lucretius' teaching, by which all delights are
blotted out in death, 'nec tibi earum / iam desiderium rerum
super insidet una' (3. 900 f.).

653. gratia : 'charm', χάρις. The contracted genitive form *cur-
rum* is not found elsewhere, and such a contraction in the
fourth declension is very rare: cf. Plaut. *Men.* 177 'mille
passum commoratu's cantharum', Lucilius 506 M (*passum*),
Mon. Anc. 5. 40 (*exercitum*).

654. nitentis : glossy, well-groomed, the result of *cura*: so
7. 275 'stabant ter centum nitidi in praesepibus altis', of
Latinus' horses. The arrangement of the nouns in the passage
is worth noting: *arma currusque* (651), *hastae* (652), *equi*
(653); *currum, armorum, equos* (653–5); the horses make a
climax.

655. eadem . . . repostos : for the same idea cf. Ovid, *Met.* 4.
445 f. 'pars aliquas artes, antiquae imitamina uitae, / exer-
cent'. For the syncopated form *repostos* see on 24, 59. In
Od. 11. 573 Odysseus sees the ghost of Orion, θῆρας ὁμοῦ
εἰλεῦντα κατ' ἀσφοδελὸν λειμῶνα, as he used to hunt in life.

656. ecce : Aeneas is surprised and pleased to catch sight of
a new group of heroes, picnicking on the grass; for scenes
of feasts in Etruscan tomb-paintings see Toynbee, op. cit.
12.

    per herbam : cf. 1. 214 f. 'fusique per herbam / implentur
ueteris Bacchi pinguisque ferinae'.

657. paeana : 'proprie Apollinis laudes, quod nunc congruit
propter *lauri nemus*' (Servius); cf. *Il.* 1. 473, where the
Achaeans hymn Apollo, καλὸν ἀείδοντες παιήονα. The allusive
connexion with Apollo (cf. 'Phoebo digna locuti', 662) suits
the general scene of music and dancing; cf. Scullard, op. cit.
pl. 16 (from Tarquinia).

658. lauris : so Mynors, Geymonat, from the St. Gall fragments

(G); the consensus of all other manuscripts (and Servius) is for *lauri*. For the construction cf. Pliny, *Epp.* 2. 17. 17 'xystus uiolis odoratus' (Mynors notes 9. 381 f. 'silua . . . dumis atque ilice nigra / horrida', *G.* 3. 333 f. 'nigrum / ilicibus crebris . . . nemus'). It is an attractive reading, drawing attention to the scent rather than to the trees. For Elysian fragrance cf. Pindar, fr. 114. 6 (of incense), Tib. 1. 3. 62 (of roses; cf. K. F. Smith ad loc.).

superne : normally 'above' or 'from above', a meaning that is possible here if we imagine the *nemus* to be on a hill-side (cf. the *iugum* of 676), with the river flowing down *per siluam* (659); it is absurd to differentiate the *silua* from the *nemus* and to refer it to some forest in the upper world, as some suppose, with *superne* meaning 'in the world above'. But Servius (approved by Norden) explains *superne* as *ad superos*, 'to the upper world', an unusual use, but cf. Pliny, *NH* 19. 76 (of turnips) 'solum . . . hoc genus superne tendit, non ut cetera in terram'; perhaps also Lucr. 1. 1105 'neue ruant caeli tonitralia templa superne', where Bailey, against Munro, takes *superne* as 'upwards'.

The Eridanus was a legendary river in the North West, not Homeric, but listed in Hesiod's river-catalogue (*Theog.* 338). On its banks the sisters of Phaethon, turned into poplars, wept amber tears at his death (Ovid, *Met.* 2. 324, 340; Hyginus, *Fab.* 154). It was reported to Herodotus (3. 115) as a source for amber, but he sniffed at the tale. When Greek geographers began to know something of the early amber-route from the Baltic to Greece via the Adriatic, the Eridanus became identified with the Padus (Po); Aeschylus took it to be the Rhône (*Rhodanus*) according to Pliny, *NH* 37. 32. See West on Hesiod, l.c.; Barrett on Eur. *Hipp.* 735 ff.; J. O. Thomson, *History of Ancient Geography*, 49 (with references).

Virgil thinks of it as the Padus, with a mysterious source; in *G.* 4. 372 it is one of the streams that Aristaeus sees rising in Cyrene's strange underwater world, 'quo non alius per pinguia culta / in mare purpureum uiolentior effluit amnis'; the flooding of 'fluuiorum rex Eridanus' (*G.* 1. 481 ff.) was one of the sinister signs at Caesar's death. The great river of his home country still retained for him something of its legendary character.

659. plurimus : 'in all his strength'. It is quite fanciful to see in the *silua* here an allusion to the poplars of the Phaethon-legend (so Norden, followed by Butler).

660. The groups of the blessed are pointedly contrasted with the groups of sinners in 608 ff., with both passages introduced by *hic*, and *dum uita manebat* (661) repeated. For *passi* in apposition to *manus* cf. 580 f. *genus . . . deiecti.*

ob patriam : *pietas* again: cf. 7. 181 f. 'aliique ab origine reges, / Martiaque ob patriam pugnando uulnera passi' (of the images in Latinus' palace). How were these heroes in Elysium differentiated from the *bello clari* in the 'neutral' region (478)?

662. uates : either prophets or poets; *Phoebo digna locuti* suits both (see Nisbet–Hubbard on Hor. *C.* 1. 1. 35, 1. 31. 2): cf. Silius 14. 28 f. 'hic Phoebo digna et Musis uenerabere uatum / ora excellentum' (of the poets of Sicily).

663. inuentas . . . artis : 'or those who found out knowledge and used it for the betterment of life'; for the postponement of *aut* see on 28. *Artis* is used in a wide sense, of any 'art' that develops man's mind and adds to a civilized way of life; cf. Silius 13. 537 ff., where through one of the ten gates of the Underworld come 'qui laetas artes uitaeque colendae / inuenere uiam nec dedignanda parenti / carmina fuderunt Phoebo'.

excoluere : cf. Sen. *de ben.* 6. 17. 2 'in optimis uero artibus, quae uitam aut conseruant aut excolunt, qui nihil se plus existimat debere quam pepigit, ingratus est'. Servius comments 'significat autem philosophos'; see Norden, pp. 34 ff., and cf. Manilius 1. 771 f. 'quique animi uires et strictae pondera mentis / prudentes habuere uiri', alluding to Solon, Lycurgus, Plato, Socrates.

The line has a clear affinity with a passage in a Bologna papyrus (second/third c. A.D.), first published by Pighi in 1947. This is a fragmentary Hellenistic poem in hexameters, evidently listing categories of souls in the Underworld; it has been termed 'Orphic'. Among the good ψυχαί are αἱ δὲ βίον σοφίῃσιν ἐκόσμεον (fol. iii v. 7), a phrasing which at once suggests the present line; there is also a category of those who lived pure lives (cf. 661), and an allusion to Apollo (cf. 662). Among the sinful are those guilty of incest (cf. 623), fratricide (cf. 608), miserliness (cf. 610), betrayal of a friend (cf. 609). Virgil may have known the actual poem, or it may be representative of a genre familiar to him: its interest and importance are obvious.

For a critical text of the papyrus see R. Merkelbach, *Mus. Helv.* viii (1951), 1 ff.; it was republished by O. Montevecchi, *Papyri Bononienses* i (1953), no. 4 (pp. 8 ff.). It is discussed, with specific reference to Virgil, by M. Treu, *Hermes* lxxxii (1954), 24 ff.; with this cf. F. Solmsen, *Proc. Am. Philos. Soc.* cxii (1968), 10 f., and *CP* lxvii (1972), 32 f. (two most helpful and lucid papers on Virgil's 'world of the dead'): see also

R. Turcan, *Rev. de l'histoire des Religions* cl (1956), 136 ff.,
and A. Setaioli, *Alcuni aspetti del VI libro dell'Eneide*
(Bologna, 1970), ch. 4.

664. aliquos : the v.l. *alios* is far less telling; service to just
'some' is the most that ordinary men can do, and it brings
its reward: a comfortably wide category.

665. niuea ... uitta : such as was worn by priests (e.g. Lao-
coon, 2. 221; cf. Val. Flacc. 1. 840 'seu uenit in uittis castaque
in ueste sacerdos') or by poets (cf. Stat. *Ach.* 1. 11 'nec mea
nunc primis augescunt tempora uittis'), marking their holy
office: so here it marks all the good.

667. Musaeum : constantly associated with Orpheus, e.g. Plato,
Apol. 41A, *Ion* 536B, *Protag.* 316D, *Rp.* 364E; cf. I. M. Lin-
forth, *The Arts of Orpheus*, 72 f., 77 ff., 106 f. There is some
evidence that he was thought to be an amanuensis of
Orpheus, writing down the Orphic poems at dictation
(Linforth, 125 ff.; cf. N. J. Richardson, *The Homeric Hymn to
Demeter* [Oxford, 1974], 78). In Eur. *Rhesus* 945 f. the Muse
terms him a reverend citizen of Athens (σὸν / σεμνὸν πολίτην,
spoken to Athena), honoured by Apollo and all the Muses
(cf. Linforth, 62). In Ar. *Ran.* 1033 Aeschylus is represented
as saying that Musaeus taught healing arts (ἐξακέσεις νόσων):
could there, perhaps, be some connexion between this tra-
dition and the fact that the Bologna papyrus lists νούσων
σωτῆρα (fol. 3 v. 11) among the categories of the good?

The naming of Musaeus here is in keeping with Virgil's
particularizing technique, as well as singling him out for his
traditional importance (but it is a little odd that the *plurima
turba* surrounds him and not Orpheus himself). H. Lloyd-
Jones (*Maia* xix [1967], 223 f.) suggests that his special pro-
minence may be due not only to his association with Orpheus
but also to his connexion with Eleusis and the Mysteries.

nam : see on 28; it is postponed to third place in 9. 803,
and (in a parenthesis, as here) in 12. 206.

668. suspicit : literally and figuratively. Musaeus towers over
his surrounding admirers, a lively realistic detail: cf. 8. 161 ff.
(Evander reminiscing) 'mirabarque duces Teucros, mirabar
et ipsum / Laomedontiaden; sed cunctis altior ibat / An-
chises.' The semi-confidential parenthesis is designed to vary
the narrative tone.

669. The Sibyl (cf. 398, note) probably did not need guidance,
but the request is a natural courtesy towards the sublime
Musaeus; cf. Ar. *Ran.* 431 ff., where Dionysus asks artlessly
of the Mystae ἔχοιτ' ἂν οὖν φράσαι νῷν / Πλούτων ὅπου 'νθάδ' οἰκεῖ; /
ξένω γάρ ἐσμεν ἀρτίως ἀφιγμένω: Norden infers that such an in-
quiry for direction was a *Katabasis*-motif.

felices animae, tuque : cf. 194 ff. 'este duces . . . tuque', 8. 71 f. 'Nymphae, Laurentes Nymphae . . . tuque': an echo in Sen. *dial.* 6. 25. 1 'integer ille . . . fugit et totus excessit paulumque supra nos commoratus, dum expurgatur et inhaerentia uitia situmque omnem mortalis aeui excutit, deinde ad excelsa sublatus inter felices currit animas.'

670. quae regio . . . quis . . . locus : cf. 1. 459 f. '"quis iam locus," inquit, "Achate, / quae regio in terris nostri non plena laboris?"' The association goes back to early Latin, and suggests the use of synonymous pairs of words in legal and sacral style; see H. Haffter, *Untersuchungen zur altlateinischen Dichtersprache* (Berlin, 1934), 81 (I owe the reference to Mr. T. E. V. Pearce): cf. Plaut. *Pseud.* 595 'hi loci sunt atque hae regiones', *Rud.* 227 'haec loca atque hae regiones', Lucil. 189 M 'loco . . . ac regione', Lucr. 2. 534, 4. 786 'regione locoque'; in a *deuotio* quoted by Macrob. *Sat.* 3. 9. 10 'in his locis regionibusque' occurs among other synonymous pairs of words.

illius ergo : 'on his account', ἐκείνου ἕνεκα. This prepositional use of *ergo* (always following its substantive) is an archaism, adding solemnity to the Sibyl's tone: so Lucr. 3. 78 'statuarum et nominis ergo', 5. 1246 'formidinis ergo'. It belongs to the language of early laws and formulae: so *funeris ergo* in a law of the Twelve Tables (Cic. *de leg.* 2. 59), *eius rei ergo, eiusdem rei ergo*, Cato, *agr.* 132. 1, 134. 3 (in prayers); Livy has it in ritual contexts, 1. 18. 6 (*honoris ergo*), 37. 47. 4 (*uictoriae naualis ergo*); Silius revived it, 6. 134 (*uirtutisque ergo*), in a speech by an aged man. See Wölfflin, *ALL* i, 175 f.

671. tranauimus : cf. *innare*, 134. Had they crossed any others of the Underworld rivers apart from Styx? The Sibyl does not speak again in the Book: her part as guide is over.

672. paucis : sc. *uerbis*; so 4. 116, 10. 16, 12. 71; Plaut. *Aul.* 1 'ne quis miretur qui sim, paucis eloquar'.

674. riparumque . . . riuis : 'cushioning banks and meadows freshened by streams'. *Torus* is used of anything that swells or undulates; here of the gentle pillowing formation of the *ripae* that make them comfortable. For the general picture cf. Lucian, *Ver. Hist.*. 2. 14 (of the Elysian Fields) λειμὼν δέ ἐστι κάλλιστος καὶ περὶ αὐτὸν ὕλη παντοία, πυκνή, ἐπισκιάζουσα τοὺς κατακειμένους, καὶ στρωμνὴ μὲν ἐκ τῶν ἀνθέων ὑποβέβληται.

675. si . . . uoluntas : cf. Lucr. 3. 46 'si fert ita forte uoluntas'; *fert* implies the trend or inclination of the mind, from the idea of a road bearing in some direction (cf. 295): so Ovid, *Met.* 1. 1 f. 'in noua fert animus mutatas dicere formas / corpora'.

676. hoc . . . iugum : he points (*hoc*) to the hill above them,

which they must climb over to see their path below: the
picture suggests an Alpine meadow high above a valley. For
superare, 'surmount', cf. 2. 302 f. 'summi fastigia tecti /
ascensu supero', 11. 513 f. 'ipse ardua montis / per deserta
iugo superans aduentat ad urbem'.

facili ... sistam : 'I shall soon set you on a comfortable
path'. Musaeus speaks with the courtesy and simplicity due
to strangers; cf. 1. 401 'perge modo et, qua te ducit uia,
derige gressum'.

677. ante ... gressum : he walks in front, showing the way; cf.
2. 753 'qua gressum extuleram', 11. 99 'gressumque in
castra ferebat'.

nitentis : the fields in the valley below have the same
luminosity as the *loci laeti* where they are now. But they also
have the sheen of good, healthy ground (*G.* 1. 153 'nitentia
culta').

678. dehinc : monosyllabic, by synizesis (so 1. 131, 256, 9. 480):
this occurs sometimes in Comedy, presumably reflecting
ordinary pronunciation; but the iambic scansion is more
common.

summa cacumina : rather grandiose; but it helps to sug-
gest contour. Norden notes that this viewing from a height
is a frequent motif in apocalyptic writings: cf. Cic. *Rep.* 6. 11
(Scipio's dream) 'ostendebat ... Karthaginem de excelso et
pleno stellarum illustri et claro quodam loco'; Plato, *Rp.*
616B ἀφικνεῖσθαι ... ὅθεν καθορᾶν ἄνωθεν διὰ παντὸς τοῦ οὐρανοῦ καὶ γῆς
τεταμένον φῶς εὐθύ, οἷον κίονα; Revelation 21. 10 ἀπήνεγκέ με ἐν
Πνεύματι ἐπ' ὄρος μέγα καὶ ὑψηλόν, καὶ ἔδειξέ μοι τὴν πόλιν τὴν ἁγίαν;
so of Christ's tempting, Matthew 4. 8 πάλιν παραλαμβάνει αὐτὸν
ὁ διάβολος εἰς ὄρος ὑψηλὸν λίαν, καὶ δείκνυσιν αὐτῷ πάσας τὰς βασιλείας
τοῦ κόσμου.

679–702. *Anchises happened just then to be reviewing the spirits
destined for rebirth in the world above, his posterity to come.
He greets Aeneas with emotion and love; Aeneas tries to embrace
him, but the ghostly wraith eludes his grasp.*

Virgil's art makes Aeneas' meeting with his father seem
almost casual: the son goes down the hill into the valley, and
there Anchises is. The whole scene is worlds away from its
prototype, Odysseus' meeting with his mother's ghost (*Od.*
11. 152 ff.). Homer shows an Odysseus who does not know
that his mother has died; the mother is surprised to see her
son there, and cannot conjecture how he has come; their
conversation is domestic, and concerned with the past alone.
In Virgil, the meeting with Anchises is the whole reason for

Aeneas' journey; Anchises has always known that he would
come; the encounter is the setting for future hope and future
greatness, with its hint—no more as yet—of the great doc-
trine of rebirth (680). The passage does not have the homely
pathos of Homer, which is even stronger in *Od*. 24. 244 ff.,
where Odysseus first meets his living father in Ithaca: it has
its own emotion, but its function is to be the prelude to an
apocalypse.

679. at pater Anchises : *at* begins a new 'chapter', a very fre-
quent Virgilian use (e.g. 4. 1, 296, 393, 504). Anchises is
termed *pater* here not as Aeneas' father (Aeneas has not
been specifically named), but as marking his responsibilities
and the respect that they ensured (see on 2. 2; cf. 5. 700,
8. 28); it is an Ennian usage (*Ann*. 54, of the Tiber; *Ann*. 117,
of Quirinus).

conualle : in the *Aeneid* only here and in 139; also, *G*. 2.
186, 488, 3. 276: other poets too use the word with some
caution. The Virgilian passages all seem to emphasize depth.

680. superumque ad lumen : 'to the light of the upper world';
cf. Ennius, *Ann*. 102 'cum superum lumen nox intempesta
teneret', Lucr. 6. 856 'cum superum lumen tanto feruore
fruatur' (of the Sun).

681. lustrabat . . . recolens : 'was passing in review with earnest
thought'. For *lustrare* see on 231; here the sense of slow,
careful movement is uppermost, but in this context it is a
highly allusive and emotive word, suggesting to a Roman
reader the quinquennial *lustratio* of the people, held by the
censors (cf. *recensebat*, 682). Anchises is like a Roman censor,
making an official list, but a list of ghosts, destined to live
again.

recolens : going over in his mind; cf. Cat. 63. 45 'ipse
pectore Attis sua facta recoluit', Ovid, *H*. 5. 113 'hoc tua
(nam recolo) quondam germana canebat'.

682. forte : seemingly accidental, but such coincidence cannot
be explained by 'accident': cf. 186, note; 1. 362 (ships
'happen' to be available just when Dido needs them), 8. 102
(Evander 'happens' to be holding a ritual festival in honour
of Hercules just when Aeneas arrives).

recensebat : cf. *G*. 4. 436 'consedit scopulo medius, nu-
merumque recenset' (Proteus making a tally of his seal-
flock). Anchises was holding a roll-call of his 'family';
suorum is amplified in *caros nepotes*, and this in turn is ex-
tended in *fataque . . . manusque*; the notion of counting
merges into a more general idea of a survey.

683. uirum : for *eorum*. The pairs of alliterative nouns frame it
with striking effect (cf. 15, 857); and there is noteworthy

assonance in *uirum, aduersum* (684), with *numerum* above, all in the same position in the line.

moresque manusque : 'their ways and works'; *manus* here of deeds in general (often of artists' or craftsmen's 'handi-work', cf. 1. 455).

685. alacris : masculine nominative, as in 5. 380 (but *alacer*, 10. 729, 12. 337), Ennius, *Sc.* 127, Ter. *Eun.* 304; so *acris* (Ennius, *Ann.* 369), *celebris* (Tac. *Ann.* 2. 88, 14. 19), *equestris* (Livy 27. 1. 11).

tetendit : the repetition from *tendentem* (684), with change of meaning, is a noticeable feature of Virgil's style. Conington thought it 'carelessness'; but both Greek and Latin authors' taste in this matter differed from the modern attitude, and they differed among themselves, each having his own prac-tice: 'Horace was as sensitive to iteration as any modern . . . Virgil was less sensitive, Ovid much less; Lucan was almost insensible' (Housman, *Lucan*, p. xxxiii). With this example cf. 1. 83, 85 (*ruunt*), 5. 780, 781 (*pectore, pectus*), 7. 9, 13 (*lumine, lumina*): see on 2. 505, with bibliographical refer-ences.

686. effusaeque genis : sc. *sunt*; *genis* = 'eyes' (more pre-cisely the eyelids; 'palpebris', Servius), as in 5. 173 'nec lacrimis caruere genae'; so Ennius, *Ann.* 532 'pandite sulti genas et corde relinquite somnum', Ovid, *ars* 2. 70 'nec patriae lacrimas continuere genae', etc.: sometimes it is difficult to decide on 'eye' or 'cheek' for the meaning, e.g. Stat. *S.* 2. 7. 133 f. 'cedat luctus atrox genisque manent / iam dulces lacrimae' (cf. A. Klotz, *ALL* xv, 411 f.).

687. tandem : Anchises had been waiting so long (but he took Aeneas' coming for granted); Servius comments 'hoc ad adfectum pertinet desiderantis': contrast *Od.* 16. 23 f. (Eumaeus speaking) ἦλθες, Τηλέμαχε, γλυκερὸν φάος· οὔ σ' ἔτ' ἐγώ γε / ὄψεσθαι ἐφάμην.

tuaque . . . parenti : 'and has the love that a father looked for brought you safely over the harsh path?' *Pius Aeneas* has reached his appointed goal; *parenti* is primarily specific, of Anchises himself, but *pietas* is the natural due of any father from any son.

exspectata : here and in 2. 282 f. 'quibus Hector ab oris / exspectate uenis?' Virgil uses the language of ordinary day-to-day experience: cf. Plaut. *Most.* 440 f. 'triennio post Aegypto aduenio domum; / credo, exspectatus ueniam familiaribus', Cic. *ad fam.* 4. 10. 1 'cura igitur ut quam pri-mum uenias; uenies enim, mihi crede, exspectatus'; Menan-der, *Mis.* 214 f. (OCT) ἔχω σε, τέκνον—ὦ ποθούμενος φανείς, / ὁρῶ σ' ὃν οὐκ ἂν ᾠόμην ἰδεῖν ἔτι.

688. ora : for the repetition (with different meaning) from *ore* (686) see on 685.

689. notas . . . uoces : for the pathetic *notas* cf. 499. So 1. 408 f. 'cur dextrae iungere dextram / non datur ac ueras audire et reddere uoces?' (Aeneas to his mother); Cat. 64. 166 (of the winds) 'nec missas audire queunt nec reddere uoces'.

690. 'This is what I kept working out in my mind, this is what I kept thinking would happen'. *Ducebam* suggests a calculation; *rebar* seems to have been thought old-fashioned by Cicero (*de or.* 3. 153).

691. dinumerans : as if crossing off days on a calendar; cf. Ovid, *Met.* 11. 573 f. 'Aeolis interea tantorum ignara malorum / dinumerat noctes'.

692. An echo of Cat. 101. 1 (see on 335); Norden notes Pacuvius 319 R 'quam te post multis tueor tempestatibus', from the *Teucer*, a play that Virgil clearly knew (see on 1. 87). *Per* must be taken with *terras* as well as with *aequora*; cf. 7. 296 f. 'medias acies mediosque per ignis / inuenere uiam': similarly 416 'informi limo glaucaque exponit in ulua', Hor. *C.* 3. 25. 2 'quae nemora aut quos agor in specus . . .?', *Epp.* 2. 1. 24 f. 'foedera regum / uel Gabiis uel cum rigidis aequata Sabinis', Stat. *Th.* 8. 384 'iamque hos clipeum, iam uertit ad illos'; see Leo, *Ausg. Kl. Schriften* i, 117 f.

693. iactatum : 'buffeted'; Virgil likes this verb in connexion with Trojan sufferings (see on 1. 3).

694. ne . . . nocerent : revealing; *regna* shows that Anchises was not thinking simply of *pericula* as hazards of voyaging, but of the even greater danger from Dido, whose temptation Aeneas, with all his *pietas*, had so nearly failed to overcome. The words show Anchises' recognition that his son had ordinary human weaknesses; and they reveal the father's anxious love, watching Aeneas from the spirit-world.

695. As Anchises thought always of his son, so Aeneas constantly thought of his father. The explicit reference is to the ghostly instructions of Anchises in 5. 731 ff., but that he had appeared in other visions also is suggested by 4. 351 ff. (and cf. 116, note).

    tristis imago : cf. 4. 353 'admonet in somnis et turbida terret imago'.

696. haec limina : 'this dwelling', Elysium: cf. 5. 733 ff. 'non me impia namque / Tartara habent, tristes umbrae, sed amoena piorum / concilia Elysiumque colo'. For the accusative without preposition see on 345; cf. 1. 553 f. 'si datur Italiam sociis et rege recepto / tendere'. The use of *adigere* with an infinitive (again, 7. 113) is not recorded before Virgil.

697. stant . . . classes : a rather odd way for Aeneas to say that he has safely passed all perils and by reaching Cumae has made his way to the Underworld. For *sal* of the sea cf. Ennius, *Ann.* 52, 385, Lucr. 4. 438 'quaecumque supra rorem salis edita pars est'; the ships are in fact beached (cf. 4), not anchored off-shore.

    da iungere dextram : cf. 1. 408 f. 'cur dextrae iungere dextram / non datur . . .?' (Aeneas to his mother): in both passages Aeneas' longing and loneliness are plain.

698. teque . . . nostro : yet Anchises' hands were stretched towards him (685); he may not touch the ghost. The words echo Aeneas' plea to Dido (465) 'siste gradum teque aspectu ne subtrahe nostro'.

699. Cf. 9. 250 f. 'sic memorans umeros dextrasque tenebat / amborum et uultum lacrimis atque ora rigabat' (Aletes to Nisus and Euryalus).

700 ff. These lines are repeated from 2. 792 ff., where the apparition of Creusa has come to comfort Aeneas; but there his wife vanishes, here his father stays with him. The intricate alliteration gives a marvellous effect of sound and beauty (especially 702). Virgil looks back to *Od.* 11. 206 ff. (Odysseus meeting his mother's ghost) τρὶς μὲν ἐφορμήθην, ἑλέειν τέ με θυμὸς ἀνώγει, / τρὶς δέ μοι ἐκ χειρῶν σκιῇ εἴκελον ἢ καὶ ὀνείρῳ / ἔπτατ'· ἐμοὶ δ' ἄχος ὀξὺ γενέσκετο κηρόθι μᾶλλον.

702. 'Just like weightless winds, very like winging sleep'. So the vision of Anchises vanishes, 5. 740 'tenuis fugit ceu fumus in auras'; so Eurydice drifts away from Orpheus, *G.* 4. 499 f. 'ceu fumus in auras / commixtus tenuis, fugit diuersa'; so the phantom of Patroclus left Achilles ἠΰτε καπνός (*Il.* 23. 100).

703–23. *Aeneas sees a vast multitude of souls on the banks of a river; Anchises tells him that they are those destined for rebirth, drinking forgetfulness from Lethe. Aeneas is puzzled, and Anchises promises to unfold the mystery.*

    After the hint given in 680, Virgil leads up to the theme of reincarnation in a gentle passage of preparation. It is beautifully done: the busy, purposeful throng, with a decorative simile; the sleepy river; the natural questioning, bringing as naturally the ultimate revelation to follow.

703. interea : 'and now'; a transition-formula to a fresh scene or part of a scene (cf. 212).

    in ualle reducta : again, 8. 609; Hor. *C.* 1. 17. 17 (conventional, but appropriate; see Nisbet–Hubbard), *Epod.* 2. 11. Presumably this *uallis* is a deep branch-valley of the *conuallis* described in 679.

704. et . . . siluae : explanatory of the *nemus*, 'whispering woodland brakes'. There is a variant *siluis*, which Conington preferred; cf. 3. 442 'Auerna sonantia siluis', where *siluis* makes sense, but here it is tautological with *uirgulta*.

705. Lethaeumque . . . amnem : Virgil does not use *Lethe*, only this type of periphrasis (cf. 714, 749); so Cat. 65. 5 'Lethaeo gurgite'.

domos placidas : these 'quiet dwellings' are a particular part of the Elysian Fields; *placidas* perhaps hints at the function of Lethe. The arrangement of the line is noteworthy, with *Lethaeum . . . amnem* enclosing the rest, and *domos placidas* brought into prominence by its position.

praenatat : 'drifts past', lazily; the verb is not recorded before Virgil. Servius objects 'non natant aquae, sed nos in ipsis natamus', excusing Virgil with Ennius' *fluctusque natantes* (*Ann.* 596): cf. *campi natantes* of the sea, *G.* 3. 198; Lucr. 5. 488, 6. 1142.

706. hunc circum : this picks up the little ἔκφρασις in the usual way; the river is the significant feature, so it is substituted for a more general *hic*.

gentes populique : 'nations and communities'; the relationship can be seen from 10. 202 'gens illi triplex, populi sub gente quaterni': so 7. 236 ff. 'multi nos populi, multae . . . / et petiere sibi et uoluere adiungere gentes'. For a study of expressions for 'people' see F. Cramer, *ALL* vi, 341 ff.

707 ff. The simile presents a scene of light and colour and excitement, as this gathering of souls is compared to bees in a flowery meadow on a fine summer day, busy with their pursuits and humming cheerfully. It has an ancestry: (*a*) *Il.* 2. 87 ff. (of the Greeks hurrying to the Council of the kings) ἠΰτε ἔθνεα εἶσι μελισσάων ἀδινάων, | πέτρης ἐκ γλαφυρῆς αἰεὶ νέον ἐρχομενάων· | βοτρυδὸν δὲ πέτονται ἐπ' ἄνθεσιν εἰαρινοῖσιν; (*b*) Apoll. Rhod. 1. 879 ff. (of the Lemnian women surrounding the Argonauts on their departure) ὡς δ' ὅτε λείρια καλὰ περιβρομέουσι μέλισσαι | πέτρης ἐκχύμεναι σιμβληΐδος, ἀμφὶ δὲ λειμών | ἐρσήεις γάνυται, ταὶ δὲ γλυκὺν ἄλλοτε ἄλλον | καρπὸν ἀμέργουσιν πεποτημέναι: Virgil is closer to Apollonius than to Homer, and his application of the simile is more sensitive than that of either poet.

Norden notes Soph. fr. 879 P βομβεῖ δὲ νεκρῶν σμῆνος ἔρχεταί τ' ἄνω, preserved by Porphyrius, *de antr. nymph.* 18, with the comment that οἱ παλαιοί called souls awaiting birth 'bees', μέλισσαι: see Pearson ad loc.; A. B. Cook, *JHS* xv (1895), 19, *Zeus* i, 469 n. 7 (souls as bees on gems). If Virgil knew such a tradition (and his obviously special interest in bees suggests that he probably did), his choice of simile here takes on particular significance.

218 COMMENTARY

707. ac ueluti : as in 2. 626 ff., 4. 402 ff., there is no pick-up
with *sic* or *haud aliter*, and an ellipse or compression of
thought must be assumed (*ac ueluti* = 'and the scene was
like what happens . . .'). Some commentators make the
simile end at *funduntur* (709), with *strepit . . . campus* as the
main statement or 'apodosis': but the structure of the two
parallel passages mentioned gives no support to this, and the
whole run of the lines points to *strepit . . . campus* being
part of the simile, a summarizing picture added in asyn-
deton, exactly as in 4. 407 'opere omnis semita feruet' is
added at the end of the simile introduced by *ac uelut*.

aestate serena : a clear summer day; so *G.* 1. 340 'uere
sereno', of bright spring weather; cf. *G.* 4. 58 f. 'ubi iam
emissum caueis ad sidera caeli / nare per aestatem liquidam
suspexeris agmen', of a swarm of bees 'floating across a clear
summer sky'.

708. uariis : 'gay', with many colours; cf. 4. 202 'uariis
florentia limina sertis', *E.* 9. 40 f. 'uarios hic flumina circum /
fundit humus flores', Cat. 61. 87 ff. 'talis in uario solet / diuitis
domini hortulo / stare flos hyacinthinus'. Ovid has *uarius* of
a mottled snake (*Met.* 4. 619), Petronius (45. 1) of a striped
pig.

709. lilia : particularizing the flowers; cf. Apoll. Rhod. 1. 879.

710. horrescit : Aeneas is startled with surprise ('cum stupore
miratur', Ti. Donatus); an unusual use of the verb, but cf.
Pacuvius, fr. 294 R, where it seems to mean a thrill of joy
(the text is uncertain), *Pan. Lat.* 4 (10). 29. 5 'cuius rei cum
imaginem cepi, dicturus horresco', where the context implies
admiration.

711. porro : 'over there', an old-fashioned usage; cf. Plaut.
Rud. 1034 'ubi tu hic habitas?—porro illic longe usque in
campis ultimis'; in a different local sense ('further on'), Pliny,
Epp. 5. 6. 18 'campi deinde porro multaque alia prata'. The
double question (*quae sint . . . quiue uiri*) is characteristically
Virgilian.

713. This is the first knowledge of rebirth that is given to
Aeneas; the allusion in 680 is an anticipation by the poet.

715. securos latices : 'waters of unmindfulness', explained in
longa obliuia; Lethe gives *securitas*, freedom from the cares
of their finished life. It is an arresting and beautiful phrase;
cf. Plato, *Rp.* 621A, where the souls camp at evening παρὰ
τὸν Ἀμέλητα ποταμόν. The line has a notably quiet, grave move-
ment, helped in its effect by the subtle arrangement of the
vowel-sounds.

obliuia : a poetic 'plural only' noun in classical Latin (un-
less an ablative singular *obliuio* is sound, Tac. *H.* 4. 9. 2),

a substitute for *obliuio* from Lucretius onwards: in Silver Latin, with the extended treatment of final *-o* as short (see on 2. 735), the noun *obliuiŏ* became possible in hexameters (e.g. Lucan 10. 403, Stat. *S.* 1. 4. 57). Silius has a take-over from Virgil, 13. 552 ff. 'hic turba piorum / . . . Lethaeos potat latices, obliuia mentis', 13. 851 f. 'animas tibi, quae potant obliuia, paucas / in fine enumerasse paro'; cf. Lucan 3. 29 f. 'me non Lethaeae, coniunx, obliuia ripae / immemorem fecere tui' (the ghost of Iulia, speaking to Pompey).

716 ff. After anticipating (713 ff.) the theory of reincarnation that begins in 724, Anchises now anticipates the Roman 'pageant' that begins in 756. He first points to all the souls on the banks of Lethe (*has*), then more precisely points to his own descendants (*hanc prolem*) among them. *Iampridem* is common to both clauses; some editors prefer to put a comma after *coram* instead of after *iampridem*, which is less satisfactory because it blurs the anaphora of *has . . . hanc*.

718. 'That you may rejoice all the more, as I do, now that you have found Italy': for *mecum* cf. 1. 281 f. 'consilia in melius referet, mecumque fouebit / Romanos'. Anchises wishes Aeneas to share his pride in the Italian stock, soon to be revealed.

719. o pater : this is enough to show who is speaking ('noua breuitas', Servius).

anne : less common than *an* in direct questions. In early Latin it regularly has a vowel following, as here and in 864; a consonant follows in Cat. 66. 27, Lucr. 4. 781 (so *G.* 1. 32, 2. 159, where it is correlative with *an*).

putandum est : Lucretian (e.g. 2. 193, 700, 809, etc.); Virgil does not use this gerund form of the verb again, and it is clearly meant to suggest the philosophic manner in anticipation of the tone of 724 ff.

720. sublimis : 'soaring upwards', predicative with *ire*; cf. 1. 415 'ipsa Paphum sublimis abit'.

tarda : 'clogging'; Aeneas (unconsciously) uses a term in keeping with the exposition that follows (731).

721. miseris : cf. *mortalibus aegris*, 2. 268, etc. It is their passion to live again in this world that makes Aeneas call them 'poor things'; a hint at his own sufferings seems to be intended. Norden takes *miseris* as proleptic, perhaps rightly.

dira cupido : cf. 373, Lucr. 3. 59 'honorum caeca cupido', 4. 1090 'tam magis ardescit dira cuppedine pectus'.

722. Cf. Lucr. 6. 245 'expediam, neque te in promissis plura morabor'; *G.* 2. 45 f. 'non hic te carmine ficto / atque per ambages et longa exorsa tenebo': the didactic manner.

723. suscipit : 'takes up', in reply; cf. Varro, *RR* 1. 2. 24

'suscipit Stolo, "tu" inquit "inuides tanto scriptori"',
Quintil. 2. 15. 28 'ille quidem conticescit, sed sermonem
suscipit Polus'.

724–51. *Anchises answers Aeneas by discoursing on the life-
principle of the Universe, a creative Mind of elemental fire,
to which ultimately the soul returns after varying forms and
degrees of purification: a few achieve this refining by remaining
in Elysium, but for most it is necessary to undergo a new birth-
cycle, and it is these whom Aeneas sees gathered on the shore of Lethe.*

Until Aeneas reaches Elysium (637 ff.) the consciousness of
being in a dim Underworld is always present: nothing re-
lieves its oppressive weight; nothing suggests that the spirits
encountered on either bank of Styx are not in their final
home or state, just as the Sibyl makes it clear that the evil
sinners in Tartarus are there for eternity. In Elysium the
darkness has lifted, but it is still a region of an Underworld
where happy spirits seem at the end of their own road to
bliss. When the possibility of reincarnation is first mentioned
(680), no explanation for it is given, and nothing has hinted
at a relationship of soul to body. The after-life, with miseries
or punishments or rewards, appears localized and final.

But now, astonishingly, all is changed and a new prospect
opens. The Underworld spirit-existence, in its various forms,
is replaced by a cosmic system of the origin and progress of
the soul in its connexion with the body; after death it is
gradually purged of the contaminations that have become
ingrained during its bodily imprisonment, and with lapse
of time, depending on individual circumstance, it ascends in
purity to the fiery element that gave it birth.

The passage is a poetic synthesis, blending the Stoic doc-
trine of the *anima mundi* with Platonic and Orphic–Pytha-
gorean teaching of rebirth (for which see Dodds, *The Greeks
and the Irrational*, 149 ff.). Structurally, its purpose is to
make possible the great procession of Romans whom An-
chises prophetically reviews (756 ff.), reassuring Aeneas after
his dismayed questioning, and showing 'Roman History' as
a destined and pre-ordained process. But in the vision that
it presents there is not only no consistency with the Under-
world of myth, but even Elysium is transformed from the
ultimate paradise into a resting-stage on the soul's journey-
ing far beyond it. Anchises ends his survey of future Romans
with the young Marcellus, and then (886 f.) 'sic tota passim
regione uagantur / aëris in campis latis': the Elysium of the
Underworld has become fused in impalpable atmosphere,
from which Aeneas departs through the Ivory Gate of Sleep

—a region partly still localized, partly a cosmological concept. Virgil, through Anchises' exposition, has deliberately questioned, even perhaps rejected, the whole conception of that world of the dead through which Aeneas has been led by the Sibyl, making the very notion of a κατάβασις seem incongruous. Here, in this speech of such visionary beauty and earnest solemnity, it is as if the poet were 'thinking aloud', giving expression to his inmost beliefs. The manner is constantly and pointedly Lucretian; the matter would have excited Lucretius' disdain (cf. Lucr. 3. 772 ff.).

See Norden, pp. 16 ff.: for a discussion from many varying standpoints see M. R. Arundel, *Proc. Virg. Soc.* iii (1963–4), 27 ff.; Bailey, *Religion in Virgil*, 274 ff.; Camps, op. cit. 90 ff., and *Proc. Virg. Soc.* vii (1967–8), 24 ff.; Cumont, *Lux Perpetua*, 72 f., 199 ff., 212 f.; Dieterich, op. cit. 153 ff.; Guthrie, *Orpheus and Greek Religion*, 186; Klingner, *Virgil* (Zürich, 1967), 490 f.; Nettleship, *Lectures and Essays* (Oxford, 1885), 135 ff.; F. Norwood, *CP* xlix (1954), 15 ff.; Otis, op. cit. 300 f.; H. W. Prescot, *The Development of Virgil's Art* (New York, 1963), 403 f.; F. Solmsen, *Proc. Am. Philos. Soc.* cxii (1968), 8 ff., and *CP* lxvii (1972), 31 ff.; R. Speaight, *A Modern Virgilian* (Virgil Society Lecture, 1958, a Memorial to Ronald Knox), 13 f.; R. D. Williams, *Greece & Rome* n.s. xi (1964), 56 ff.

724. **principio** : a Lucretian 'signature' for the philosophic exposition; cf. *G.* 2. 9, 4. 8, Cic. fr. 11. 1 ff. Tr. 'principio aetherio flammatus Iuppiter igni / uertitur et totum conlustrat lumine mundum, / menteque diuina caelum terrasque petessit'. The stages of the argument (*inde*, 728; *hinc*, 733; *non tamen*, 736; *ergo*, 739) also suggest Lucretius, though without the leisurely Lucretian straggle.

terras : the v.l. *terram* (so Ribbeck, Sabbadini) has good support also; but cf. 1. 58 'maria ac terras caelumque profundum', 4. 269, 7. 571, Lucr. 5. 693, Cic. l.c. above.

camposque liquentis : a Lucretian type of periphrasis (see on *praenatat*, 705); for the metaphor cf. 8. 695 'arua . . . Neptunia', Cic. fr. 34. 129 Tr. 'Neptunia prata'.

725. **globum lunae** : so Lucr. 5. 68 f. 'terram caelum mare sidera solem / lunaique globum'; Claudian 7. 163 f. 'liquido signauit tramite nubes / ingrediturque globum lunae' (of Theodosius on his way to heaven).

Titaniaque astra : grand Epic for the Sun, child of the Titan Hyperion (Hesiod, *Th.* 374), himself termed *Titan* (4. 119; Ovid, *Met.* 1. 10, etc.; so the Moon is *Titanis*, Stat. *Th.* 1. 337). The unexpected plural makes possible the sonorous and allusive epithet (cf. Ovid, *Met.* 14. 172

'caelumque et sidera solis'). But some interpret as 'sun and stars' (see M. R. Arundel, l.c. 28); Nettleship suggests 'stars shining like the sun', with their own light.

726. spiritus . . . alit: the Stoic principle of the *anima mundi*, set out in *G.* 4. 219 ff. (of the mysterious qualities of bees):

> his quidam signis atque haec exempla secuti
> esse apibus partem diuinae mentis et haustus
> aetherios dixere; deum namque ire per omnis
> terrasque tractusque maris caelumque profundum;
> hinc pecudes, armenta, uiros, genus omne ferarum,
> quemque sibi tenuis nascentem arcessere uitas;
> scilicet huc reddi deinde ac resoluta referri
> omnia, nec morti esse locum, sed uiua uolare
> sideris in numerum atque alto succedere caelo.

The Stoics held that the universe is material, corporeal, activated and made creative by a pervading fiery ether, its *anima*, from which the human soul has been detached: at the death of the mortal body, the soul returns to its original element of fire. In *G.* 4. 221 this activating *anima* is specifically termed *deus*; cf. Plato, *Tim.* 30B, where the κόσμος is said to be ζῷον ἔμψυχον ἔννουν τε τῇ ἀληθείᾳ διὰ τὴν τοῦ θεοῦ γενέσθαι πρόνοιαν. See Cumont, op. cit. 113 ff.

spiritus: πνεῦμα; cf. Cic. *de nat. deor.* 2. 19 'haec ita fieri omnibus inter se concinentibus mundi partibus profecto non posset, nisi ea uno diuino et continuato spiritu continerentur': the *spiritus* is material, 'the warm air or ether which penetrates and gives life to all things and connects them together in one organic whole; just as man's body is unified by the living soul, which is also material' (Mayor ad loc.). See Arundel, l.c. 28 f.; Richter on *G.* 4, l.c.; J. M. Rist, *Stoic Philosophy*, 86 ff.

alit: cf. Cic. *de nat. deor.* 2. 41 'ille [sc. *ignis*]. corporeus uitalis et salutaris omnia conseruat, alit, auget, sustinet sensuque afficit'; Sen. *NQ* 6. 16. 1 'non esse terram sine spiritu palam est: non tantum illo dico, quo se tenet ac partes sui iungit, qui inest etiam saxis mortuisque corporibus, sed illo dico uitali et uegeto et alente omnia'.

infusa per artus: a Lucretian line-ending, e.g. 3. 283 'inter se uigeant commixta per artus', 3. 393 'semina corporibus nostris immixta per artus'. Here *artus* means the separate parts of the *corpus* of the Universe: cf. Posidonius, fr. 21 E–K (Diog. Laert. 7. 138) τὸν δὴ κόσμον διοικεῖσθαι κατὰ νοῦν καὶ πρόνοιαν . . . εἰς ἅπαν αὐτοῦ μέρος διήκοντος τοῦ νοῦ, καθάπερ ἐφ' ἡμῶν ψυχῆς; fr. 100 E–K θεός ἐστι πνεῦμα νοερὸν διῆκον δι' ἁπάσης οὐσίας (I owe these references to Mr. D. A. Russell).

727. 'Mind activates the whole mass, commingling with the vast frame': *mens* (νοῦς) is synonymous with the Stoic *spiritus*, and the clause *totamque . . . miscet* amplifies *spiritus intus alit*.

agitat : cf. Cic. *de nat. deor.* 2. 31 'absurdum est dicere . . . mundum esse sine sensu, qui . . . acerrimo et mobilissimo ardore teneatur, praesertim cum is ardor, qui est mundi, non agitatus ab alio neque externo pulsu sed per se ipse ac sua sponte moueatur'; Diog. Laert. 7. 157 (of Zeno) πνεῦμα ἔνθερμον εἶναι τὴν ψυχήν· τούτῳ γὰρ ἡμᾶς εἶναι ἐμπνόους καὶ ὑπὸ τούτου κινεῖσθαι.

magno . . . miscet : in procreation; cf. *G.* 2. 325 ff. 'tum pater omnipotens fecundis imbribus Aether / coniugis in gremium laetae descendit, et omnis / magnus alit magno commixtus corpore fetus' (of springtime).

728. inde . . . genus : cf. 1. 742 f. (Iopas' song) 'hic canit errantem lunam solisque labores, / unde hominum genus et pecudes'.

uolantum : cf. Lucr. 2. 1082 f. 'mutas / squamigerum pecudes et corpora cuncta uolantum'; Ennius, *Ann.* 81 'seruat genus altiuolantum' (of Romulus).

729. 'And all the curious creatures that the sea bears beneath its gleaming surface'; *monstra* need not imply size, only what is strange or uncanny (so *monstrum* of a gadfly, *G.* 3. 152).

marmoreo : cf. *Il.* 14. 273 ἅλα μαρμαρέην; *marmor* of the sea occurs in Ennius, *Ann.* 384, but Virgil seems to have first applied the epithet.

730. igneus : the nature of the *spiritus* or *mens* is now made explicit: it is the pure elemental fire (cf. 747), the πνεῦμα νοερὸν καὶ πυρῶδες of Posidonius (fr. 101 E–K).

ollis : the extreme archaism (see on 321) deepens the solemn tone; probably it is pronominal, not adjectival with *seminibus* below; 'of fire is their force, heavenly the seeds' lifespring'. *Caelestis origo* defines the nature of the *igneus uigor*.

731. seminibus : the particles of the divine fire; cf. Varro, *LL* 5. 59 'animalium semen ignis is qui anima ac mens' (from Zeno, = fr. 126 SVF).

quantum . . . tardant : 'as far as the harming body does not clog them'. There is a compression of thought in *quantum non*; the clause 'does not strictly cohere with what precedes, as the influence of the body would not affect the principle of the soul, but only the extent of its operation, which is evidently Virgil's real meaning' (Conington): the *igneus uigor* is present, but it cannot function properly because of the weaknesses of the body. Note that Virgil has quietly slipped into an exposition of the *hominum genus* only.

732. hebetant : the earthly limbs 'blunt' the fire's sharpness. The verb is not recorded before Virgil; cf. 2. 604 ff. 'omnem, quae nunc obducta tuenti / mortalis hebetat uisus tibi et umida circum / caligat, nubem eripiam'. *Terreni* and *moribunda* explain *noxia* above; cf. Lucr. 2. 1114 f. 'terreno corpore terra / crescit', 3. 128 f. 'est igitur calor ac uentus uitalis in ipso / corpore qui nobis moribundos deserit artus'.

733. hinc : i.e. from the harmful contagion of the body, which brings fears and desires, sorrow and joy (cf. the argument in Plato, *Phaedo* 66). Servius attributes this quadripartite classification of emotions to 'Varro et omnes philosophi': see Cic. *Tusc.* 3. 24, 4. 11; Hor. *Epp.* 1. 6. 12 'gaudeat an doleat, cupiat metuatue, quid ad rem?'; Plato, *Phaedo* 83B ἡ τοῦ ὡς ἀληθῶς φιλοσόφου ψυχὴ οὕτως ἀπέχεται τῶν ἡδονῶν τε καὶ ἐπιθυμιῶν καὶ λυπῶν καὶ φόβων, καθ᾽ ὅσον δύναται.

The line has an interesting rhythm: the dominant break is at the 'weak' caesura in the third foot, with the fourth-foot caesura hardly noticeable since *dolent gaudentque* are so closely connected (cf. 117, note); there is an unusually late sense-break in the fifth foot; and the arrangement of the pairs of verbs combines with the rhythm to suggest a swaying effect, as if of instability.

auras : the heavenly air from which they have sprung: 'obliuiscuntur naturae suae, quam *auras* uocauit' (Servius).

734. dispiciunt : 'descry'; cf. Lucr. 2. 741 f. 'caecigeni, solis qui lumina numquam / dispexere'.

clausae . . . caeco : as if *animae* had preceded. Orphic terminology: the soul is immured in the dark prison-house of the body. Plato, discussing the word σῶμα (*Crat.* 400C), first gives two anonymous etymologies that connect it with σῆμα, meaning either the 'tomb' of the soul, buried in the body, or a 'sign' made by the soul communicating through the body (διότι αὖ τούτῳ σημαίνει ἃ ἂν σημαίνῃ ἡ ψυχή). But his own view is that the name σῶμα is due to οἱ ἀμφὶ Ὀρφέα, who connect it with σῴζειν, holding that the soul is doing some kind of penance, and that the body is an enveloping container, keeping it under guard, like a prison (τοῦτον δὲ περίβολον ἔχειν, ἵνα σῴζηται, δεσμωτηρίου εἰκόνα) until it has paid what it owes; cf. *Grg.* 493A, *Phaedo* 82E, *Phaedr.* 250C ἀσήμαντοι τούτου ὃ νῦν δὴ σῶμα περιφέροντες ὀνομάζομεν, ὀστρέου τρόπον δεδεσμευμένοι: see Guthrie, op. cit. 156 f.; Linforth, op. cit. 147 f.; Dodds, op. cit. 169 n. 87. For similar language cf. Cic. *de rep.* 6. 15 (Scipio's Dream) 'nisi enim deus is . . . istis te corporis custodiis liberauerit, huc tibi aditus patere non potest', *Tusc.* 1. 75 'hoc et dum erimus in terris erit illi caelesti uitae simile et cum illuc ex his uinclis emissi feremur minus tardabitur cursus animorum'; Sen. *Epp*. 65. 16 'nam corpus hoc animi pondus ac poena est; premente illo urguetur, in uinclis est, nisi accessit philosophia et illum respirare rerum naturae spectaculo iussit et a terrenis ad diuina dimisit'.

735. quin et : 'yes, and even . . .'; this use, for *quin etiam*, begins with Virgil and Horace (HSz, 677); sometimes it simply connects, with no implication of emphasis (7. 750 'quin et Marruuia uenit de gente sacerdos'; see Rothstein on Prop. 2. 34. 93).

 supremo . . . lumine : 'on their last day' (for *lumine* cf. 356); cf. Lucr. 1. 545 f. 'esse immortali primordia corpore debent, / dissolui quo quaeque supremo tempore possint'.

 uita reliquit : cf. Lucr. 5. 63 'cernere cum uideamur eum quem uita reliquit'; Ennius, *Ann*. 149 'postquam lumina sis oculis bonus Ancus reliquit' (quoted at Lucr. 3. 1025).

736. miseris : sc. *animabus*; Anchises picks up Aeneas' *miseris* (721). Virgil now begins to turn to the Pythagorean theory of purgation and transmigration. The alliterative pattern of this group of lines is strikingly subtle.

737. corporeae . . . pestes : cf. Plato, *Phaedo* 81B ἐὰν . . . μεμιασμένη καὶ ἀκάθαρτος τοῦ σώματος ἀπαλλάττηται . . . οὕτω δὴ ἔχουσαν οἴει ψυχὴν αὐτὴν καθ' αὑτὴν εἰλικρινῆ ἀπαλλάξεσθαι; (see M. R. Arundel, l.c. 32 f.).

737 f. penitusque . . . miris : 'but it must be the case that many evils, long set hard, are deep ingrained in them, in strange uncanny ways'. The force of *-que* is adversative; *necesse est* has a Lucretian tone.

738. A strangely haunting line. The idea in *concreta* ('coniuncta et conglutinata', Servius) is restated in *inolescere*: this verb is not recorded before Virgil, and is very rarely used in classical Latin; in *G*. 2. 77 'udoque docent inolescere libro' it is used of a grafted shoot becoming set in an adoptive tree and growing up with it; Silius has it of branches hardening into stone in a stream, 8. 580 f. 'quo gurgite tradunt / durities lapidum mersis inolescere ramis'. On *G*. 2. 77 Servius glosses *inolescere* by συμφύειν; cf. Plato, *Rp*. 609A σχεδὸν πᾶσι σύμφυτον ἑκάστῳ κακόν τε καὶ νόσημα, *Tim*. 42A ὁπότε δὴ σώμασιν ἐμφυτευθεῖεν ἐξ ἀνάγκης . . . πρῶτον μὲν αἴσθησιν ἀναγκαῖον εἴη μίαν πᾶσιν ἐκ βιαίων παθημάτων σύμφυτον γίγνεσθαι.

 modis . . . miris : an epithet of quality with *modis* is an early Latin usage, and seldom occurs later. For a full discussion of the phrase see on 1. 354 'coniugis ora modis attollens pallida miris' (of Sychaeus' ghost); it recurs in 7. 89 (of the visions of Faunus' priest), 10. 822 (of the dying Lausus), *G*. 1. 477 (of the apparitions at Caesar's death), *G*. 4. 309 (of the mysterious 'bougonia'); Lucretius uses it,

1. 123 'quaedam simulacra modis pallentia miris', which
may perhaps be a quotation from Ennius (cf. M. Wigodsky,
op. cit. 73 n. 368). Both poets invest it with a strange, almost
mystical quality in its contexts, but it is unlikely that this
was its original tone: examples from Comedy show that it
was a cliché of ordinary speech for something queer or out
of the way (e.g. Plaut. *Merc.* 225, *Mil.* 539, *Rud.* 593). After
Virgil the phrase disappears from classical poetry.

739 ff. After death the soul must be cleansed of the ingrained
bodily impurities, either by air, or by water, or by fire. St.
Augustine comments (*de ciu. Dei* 21. 13) 'qui hoc opinantur
nullas poenas nisi purgatorias uolunt esse post mortem, ut
quoniam terris superiora sunt elementa, aqua, aer, ignis, ex
aliquo istorum mundetur per expiatorias poenas quod ter-
rena contagione contractum est'. Norden (p. 28) sees traces
of the idea in Empedocles; cf. M. R. Arundel, l.c. 33. See
Cumont, op. cit. 209 ff.

739. exercentur : 'they are plied' with unremitting *poenae*; for
the verb see on 543: the souls are kept 'on the go', as it were.

740. expendunt : cf. 11. 257 f. 'infanda per orbem / supplicia et
scelerum poenas expendimus omnes'.

    inanes : nominative ('in their flimsy state'). But *inanis*
(accusative) is preferable, of the 'unsubstantial winds'; cf.
10. 82 'nebulam et uentos obtendere inanis' (so with *auras*,
7. 593; with *nubila*, *G.* 4. 196): the epithet seems pointless as
applied to the 'animae', and *inanis uentos* is balanced by
gurgite uasto below.

741. suspensae : cf. Plato, *Grg.* 525c, of hardened sinners,
ἀτεχνῶς παραδείγματα ἀνηρτημένους ἐκεῖ ἐν Ἅιδου ἐν τῷ δεσμωτηρίῳ;
Diog. Laert. 8. 21, where Pythagoras is said to have seen the
soul of Homer in the Underworld κρεμαμένην ἀπὸ δένδρου
(Dieterich, op. cit. 129): but in these passages there is no
suggestion of purification, only the idea of punishment.

    aliis : a characteristic switch of construction from *aliae*.

    sub ... uasto : 'under a waste of waters': they need more
than just a dip. *Gurges* need not mean a 'whirlpool'; it is
a 'flood', sometimes quite small (Henry on 1. 118, or 122 in
his numbering).

742. infectum ... scelus : 'the dye of sin is washed out': a vivid
and unusual turn of phrase, for *scelus quo infectae sunt*.
Seneca has an echo, *Epp.* 59. 9 'diu in istis uitiis iacuimus,
elui difficile est; non enim inquinati sumus sed infecti'.

    exuritur : 'is burnt away'; so Silius 13. 871 f. 'perfidiae
Poenus quibus aut Phlegethontis in undis / exuret ductor
scelus...?'; cf. Pliny, *NH* 19. 19 (on asbestos napkins)
'uiuum id uocant [*sc.* linum], ardentesque in focis conuiuiorum

uidimus mappas sordibus exustis splendescentes igni magis
quam possent aquis'. For fire as a purifying element cf.
Ovid, *F*. 4. 785 f. 'omnia purgat edax ignis uitiumque
metallis / excoquit'.

743. quisque suos patimur manis: with this punctuation
(Mynors, 1972; in his 1969 text lines 743-4 are in parenthesis)
the famous words sum up the exposition of the four preceding
lines: see further below. If one single phrase had to be chosen
from the whole *Aeneid* to illustrate the elusiveness of Virgil,
it might well be this.

Servius offers two explanations. The first makes *patimur
manis* a compression of 'supplicia quae sunt apud manes',
i.e. the idea already expressed in *supplicia expendunt* (740);
Servius adds an analogy, 'ut si quis dicat *iudicium patimur* et
significet ea quae in iudicio continentur'. This was early
misinterpreted as an actual equation of *manis* with *supplicia*
(so L. & S., even now): in Stat. *Th*. 8. 84 f. Pluto chokes with
rage at the unauthorized intrusion of the living Amphiaraus
into the Underworld: '"At tibi quos" ¦inquit "Manis, qui
limite praeceps / non licito per inane ruis?"'; the remark-
able aposiopesis (cf. *Aen*. 1. 135) implies simply 'what place
in the world of the *Manes* shall I assign to you, when you
have no business to be here?'; but Lactantius Placidus (sixth
century) comments '*quos inquit Manes* pro poenis posuit. id
est, quos cruciatus patieris?', and then quotes Virgil's
phrase. There seems also the same misinterpretation in
Ausonius, *Ephem*. 3. 55 ff. 'si ... sensus / formido excruciat
tormentaque sera gehennae / anticipat patiturque suos mens
saucia manes'.

Servius regards his second explanation as *uerius*: '*manes*
genios dicit, quos cum uita sortimur'; at birth, he says, we
are allotted two *genii*, one prompting to good, the other to
evil, and after death it is these *genii* whose effect decides
our future state ('quibus adsistentibus ... aut adserimur in
meliorem uitam aut condemnamur in deteriorem; per quos
aut uacationem meremur aut reditum in corpora'). Possibly
Ti. Donatus had something of the same idea in his mind in a
much less elaborate *interpretatio*, 'concinne complexus est
unumquemque talis sentire manis qualis ad inferos uenerit,
si bonus, bonos, sin malus, malos'.

This somewhat confused theory seems based on the Greek
concept of the personal δαίμων, which was immortal, regarded
as equivalent to the Roman *genius*, which in its original con-
ception was mortal: cf. Kiessling–Heinze on Hor. *Epp*. 2. 2.
187. Servius then equates the *genius* with the *di manes* of the
individual after death: for this identification see Bömer on

Ovid, *F.* 2. 545; its relevance to the present passage is rejected by H. J. Rose (see *Harvard Theological Review* xxxvii [1944], 45 ff.). There is a strong indication that a person's *di manes* could be identified with his δαίμων in the remarkable ending of the *Laudatio Turiae* (*CIL* 6. 1527. 69), 'te di manes tui ut quietam patiantur atque tueantur opto'. On this see M. Durry, *Éloge funèbre d'une matrone romaine* (Paris, Budé, 1950), 62 f.; it is considered the best parallel to Virgil's phrase by Latte, *Rom. Religionsgesch.*, 287 n. 3. Durry dates the inscription to between 8 and 2 B.C.: for its moving content see Warde Fowler, *Social Life at Rome in the Age of Cicero* (London, 1908), 159 ff., and cf. his *Roman Essays and Interpretations* (Oxford, 1920), 126 ff., *Religious Experience of the Roman People*, 389.

Norden (pp. 33 f.) concluded that *manis* here = δαίμονα, on different grounds, though he quotes Servius' second explanation in support: he bases his view on Plato, *Phaedo* 107D, where after death each individual is led to a place of judgment by ὁ ἑκάστου δαίμων, ὅσπερ ζῶντα εἰλήχει, 113D ἐπειδὰν ἀφίκωνται οἱ τετελευτηκότες εἰς τὸν τόπον οἷ ὁ δαίμων ἕκαστον κομίζει, etc.; he notes also Plutarch, *de Socratis genio* 22, 592BC, where control of punishments after death lies with each man's δαίμων, according to his bodily conduct in life.

In spite of the attractions of this interpretation, it causes misgivings; for it imports into Virgil's use of *manes* a conception that has no parallel elsewhere in the *Aeneid* (cf. Bailey, op. cit. 278), and its justification would have to lie in the Greek background and manner of Anchises' speech. Virgil has *manes* of the collective spirits of the dead (e.g. 8. 246), of the world in which these spirits dwell (e.g. 4. 387), and of the individual spirit of a person (e.g. 119, 3. 303, 5. 99, 10. 534). In the present passage it is reasonable to think that Virgil has extended the last of these uses to express the individual spirit's experience in the cleansing process that he has just described: *quisque suos patimur manis* = 'we endure, each of us, a personal ghostly treatment'; or, as Warde Fowler puts it (*Religious Experience*, 386; he stresses the importance of *quisque*, 399 n. 26) 'each individual of us must endure his own individual ghosthood'. With a different approach, H. J. Rose (*Harvard Theological Review*, l.c.) takes *manis* as 'ghost-land', and thinks that Servius' first explanation comes near the right idea: this suits *patimur* less well. It is desirable to emphasize that the phrase must not be divorced from its context.

For discussions see Henry, ad loc.; Nettleship, ad loc., and *Contr. Lat. Lex.* s.v. *manes*; Butler, ad loc.; E. Marbach,

Phil. Woch. xlix (1929), 363 ff.; W. Nestle, *Phil. Woch.* l
(1930), 126; A. Setaioli, *Atene e Roma* xii (1967), 169 ff.;
Dieterich, op. cit. 155; Bailey, op. cit. 277 f. For the passage
from the *Laudatio Turiae* see Cumont, *Lux Perpetua*, 394.

suos . . . manis: there is no singular of *manes*. Rose found
the whole phrase 'clear and even conventional (for Virgil)';
however that may be, it is certainly likely that it would not
have been so much of a problem to Virgil's contemporaries
as it is to us: consider such passages as Ovid, *Met.* 9. 406
'subductaque suos manes tellure uidebit' (of Amphiaraus,
arriving in the Underworld), *Tr.* 5. 14. 12 'nil feret ad Manis
diuitis umbra suos'; Stat. *Th.* 5. 742 f. 'det pulchra suis
libamina uirtus / manibus' (Amphiaraus, speaking of the
dead baby Archemorus); Silius 5. 213 'manibus ipsa suis
praesumpta piacula mittit' (of the Roman soldiery, attacking
the Carthaginians at Trasimene); with Stat. *Th.* 7. 709 ff. 'in-
numeram ferro plebem . . . / . . . immolat umbris / ipse suis'
(of Amphiaraus).

patimur: Anchises himself has had to undergo his own
form of purification, among all the other souls.

743 ff. The arrangement and punctuation of these lines have
been much discussed, often with needless complication.
Ribbeck transposed 745–7 to follow 742 (see Geymonat's
app. crit. for other violent theories), and many editors make
743–4 a parenthesis (so Geymonat, and Mynors's 1969 text);
both arrangements then make *donec . . . ignem* (745 ff.) follow
on the verbs of 740 ff. (*panduntur . . . exuritur*): Ribbeck's
transposition ignores the obvious problem of how Anchises
is already in Elysium (see Butler, p. 230), while the paren-
thetic placing of 743–4 is inartistic in itself and does nothing
to elucidate the argument.

The present text, punctuated in basic agreement with
Norden, makes *donec* follow on *mittimur . . . tenemus* (744),
with this result: after their individual elemental purification
(739–42), summed up in *quisque suos patimur manis*, the
souls are next sent to range over Elysium; a few stay there,
until *perfecto temporis orbe* (745) they are wholly refined into
pure fire, their original state before entering the body; the
rest (*has omnis*, 748, the vast concourse of souls about whom
Aeneas has inquired) drink of Lethe and are reborn, after
a cycle of a thousand years.

This provides a reasonably satisfactory coherence, accord-
ing in general with Orphic ideas: for to the Orphics, Elysium
was 'no more than a brief resting-ground' (Guthrie, op. cit.
184), itself a place of purification but distinct from a yet
higher dwelling, the αἰθήρ, which was the final home of the

finally purified soul. Guthrie discusses the lines with per-
suasive clarity (op. cit. 186, 192 n. 19): if the passage is seen
in this Orphic setting, many of its alleged difficulties appear
as phantoms, and much argumentation is shown as irrelevant
(cf. R. D. Williams, *Greece & Rome*, 2nd ser. xi [1964], 57 f.).

See Norden, pp. 16 ff.; his views are summarized in a use-
ful note by Butler (pp. 228 ff.), and contrasted with others:
see also Bailey, op. cit. 279; Dieterich, op. cit. 155 ff. (partly
in disagreement with Norden); H. T. Plüss, *Vergil und die
epische Kunst* (Leipzig, 1884), 169; T. G. Tucker, *CQ* vii
(1913), 54; E. A. Hahn, *TAPA* lv (1924), p. xxviii.

744. mittimur : this, like *patimur*, must imply all the souls in
process of purification; Virgil bypasses altogether the cate-
gory of those whose irredeemable sins condemn them for
ever to Tartarus. At first sight, Virgilian style would suggest
that *pauci* should be taken with *mittimur* as well as with
tenemus: but this is incompatible with the thronging mass
of souls now in Elysium but awaiting rebirth. It would be
preferable to punctuate with a comma after *Elysium* (so
Norden in his text, but not in his exposition, p. 17) and no
comma after *tenemus* (so Guthrie, after inserting the previous
comma).

pauci . . . tenemus : 'the few' are those who stay in Elysium
needing only the refinement that they are fitted to receive
there, without the need for rebirth; Anchises is one of these:
they are contrasted with the crowding souls of 748 ff. The
laeta arua resume the *locos laetos* of 638; 'the few' presumably
includes the *felices animae* of that passage, gathered round
Orpheus and Musaeus, among them *sacerdotes casti* and *pii
uates*, all clearly apart from the souls destined for rebirth
(679, 704).

745. longa dies : for the feminine see on 429. The vague expres-
sion is explained in *perfecto temporis orbe*, a definite cycle of
time. Plato (*Phaedrus* 248E) assigns ten thousand years to
the cycle needed for the soul to return to the place from
which it came (but for a philosopher three thousand only
may be necessary). But the poet cannot be so explicit, nor is
he in such a precise context.

746. concretam . . . labem : the 'hardened stain' (cf. 738) at
last attains its complete refining. Virgil does not say in so
many words that in this way 'the few' need no rebirth, but
it is to be inferred. (Ovid knew his Virgil: *ars* 2. 653 'eximit
ipsa dies omnis e corpore mendas', in a frivolous context.)

746 f. purumque . . . ignem : 'leaving in its pure state the
ethereal sentient power, the elemental fiery breath': the
soul at last returns to the ether from which it sprang. Servius

glosses *aetherium sensum* as ᾽πῦρ νοερόν, ignem sensualem, id est deum; per quod quid sit anima ostendit᾽.

747. aurai simplicis ignem : a restatement of *aetherium sensum*; both *sensus* and *aura* are the *spiritus* or *mens* of 726 f., the *igneus uigor*, the πνεῦμα πυρῶδες, of 730. The archaic form *aurai* (a trisyllable) is wonderfully chosen for 'tone'; such forms occur in early inscriptions, in Ennius (cf. the quotation on 179 ff.), and especially in Lucretius (see Bailey, proleg. 75 ff.): so *aulai* (3. 354), *aquai* (7. 464), *pictai uestis* (9. 26). Quintilian observes (1. 7. 18) that Virgil uses the form 'amantissimus uetustatis'.

748. has omnis : in antithesis with the *pauci* of 744 (this has been made clearer by the substitution of a colon at the end of 747—so Norden, p. 17—for the full stop of OCT). Anchises now replies to Aeneas' question (719 ff.), pointing to the souls gathered on the banks of Lethe. I owe to Mr. D. A. Russell an interesting parallel in both subject and form of sentence, Plutarch, *de def. orac.* 415 BC ἐκ δὲ δαιμόνων ὀλίγαι μὲν ἐν χρόνῳ πολλῷ δι᾽ ἀρετὴν καθαρθεῖσαι παντάπασι θειότητος μετέσχον, ἐνίαις δὲ συμβαίνει μὴ κρατεῖν ἑαυτῶν ἀλλ᾽ ὑφιεμέναις καὶ ἐνδυομέναις πάλιν σώμασι θνητοῖς ἀλαμπῆ καὶ ἀμυδρὰν ζωὴν ὥσπερ ἀναθυμίασιν ἴσχειν. Cf. Norden, p. 40.

mille . . . per annos : the thousand-year period before rebirth is Platonic: see *Phaedrus* 249AB, *Rp.* 615A; the cycle of ten thousand years (cf. 745, note) is divided into ten periods, each occupying one incarnation (see Guthrie, op. cit. 167).

rotam uoluere : 'sermo Ennii', Servius (not in extant fragments). Nettleship notes Silius 6. 120 f. 'talis lege deum cliuoso tramite uitae / per uarios praeceps casus rota uoluitur aeui'. Virgil's expression suggests the Orphic κύκλος γενέσεως; in one of the Orphic gold plates from Thurii the pure soul on arriving in the Underworld is represented as saying κύκλου δ' ἐξέπταν βαρυπενθέος ἀργαλέοιο (see Guthrie, op. cit. 175, 208; text in Kern, *Orphicorum Fragmenta* [Berlin, 1922], fr. 32).

749. Lethaeum ad fluuium : in the Myth of Er (Plato, *Rp.* 621A) the souls must all drink a certain amount of water from the Ἀμέλης ποταμός: τοὺς δὲ φρονήσει μὴ σῳζομένους πλέον πίνειν τοῦ μέτρου. Cf. Guthrie, op. cit. 177, 183.

deus : perhaps Mercury (i.e. Hermes ψυχοπομπός), as Servius suggests; it is worth remark that Virgil uses *euocare* once only elsewhere, 4. 242 'hac [sc. *uirga*] animas ille euocat Orco', in a context referring specifically to Mercury.

agmine magno : picking up Aeneas' questioning in 712 'quiue uiri tanto complerint agmine ripas'; Norden improbably suggests that Virgil uses *agmen* because *euocare* occurs as a military t.t.

750. scilicet : explanatory ('you see', 'you must know'),
Lucretian in tone. The emphasis is on *immemores*; for *supera
conuexa* see on 241.

751. rursus : this is best taken with *reuisant*; Norden connects
it with *uelle reuerti*, putting a comma after *reuisant*; the
pleonasm is a marked feature of Latin style, e.g. Plaut.
Poen. 79 'reuortor rursus denuo Carthaginem', Lucr. 4. 310
'inde retro rursum redit', Cic. *Rosc. Am.* 41 'rursus igitur
eodem reuertamur' (see HSz, 798).

    uelle : a specific reference to Aeneas' question 'quae lucis
miseris tam dira cupido?' (721); their draught of Lethe has
made the souls forget their extra-bodily experience, and they
have an urge to return to their dwelling in the body (cf.
Cumont, op. cit. 200). Such an urge becomes more compre-
hensible to Aeneas as Anchises unrolls the future glories of
Rome which his descendants will ensure.

752–5. *Anchises takes Aeneas and the Sibyl into the heart of the
gathering of souls, and from a knoll points each one out.*

    These four gentle lines (rather like a stage direction) lower
the emotional tone, and provide an interval before it rises
again.

753. conuentus : only here in Virgil, and very rare in poetry
(Cat. 64. 32; Lucr. 1. 611, 4. 784; not in Ovid, nor in the
elegists, nor in Silver Epic).

754. tumulum : again the idea of height, as in 676; Anchises
picks a good viewpoint for looking intently at the souls as
they come before him *(aduersos legere)*, identifying each in
turn, like an affectionate father.

756–853. *Anchises shows Aeneas the souls of the great men now
awaiting birth who will build the glory of Rome: the Alban
Kings, leading to Romulus (760–87); the gens Iulia, marked
out by the splendour of Augustus (788–807); the early Kings of
Rome, and men of the early Republic (808–25); Caesar and
Pompey (826–35); a throng of other famous Romans, dis-
tinguished in civil or military achievement, ending with Q.
Fabius Maximus (836–46). An epilogue (847–53) proclaims the
special duty and responsibilities of Rome to the world.*

    This inspired vision of Roman history has no really logical
connexion with the eschatology that precedes it; but it gains
immeasurable impressiveness from the awe and mystery of
its apparent setting, as the ghostly figures of these unborn
Romans file past Anchises in grave procession. It is a poetic
counterpart to Roman sculptured reliefs, such as the Ara
Pacis, on part of which Augustus is seen in the presence of

members of his family. It recalls also the Roman tradition of
the *maiorum imagines* in great families, which played a dis-
tinctive and significant role at their funeral ceremonies (see
the notable description in Polybius 6. 53, with Walbank's
commentary; Pliny, *NH* 35. 6 f.; Toynbee, op. cit. 47 f.).
More directly, it is a powerful and evocative illustration
of the moral significance traditionally attached to *exempla*,
so often appealed to in exhortatory contexts of various
kinds: e.g. Cic. *Cael.* 39, *Sest.* 143, *de off.* 1. 61, *de nat. deor.*
2. 165, *Tusc.* 1. 110; Livy 9. 17. 8; Quintilian 12. 2. 30;
Sen. *Contr.* 2. 1. 8, *Suas.* 7. 6; Pliny, *Pan.* 13; Juvenal 2. 154,
11. 90 f. Polybius ends his account of an exalted personage's
funeral memorably, οὗ κάλλιον οὐκ εὐμαρὲς ἰδεῖν θέαμα νέῳ φιλοδόξῳ
καὶ φιλαγάθῳ. τὸ γὰρ τὰς τῶν ἐπ' ἀρετῇ δεδοξασμένων ἀνδρῶν εἰκόνας
ἰδεῖν ὁμοῦ πάσας, οἱονεὶ ζώσας καὶ πεπνυμένας, τίν' οὐκ ἂν παραστήσαι; τί
δ' ἂν κάλλιον θέαμα τούτου φανείη; and Sallust (*Iug.* 4. 6) ob-
serves in a similar context 'memoria rerum gestarum eam
flammam egregiis uiris in pectore crescere neque prius sedari
quam uirtus eorum famam atque gloriam adaequauerit': we
may be sure that Virgil's contemporaries would see this
speech as a resonant call to build future greatness on the
firm basis of a splendid past, a moral challenge to them and
to their posterity.

Virgil has carefully avoided a strictly consecutive chrono-
logy; the speech has contours, as it were, with now a quiet,
almost factual tone, now impassioned at a peak of emotion:
thus on Augustus it rises to something like hymn-style, and
in the oblique allusion to Caesar and Pompey it becomes a
direct and urgent personal address. Augustus himself is not
the climax, but the central figure standing between two
flanking passages of narrative that are of almost equal length.
The climax is not a person but an ideal, the expression of
Roman ethos and Roman mission. At moments personal ap-
pearance or characteristics are described, as if from a por-
trait or sculpture (e.g. 760, 772, 779, 809, 815). By an illusion
of movement Virgil gives the speech a processional structure;
Anchises introduces the souls as they come forward, one by
one: *uides* (760), *uiden* (779), *aspice* (788, 825); *quis procul
ille* (808), *subibit* (812), *uis . . . uidere* (817 f.), *cernis* (826),
quo fessum rapitis? (845). The movement is slowed as he
dwells on individual personages (e.g. Silvius, 763; Romulus,
778; Augustus, 791; Brutus, 818); at other times the names
come in swiftly gathering groups (767 ff., 824 f., 836-45).
The whole is a great work of high poetic art and action.

There are two other passages in the *Aeneid* that comple-
ment this one, Iuppiter's prophecy to Venus with its promise

of *Roma aeterna* (1. 257 ff.) and the description of the Shield made for Aeneas by Vulcan at Venus' request (8. 626–728; for its relationship to Anchises' speech cf. J. G. Griffith, *Proc. Virg. Soc.* vii [1967–8], 57 ff.). Virgil may have known and used Hor. *C.* 1. 12, a poem with its own group of famous Romans, to whose traditions Augustus is heir (see Nisbet–Hubbard, introductory comment, p. 145). For post-Virgilian imitations see Manilius 1. 777 ff.; Silius 13. 721 ff., 806 ff. (a group of Roman women), 853 ff.; and Dante, *Inferno* 4. 121 ff.

Norden analyses the speech from the standpoint of rhetoric, as a λόγος παραινετικός. For a detailed discussion see H. T. Plüss, *Vergil und die epische Kunst*, 167–256; also Camps, op. cit. 88 f., and *Proc. Virg. Soc.* vii (1967–8), 25 f.; Otis, op. cit. 301 ff.; Klingner, *Virgil*, 492 ff.; R. D. Williams, *Greece & Rome*, 2nd ser. xi (1964), 58 ff.; E. Skard, *Symb. Osl.* xl (1965), 53 ff. (an interesting paper); M. von Albrecht, *Wiener Studien* lxxx (1967), 156 ff.

756. nunc age : a didactic formula, introducing a new exposition: so Lucr. 2. 62, 3. 417, 4. 673, etc., *G.* 4. 149 f. 'nunc age, naturas apibus quas Iuppiter ipse / addidit expediam', Silius 11. 1 ff. 'nunc age, quos clades insignis Iapyge campo / uerterit ad Libyam populos . . . / expediam'.

Dardaniam prolem : 'Albanos reges, qui tredecim fuerunt de Aeneae et Lauiniae genere; unde ait *Itala de gente*' (Servius). The fusion of Trojan with Italian stock is given significant prominence.

deinde : 'in after time', following Aeneas himself; for the prosody see on 434.

757. maneant : 'are in store' (cf. 84 'terrae grauiora manent').

Itala : the first syllable is short (the original prosody); see on 61, 92, and contrast 3. 185 'Ĭtala regna', 7. 643 f. 'Ĭtala . . . terra', 9. 698 'uolat Ĭtala cornus'. Norden notes Hor. *Sat.* 1. 7. 32 'Ĭtalo . . . aceto' as the earliest recorded occurrence of the adjective; Virgil's contemporary Crinagoras (see Gow–Page, *Garland of Philip*, ii. 212) has αἰχμητὴς Ἰταλός (*A P* 7. 741. 3).

758. inlustris : 'hoc nomen notitiae fuit, non meriti: unde etiam in meretricibus inuenitur' (Servius, engagingly). The construction gives a variation from the two dependent clauses, summarizing both.

nostrumque . . . ituras : 'future heirs of our name and fame' (*nomen* implies both). The line recalls 680.

759. expediam dictis : so 3. 379, where, as here, *dictis* is virtually 'prophecy'.

760. uides : Silvius comes forward; for the technique (to suggest movement) see introductory note above.

pura . . . hasta : as if Virgil was describing a statue. Servius explains, on Varro's authority, that *pura* = 'sine ferro', i.e. a spear with no metal tip: 'nam hoc fuit praemium apud maiores eius qui tunc primum uicisset proelio'; Ti. Donatus notes 'nuntia scilicet non belli sed pacis'. Servius' *tunc primum* does not accord with a tradition that L. Siccius Dentatus, tr. pl. 454 B.C., gained a *hasta pura* eighteen times (Pliny, *NH* 7. 102, Gellius, 2. 11. 2). It appears as a military decoration in many imperial inscriptions; cf. Prop. 4. 3. 67 f. 'tua sic domitis Parthae telluris alumnis / pura triumphantis hasta sequatur equos', Sueton. *Claud.* 28 'etiam Britannico triumpho inter militares uiros hasta pura donauit' (an award to the eunuch freedman Posides). See W. Helbig, *Zur Geschichte der hasta donatica* (Berlin, 1908), for which cf. *CR* xxiv (1910), 29; Walbank on Polybius 6. 39. 3.

761. proxima . . . loca : 'holds the nearest allotted place in the world of light', explained in *primus . . . surget*. By *sorte* Virgil probably means the destined order of precedence, not that lots were actually drawn (a notion that Lucretius sardonically mocks, 3. 778 ff.).

762. aetherias : i.e. of the upper world (cf. 436); so 1. 546 f. 'si uescitur aura / aetheria' (= 'if he is still alive'): contrast the quite different use of the word in 747.

Italo . . . sanguine : Silvius will be the first descendant of mixed Trojan and Italian stock.

763. Albanum nomen : the name Silvius became a tradition: Livy 1. 3. 7 'mansit Siluiis postea omnibus cognomen qui Albae regnarunt' (similarly Servius, on 760).

postuma : 'late-born', as the next line makes clear. But another tradition, going back to Cato (Servius, on 760), made Silvius a posthumous child, and the meaning of *postuma* here was debated in antiquity (see Gellius 2. 16. 5, where the sense 'last born' is defended). For this version see Dion. Hal. *ant. Rom.* 1. 70; another tradition (Livy 1. 3. 6; Ovid, *F.* 4. 41 f.) made Silvius a son of Ascanius.

764. longaeuo : see on 321. The epithet is not consistent with 1. 265 f., where Aeneas is given a reign of three years only, *Rutulis subactis*. But old age sets in early at poetic need. The line is the first to name Lavinia (contrast 93, 2. 783).

765. educet : 'shall rear'; cf. 779, 7. 763 'eductum Egeriae lucis', 9. 584 'eductum Martis luco', Plaut. *Curc.* 518 'bene ego istam eduxi meae domi', Ter. *Ad.* 48 'eduxi a paruolo' (on which Donatus comments 'quod nos educare, educere ueteres dicebant', quoting this line). As Norden points out, *educere* has obvious metrical advantages over *educare*.

siluis : so Livy 1. 3. 6 'Siluius deinde regnat Ascani filius, casu quodam in siluis natus', Ovid, *F.* 4. 41 f.: an 'etymological' explanation of the name. Ogilvie (on Livy, l.c.) suggests that the landscape of early Latium may have inspired the name.

766. unde : 'from whom', as in 1. 6 (probably), 5. 123, 5. 568 (all with *genus*, as here): an archaic use, in elevated tone; see Nisbet–Hubbard on Hor. *C.* 1. 12. 17, with references.

Longa . . . Alba : founded by Ascanius (1. 270 f., 8. 48, Livy 1. 3. 3). Ogilvie (on Livy, l.c.) accepts the view that the city was on the site of the modern Castel Gandolfo, twelve miles south-east of Rome. Naturally, Anchises does not name Ascanius as the first Alban king (cf. Ovid, *Met.* 14. 609, *F.* 4. 39 f.): he was no ghost waiting to be reborn. The line of Alban Kings is omitted in Iuppiter's prophecy (1. 257 ff.), where the main purpose is to reveal the safe arrival of Aeneas in Italy and the ultimate founding of Rome; here Virgil is concerned to show the Italian–Trojan origins of the Roman people. The tradition of the king-list is varied and complicated: see Ogilvie on Livy 1. 3. 6, and cf. Heinze, 158 n. 1, Bömer on Ovid, *F.* 4. 39.

767. proximus : 'standi ordine, non nascendi' (Servius). After singling out Silvius, Virgil now names a group together, not in historical order; Procas has jumped the queue. 'Troianae gloria gentis' is an epic flourish; nothing is known to suggest that Procas had any special distinction.

768. Capys : a Trojan name (1. 183, 2. 35, 9. 576, 10. 145); in *Il.* 20. 239 it is said to be the name of Anchises' father. For the 'etymological' legend that a Capys (probably not this Alban king) founded Capua (cf. 10. 145, Sueton. *Iul.* 81) see Ogilvie on Livy 4. 37. 1, Bömer on Ovid, *F.* 4. 45.

Numitor : the final syllable is long, as if it were a Greek form. Tradition made him grandfather of Romulus; see Livy 1. 3. 10, and Ogilvie ad loc., Dion. Hal. *ant. Rom.* 1. 76. 1 ff.

reddet : this king will be another Aeneas in name, character, and deeds; cf. 12. 348 'nomine auum referens, animo manibusque parentem'.

769. Siluius Aeneas : son of the king named in 763; his reign lasted 31 years (Dion. Hal. *ant. Rom.* 1. 71. 1). The description of him here echoes the Sibyl's words of Aeneas himself (403).

770. si . . . Albam : this seems an allusion to a tradition reported by Servius, that he was kept out of his kingdom by a *tutor*, 'qui eius inuasit imperium: quod ei uix anno quinquagesimo tertio restituit'. Anchises pretends to be worried, a neat touch. For the elision of *si* cf. 2. 102, 4. 669, 11. 166, *E.* 3. 48: see Soubiran, op. cit. 410, 412; Norden's table (p. 457) gives eleven instances in Virgil.

regnandam : 'for ruling'; this gerundive from an intransi-
tive verb seems unique, but cf. *regnata* (793, 3. 14), *regnabitur*
(1. 272, impersonal; see note): so *triumphata* (836, with
G. 3. 33), *bacchatam* (3. 125, with *G.* 2. 487), *ululata* (4. 609;
note). See HSz, 32.

771 f. An illusion of a whispered comment as the *iuuenes* come
forward to be introduced.

772. ciuili ... quercu : the 'civic crown' ('*ciuica* debuit dicere',
Servius) was one of the highest military decorations, a
wreath of oak-leaves awarded for saving a citizen in battle:
see Gellius 5. 6. 11 ff., Pliny, *NH* 16. 7 ff. ('militum uirtutis
insigne clarissimum'), Polybius 6. 39. 6 (see Walbank).
Augustus was granted it (*Mon. Anc.* 34. 2 'corona ciuica
super ianuam meam fixa est'); cf. Sen. *de clem.* 1. 26. 5
'nullum ornamentum principis fastigio dignius pulchriusque
est quam illa corona ob ciues seruatos'). Caesar received it in
80 B.C., *in expugnatione Mytilenarum* (Sueton. *Iul.* 2); Tiber-
ius refused it (id. *Tib.* 26. 2). See Bömer on Ovid, *F.* 1. 345.

773 ff. A cluster of townships, members of the Latin League
with Alba Longa at its head. Virgil's antiquarian interests
combine with his feeling for the romance of place-names
and for ancient Italian sturdiness (cf. *G.* 2. 532 f.). The little
list anticipates the ethos of the Catalogue in 7. 647 ff.

773. Nomentum : again, 7. 712 (in the Sabine contingent);
Livy (1. 38. 4) lists it among the towns 'de Priscis Latinis
aut qui ad Latinos defecerant capta', following the defeat
of the Sabines by Tarquinius. It stood thirteen miles north
of Rome, guarding the crossing of the Allia (Ogilvie, Livy,
l.c.), the modern Mentana. Here was the villa at which
Martial pokes affectionate fun (12. 57. 1 f. 'cur saepe sicci
parua rura Nomenti / laremque uillae sordidum petas,
quaeris?').

  Gabios : near the modern Torre di Castiglione, twelve
miles east of Rome (Ogilvie on Livy 1. 53. 4). Virgil's tone of
pride contrasts with Hor. *Epp.* 1. 11. 7 f. 'scis Lebedus quid
sit; Gabiis desertior atque / Fidenis uicus'; cf. Lucan 7. 391 ff.
(on the legacy of civil war) 'tunc omne Latinum / fabula
nomen erit; Gabios Veiosque Coramque / puluere uix tectae
poterunt monstrare ruinae'. See T. Ashby, *PBSR* i (1902),
180 ff.

  Fidenam : normally plural, and with the first syllable long
(as in Hor. *Epp.* l.c.); for the singular cf. Silius 15. 91 'impar
Fīdenae', Tac. *Ann.* 4. 62. It was some five miles north of
Rome, near the modern Castel Giubileo, and in early times
it was a formidable menace to Rome (Ogilvie on Livy 1. 14.
4 ff., 2. 19. 2, 4. 22. 2, 4. 31. 6 ff.).

774. Cf. *G.* 2. 156 'tot congesta manu praeruptis oppida saxis'.
Collatia (on the site of the modern Lunghezza) commanded
a crossing of the Anio (Ogilvie on Livy 1. 38. 1); here Sex.
Tarquinius first set eyes on the young Lucretia, 'nocte sera
deditam lanae inter lucubrantes ancillas in medio aedium
sedentem' (Livy 1. 57. 9; a Virgilian picture, cf. *G.* 1. 390 ff.).

　　imponent . . . arces : a highly rhetorical exaggeration (cf.
A. W. Van Buren, *CR* xxxiv [1920], 128) : cf. Hor. *Epp.* 2. 1.
250 ff. (written after 17 B.C.) 'nec sermones ego mallem /
repentis per humum quam res componere gestas, / ter-
rarumque situs et flumina dicere et arces / montibus im-
positas' (a context characterizing elevated poetic style). The
periphrasis *Collatinas arces* ingeniously gets round the metri-
cal problem of an accusative of Collatia; and the resul-
tant line, grandly referring to one single place, makes an
artistic division between the two lines containing grouped
names, so that the effect of 'cataloguing' is avoided.

775. **Pometios** : elsewhere Pometia or Suessa Pometia. It lay
on the borders of the Latin and Volscian regions (Ogilvie on
Livy 1. 41. 7); for its capture by Rome see Livy 2. 25. 5.

　　Castrumque Inui : perhaps near Ardea (where the modern
name of a stream, Fosso d'Incastro, may be a relic of the
name); cf. Silius 8. 359 'quos Castrum Phrygibusque grauis
quondam Ardea misit' (with Collatia in close context), Ovid,
Met. 15. 727 f. 'donec Castrumque sacrasque / Lauini sedes
Tiberinaque ad ostia uenit'. Servius identifies 'Inuus' with
Pan (cf. Livy 1. 5. 2, Macrob. *Sat.* 1. 22. 2).

　　Bolamque Coramque : the site of Bola is not identifiable:
see Ogilvie on Livy 4. 49. 3. Cora, the modern Cori, was on
the north-western edge of the Volscian mountains (Ogilvie
on Livy 2. 16. 8); cf. N. Horsfall, *JRS* lxiii (1973), 71.

776. A curiously flat-toned line, with an almost primitive as-
sonance in *erunt, nunc sunt*. But there is crisp antithesis in
nomina (famous names) . . . *sine nomine* (nameless); cf. 12.
134 ff. 'at Iuno ex summo (qui nunc Albanus habetur; / tum
neque nomen erat neque honos aut gloria monti) / pro-
spiciens tumulo'.

777. **quin et** : see on 735; here it is merely connective. Virgil
introduces Romulus with a new formula, and the tone begins
to rise, preparing for the exaltation of Rome. Presumably
the meaning of *auo comitem sese addet* is that Romulus will
be born in the lifetime of his grandfather (Numitor) on
earth; for *Mauortius* (from the archaic *Mauors*) cf. 1. 276 f.
'Romulus excipiet gentem et Mauortia condet / moenia
Romanosque suo de nomine dicet'.

778. **Ilia** : another name for the Vestal Rhea Silvia, daughter of

Numitor (see on 1. 274; Bömer on Ovid, *F.* 2. 383; K. F. Smith on Tib. 2. 5. 51 ff.): Virgil's choice of the name stresses the Trojan aspect of Romulus' mother's descent, and the mention of Assaracus (cf. 650) adds further Trojan colour. For a characteristically bland account of the Vestal's seduction by Mars, and of Romulus' birth, see Ovid, *F.* 3. 11 ff.

779. **uiden** : for *uidesne* (contrast the parenthetic *uides*, 760), in the quickened casual pronunciation of the man-in-the-street, the second syllable being shortened by *breuis breuians*: see Lindsay, *Early Latin Verse*, 42. It is remarkable to find it in Epic, and in a passage of high tone; Servius states that Virgil uses it 'secutus Ennium', but no Ennian example survives. It is designed to give dramatic conversational realism to Anchises' talk with Aeneas. For its use in Comedy cf. Plaut. *Curc.* 311 'uiden ut expalluit?', *Most.* 1172 'uiden ut adstat furcifer?', Ter. *Eun.* 241 'uiden me ex eodem ortum loco?', 783 'uiden tu, Thais, quam rem hic agit?', etc. Catullus brought it into Lyric, 61. 77 f. 'uiden ut faces / splendidas quatiunt comas?', 94 f. 'uiden? faces / aureas quatiunt comas' (like a commentator on a procession), and into his semi-dramatic hexameter marriage-poem, 62. 8 'uiden ut perniciter exsiluere?'

In these passages, the construction with *ut* is paratactic; *uiden* is quasi-parenthetic, merely calling attention to the fact announced by *ut*, which is followed by an indicative verb (similarly *aspice*, 855, *E.* 5. 6; *nonne uides?*, *G.* 1. 56; *aspicite*, Cat. 62. 12): but in Tib. 2. 1. 25 f. 'uiden ut felicibus extis / significet placidos nuntia fibra deos?' (the only other classical occurrence of *uiden*), the subordinating construction is used, with a subjunctive verb.

geminae ... cristae : a cryptic allusion. Henry quotes Val. Max. 1. 8. 6 (of an apparition in battle, thought to be Mars) 'inter cetera huiusce rei manifesta indicia galea quoque duabus distincta pinnis, qua caeleste caput tectum fuerat, argumentum praebuit'.

780. **pater ... honore** : 'the father of the gods himself already marks him out with his own majesty': i.e. Romulus is destined to become a god. Ti. Donatus interprets 'uide ... quomodo eum iam pater superum id est Iuppiter honore suo et maiestate perconfundat'. But there has been much discussion concerning the case and meaning of *superum*, and of the identity of *pater*.

Servius took *superum* as accusative, = *deum*. But there is no parallel for this meaning in the singular, and the interpretation 'child of upper air' (Conington, on a suggestion by Henry) is absurd: all these souls were destined for the upper air. *Superum* can only be the archaic genitive plural, as Ti. Donatus saw (cf. 1. 4).

Conington and others, following Servius, take *pater* to mean Mars. This involves taking *superum* with *honore*, and ignoring *suo*; and the function of Mars is then obscure. *Pater ipse superum* must be taken together, referring to Iuppiter; *suo* then offers no problem, for *ipse* often attracts an oblique case of *suus* to its side with an apparent upset to the word-order (cf. 4. 233 'nec super ipse sua molitur laude laborem', 12. 638 'uidi oculos ante ipse meos'; an extreme instance in Ovid, *Her.* 12. 18 'et caderet cultu cultor ab ipse suo'). Norden accepted this interpretation in his second edition; see also F. Skutsch, *Aus Vergils Frühzeit* (Leipzig–Berlin, 1906), ii. 97 ff., and Leo, *Hermes* xlii (1907), 56 f. (= *Kleine Schriften*, ii. 91 f.).

honore : probably no more than 'majesty', as Ti. Donatus saw. Norden takes it to mean a kingly sceptre, quoting *Ciris* 268 f. 'ille, uides, nostris qui moenibus assidet hostis, / quem pater ipse deum sceptri donauit honore' (a line which supports the interpretation of *superum* here as genitive); but this is not really necessary.

781. en : a dramatic gesture, as if Anchises visualizes the future Rome before him.

auspiciis : the omen of the twelve vultures which appeared to Romulus, after six had appeared to Remus, when they sought an augury to give guidance on the rule of the new city: see Livy 1. 6. 4 ff., Ovid, *F.* 4. 817 f.; Ogilvie on Livy 1. 6. 3–7. 3, Bömer on Ovid, *F.* 4. 809 ff.

incluta : cf. 479, note. Virgil's line recalls Ennius, *Ann.* 502 'augusto augurio postquam inclita condita Roma est'.

782. Rome in her glory shall make her rule as wide as earth, her spirit as high as heaven: a restatement of 1. 286 f. 'nascetur pulchra Troianus origine Caesar, / imperium Oceano, famam qui terminet astris'. For *Olympus* of the sky cf. 1. 374 'ante diem clauso componet Vesper Olympo', *G.* 1. 450 'emenso cum iam decedit Olympo' (of the Sun); Servius comments 'magnanimitate aequabitur caelo'.

783. So *G.* 2. 534 f. 'rerum facta est pulcherrima Roma, / septemque una sibi muro circumdedit arces'; the juxtaposition *septem*)(*una* is effective. For the Seven Hills of Rome see K. F. Smith on Tib. 2. 5. 55.

784. felix prole uirum : 'blessed and fruitful in manly progeny': *felix* combines the ideas of good fortune and fertility, and the phrase corresponds to *laeta deum partu* in the following simile (786); the epithet gains much force from its position. *Proles* often has a nuance of vigour and lustiness; here it has

something of the stateliness that made Cicero (*de or.* 3. 153)
include it among words 'quibus loco positis grandior atque
antiquior oratio saepe uideri solet'; cf. 648 'genus antiquum
Teucri, pulcherrima proles'.

784 ff. This remarkable and rich simile owes something to
Lucr. 2. 606 ff. (the procession of the *magna deum mater*)
' muralique caput summum cinxere corona, / eximiis munita
locis quia sustinet urbis: / quo nunc insigni per magnas
praedita terras / horrifice fertur diuinae matris imago. / . . .
(624) ergo cum primum magnas inuecta per urbis / munificat
tacita mortalis muta salute, / aere atque argento sternunt
iter omne uiarum'.

The cult of Cybele, one of whose cult-places was at Mt.
Berecyntus in Phrygia, was brought to Rome in 204 B.C.
(Livy 29. 11. 6 f., 14. 5 ff.). Its fascination for Roman poets
(and its importance) is clear from Lucr. l.c., Cat. 35. 13 f.
(a poem on it by Caecilius), Cat. 63 (the 'Attis'; see Fordyce's
introductory note), Ovid, *F.* 4. 181 ff.; Varro's Menippean
satire *Eumenides* also dealt with it (Bücheler–Heraeus, frs.
117 ff.). For Virgil the cult of the Mother-goddess held a dif-
ferent interest (he ignores the orgiastic aspect of her wor-
ship), from its Phrygian origin. In 2. 788 Creusa is wafted
away to serve *magna deum genetrix*; in 3. 111 ff. Anchises
speaks of her worship and of her lion-drawn chariot; in 7. 139
she is one of the deities invoked by Aeneas on his arrival at
the site of Lavinium; in 9. 82 ff. she appeals to her son
Iuppiter to save the Trojan ships from burning; in 9. 619
Turnus taunts the Trojans with her Phrygian ritual; in
10. 234 it is she who has turned Aeneas' ships into sea-
nymphs; in 10. 252 ff. Aeneas prays to her in solemn and
formal style, 'alma parens Idaea deum, cui Dindyma cordi /
turrigeraeque urbes biiugique ad frena leones, / tu mihi
nunc pugnae princeps, tu rite propinques / augurium Phry-
gibusque adsis pede, diua, secundo'.

Virgil clearly thought of the Magna Mater as a tutelary
deity of the Trojans: Latte's view, however, that he first
linked her with the Trojan legend (*Röm. Religionsgesch.*
260 n. 3) is doubted by Weinstock (*JRS* li [1961], 213). His
choice of just this simile to illustrate the all-embracing
world-dominion of Rome (and in such a context) is bold and
even startling. It shows his concern to enrich the 'Trojan
history' of the Roman people, and perhaps also his desire
to set full Roman sanction on what was still regarded as a
foreign cult: see M. Grant, *Proc. Virg. Soc.* iii (1963–4), 7 f.

785. curru : traditionally drawn by lions (3. 113, Cat. 63. 76,
Ovid, *F.* 4. 215 f.), which symbolized the civilizing power

of the goddess (Ovid, l.c.; Varro, quoted by St. Augustine, *de ciu. Dei* 7. 24 'leonem . . . adiungunt solutum ac mansuetum, ut ostendant esse nullum genus terrae tam remotum ac uehementer ferum quod non subigi colique conueniat'). For a fine illustration see Rostovtzeff, *History of the Ancient World* (Oxford, 1928) ii, pl. xv; for representation on coins see Bömer on Ovid, *F.* 4. 215.

    turrita : so Prop. 4. 11. 52, Ovid, *Met.* 10. 696, *F.* 4. 219 ff. '"at cur turrifera caput est onerata corona?"', etc. (see Bömer ad loc.). Cybele wore a battlemented crown, the *corona muralis* of Lucr. 2. 606 (above); see Frazer, *Fasti of Ovid*, v, pl. 49 (from Formiae). This symbol became attributed to the concept of *dea Roma*; cf. Lucan 1. 186 ff. (Caesar's vision of Roma before crossing the Rubicon) 'ingens uisa duci patriae trepidantis imago / clara per obscuram uoltu maestissima noctem / turrigero canos effundens uertice crines' (imitated by Silius 4. 410 f. 'ipsam turrigero portantem uertice muros / credite summissas Romam nunc tendere palmas'): see R. J. Getty, *Proc. Camb. Phil. Soc.* 1939, 3 ff., Bömer on Ovid, l.c.

786. laeta . . . partu : a counterpart to *felix prole uirum* (784); *laeta*, like *felix*, implies both happy pride and fruitfulness.

787. caelicolas : an Ennian compound (*Ann.* 491), virtually paraphrased in the variation *supera alta tenentes*. The parallel structure of 786–7, with the anaphora of *omnis*, produces a remarkably joyous, musical effect in balanced, ringing rhythms.

788 ff. Virgil now abandons chronological order, to pass directly from Romulus to Augustus, the second founder of Rome; when Octavian took the name Augustus, certain persons had wished him to be called Romulus, 'quasi et ipsum conditorem Urbis' (Sueton. *Aug.* 7. 2). The full function of the preceding simile is now seen: Rome's dominion shall be as all-embracing and as proudly protective of the Roman family of nations as that of the Mother of the Gods; Augustus shall be its embodiment. The passage is highly wrought, ornate and allusive, filled with geographical romance, hinting at a comparison of Augustus with Alexander: except that it is not a direct address to Augustus, its manner is that of a hymn of praise (cf. 8. 293 ff., the Arcadians' hymn to Hercules). Norden's commentary here is supplemented by fuller treatment in *Rh. Mus.* liv (1899), 467 ff. (= *Kleine Schriften*, 422 ff.); see also G. Williams, op. cit. 428 f.

788. huc . . . hanc . . . gentem : Anchises points to a new group of souls, not now of Alba but of *illa incluta Roma*.

    geminas . . . acies : i.e. 'look keenly'; *acies* has its strict

sense of the pupil of the eye: the pleonasm in *geminas* has
a certain force here, as perhaps it has in Cat. 63. 75 'geminas
deorum ad aures noua nuntia referens', *Culex* 150 'geminas
auium uox obstrepit auris'; but sometimes it seems a mere
mannerism, e.g. Cic. *Arat.* 48 'serpens geminis secat aëra
pinnis'.

gentem : the *gens Iulia*, to which Augustus belonged by
adoption. The reference in *Caesar* below is clearly to Augus-
tus; an allusion to Iulius in this context would in any case
have blurred the juxtaposition of Romulus and Augustus;
and Iulius has his place in 830 ff., where Virgil's unhappiness
concerning him is plain. There is no such ambiguity here as
there is in 1. 286 'nascetur pulchra Troianus origine Caesar'
(see note there; but I am now less inclined to take it as an
allusion to Iulius).

791. hic uir, hic est : the second *hic* preserves the prosody of a
short syllable before an initial vowel that it has in Plautus: so
4. 22 'solus hic inflexit sensus'; Lucr. 2. 387 'noster hic e
lignis ortus', 2. 1066, 4. 921, 6. 9; Tib. 1. 10. 39 'quam potius
laudandus hic est'. The normal classical prosody is *hĭc* (i.e.
hicc, by analogy with *hocc*): see W. S. Allen, *Vox Latina*
(Cambridge, 1965), 76 f.; Lindsay, *Early Latin Verse*, 119,
163; *Thes.L.L.* s.v. 2696. 35 ff.

quem . . . audis : curiously circumstantial, as if Anchises
had had many conversations with his son on the subject.

792. diui genus : 'child of a god' (cf. 500, 839): Octavian be-
came *diui filius* after his adoptive father Iulius was officially
deified in 42 B.C. The pause at the diaeresis after *genus* helps
to throw emphasis on the virtual title.

Heyne comments 'in Augusto uero repraesentando se ipsum
superauit poeta . . . quam grauia haec omnia laudum argu-
menta, et quam splendide uerbis et rerum phantasmatibus
declarata!'

792 ff. Augustus shall be the founder of a renewed Golden Age
of Saturn: cf. 8. 319 ff. 'primus ab aetherio uenit Saturnus
Olympo / . . . is genus indocile ac dispersum montibus altis /
composuit legesque dedit . . . / aurea quae perhibent illo sub
rege fuere / saecula: sic placida populos in pace regebat'
(cf. Warde Fowler, *Aeneas at the Site of Rome* [Blackwell,
Oxford, 1918], 70), a passage that clearly illustrates the im-
plications of the present lines.

But Virgil's words have a special social significance; the
Golden Age of Saturn symbolized the purity and simplicity of
early Italian life, the ways that had made Rome great (*G.* 2.
538 'aureus hanc uitam in terris Saturnus agebat'). It is
highly probable that in *aurea condet saecula* there is an

allusion to Augustus' social and moral reforms, attempted
unsuccessfully in 28 B.C. but given fresh impetus in 22 B.C.,
then postponed until 18 B.C. when his legislative programme
was finally carried through and celebrated by the revival of
the *ludi saeculares* in the next year, made memorable by
Horace's *carmen saeculare*: see Syme, *Roman Revolution*,
339, 443; H. Mattingly, *C R* xlviii (1934), 161 ff.; P. Grimal,
Rev. des Études anciennes lvi (1954), 40 ff.; R. Merkelbach,
Mus. Helv. xviii (1961), 90 ff. For a discussion of the concept
of a 'Golden Age' and its origin see H. C. Baldry, *CQ* n.s.
ii (1952) 83 ff.

793. For the postponement of *qui* cf. *E.* 3. 86 f. 'pascite
taurum, / iam cornu petat et pedibus qui spargat harenam',
G. 3. 387 f. 'quamuis aries sit candidus ipse, / nigra subest udo
tantum cui lingua palato': the arrangement here sets strong
emphasis on *aurea*. For the passive form *regnata* see on 770.

794. Garamantas : Greek accusative, with short final syllable.
The Garamantes were a Tripolitanian people, the modern
Fezzan; their name is often used quite generally for 'African':
cf. 4. 198 (of Iarbas) 'hic Hammone satus rapta Garamantide
nympha', Silius 1. 142 (of Hamilcar) 'fert Herculeis Gara-
mantica signa columnis'. Here they picturesquely suggest
the southern bounds of the Mediterranean world ('extremi
Garamantes', *E.* 8. 44; cf. Lucan 4. 334). In 19 B.C. the
proconsul L. Cornelius Balbus triumphed for an expedition
against them (Pliny, *NH* 5. 36; Syme, *Roman Revolution*,
339; J. O. Thomson, *History of Ancient Geography*, 264): but
no safe inference can be drawn as to the date of composition
of this passage.

    Indos : then, as now, India held a mysterious glamour: cf.
G. 1. 57, *G.* 2. 116, 122 f. 'quos Oceano propior gerit India
lucos, / extremi sinus orbis'; but Italy surpasses its wonders,
G. 2. 137 f. 'nec pulcher Ganges atque auro turbidus Hermus /
laudibus Italiae certent, non Bactra neque Indi'. For Roman
trade with India see J. O. Thomson, op. cit. 298 ff.

    The allusion is primarily to India as 'extremi sinus orbis',
like that to the Garamantes. But it could hint at the em-
bassies received by Augustus from Indian rulers (*Mon. Anc.*
31, Sueton. *Aug.* 21. 3), one of which was *c.* 25 B.C. (cf.
Nisbet–Hubbard on Hor. *C.* 1. 12. 56 and p. xxxiv). It
might even suggest preparations for attacking the Parthians:
cf. 7. 605 f. 'seu tendere ad Indos / Auroramque sequi Par-
thosque reposcere signa' (the standards lost at Carrhae were
recovered in 20 B.C.; cf. 1. 289, note). It would certainly
offer a comparison of Augustus' conquests with those of
Alexander.

795. extra sidera : i.e. beyond the Zodiac: Servius comments 'nulla terra est quae non subiaceat sideribus; unde perite addidit *extra anni solisque uias*, ut ostenderet xii signa in quibus est circulus solis' (cf. *G.* 1. 231 ff.): see Housman, *CR* xx (1906), 44 f. (= *Classical Papers*, 650 ff.), and his astronomical appendix to his text of Lucan, p. 328. In an ecstatic vision Anchises sees this distant land, beyond the known bounds of the world, to which Augustus shall extend his rule.

796. extra . . . uias : Servius takes Virgil to mean Ethiopia, quoting Lucan 3. 253 ff. 'Aethiopumque solum, quod non premeretur ab ulla / signiferi regione poli, nisi poplite lapso / ultima curuati procederet ungula Tauri'. Statius has a similar hyperbole, *S.* 4. 3. 155 ff. (of Domitian) 'ibis qua uagus Hercules et Euhan / ultra sidera flammeumque solem, / et Nili caput et niues Atlantis'. Housman (l.c.) censures all three poets for imagining the Zodiac as coincident with the Tropic of Cancer.

The language suggests traditional encomia of Alexander: Norden (*Rh. Mus.* l.c., 469, = *Kl. Schr.* 424) notes Aeschines, *in Ctes.* 165 ὁ δ᾽ Ἀλέξανδρος ἔξω τῆς ἄρκτου καὶ τῆς οἰκουμένης ὀλίγου δεῖν πάσης μεθειστήκει; cf. Sen. *Suas.* 1. 2 'tempus est Alexandrum cum orbe et cum sole desinere'.

caelifer : first recorded here: also of Atlas, Ovid, *F.* 5. 83, Silius 15. 142, Stat. *Th.* 5. 430. Ti. Donatus somewhat disrespectfully describes Atlas as 'baiulus caeli'.

Atlas : he stood πείρασιν ἐν γαίης πρόπαρ᾽ Ἑσπερίδων λιγυφώνων (Hesiod, *Theog.* 518; see West ad loc.).

797. A splendid line, repeated from 4. 481 f. 'ultimus Aethiopum locus est, ubi maximus Atlas / axem umero torquet stellis ardentibus aptum'. The phrasing is from Ennius, *Ann.* 29 'qui caelum uersat stellis fulgentibus aptum', 159 'caelum suspexit stellis fulgentibus aptum', 339 'hinc Nox processit stellis ardentibus apta' (borrowed by Virgil, 11. 201 f. 'nox umida donec / inuertit caelum stellis ardentibus aptum'): see Bowra, *CQ* xxiii (1929), 68 f. So too Lucr. 6. 357 f. 'autumnoque magis stellis fulgentibus apta / concutitur caeli domus'. For the participial *aptum* ('fitted with'), frequent in Lucretius, see *Thes.L.L.* s.v., 328. 49 ff. With *axem torquet* cf. Varro Atacinus, fr. 14. 1 Morel 'uidit et aetherio mundum torquerier axe'.

Servius is no doubt right in assuming that Virgil is thinking of Ethiopia (cf. 4. 481, above). The Ethiopians were originally a strange mythical people, living vaguely across Africa from east to west; in *Od.* 1. 23 f. they are ἔσχατοι ἀνδρῶν / οἱ μὲν δυσομένου Ὑπερίονος, οἱ δ᾽ ἀνιόντος (cf. Pliny,

NH 5. 43, and see West on Hesiod, *Theog.* 985); according
to Herodotus (4. 183. 4) they were hunted by the Gara-
mantes. An association of Ethiopia with a visionary region
'extra anni solisque uias' would accord well with the tone
of the passage; it suits Virgil's poetic purpose to imagine
Atlas there—the fabled giant, not the mountain as Housman
seems to have supposed: cf. Norden, *Rh. Mus.* l.c., 470 ff.
(= *Kl. Schr.* 426 ff.).

798. in aduentum : 'expecting his coming'; not a common use
of *in* (cf. Hor. *Epp.* 1. 3. 36 'pascitur in uestrum reditum
uotiua iuuenca').

    iam nunc : cf. *G.* 1. 42 'uotis iam nunc adsuesce uocari':
Anchises impatiently anticipates reality.

    Caspia regna : perhaps an allusion to an embassy from
Scythia to Augustus in 25 B.C. (*Mon. Anc.* 31. 2; Norden,
Rh. Mus. l.c., 477 ff. = *Kl. Schr.* 432 ff.). But again (like
Maeotia tellus in 799, i.e. the region round the Sea of Azov),
it need be no more than romantic rhetorical geography, used
to indicate distant Eastern worlds, much as Horace speaks
of the Massagetae (*C.* 1. 35. 40; see Nisbet–Hubbard ad loc.).
It suggests another comparison with Alexander (cf. J. O.
Thomson, op. cit. 127).

799. responsis : 'because of oracles'. Norden refers this to
current 'Sibylline' prophecies (*Rh. Mus.* l.c., 478 ff. = *Kl.
Schr.* 433 ff.). That there was a vast accretion of 'super-
natural' lore concerning Augustus is clear from Sueton.
Aug. 94; a Sibylline oracle conveniently turned up when he
was preparing to celebrate the *ludi saeculares* in 17 B.C. (see
Fraenkel, *Horace*, 365 f.; text in Kiessling–Heinze on the *car-
men saeculare*, 467).

800. septemgemini : from Cat. 11. 7 f. 'quae septemgeminus
colorat / aequora Nilus' (with Scythians and Parthians in
the previous line); cf. Aesch. *fr.* 304 Νεῖλος ἑπτάρους, Moschus
2. 51 ἑπταπόρῳ παρὰ Νείλῳ: so of Rome, Stat. *S.* 1. 2. 191 'quis
septemgeminae posuisset moenia Romae?', 4. 1. 6 f. 'septem-
gemino iactantior aethera pulset / Roma iugo'.

    turbant : 'are in turmoil'; a curious intransitive use: cf.
Lucr. 3. 492 f. (of an epileptic) 'ui morbi distracta per artus /
turbat agens anima spumas'; Varro, *RR* 3. 17. 7 'cum mare
turbaret'; Tac. *Ann.* 3. 47 'si una alteraue ciuitas turbet'. For
the frightened Nile cf. Prop. 3. 11. 51 (of Cleopatra) 'fugisti
tamen in timidi uaga flumina Nili', Ovid, *Met.* 2. 254 'Nilus
in extremum fugit perterritus orbem' (when Phaethon set the
world on fire).

801 ff. The *laus Augusti* is rounded off in the approved manner
of rhetoric with a pair of *exempla* (cf. 119 ff.), Hercules and

Bacchus, both hinting at a comparison with Alexander. Horace associates both with Augustus, as benefactors of mankind (*C.* 3. 3. 9 ff.); cf. Cic. *de nat. deor.* 2. 62 'suscepit . . . uita hominum consuetudoque communis ut beneficiis excellentes uiros in caelum fama ac uoluntate tollerent. hinc Hercules . . . hinc Liber etiam . . . hinc etiam Romulus', *de off.* 3. 25 'Herculem illum, quem hominum fama beneficiorum memor in concilio caelestium collocauit'. Both occur in encomia of Alexander: Norden (*Rh. Mus.* l.c., 470 = *Kl. Schr.* 425) notes the rhetorician Menander (388. 6 Spengel) ὁ Ἀλέξανδρος ὁ μηδὲ Ἡρακλέους λειπόμενος μηδὲ Διονύσου νομισθεὶς εἶναι χείρων, Lucian, *dial. mort.* 14. 6 (Alexander speaking) Ἡρακλεῖ καὶ Διονύσῳ ἐνάμιλλον τιθέασί με.

802 f. Virgil chooses examples from the Labours of Hercules in which he gave men peace from plaguing monsters: contrast Lucretius' attitude (5. 22 ff.).

802. fixerit : 'shot'; so *figere dammas*, *G.* 1. 308; *figere ceruos*, *E.* 2. 29. Hercules' third Labour was to bring the hind of Cerynaia to Mycenae, alive (Apollod. *Bibl.* 2. 5. 3); Virgil follows a version by which the hind was killed (so Eur. *HF* 378).

aeripedem : a Virgilian coinage, borrowed by Silius 3. 38 f. 'altos / aeripedis ramos superantia cornua cerui' (in the depicting of the Labours on the temple-gates at Gades); Ovid has it of the brazen-footed bulls at Colchis (*Met.* 7. 104 f.). The hind had horns of gold (Apollod. l.c.; Pindar, *O.* 3. 51, where Hercules is said to have sought it 'behind the North Wind'; Callim. *h.* 3. 102).

Erymanthi : polysyllabic ending, with the Greek name. The fourth Labour was the capture of the Erymanthian boar (Apollod. *Bibl.* 2. 5. 4). Pausanias (8. 24. 5) knew a story, which he disbelieved, that the boar's tusks were dedicated in Apollo's temple at Cumae.

803. Lernam : for the killing of the Hydra see on 287.

804. pampineis : not recorded before Virgil. Bacchus' reins were made of vine-shoots, *pampini*; cf. Prop. 3. 17. 26 *pampinea . . . rate*, of Bacchus' ship, travelling to Naxos, when a vine twined round the mast (*Hom. h.* 7. 38 f.). For Bacchus' discovery of the vine, and his travels, see Frazer on Apollod. *Bibl.* 3. 5. 1.

805. Nysae : the legendary mountain where Dionysus was said to have been brought up by nymphs, situated variously in Egypt (*Hom. h.* 1. 9), Ethiopia (Hdt. 2. 146), Arabia (Diodorus, 3. 59. 2, etc.), India (Pliny, *NH* 6. 79), Asia (Apollod. *Bibl.* 3. 4. 3; see Frazer).

tigris : for Bacchus' team of tigresses cf. *E.* 5. 29, Hor. *C.*

3. 3. 14; for a mosaic from Saragossa depicting it see J. M. C.
Toynbee, *Animals in Roman Life and Art* (London, 1973), 70
(and, for a team of leopards, 84 ff., pls. 25, 26). Sometimes he
drives lynxes (Ovid, *Met.* 4. 25, Prop. 3. 17. 8; cf. *G.* 3. 264);
for an imagined Bacchic zoo see Ovid, *Met.* 3. 668 f. 'quem
circa tigres simulacraque inania lyncum / pictarumque iacent
fera corpora pantherarum'. The beasts symbolize Bacchus'
power to tame and civilize: it is a pointed *exemplum*. Alexan-
der's eastern conquests are hinted at in the mention of Nysa
(see Curtius 8. 10. 13 for his reported ascent of the moun-
tain); it is recorded further that on his arrival in India certain
princes met him with the words 'illum tertium Ioue genitum
ad ipsos peruenisse; Patrem Liberum atque Herculem fama
cognitos esse, ipsum coram adesse cernique' (Curtius 8. 10. 1).

806 f. Anchises ends his prophecy of Augustus, in the manner
of rhetoric, with a moral exhortation drawn from the *exem-
pla*, not in any spirit of chiding but in loving encourage-
ment: Aeneas need have no further doubts or hesitations,
he has seen the glorious vision through his father's eyes. In
dubitamus ('pro *dubitas*; miscuit personam suam', Servius)
Anchises, ghost though he is, identifies himself with his son's
emotions, an affectionate and tender touch, characteristic of
Virgil's whole picture of their relationship. It was a fine
stroke of the poet to place the exhortation just here, and
not at the conclusion of the whole survey as a less visionary
writer might have done: this is where its force is strongest,
with Augustus to inspire and comfort.

806. et dubitamus : for *et* in exhortatory protest cf. *G.* 2. 433
'et dubitant homines serere atque impendere curam?' after
an enumeration of Nature's bounties; sometimes it intro-
duces expostulation, e.g. 1. 48 f. 'et quisquam numen Iuno-
nis adorat / praeterea aut supplex aris imponet honorem?'
Ovid, *Am.* 3. 8. 1 'et quisquam ingenuas etiamnunc suspicit
artes?'

    uirtutem ... factis : 'to enlarge worth by action'; cf. 10.
468 f. 'sed famam extendere factis, / hoc uirtutis opus':
Aeneas has the needed *uirtus*—it is there to be used. The
v.l. *uirtute extendere uires* has sound support, and is preferred
by Conington, Ribbeck, Sabbadini, and Geymonat: but it
seems to put the wrong emphasis on both nouns.

808 ff. Anchises now takes up the tale that was interrupted
at 788, foretelling the Kings of Rome and, by a smooth
transition (818), the great men of the early Republic.

808. quis ... autem : a type of dramatic formula that occurs
often in Comedy when a new character appears: e.g. Plaut.
Cist. 534 'sed quis hic est qui recta platea cursum huc con-

tendit suom?', *Epid.* 435 f. 'sed quis illic est quem huc
aduenientem conspicor / suam qui undantem chlamydem
quassando facit?' Further, if the words were read without
the dactylic hexameter's ictus, they could be the opening
of a senarius, so that the illusion of conversational drama is
increased: see on 2. 101; Fraenkel, *Horace*, 349.

   ramis . . . oliuae : for the olive as a priestly symbol cf.
7. 417 f. (of Allecto, disguising herself as Iuno's priestess)
'induit albos / cum uitta crinis, tum ramum innectit oliuae',
7. 750 f. 'sacerdos / fronde super galeam et felici comptus
oliua'; in 5. 774 Aeneas makes sacrifice 'caput tonsae foliis
euinctus oliuae'.

809. sacra ferens : he bears the holy emblems of his office
(perhaps an image of the divinity); cf. 8. 85 'mactat sacra
ferens' (Aeneas sacrificing the White Sow), Hor. *Sat.* 1. 3.
10 f. 'uelut qui / Iunonis sacra ferret': so the poet as the
Muses' priest prays for their favour, *G.* 2. 476 'quarum sacra
fero ingenti percussus amore'.

   crinis . . . menta : the description of personal appearance
is in the manner of drama (cf. Plaut. *Epid.* l.c.). Anchises
recognizes Numa from a distance; the identification made
a name superfluous.

   incanaque menta : so *G.* 3. 311 'barbas incanaque menta',
of a goat, dignifying him as patriarch of the flock. The adjec-
tive is rare; cf. Plaut. *Rud.* 125 'ecquem tu hic hominem
crispum incanum uideras?', another reminder of Virgil's
closeness to drama. The plural *menta* is conditioned by the
metrical advantage of the plural epithet; it is unusual, un-
like such plurals as *corda, colla, pectora*, with reference to
a single person (cf. Maas, *ALL* xii, 541). Servius has a tale
that Numa was white-haired *a prima aetate*.

810. regis Romani : Numa Pompilius, distinguished for his
iustitia and *religio* (Livy 1. 18. 1) 'qui regno ita potitus urbem
nouam conditam ui et armis, iure eam legibusque ac moribus
de integro condere parat' (Livy 1. 19. 1). The allusive descrip-
tion of his priestly appearance is relevant both to his legen-
dary religious foundations and to his personal priesthood
(Livy 1. 20. 1 'tum sacerdotibus creandis animum adiecit,
quamquam ipse plurima sacra obibat, ea maxime quae nunc
ad Dialem flaminem pertinent'). For the historicity of
Numa's reign see Ogilvie on Livy 1. 18–21.

   primam . . . urbem : cf. 7. 61 'primas cum conderet arces':
the priority is transferred to the city from the man, as in
Silius 13. 534 'primas fundarunt moenibus urbes'. In Sen.
Apocol. 10 Augustus is made to claim 'legibus urbem fundaui',
a second Numa as well as being a second Romulus.

811. Curibus : a Sabine town, on the left bank of the Tiber, where Numa lived before he was summoned to become King (Livy 1. 18. 1 ff.): see Ogilvie on Livy 1. 13. 5, where the ancient derivation of *Quirites* from *Cures* is disputed (cf. Bömer on Ovid, *F.* 2. 475). The ablatives *Curibus, terra* depend on *missus* (812): the OCT wrongly punctuates with a comma after *terra* and none after *fundabit*.

812. imperium magnum : in marked contrast with *Curibus paruis et paupere terra*. Great emphasis is put on *magnum* by the sweep to the fourth-foot caesura and the strong pause that follows, with complete break in sense. A further striking effect is produced by the juxtaposition of noun and adjective, with the assonance caused by repeated *-um* and emphasized by the ictus.

This whole passage on Numa was said to have been lighted on by Hadrian when he consulted the *sortes Vergilianae* to discover Trajan's feelings towards him (Spartianus, *Hadr.* 2. 8).

813 f. With this vignette of Tullus Hostilius cf. Livy 1. 22. 2 'hic non solum proximo regi dissimilis sed ferocior etiam quam Romulus fuit. cum aetas uiresque tum auita quoque gloria animum stimulabat. senescere igitur ciuitatem otio ratus undique materiam excitandi belli quaerebat': for the traditions of his reign see Ogilvie on Livy 1. 22–31; the fall of Alba to Tullus' army is one of Livy's most moving episodes (1. 29).

813. residesque mouebit : a variation on *otia rumpet*; the sense of *resides* ('stagnating') is in turn varied in *desueta* ('out of practice'). Varro uses *reses* of stagnant water (*RR* 3. 17. 8), contrasted with a flowing stream; for the association with *desuetus* (a word first recorded in Virgil) cf. 1. 722 'iam pridem resides animos desuetaque corda', 7. 693 f. 'iam pridem resides populos desuetaque bello / agmina in arma uocat', Ovid, *Met.* 14. 436 'resides et desuetudine tardi'.

815. iactantior : the positive *iactans* as an adjective is not used in classical poetry; for the comparative cf. *Hor. Sat.* 1. 3. 49 f. 'ineptus / et iactantior hic paulo est', Stat. *S.* 4. 1. 6 f. 'septemgemino iactantior aethera pulset / Roma iugo'.

For the reign of Ancus Marcius see Ogilvie on Livy 1. 32–4. Nothing in Livy's tradition explains Virgil's reference to him here as 'nimium gaudens popularibus auris'. Norden suggested a confusion with Servius Tullius (omitted in Virgil's king-list), who ἐπὶ τὸ δημαγωγεῖν καὶ θεραπεύειν τοὺς ἀπόρους τῶν πολιτῶν ἐτρέπετο (Dion. Hal. *ant. Rom.* 4. 8. 3). Such a historical blunder seems improbable: and the whimsical, not to say amusing, conception of such *populares aurae* among the ghosts points to some definite (if apocryphal) family legend current at some time in the *gens Marcia*, a plebeian house. See O. Skutsch, *Entretiens Hardt* xvii (1972), 14 ff., E. Badian, ib. 34 f.; Skutsch thinks it possible that the Latin leader Ancus Poplicius, mentioned in Dion. Hal. *ant. Rom.* 3. 34. 3, is to be identified with the king, and that Virgil's allusion arose from the implications of the name Poplicius.

816. popularibus auris : a frequent metaphor: cf. Cic. *har. resp.* 43 'Sulpicium . . . longius quam uoluit popularis aura prouexit'; Livy 3. 33. 7 'ut plebicola . . . omnisque aurae popularis captator euaderet' (of Appius Claudius); Hor. *C.* 3. 2. 20 'arbitrio popularis aurae'; Lucan 1. 132 f. (of Pompey) 'multa dare in uulgus, totus popularibus auris / inpelli'; [Ovid], *Hal.* 69 f. 'nonne uides uictor quanto sublimius altum / adtollat caput et uulgi se uenditet aurae?' (of a racehorse).

817. uis : a new way of varying the introductions, and a pointed one: the Tarquins are distasteful to mention (and are quickly passed over, with the inference of a negative reply to Anchises' question); the story of Brutus is ghastly, but he did the State high service (and a positive reply is assumed).

Tarquinios : Priscus and Superbus (Livy 1. 35 ff., 1. 49 ff.): see Ogilvie's introductions to both passages.

animamque superbam : Virgil has transferred to Brutus the *superbia* of the second Tarquin. This is the natural interpretation: but Servius plainly took the words to refer to Tarquin; Ti. Donatus explains 'superbiae uitium magis Tarquiniis adplicatur secundum ueterum fabulam, non Bruto', which shows that both views existed. Norden accepts Servius, putting a comma at the end of the line, making *Bruti* (818) dependent on *fasces*, and taking *-que* (818) as a postponed connective; so too Sabbadini and Geymonat (but Sabbadini in his commentary [1927] took the other view). This seems quite untenable: it involves a most disconcerting postposition of *-que* (theoretically possible; see Norden, p. 404 n. 4), and destroys the natural rhythm of both lines, besides depriving Virgil of an arresting point.

The meaning of *animam superbam* as applied to Brutus is ambivalent. Virgil normally uses the epithet in a bad sense, of overweening pride: so of Turnus, 10. 514, 12. 326; of Mezentius, 11. 15; of Metabus, 11. 539; Dido terms Aeneas *hostem superbum*, 4. 424; Camilla taunts an enemy 'uane Ligus, frustraque animis elate superbis' (11. 715). But he also has it of men 'glorying in' rewards or achievements (5. 268, 473, 8. 202), an innocent pride; and twice it bears an honourable sense of proud distinction, 2. 556 f. (of Priam) 'tot quondam populis terrisque superbum / regnatorem Asiae', 3. 475 'coniugio, Anchisa, Veneris dignate superbo' (Helenus speaking). Here Virgil is torn between admiration for the proud spirit of the man who gloried in the overthrow of a tyrant, and horror at the unbending spirit of the father who had his own sons executed: *animam superbam* contains both implications. The dilemma would be sharpened by the memory of another Brutus, an *ultor* likewise: what were Virgil's thoughts of him?

For some discussion see Plüss, op. cit. 229 ff.; W. F. J. Knight, *CR* xlvi (1932), 55 ff., R. S. Conway, ib. 199 ff.

818. fascisque . . . receptos : for the *fasces* see Ogilvie on Livy 2. 1. 7. They were 'recovered' from the kings: i.e. the ruling authority was transferred from kings to consuls. For the historicity of L. Iunius Brutus see Walbank on Polybius 3. 22. 1–3, Ogilvie on Livy 1. 56. 3.

819. consulis imperium : 509 B.C. (Livy 1. 60. 4; see Ogilvie).
saeuasque securis : the lictors' axes (see Ogilvie on Livy 1. 8. 2): cf. Lucr. 3. 995 ff. 'Sisyphus in uita quoque nobis ante oculos est / qui petere a populo fascis saeuasque securis / imbibit', 5. 1233 ff. 'usque adeo res humanas uis abdita quaedam / obterit et pulchros fascis saeuasque securis / proculcare ac ludibrio sibi habere uidetur'.

820. natosque pater : for the juxtaposition cf. 8. 383 'arma rogo, genetrix nato', 10. 466 'genitor natum dictis adfatur amicis'.
noua bella : the sons of Brutus plotted with other high-born young men to bring back the Tarquins (Livy 2. 4); *noua* implies both 'renewed' and 'strange' (from their position and their impiety).

821. Sound and rhythm and meaning make this a memorable line: the solemn spondees, the sharp alliteration, the juxtaposition of *poenam* with *pulchra*—all is effective. For the story see Livy 2. 5. 6 ff.
pulchra : with a moral sense, 'noble'; here the *anima superba* of Brutus is justified: cf. 2. 317 'pulchrumque mori succurrit in armis', 9. 401 'pulchram properet per uulnera mortem'; Lucan 9. 390 ff. (Cato speaking) 'hi mihi sint comites, quos ipsa pericula ducent, / qui me teste pati uel quae tristissima pulchrum / Romanumque putant'.
libertate : cf. Livy 2. 1. 1 'liberi iam hinc populi Romani res pace belloque gestas, annuos magistratus, imperiaque legum potentiora quam hominum peragam' (after the expulsion of Tarquin).

Livy states (2. 5. 8) 'consules in sedem processere suam, missique lictores ad sumendum supplicium. nudatos uirgis caedunt securique feriunt, cum inter omne tempus pater

uoltusque et os eius spectaculo esset, eminente animo
patrio inter publicae poenae ministerium'. The execution
became a theme for the rhetoric-schools: see *ad Herenn.*
4. 66, Quintilian 5. 11. 7, Sen. *Contr.* 10. 3. 8; cf. Val. Max.
5. 8. 1 'exuit patrem ut consulem ageret, orbusque uiuere
quam publicae uindictae deesse maluit'.

822 f. 'Poor man, however later ages shall judge that deed:
patriotism will prevail, and a measureless desire for honour'.
Servius comments 'etiamsi lauderis a posteris: extorquere
debet naturae uim amor patriae'. St. Augustine has a sensi-
tive exposition, *de ciu. Dei* 3. 16 'quod factum Vergilius
postea quam laudabiliter commemorauit, continuo clemen-
ter exhorruit. cum enim dixisset *natosque pater noua bella
mouentis / ad poenam pulchra pro libertate uocabit,* mox deinde
exclamauit et ait *infelix, utcumque ferent ea facta minores.*
quomodolibet, inquit, ea facta posteri ferant, id est prae-
ferant et extollant, qui filios occidit infelix est. et tamquam
ad consolandum infelicem, subiunxit, *uincit amor patriae
laudumque immensa cupido'.* The dilemma of the *anima
superba* could hardly be better set out, nor Virgil's better
understood.

822. ferent : a neutral word ('take', 'interpret'); here praise is
implied (but in spite of it Brutus is *infelix*).

824 ff. After singling out Brutus, Virgil interposes a cluster of
famous republican names: typical of his method.

824. quin : with *aspice* (cf. Ovid, *Met.* 7. 70 f. 'quin adspice,
quantum / adgrediare nefas!'). This use with an imperative
was originally colloquial, often marking impatience or an-
noyance: Virgil brought it into elevated style (HSz, 676; see
on 4. 99). Anchises hurries on from the painful subjects of the
preceding lines.

Decios : father (Livy 8. 9; 340 B.C.) and son (Livy 10. 28;
295 B.C.), famous *exempla* of self-immolation *(deuotio)* 'pro
salute populi Romani uictoriaque' (Cic. *Sest.* 48); that a
grandson followed suit is an invention (Cic. *Tusc.* 1. 89;
see Dougan ad loc.): cf. Manilius 1. 789 'certantesque Deci
uotis'.

Drusos : an evocative name in the *gens Liuia.* The primary
reference is to M. Livius Drusus, tr. pl. 91 B.C.; cf. Lucan
6. 795 f. 'laetantis, popularia nomina, Drusos / legibus in-
modicos': see *ad Herenn.* 4. 31 for a declamation-theme on
his death, coupled with the Gracchi and Saturninus. Servius
saw an allusion to Augustus' stepson Nero Claudius Drusus;
he refers also to M. Livius Salinator, victor at the Metaurus
in 207 B.C. (not himself a Drusus, but a glorious ancestor of
the family; cf. Hor. *C.* 4. 4. 37 ff.).

saeuumque securi : for Manlius Torquatus' execution of his disobedient son see Livy 8. 7. 19: the remarkable echo from 819 stresses the parallelism between two stern fathers. Quintilian (5. 11. 10) names him as an *exemplum* in rhetoric (cf. Sen. *Contr.* 9. 2. 19, 10. 3. 8).

825. referentem signa : one of the many legendary feats of Camillus was the recovery of the gold said to have been the price of the Gauls' withdrawal from Rome in 390 B.C.; for the tangled story see Ogilvie on Livy 5. 48–50. Virgil has substituted Roman standards for the gold. Both *signa* and gold are mentioned by Servius, and by the fourth-century historian Eutropius (1. 20. 3), who might be reflecting Virgil as Norden holds. There is possibly a similar allusion in Prop. 3. 11. 67 'nunc ubi Scipiadae classes, ubi signa Camilli?' (if *signa* there is not simply used for 'army'), in a context of direct adulation of Augustus: that book was published in 22/21 B.C., a year or so after Virgil read *Aen.* 6 to Augustus.

It is highly probable that Virgil's variation deliberately alludes to the recovery of the standards lost to the Parthians at Carrhae, achieved by negotiation in 20 B.C., or at least to the anticipation of their recovery (cf. 7. 606 'Parthosque reposcere signa', Prop. 3. 4. 9 'omina fausta cano. Crassos clademque piate!'). Münzer suggests (*RE* s.v. *Furius*, 44) that among the statues of famous Romans in the *forum Augusti* (for which cf. Syme, *Roman Revolution*, 449) there was one of Camillus shown with the *signa* as symbolic of the hope placed in Augustus as the saviour of Roman honour. The defeat of Crassus at Carrhae and the loss of the standards was deeply traumatic; a modern parallel might be Pearl Harbour, or Sedan. Virgil's contemporaries would know what he meant.

826 ff. Virgil again interrupts chronology, as with Augustus, to give prominence to Caesar and Pompey: no names, but *paribus armis* gives the clue, and *socer . . . gener* (830 f.) is explicit.

826. paribus : of civil war: *G.* 1. 489 f. 'ergo inter sese paribus concurrere telis / Romanas acies iterum uidere Philippi'; Lucan 1. 7 'pares aquilas et pila minantia pilis'.

fulgĕre : so *effulgĕre*, 8. 677. This archaic form occurs in early poetry and in Lucr. 5. 1095, 6. 165 (cf. Bailey, *proleg.* 85 f.); it is revived in Val. Flacc. 8. 284.

827. concordes : contrast Lucan 1. 87 (of the Triumvirate) 'o male concordes nimiaque cupidine caeci'. In his earlier political career Caesar was on good terms with Pompey (cf. Syme, op. cit. 35 f.), whom his daughter Iulia married in 59 B.C.

dum nocte prementur : 'during all their time with the weight of night upon them', i.e. in their ghostly existence before rebirth. There is sound authority also for the v.l. *premuntur* (so too Servius, Ti. Donatus), preferred by Norden and Sabbadini: the future (so too Geymonat) gives a certain contrast with *nunc* ('now and for the rest of their time in darkness').

828 f. Cf. Silius 13. 864 ff. (Scipio in the Underworld sees Pompey and Caesar) 'quantas moles, cum sede reclusa / hinc tandem erumpent, terraque marique mouebunt! / heu miseri, quotiens toto pugnabitis orbe! / nec leuiora lues quam uictus crimina uictor': a typically Silver 'improvement'. For Anchises' pretended misgiving in 'si lumina uitae attigerint' cf. 770 (but here the reason is horrified reluctance to contemplate what will happen).

830 f. socer . . . gener : the marriage-relationship between Caesar and Pompey added a special family *impietas* to the wider *impietas* of civil war; cf. 7. 317 'hac gener atque socer coeant mercede suorum' (a savage allusion by Iuno to Aeneas and Latinus).

Virgil has given Epic cachet to what was originally a gibe of the lampoonists: Cat. 29. 24 'socer generque, perdidistis omnia' (in his squib against Mamurra), quoted in *Catalepton* 6. 5 f. 'ut ille uersus usquequaque pertinet: "gener socerque, perdidistis omnia"'. Lucan seized upon it for 'point' (1. 289 f. 'socerum depellere regno / decretum genero est', 4. 802, 10. 417); so Martial 9. 70. 3 f. 'cum gener atque socer diris concurreret armis / maestaque ciuili caede maderet humus'; it was revived by Sidonius, *C.* 9. 239 ff. 'pugnam tertius ille Gallicani / dixit Caesaris, ut gener socerque / cognata impulerint in arma Romam' (of Lucan).

830. aggeribus . . . Monoeci : an Epic way of referring to Gaul; Virgil is not concerned with Caesar's actual position at the outbreak of the war (cf. Lucan 1. 183 'iam gelidas Caesar cursu superauerat Alpes'). The *arx Monoeci* is the promontory of Monaco, south of the Maritime Alps, at the western end of the Ligurian coast; there was a harbour there called *portus Herculis*, with a temple on the cliff (see Servius); cf. Silius 1. 585 f. 'Herculei ponto coepere exsistere colles, / et nebulosa iugis attollere saxa Monoeci', Tac. *H.* 3. 42 'Fabius Valens e sinu Pisano . . . portum Herculis Monoeci depellitur'. Servius comments on *aggeribus* 'a munimentis Alpium; haec enim Italiae murorum exhibent uicem'.

831. aduersis . . . Eois : 'in formation with confronting forces from the East': with dramatic simplification Virgil presents the war as a conflict between West and East. After Pompey

had reached Brundisium before Caesar in 49 B.C. he crossed
the Adriatic and made his headquarters at Thessalonica,
where he gathered a strong army and a fleet. But an 'eastern'
aura had been attached to Pompey since his Mithridatic
campaigns and his settlement of Syria and Judaea.

832. pueri : 'my children': the patriarch appeals sadly to his
young descendants.

ne . . . bella : 'never let so dread a war be natural to your
hearts': a striking inversion for *ne tantis animos adsuescite
bellis* (which Virgil could have written, by omitting a re-
peated *ne*). They must not take a civil war as a matter of
course. Ti. Donatus interprets 'nolite, pueri, male adsue-
scere, non expedit ut talia bella gerere discatis'.

833. neu . . . uiris : 'nor turn your sturdy strength against
your country's core'. The line well shows the power of initial
alliteration discreetly used: cf. Lucr. 5. 993 'uiua uidens
uiuo sepeliri uiscera busto', Lucan 1. 2 f. 'populumque
potentem / in sua uictrici conuersum uiscera dextra'. The
effect is passionate and moving.

ualidas . . . uiris : so Ennius, *Ann.* 300 '⟨fortuna⟩ uaria
ualidis ⟨cum⟩ uiribus luctant', Lucr. 1. 286 f. 'ita magna
turbidus imbri / molibus incurrit ualidis cum uiribus amnis',
Cic. *Arat.* 67 'at ualidis aequor pulsabit uiribus Auster'. The
epithet is almost a cliché.

uiscera : cf. Silius 3. 709 'altius Ausoniae penetrare in
uiscera gentis'.

834. Anchises appeals to Caesar, the descendant of his own
line (through Iulus), to take the initiative in forbearance.
Clemency towards the Pompeians was Caesar's deliberate
policy, and *parce* reflects this obliquely: cf. his letter to
Oppius Cornelius (49 B.C.), Cic. *ad Att.* 9. 7c. 1 'mea sponte
facere constitueram ut quam lenissimum me praeberem et
Pompeium darem operam ut reconciliarem. temptemus hoc
modo si possimus omnium uoluntates reciperare et diuturna
uictoria uti, quoniam reliqui crudelitate odium effugere non
potuerunt neque uictoriam diutius tenere praeter unum L.
Sullam, quem imitaturus non sum. haec noua sit ratio uin-
cendi ut misericordia et liberalitate nos muniamus'; in *Deiot.*
34 Cicero terms Caesar *clementissimum in uictoria*. But his
clemency was not always appreciated (Syme, op. cit. 51).

genus . . . Olympo : cf. 5. 800 f. 'fas omne est, Cytherea,
meis te fidere regnis, / unde genus ducis'; Norden notes a
fragment of early Tragedy, *trag. fr. incert.* 124 R 'a Tantalo
ducat genus'. The rhythm is dominated by the 'weak' cae-
sura after *parce*, with sense-pause.

835. sanguis meus : cf. Hor. *Carm. Saec.* 50 'clarus Anchisae

Venerisque sanguis' (of Augustus). The words are in apposition to the vocative *tu*; cf. Stat. *Th.* 3. 239 'uos o superi, meus ordine sanguis': so, e.g., Plaut. *Cist.* 52 f. 'sed tu inter istaec uerba, / meus oculus, mea Selenium', Augustus ap. Gell. 15. 7. 2 'aue, mi Gai, meus asellus iucundissimus'; see HSz, 25; Löfstedt, *Synt.* i, 99 f.; *Thes.L.L.* s.v. *meus*, 914. 61 ff.

For the incomplete line see on 94; this is one of those that are extraordinarily effective and moving as they stand.

836 ff. Virgil now turns back, to a fresh cluster of great names, thronging in quick succession. He begins with conquerors of Greece, who in time will avenge the ruins of Troy: cf. 1. 283 ff. (Iuppiter speaking) 'ueniet lustris labentibus aetas / cum domus Assaraci Pthiam clarasque Mycenas / seruitio premet ac uictis dominabitur Argis'.

836. ille : abrupt, with no introductory particle or phrase; if Virgil had been able to complete the preceding line the abruptness would perhaps have been removed. He alludes to L. Mummius, who sacked Corinth in 146 B.C.: Livy. *per.* 52 'L. Mummius de Achaeis triumphauit, signa aerea marmoreaque et tabulas pictas in triumpho tulit'; the triumph started off Roman interest in works of art (cf. Pliny, *NH* 35. 24 'tabulis . . . externis auctoritatem Romae publice fecit primus omnium L. Mummius', 37. 12 'uictoria . . . illa Pompei primum ad margaritas gemmasque mores inclinauit . . . sicut L. Mummi ad Corinthia et tabulas pictas').

triumphata . . . Corintho : cf. *G.* 3. 33 'bisque triumphatas utroque ab litore gentis'; for the passive participle from the intransitive *triumphare* cf. 770, note, 4. 609, note. The plural *Capitolia* is due to the metre; so *Romana Palatia* (*G.* 1. 499): again, 8. 347 f. 'Capitolia . . . aurea', 8. 653 'Capitolia celsa'; contrast 9. 448 f. 'dum domus Aeneae Capitoli immobile saxum / accolet'.

838. Argos : Virgil regularly has this masculine plural form (for the Greek neuter *Ἄργος*); cf. *Thes.L.L.* s.v. *Argos* for the practice of different authors. Argos and Mycenae are used for 'Greece' in general, in Virgil's coloured way: the allusion is in fact to the victory of L. Aemilius Paullus over Perseus of Macedon at Pydna in 168 B.C., treated in high Epic style as vengeance for Troy.

839. Aeaciden : Perseus claimed descent from Pyrrhus, king of Epirus, himself a claimant for descent from Achilles' son Pyrrhus (Neoptolemus), termed *Aeacida* by Ennius, *Ann.* 179; cf. Prop. 4. 11. 39 'Persen proauo stimulantem pectus Achille' (for the difficulties of the line see Butler–Barber):

so Silius 15. 292 'Aeacidum sceptris proauoque tumebat Achille' (of Perseus' father Philip).

genus . . . Achilli : cf. Silius 14. 94 f. (of Hieronymus of Syracuse) 'Pyrrhus origo dabat stimulos proauique superbum / Aeacidae genus atque aeternus carmine Achilles'. For *armipotentis* see on 500; for the genitive form *Achilli* see Leumann, *Kleine Schriften*, 116 f.

Gellius reports (10. 16. 16 ff.) that Hyginus severely censured Virgil, assuming *Aeaciden* to refer to Pyrrhus: '"confudit" inquit "et personas diuersas et tempora"': poor Virgil.

840. ultus : for the idea of vengeance cf. *AP* 9. 102, on the ruins of Mycenae, τίσασα Πριάμου δαίμοσιν ὀψὲ δίκας: see Gow–Page, *Garland of Philip* ii, pp. 428, 431 for this and similar epigrams.

templa et temerata : for postponed *et* cf. 426. Virgil alludes to the violation of Cassandra in Athena's temple by the Locrian Ajax (see on 1. 41, 2. 403): *temerare* is not recorded before Virgil (cf. Ovid, *Met.* 8. 742 'dicitur et lucos ferro temerasse uetustos', of Erysichthon; Livy 26. 13. 13 'arae foci deum delubra sepulcra maiorum temerata ac uiolata').

841. quis . . . relinquat? : the apostrophe is a new and lively variation for introducing fresh names; cf. *G.* 2. 101 f. (in the list of vines) 'non ego te . . . / transierim, Rhodia, et tumidis, bumaste, racemis' (where the metrical advantage of the figure is clear). For a suggestion that this passage contains direct quotations from Ennius see L. J. D. Richardson, *CQ* xxxvi (1942), 40 ff.; cf. M. Wigodsky, op. cit. 72 n. 362.

magne Cato : the Censor. Cossus won the *spolia opima* (see on 855, 859) by killing Tolumnius (? 426 B.C.; see Ogilvie on Livy 4. 20. 5 ff.); cf. Prop. 4. 10. 23 f. 'Cossus at insequitur Veientis caede Tolumni, / uincere cum Veios posse laboris erat'.

tacitum : 'in silence'; the participial use with a personal object is unusual (contrast Livy 6. 12. 3 'quod cum ab antiquis tacitum praetermissum sit'). The interlaced alliteration of the line is notable; the repeated *t* (also in 840) is very marked.

842. Gracchi genus : not only the two great tribunes, but their father also, Ti. Sempronius, consul 177, censor 169, 'homo prudens ac grauis . . . et saepe alias et maxime censor saluti rei publicae' (Cic. *de or.* 1. 38; cf. *Brut.* 79). An earlier Ti. Sempronius (consul 215 and 213) had a distinguished military record against Hannibal.

842 f. geminos . . . Scipiadas : the elder Scipio Africanus, victor of Zama (202 B.C.), and the younger, destroyer of Carthage

(146 B.C.): Servius, however, thought that Virgil meant the two Scipiones killed in Spain in 211 B.C. (for the date see Walbank, *Polybius* ii, p. 8), an idea ruled out by *cladem Libyae* below.

The hybrid form *Scipiadas* (cf. Lucilius 1139, Lucr. 3. 1034, Hor. *Sat.* 2. 1. 72, Manilius 1. 792) replaces the metrically impossible *Scipiones* (so *Memmiadae* for *Memmio*, Lucr. 1. 26). The singular *Scipio* gave equal difficulty until the practice of shortening final *o* came into vogue (see on 2. 735), as in Ovid, *ars* 3. 410 and often in Silius: but Ennius solved the problem by shortening the final syllable in hiatus on the Greek pattern, 'Scipio inuicte' (*Var.* 3; Cic. *orat.* 152).

For the mannered arrangement of adjective, appositional phrase, noun cf. *E.* 1. 57 'raucae, tua cura, palumbes', *E.* 9. 9 'ueteres, iam fracta cacumina, fagos'; Ovid, *Met.* 8. 372 'gemini, nondum caelestia sidera, fratres': see G. Williams, op. cit. 726 f., where the device is traced to Hellenistic poetry; Vahlen, *opusc. acad.* i, 119 f.; Hollis on Ovid, *Met.* 8. 226; cf. 1. 435, note. Here, as an added complexity, *cladem Libyae* is appended in another apposition.

842. duo fulmina belli : 'two thunderbolts of war': so Lucr. 3. 1034 'Scipiadas, belli fulmen, Carthaginis horror' (of the elder Africanus) in a context that has clear Ennian colour.

The family name Scipio means 'support', 'staff': according to Macrob. *Sat.* 1. 6. 26 it was first borne by a Cornelius who acted as a *baculum* to his blind father. It is likely that *fulmina* contains allusively a Greek word-play on the name (σκῆπτρον = *scipio*; cf. Soph. *O.T.* 456 σκήπτρῳ προδεικνὺς γαῖαν, of the blind Oedipus: σκηπτός = *fulmen*): see Kenney and Munro on Lucr. l.c. The notion of 'support' is evidently latent in Cic. *Balb.* 34 (referring to the event of 211 B.C.) 'cum . . . Carthago nixa duabus Hispaniis huic imperio immineret et cum duo fulmina nostri imperi subito in Hispania, Cn. et P. Scipiones, exstincti occidissent', and probably in Silius 7. 106 f. (with the same allusion) 'ubi nunc sunt fulmina gentis / Scipiadae?' See further O. Skutsch, *Studia Enniana* (London, 1968), 145 ff., where the idea is traced to Ennius, with the added possibility that *fulmen* in Cic. l.c. may be equivalent to *fulmentum* ('prop'). The passages quoted are discussed, with others, by C. Thulin, *ALL* xiv, 511 f. (see also Skutsch's references, l.c. 150).

843. cladem Libyae : cf. Manilius 1. 792 'Scipiadaeque duces, fatum Carthaginis unum'; Val. Max. 3. 2 ext. 5 'Epaminondas maxima Thebarum felicitas, idemque Lacedaemonis prima clades'.

paruoque potentem : cf. 9. 607 'patiens operum paruoque adsueta iuuentus'.

844. **Fabricium** : C. Fabricius Luscinus, consul 282, 278, censor 275: a familiar exemplar of ancient Roman austerity and integrity. For his uprightness in the war with Pyrrhus cf. Cic. *de off.* 3. 86, Plutarch, *Pyrrhus* 20, Val. Max. 4. 3. 6.

sulco . . . serentem : C. Atilius Regulus, consul 257, said to have been sowing on his farm when he was summoned to the consulship, and he was therefore given the *agnomen* Serranus (a typical example of wishful 'etymology'): see Cic. *Rosc. Am.* 50, *Sest.* 72, Pliny, *NH* 18. 20, Val. Max. 4. 4. 5. It is generally held that the name is derived from the Umbrian town of Saranum (cf. Landgraf on Cic. *Rosc. Am.*, l.c.).

For the rhyming assonance *potentem . . . serentem* (not very obtrusive, since *potentem* runs on so closely to *Fabricium*) cf. 469, note. For the triple initial alliteration in the second half of the line cf. 3. 183 'casus Cassandra canebat', 8. 603 'Tyrrheni tuta tenebant', 9. 635 'Rutulis responsa remittunt': Wölfflin (*ALL* xiv, 515 ff.) suggests that it is a feature that may be traced back to the Saturnian metre.

845. **quo . . . Fabii?** : a vivid, animated final introduction; from a vast throng of representatives of the *gens Fabia* (cf. Ogilvie on Livy 2. 48) who whirl him away exhausted by their endless fame, Anchises chooses as his last *exemplum* the hero of Rome's recovery after Trasimene and Cannae, Q. Fabius Maximus Cunctator. For the rhetorical flourish cf. Ovid, *Met.* 8. 491 f. 'ei mihi, quo rapior? fratres, ignoscite matri: / deficiunt ad coepta manus', Hor. *C.* 3. 25. 1 f. 'quo me, Bacche, rapis tui / plenum?'

846. A quotation from Ennius, with slight changes to suit the new setting: *Ann.* 370 'unus homo nobis cunctando restituit rem'. The famous line is evocative of Roman strength and Roman pride, and by using it here Virgil pays his own debt of *pietas* to his great poet-ancestor. It is often quoted: see Vahlen ad loc.; Livy's use of it shows his Epic attitude to history, 30. 26. 9 'sicut dubites utrum ingenio cunctator fuerit an quia ita bello proprie quod tum gerebatur aptum erat, sic nihil certius est quam unum hominem nobis cunctando rem restituisse, sicut Ennius ait'.

847-53. This epilogue to Anchises' prophecy is the most famous sustained passage in the whole *Aeneid*. It proclaims Rome's duty to the world of the poet's future, the *Pax Romana* of his poetic vision, the conjunction of two complementary cultures, each with its special gifts for mankind, its own civilizing power. Its construction is carefully wrought: four lines to Greece ('alii'), three to Rome; a casual-seeming parenthesis in each part, in the second line of each and in the same position of the line; the verbs in the first part are in balanced arrangement, with *excudent, orabunt* opening their clause, *ducent, describent* in an inner position, and the concluding line framed by *describent, dicent*; in the second part *regere imperio, pacique imponere morem* stand in the first and second half of their respective lines, and the final line contains two verbs, *parcere, debellare*, giving it ultimate weight. There is abundant alliteration and assonance, a craftsman's mosaic of sound. The passage is in 'priamel' form, a stylistic device in which there is an opening 'preamble' describing what others do or prefer, leading to a contrasting climax expressing the writer's own attitude, this being the real purpose of the piece: so, e.g., Hor. *C.* 1. 7. 1 ff. 'laudabunt alii . . . / sunt quibus unum opus est . . . / me . . .' (see Nisbet– Hubbard ad loc. and on *C.* 1. 1; Fraenkel, *Horace*, 230 f., and on Aesch. *Ag.* 899–902).

Virgil looks at the Greek genius with respect and honour, and without jealousy: for him a civilized world meant a Greco-Roman world. His patriotism is of a very different type from that of Cicero, who justified his decision to expound philosophy in Latin by saying (*Tusc.* 1. 1 ff.) 'meum semper iudicium fuit omnia nostros aut inuenisse per se sapientius quam Graecos aut accepta ab illis fecisse meliora, quae quidem digna statuissent in quibus elaborarent', etc. But Cicero himself would have been one with Virgil in finding incomprehensible the mentality of old Cato, who termed the Greeks *nequissimum et indocile genus*, saying 'quandoque ista gens suas litteras dabit, omnia corrumpet' (Pliny, *NH* 29. 14). Whether Virgil's contemporaries shared his vision with full sympathy and understanding is doubtful: see M. Grant, *Proc. Virg. Soc.* iii (1963–4), 10 f.

847. excudent : 'shall shape': the verb (which Virgil brought into poetry) is strictly not applicable to bronze-casting, since its proper sense is 'hammer out'; cf. Quintilian 2. 21. 10, where *excusor* is used of a worker in bronze for *uasa*, contrasted with a bronze-caster (*statuarius*). For another unexpected use cf. *G.* 4. 57 (of bees) 'excudunt ceras et mella tenacia fingunt'. See Bömer, *Hermes* lxxx (1952), 117 ff.

spirantia : cf. *G.* 3. 34 'Parii lapides, spirantia signa', Martial 7. 84. 2 'spirat et arguta picta tabella manu'; so *A P* 9. 724. 2 πλάττεις ἔμπνοα καὶ σὺ Μύρων (of Myron's celebrated lifelike cow; cf. Petron. 88. 5 'Myron qui paene animas hominum ferarumque aere comprehendit'; for the epigrams on the subject see Overbeck, *Die Antiken Schriftquellen*, nos. 550–88; Gow-Page, *Hellenistic Epigrams* ii, p. 63).

mollius : of delicate, supple work; cf. Cic. *Brut.* 70 'Cala-
midis dura illa quidem, sed tamen molliora quam Canachi',
Quintilian 12. 10. 7 'duriora . . . Callon atque Hegesias, iam
minus rigida Calamis, molliora adhuc supra dictis Myron
fecit'.

aera : for Greek artists in bronze see Pliny, *NH* 34, *passim*.

848. **credo equidem** : 'yes, I am sure'; the parenthesis makes
the structure momentarily informal, giving an impression of
lively talk and gesture. For the early variant *cedo* see Fraen-
kel, *JRS* xxxviii (1948), 132 (= *Kl. Beitr.* ii, 342).

uiuos . . . uultus : *uiuos* corresponds to *spirantia* above; cf.
Stat. *S.* 4. 6. 26 f. 'laboriferi uiuant quae marmora caelo /
Praxitelis' *AP* 16. 159. 1 τίς λίθον ἐψύχωσε; (of the Cnidian
Aphrodite). For his own purposes Virgil grants generally to
the Greeks an art-form that in one respect could be claimed
as essentially Roman, the 'veristic' type of republican por-
traiture with its remarkable facial detail, developed under
the influence of late Hellenistic art (see *OCD*, s.v. *Portraiture*) :
cf. Polybius 6. 53. 5 (of the Roman ancestral *imagines*) ἡ δὲ
εἰκὼν ἔστι πρόσωπον εἰς ὁμοιότητα διαφερόντως ἐξειργασμένον, καὶ κατὰ
τὴν πλάσιν καὶ κατὰ τὴν ὑπογραφήν.

ducent : 'shall mould'; another unexpected use (cf. Bömer,
Hermes, l.c.) : the marble is made ductile, as if it were metal.
For the normal use cf. 7. 633 f. 'alii thoracas aënos / aut
leuis ocreas lento ducunt argento', Hor. *Epp.* 2. 1. 239 ff. 'ne
quis se praeter Apellen / pingeret, aut alius Lysippo duceret
aera / fortis Alexandri uultum simulantia'; with Virgil here
cf. Claudian, *carm. min.* 7. 7 f. (on a marble *quadriga*) 'una
silex tot membra ligat ductusque per artem / mons patiens
ferri uarios mutatur in artus'.

849. **orabunt . . . melius** : what would Cicero have made of
this? In speaking of his early predecessors in oratory he re-
marks (*Tusc.* 1. 5) that they were 'ita magnos nostram ad
aetatem ut non multum aut nihil omnino Graecis cederetur';
but he is always generous to Demosthenes (e.g. *Brutus* 35,
Orator 110). Quintilian has no doubts: while admitting 'De-
mosthenen in primis legendum uel ediscendum potius' (10.
1. 105), he claims of Romans 'oratores . . . uel praecipue
Latinam eloquentiam parem facere Graecae possunt; nam
Ciceronem cuicumque eorum fortiter opposuerim'. The fact
remains that Roman oratory was completely informed and
shaped by Greek principles; and the very difference in the
quality of the two languages put Latin on the defensive (see
the interesting passage in Quintilian 12. 10. 27 ff.).

meatus : 'journeyings', with *caeli* generalizing for the
heavenly bodies; cf. Lucr. 1. 128 f. 'solis lunaeque meatus /

qua fiant ratione'; Lucan 1. 663 f. 'cur signa meatus / de-
seruere suos?'

850. describent radio : 'shall mark out with a pointer'; cf.
E. 3. 40 f. 'quis fuit alter / descripsit radio totum qui gentibus
orbem?', Claudian, *Paneg. Man.* 274 f. 'qua saepe magistra /
Manlius igniferos radio descripserat axes'. Astronomy offered
Virgil a somewhat easier disclaimer.

851. The 'preamble' is over, and the poet's purpose is dis-
closed: *tu* is in the didactic manner, strongly antithetical to
alii (847); cf. 12. 436 ff. (Aeneas to Ascanius) 'nunc te mea
dextera bello / defensum dabit et magna inter praemia ducet. /
tu facito, mox cum matura adoleuerit aetas, / sis memor',
etc., where the didactic tone is also marked by the formal
imperative *facito*.

    regere imperio : an echo (unconscious?) of Lucr. 5. 1129 f.
'ut satius multo iam sit parere quietum / quam regere im-
perio res uelle et regna tenere'. Livy catches something of
the Virgilian tone in Romulus' words at his mysterious
epiphany, 1. 16. 7 'abi, nuntia Romanis, caelestes ita uelle
ut mea Roma caput orbis terrarum sit; proinde rem mili-
tarem colant sciantque et ita posteris tradant nullas opes
humanas armis Romanis resistere posse'.

    Romane : Anchises now speaks not to Aeneas alone but to
each future Roman, exhorting each to his duty. There is a
like solemnity in Hor. *C.* 3. 6. 1 f. 'delicta maiorum inmeritus
lues, / Romane, donec templa refeceris'; so in oracles, Livy
5. 16. 9 'Romane, aquam Albanam caue lacu contineri',
Ovid, *Met.* 15. 637 'quod petis hinc, propiore loco, Romane,
petisses', *F.* 4. 259 'Mater abest, Matrem iubeo, Romane,
requiras'. In the Sibylline oracle that was so conveniently
discovered to authorize the *ludi saeculares* of 17 B.C. it is
noteworthy that one line begins μεμνῆσθαι, 'Ρωμαῖε (text in
Kiessling–Heinze, introduction to Hor. *Carm. Saec.*; Diels,
Sibyllinische Blätter, 133 ff.; cf. Fraenkel, *Horace*, 365 f.).
The whole tone of Anchises' expression of the Roman mission
suggests an utterance of a divine sanction: cf. F. Altheim,
History of Roman Religion (London, 1938), 416 ff.

852. hae . . . artes : '*these* skills you shall have'; the emphasis is
on the subject, as the dative construction shows. The paren-
thesis (balancing *credo equidem*, 848) gives an illusion of
modest, almost apologetic explanation for the 'only thing'
left to Rome, finer than all the accomplishments that Virgil
is content to assign to 'alii'.

    pacique . . . morem : 'and to set the stamp of civilized
usage upon peace': peace is to have responsible rules of be-
haviour, a settled system of law and order. For the meaning

of *morem*, a word of deep and pregnant implication, cf. 8. 316
(of primitive men) 'quis neque mos neque cultus erat', with
1. 264 'moresque uiris et moenia ponet' (in Iuppiter's pro-
phecy concerning Aeneas; see note ad loc.).

The reading *pacisque* (so Conington and others), alleged to
have Servius' authority, has in fact no such support: see
Fraenkel, *Mus. Helv.* xix (1962), 133 f. (= *Kl. Beitr.* ii,
143 f.), where the implication of *morem* is also discussed.

853. parcere . . . superbos : 'to be merciful to the submissive,
and to crush in war those who are arrogant': the final de-
finition of the fusion of *pax* with *imperium*.

Virgil has given, memorably, an epigrammatic precision to
principles of policy familiar from other sources: cf. Cic. *de off.*
1. 35 'suscipienda quidem bella sunt ob eam causam ut sine
iniuria in pace uiuatur, parta autem uictoria conseruandi ii
qui non crudeles in bello, non immanes fuerunt . . . et cum
iis quos ui deuiceris consulendum est, tum ii qui armis positis
ad imperatorum fidem confugient . . . recipiendi', etc.; Poly-
bius 18.37.7 πολεμοῦντας γὰρ δεῖ τοὺς ἀγαθοὺς ἄνδρας βαρεῖς εἶναι καὶ
θυμικούς . . . νικῶντάς γε μὴν μετρίους καὶ πραεῖς καὶ φιλανθρώπους
(see Walbank ad loc.); Livy 30. 42. 17 'plus paene parcendo
uictis quam uincendo imperium auxisse' (Hasdrubal, on the
Romans), 37. 45. 8 f. 'maximo semper animo uictis regibus
populisque ignouistis; . . . positis iam aduersus omnes mor-
tales certaminibus haud secus quam deos consulere et parcere
uos generi humano oportet' (ambassadors from Antiochus,
190 B.C.). It was left to Horace to apply the principle
specifically to Augustus, *Carm. Saec.* 49 ff. 'quaeque uos
bubus ueneratur albis / clarus Anchisae Venerisque sanguis, /
impetret, bellante prior, iacentem / lenis in hostem' (cf.
Fraenkel, *Horace*, 376): Augustus himself could claim (*Mon.
Anc.* 26. 2) 'Alpes a regione ea, quae proxima est Hadriano
mari, ad Tuscum pacari feci nulli genti bello per iniuriam
inlato'.

debellare : first recorded in Virgil; the compound implies
carrying war through to its due end (and so establishing
peace).

854–92. *Anchises adds one further figure, M. Claudius Marcellus,
consul 222 B.C. Aeneas asks who the sad companion is, walking
at his side, and learns that this is a young Marcellus who will
barely grow to manhood before death takes him. Then Anchises
tells his son of wars that await him, and how he must act in Italy.*

Consistently with his method, Virgil does not allow the
scene to end on the high summit of these last lines: his sense

of contour demanded a descent, and the exaltation slowly
subsides, to end in grief as well as pride. The inference is
that the whole vision of heroes from 756 onwards did not
take final shape until after the young Marcellus' death in
23 B.C.: see Norden for other arguments that this passage is
not an afterthought but an integral part of Virgil's plan for
the 'Heldenschau'.

854. mirantibus : because of the impact of the preceding lines.

855. Cf. *E.* 5. 6 f. 'aspice, ut antrum / siluestris raris sparsit
labrusca racemis': for the indicative after *ut* see on *uiden*, 779.
Anchises points to M. Claudius Marcellus, consul 222 B.C. and
four times later, victor over the Insubres, captor of Syracuse:
cf. Hor. *C.* I. 12. 45 f. 'crescit occulto uelut arbor aeuo / fama
Marcelli' (see Nisbet–Hubbard ad loc.).

　　spoliis . . . opimis : the *spolia opima* ('Rich Spoils') were
won by a Roman commander with full *imperium* from an
enemy commander in personal combat (Livy 4. 20. 6 'ea rite
opima spolia habentur, quae dux duci detraxit nec ducem
nouimus nisi cuius auspicio bellum geritur'). Marcellus won
his at Clastidium in 222 B.C., killing the Gaulish leader Vir-
domarus (Plutarch, *Marcell.* 8, Prop. 4. 10. 39 ff.; see Wal-
bank on Polybius 2. 34. 6). They had previously been won
by Romulus (Livy I. 10. 4 ff.), and by Cossus (cf. 841): see
further on 859.

856. ingreditur : he comes forward proudly, *spoliis insignis*;
like *incedere* (see on I. 46) the verb takes colour from its con-
text: the fierce Mezentius 'turbidus ingreditur campo' (10.
763), the thoroughbred colt 'altius ingreditur' (*G.* 3. 76),
Aeneas walks slowly and sadly (157).

　　uictorque uiros : the tone is Ennian; cf. *G.* 3. 9 'uictorque
uirum uolitare per ora', an adaptation of Ennius, *Var.* 18
'uolito uiuus per ora uirum'.

　　supereminet : not recorded before Virgil; so of Diana, I.
501 'gradiensque deas supereminet omnis'.

857. A grim line with gathered spondees and balanced allitera-
tion. The Ennian tone continues (cf. *Ann.* 466 'qui rem
Romanam Latiumque augescere uultis', 500 'moribus anti-
quis stat res Romana uirisque').

　　tumultu : in the special sense of a Gallic rising; cf. Cic.
Phil. 8. 3 'maiores nostri tumultum Italicum quod erat
domesticus, tumultum Gallicum quod erat Italiae finitimus,
praeterea nullum nominabant'.

858. sistet : 'shall hold fast' ('confirmabit, corroborabit', Ser-
vius). The battle at Clastidium was a cavalry affair (Plu-
tarch, *Marcell.* 6 f.), so *eques* here. Some editors punctuate
after *sistet*, but this is against natural Virgilian rhythm and

denies the proper emphasis to *sternet*: see Norden and Henry ad loc., G. B. Townend, *Proc. Virg. Soc.* ix (1969–70), 79; the ancient manuscripts M and F support the punctuation adopted here.

Poenos : at Nola, and in the Sicilian campaign.

rebellem : first recorded here; cf. 12. 185 f. 'nec post arma ulla rebelles / Aeneadae referent'. The Gauls 'renewed the war' after peace-negotiations (Plutarch, *Marcell.* 6 γενομένης εἰρήνης ἀνακαινίσαι τὸν πόλεμον οἱ Γεσσάται δοκοῦσι; or *rebellem* could refer to fresh warfare after earlier campaigns.

859. 'And he shall hang up a third set of captured arms to Father Quirinus'; cf. Manil. 1. 787 f. 'tertia palma / Marcellus Cossusque prior de rege necato'. But the normal tradition made Marcellus dedicate his *spolia opima* to Iuppiter Feretrius (Prop. 4. 10. 39 f.; Plutarch, *Marcell.* 7), as Romulus and Cossus, the only earlier winners, had done (Livy 1. 10. 6, 4. 20. 5). So Virgil causes a problem.

The original conditions for the award were stringent (see on 855). But at some early period they were modified, distinctions of classification being made between *spolia prima* or *opima* in the strict sense, offered to Iuppiter Feretrius, *secunda* offered to Mars, and *tertia* offered to Ianus Quirinus. The evidence for this emerges from a confused comment by Servius here, and from a mutilated quotation from Varro in Festus 204 L which is clearly behind a similar statement in Plutarch, *Marcell.* 8; the enactment was attributed to a 'lex Numae' by the pontifices (see Ogilvie on Livy 1. 10). For these texts see Butler here and in *CR* xxxiii (1919), 61 ff.: he concludes that Virgil, misunderstanding the 'lex' or misled by some source, assumed a chronological meaning for *spolia tertia* instead of a classification. Norden, on a different reconstruction of the evidence, infers that a contaminated version of the two traditions of the *spolia opima* existed, which Virgil followed. But it is most dangerous to assume that Virgil did not understand an ancient record, especially one that is now so obscurely preserved; and Norden's theory rests mainly on a hypothetical exposition of a passage in the lost book of Livy in which Marcellus' exploit was recorded (cf. Servius here; Livy, *per.* 20). Neither view explains why Virgil was so deceived or muddled, more especially as in 29 B.C. Augustus claimed to have seen the actual *spolia opima* of Cossus, dedicated in their proper place, the temple of Iuppiter Feretrius (for the tricky story see Ogilvie on Livy 4. 20. 5 ff.; Syme, *Roman Revolution*, 308). Neither is acceptable.

Quirinus (a Sabine god) is a mysterious personage (see

Ogilvie on Livy I. 16): Virgil must have used the name here
in an allusive way which his contemporaries would have
understood. It was the name traditionally given to Romulus
after his apotheosis (Ogilvie, l.c.; Nisbet–Hubbard on Hor.
C. 1. 2. 46; Bömer on Ovid, F. 2. 475; O. Skutsch, Studia
Enniana, 130 ff.): Virgil himself uses it for Romulus, 1. 292
'Remo cum fratre Quirinus'. Surely this is the allusion here
(cf. Cerda's spirited note): Marcellus shall hang up his
spolia 'in Romulus' honour' (for such a dative cf. G. 2. 388 f.
'te, Bacche, uocant . . . tibique / oscilla . . . suspendunt')—
that is, honouring the builder of the temple of Iuppiter
Feretrius, Romulus himself, who had laid down that future
winners of the spolia opima should follow his example and
dedicate them there (Livy I. 10. 6). In this way, it seems to
me, Virgil obliquely alludes to the traditional place of dedica-
tion; it would have surprised him to discover that anyone
should have thought him ignorant of what everyone else
knew as a fact. The 'lex Numae' is a red herring.

For discussions of the spolia opima see Ogilvie on Livy
4. 20. 5-11; Latte, op. cit. 204 f. For Iuppiter Feretrius see
Ogilvie on Livy I. 10; Butler–Barber on Prop. 4. 10 (intro-
duction); Latte, op. cit. 126; Warde Fowler, Religious Ex-
perience, 129 f.; Walbank, Polybius i, p. 353.

860 ff. Virgil now leads up to the last figure in Anchises' vision,
the young Marcellus, who died, in his twentieth year, in
23 B.C., 'breuis et infaustos populi Romani amores' (Tac.
Ann. 2. 41). The passage is constructed with high art: it is
Aeneas who draws attention to the young man, as if Anchises
could not bear to point him out; and the explanation is given
in mounting suspense, until the final revelation tu Marcellus
eris (883). No wonder that when Marcellus' mother Octavia
heard Virgil reading the lines to Augustus 'defecisse fertur
atque aegre focilata' (uita Donati, 32).

860. atque hic : a sudden dramatic moment (see on 162).

namque : postponed, as in 72, 117 (see on 28). The paren-
thetic description is a lively variation of the introductory
technique.

861. egregium . . . iuuenem : so Pallas and Lausus are egregii
forma (10. 435), and Turnus has decus egregium formae (7.
473). Marcellus appears fulgentibus armis, like Caesar and
Pompey (826).

862. frons : 'expression'; cf. 11. 238 'haud laeta fronte Latinus'.
The picture is restated and emphasized in deiecto lumina
uultu.

864. anne : see on 719.

865. qui strepitus : quis has good manuscript authority also, but the exclamatory *qui* is plainly right (cf. Löfstedt, *Synt.* ii. 87).

quantum ... ipso : perhaps 'how great his single worth!' Servius glosses *instar* by 'similitudo'; Ti. Donatus has 'corporis forma': neither is satisfactory here. *Instar* implies equivalence to something else, in weight, size, etc.; it may be a verbal substantive from *instare* in a transitive sense, of putting something on a scale (Nettleship, *Contr. Lat. Lex.*, s.v.). It is normally used with a genitive of the object compared (e.g. 2. 15 'instar montis equum'; see note ad loc.): here, remarkably, there is no genitive, and the corresponding object in the 'balance' must be inferred from what precedes (see K. Alt, *Mus. Helv.* xvi [1959], 159 ff.). The equivalence is between Marcellus personally, alone (*in ipso*) and the many crowding round him: he, singly, balances them all; cf. 7. 706 f. 'magnum / agmen agens Clausus magnique ipse agminis instar' (Clausus by himself is equivalent to an army), Justin 4. 4. 7 'mittitur Gylippus, solus, sed in quo instar omnium auxiliorum erat'. Translation is difficult, because the idea of 'counterweight' is inappropriate to a ghost.

An epithet with *instar* is unusual: cf. Livy 28. 17. 2 'paruum instar eorum quae spe . . . concepisset receptas Hispanias ducebat' (of Scipio); Stat. *Th.* 6. 369 f. 'ingens certaminis instar / quadriiugi'. For the word in general see also Wölfflin, *ALL* ii, 581 ff.; HSz, 218.

866. Cf. 2. 360 'nox atra caua circumuolat umbra' (in the night-battle at Troy); Hor. *Sat.* 2. 1. 57 f. 'seu me tranquilla senectus / exspectat seu mors atris circumuolat alis' (perhaps in Virgil's mind; Horace published his book about 30 B.C.). In 2. 360 *nox atra* is actual night; here it is the darkness that symbolizes death.

867. lacrimis ... obortis : an Epic formula (again, 3. 492, 4. 30, 11. 41); cf. Livy 1. 58. 7 (of Lucretia) 'aduentu suorum lacrimae obortae': the force of the compound is that tears check speech. With *ingressus* (finite) supply *dicere* (cf. 4. 107 'sic contra est ingressa Venus'), an unusual brachylogy; cf. Macrob. *Sat.* 3. 14. 2 'Marius sic ingressus est', followed by his speech.

868. o gnate : an emotional address; the spondees in this and the next line mark Anchises' grieving reluctance to tell the tale.

C. Claudius Marcellus was Octavia's son, nephew and son-in-law of Augustus, born 42 B.C.; rival to Agrippa as a possible heir to the Principate (cf. Syme, *Roman Revolution*, 341 ff.); his early death in 23 B.C. shattered dynastic plans. Servius (on 861) notes 'ad funeris huius honorem Augustus sescentos lectos intra ciuitatem ire iussit ... cum ingenti

pompa adlatus et in campo Martio est sepultus'; Augustus
himself spoke a funeral oration (DServius on 1. 712; Cassius
Dio 53. 30), and we may reasonably suppose that Virgil was
present. Octavia made a library his memorial, Augustus
a theatre (Plutarch, *Marcell.* 30). He was highly gifted: Vell.
Pat. 2. 93. 1 'decessit admodum iuuenis, sane, ut aiunt, in-
genuarum uirtutum laetusque animi et ingenii fortunaeque
in quam alebatur capax'; Sen. *ad Marciam* 2. 3 'animo
alacrem, ingenio potentem, sed frugalitatis continentiaeque
in illis aut annis aut opibus non mediocriter admirandae,
patientem laborum, uoluptatibus alienum, quantumcumque
imponere illi auunculus et, ut ita dicam, inaedificare uoluis-
set, laturum'. Octavia's grief was lifelong: Sen. l.c. 2. 4
'nullum finem per omne uitae suae tempus flendi gemendique
fecit, nec ullas admisit uoces salutare aliquid adferentis ...
intenta in unam rem et toto animo adfixa talis per omnem
uitam fuit qualis in funere'; if this seems excessive, we
should remember Queen Victoria and the Prince Consort.

   Norden has a valuable analysis of this 'epicedion Marcelli'
according to the principles of Greek rhetoric. In its genuine
emotion it is worlds away from Propertius' formal elegy on
Marcellus (3. 18); Servius comments 'constat hunc librum
tanta pronuntiatione Augusto et Octauiae esse recitatum ut
fletu nimio imperarent silentium, nisi Vergilius finem esse
dixisset'. The passage is a noble example of the ancient
'literature of grief' (for which see the important discussion
by Nisbet–Hubbard on Hor. *C.* 1. 24).

869. The Fates will allow the world only a glimpse of Mar-
cellus. Protests against the *di inuidi* are a feature of the
genre (Menander rhetor 3. 435. 9 ff. Sp.; see Norden, p. 342);
so Hor. *C.* 1. 24. 11 f. 'tu frustra pius heu non ita creditum /
poscis Quintilium deos'.

870. Romana propago : 'the Roman stock'; cf. 12. 827 'sit
Romana potens Itala uirtute propago': an elevated, archaic
phrase, as in Lucr. 1. 42 'Memmi clara propago'.

871. propria : 'lasting', as a permanent possession; cf. 1. 73
'conubio iungam stabili propriamque dicabo' (where *pro-
priam* puts the meaning of *stabili* in a different way): so
Hor. *Sat.* 2. 6. 5, a prayer 'ut propria haec mihi munera
faxis' (i.e. 'gifts for me to keep'), Cic. *leg. Man.* 48 'quod ut
illi (*sc.* Pompeio) proprium ac perpetuum sit ... uelle et
optare debetis'.

   dona : cf. Prop. 3. 18. 15 f. 'occidit, et misero steterat
uicesimus annus : / tot bona tam paruo clausit in orbe dies'.
872. Mauortis : the order of words and the need for a qualifica-
tion of *magnam urbem* are against Conington's suggestion

that this could be taken ἀπὸ κοινοῦ with *campus* below (i.e. the
Campus Martius, often without the epithet). The allusion is
to Romulus' birth and to the cult of Mars at Rome (so
1. 276 f. 'Romulus excipiet gentem et Mauortia condet /
moenia'), for which see Bailey on Ovid, *F.* 3, pp. 33 ff.; for
the phrase cf. *A P* 9. 90. 3 f. οὔριον εὐχομένοισι δίδου πλόον Ἄρεος
ἄχρις / ἐς πόλιν.

873. aget gemitus : the Campus is personified, strikingly; cf.
Cic. *Cael.* 60 'nonne ipsam domum metuet ne quam uocem
eiciat . . . ?', *Marcell.* 10 'parietes . . . huius curiae tibi gratias
agere gestiunt'.

    Tiberine : cf. Ennius, *Ann.* 54 'teque pater Tiberine tuo
cum flumine sancto' (see on 2. 782). The characteristic
apostrophe varies the construction from the parallel clause
quantos . . . gemitus, and both clauses occupy equal space,
carefully balanced. This personification is simpler than that
of *campus*, since it is the river-god who is addressed.

874. funera : strongly emphasized by position and by the
following pause. For the 'poetic' plural (much preferred to
the singular by Virgil) cf. Ennius' epitaph (*Var.* 17 f.) 'nemo
me lacrimis decoret nec funera fletu / faxit'; here it perhaps
suggests grandeur, but the preference given to it is generally
due to the metrical advantage offered by the plural, especially
with an epithet.

    praeterlabere : Virgil introduced the verb to poetry (again,
3. 478); it reappears once in Epic, Stat. *Th.* 1. 271. The long,
heavy word gives the line a slow march, and the funereal
sound is accentuated by the assonance in *cum tumulum*.
It is noteworthy that in 870, 872, 874 *nimium, uirum,
tumulum* stand at the same point in the line, with *-um*
bearing the ictus; similarly, though not all in the same
position, *uirum* (863), *comitum* (865), *luctum* (868): a funeral
knell.

875 f. Iliaca . . . Latinos . . . Romula : an ingenious racial asso-
ciation, Trojan, Italian, Roman.

876. in tantum . . . auos : 'shall exalt his ancestry so high by
his promise': Servius saw the meaning, 'erigit generis anti-
quitatem, et rhetorice spem laudat in puero, quia facta non
inuenit'; Marcellus will add lustre to his line, but not by
achievement, only by what he bade fair to achieve. The inter-
pretation that *auos* = his ghostly ancestors, filled with hope
for him, is an improbable conceit, admirably disposed of by
Henry in a merry note.

    Romula : the adjective is not recorded before Virgil; so
Prop. 3. 11. 52 'Romula uincla', Hor. *Carm. Saec.* 47 'Romulae
genti date remque prolemque'.

quondam : 'one day', of future time: so Hor. *Sat.* 2. 2. 82
'hic tamen ad melius poterit transcurrere quondam'; simi-
larly *olim*, 1. 289, 4. 627.

877. se . . . iactabit : cf. *G.* 1. 102 f. 'nullo tantum se Mysia
cultu / iactat'.

878. Marcellus will embody an ideal of ancient honour: he will
fulfil his duty to gods and man (*pietas*), he will keep his word
(*fides*), he will be a brave soldier; but all will be lost to Rome
by his early death (*heu*). *Prisca* (with *pietas* as well as with
fides) suggests the purity of 'old-fashioned' ways; cf. Hor.
Carm. Saec. 57 ff. 'iam Fides et Pax et Honos Pudorque /
priscus et neglecta redire Virtus / audet'.

879 ff. Young as he was, Marcellus took part in the Cantabrian
campaign of 26 B.C. (led by Augustus in person; see Syme,
Roman Revolution, 332), together with the future Princeps,
Tiberius: see Gow–Page on *A P* 6. 161 (*Garland of Philip* ii,
p. 220), an epigram by the contemporary poet Crinagoras.
In *A P* 9. 945 Crinagoras presents the boy Marcellus with
a copy of Callimachus' *Hecale*: for the poet and his
many contacts with high Roman society see Gow–Page, l.c.,
pp. 210 ff.

881. seu . . . foderet : the construction is varied; *seu = uel si*:
see Housman, *CQ* vii (1913), 20 (= *Classical Papers*, 853),
for this use. The line provides an elaborate contrast to the
simple *pedes iret*.

  spumantis : Epic horses (like Epic boars, 1. 324, 4. 158)
tend to 'foam'; cf. 11. 770, 12. 372, 651 (and in 4. 135,
5. 817 the *frena* themselves are *spumantia*).

  armos : 'forequarters'. Servius comments 'equi armos pro
equo posuit, non enim possunt armi calcaribus fodi', and it
is generally assumed that *armos* is casually put for *latera*
('flanks'), for metrical convenience. But Henry, quoting an
anonymous comment ' 'Tis insufferable that to make a har-
monious verse a poet shall say that a gentleman spurred the
shoulders of his horse instead of his sides', notes Hor. *Sat.*
1. 6. 106, of a mule 'mantica cui lumbos onere ulceret atque
eques armos': he concludes that the natural meaning is 'the
lower part of the *armi*, that part of the forequarter . . .
directly under or even in front of the rider, which was
spurred by the horseman, not encumbered in those ancient
times with stirrups, nor taught that it is graceful and elegant
to ride with the toes turned inwards . . . but sitting at ease
. . . with the toes out and the heels in and the legs thrown
very much forward'. This is exactly confirmed by the Balbi
equestrian statues from Herculaneum in the Naples Museum,
so Professor J. M. C. Toynbee tells me: for this group see her

Animals in Roman Life and Art, 173, and J. J. Deiss, *Herculaneum* (London, 1968), 146, 147.

882. miserande puer : Anchises now turns dramatically from Aeneas to the ghostly figure of Marcellus and addresses him.

si qua . . . rumpas ! : the comma after *rumpas* in OCT and other texts is misleading: the words are certainly a wish, not a conditional phrase; cf. 187 f. 'si nunc se nobis ille aureus arbore ramus / ostendat nemore in tanto!' Anchises says in effect 'Pitiable boy (how I wish that in some way you could break the implacability of fate!), you are to be Marcellus', with all that the name implies for Virgil's contemporaries (and for Augustus and Octavia as they heard the lines). Attempts to explain *si . . . rumpas* as a protasis to *tu Marcellus eris* get nowhere, as Conington's notes show very clearly. The present punctuation is Wagner's; Ladewig, R. D. Williams, and Geymonat accept it; the moving simplicity of Anchises' revelation is ruined by any other interpretation. See, however, H. J. Rose, *CR* xlv (1931), 51 f. (and the riposte by G. Engleheart and J. H. Vince, ib. 126 f.). Page has an admirable note.

883 ff. Anchises ends by envisaging himself at the actual funeral of Marcellus: a powerfully imaginative and evocative passage, in which Virgil's own involvement is plain, and a most moving colophon to the whole prophetic apocalypse.

883. manibus . . . plenis : as if servants were present to hand him the flowers: 'adfectum dolentis expressit dicendo *date*, cum non essent praesto qui darent' (Ti. Donatus). *Manibus plenis* ('in armfuls') implies lavishness, as in Cic. *ad Att.* 2. 25. 1 'Hortalus quam plena manu . . . quam ornate nostras laudes in astra sustulit'. Some commentators take *date* with *spargam* as dependent jussive, with *purpureos flores* in apposition to *lilia* as object of *spargam*; they compare 4. 683 f. 'date, uulnera lymphis / abluam', but there *uulnera* cannot be the object of *date*, here *lilia* can be, and it is perverse not to accept the straightforward interpretation that Ti. Donatus indicates.

lilia : cf. *AP* 7. 485. 1 βάλλεθ' ὑπὲρ τύμβου πολιὰ κρίνα, Nicander, fr. 74. 70 λείριά τε στήλησιν ἐπιφθίνοντα καμόντων perhaps symbolic of a short life, cf. Val. Flacc. 6. 492 ff. 'lilia per uernos lucent uelut alba colores / praecipue, quis uita breuis totusque parumper / floret honor'.

For flowers as gifts to the dead see Lattimore, *Themes in Greek and Latin epitaphs*, 135 ff.; for elaborate sepulchral gardens see Toynbee, *Death and Burial in the Roman World*, 94 ff. Pliny has a nice story (*NH* 21. 10) of a Scipio who died in office as tribune, leaving no money to pay for his funeral,

'asses ergo contulit populus ac funus elocauit, quaque prae-
ferebatur flores e prospectu omni sparsit'.

884. **purpureos :** cf. 5. 79 'purpureosque iacit flores' (Aeneas
making offering to his father's spirit). The meaning may be
simply 'bright', 'dazzling' (see on 641); but Pliny (*NH* 21.
25) has *purpurea lilia* of the narcissus, for which κρίνον and
λείριον are sometimes synonymous (Gow on Nicander, l.c.),
and contrasts it with the white lily: it is safer to take the
colour here as actual purple, or perhaps bright red.

spargam : subjunctive, as the parallel *accumulem* shows.
885. **saltem :** its pathos is deepened by *inani munere*.

accumulem : contrast 5. 331 f. 'Acesten / muneribus
cumulat magnis': perhaps Virgil preferred the compound
here to get elision of the final syllable in *saltem*, so avoiding
the effect of *saltém cumulém* (and the elision itself is sugges-
tive of a sob).

fungar : the only occurrence of the verb in Virgil: curious.
886. **munere :** Anchises' final word is put into high relief by its
position; the gift is emphasized, 'empty' though it is. The
technique is very Virgilian: cf. 4. 276, 570, 8. 583, 10. 495,
776, in all of which, as here, a speech ends on a word run on
from the previous line; similarly, but in mid-speech, *funera*
(4. 618), *munera* (4. 624). Anchises ends on a note of family
pietas, very simply.
887. **aëris in campis :** 'in the wide fields of air': a startling
expression for an Elysium set in the Underworld (cf. intro-
ductory note on 724 ff.). It is improbable that by *aer* Virgil
alludes to the *largior aether* of 640, as some imagine, or that
he uses it like the Homeric ἀήρ, 'mist' (the ἠερόεντα κέλευθα of
Od. 20. 64, quoted by Page, is not relevant). The striking
phrase combines the conception of a still localized Elysium
with an insubstantiality that helps to prepare for the
strangeness of Aeneas' departure (893 ff.).

Servius comments 'locutus autem est secundum eos qui
putant Elysium lunarem esse circulum'; on 5. 735 he says
that Elysium is 'secundum theologos circa lunarem cir-
culum, ubi iam aer purior est', and then quotes the present
phrase. Norden (pp. 23 ff.) discusses this in the light of
Plutarch's cosmological myth *de facie in orbe lunae uisa*, in
which (943c) the soul after separation from the body is repre-
sented as wandering in the region between the earth and
the moon, the ἀήρ: the time spent there varies, but the un-
just receive punishment, the just stay, long enough to be
purified of such bodily taints as they have incurred, ἐν τῷ
πραοτάτῳ τοῦ ἀέρος ὃν λειμῶνας Ἅιδου καλοῦσι, and then ascend
to the moon; that part of the moon which looks towards

heaven is called the Elysian Plain (944C ὀνομάζεσθαι δὲ τὰ
μὲν πρὸς οὐρανὸν τῆς σελήνης Ἠλύσιον πεδίον) : see Guthrie, op. cit.
186, 193 n. 20, and for a summary and discussion of the
treatise see D. A. Russell, *Plutarch* (London, 1973), 69 ff.;
cf. Cumont, op. cit. 175 ff., 208 f.

It is extremely probable that Virgil's *aëris campi*, though
factually in an Underworld Elysium, yet allusively reflect
such cosmological theories of the soul's ascent to Heaven:
Butler unwisely dismisses Norden's views; Guthrie has no
such scepticism. Virgil would not have chosen these words
at random, or casually.

Ausonius (*Cup. Cruc.* 1 f., Peiper p. 110) read his Virgil
somewhat inattentively, 'aëris in campis, memorat quos
Musa Maronis, / myrteus amentes ubi lucus opacat amantes'.

lustrant : movement is clear as they survey everything in
their walk together (see on 231, 681).

888 ff. The tone begins to take on a diminuendo. The present
participle *uenientis* (889), where a future might have been
expected, shows that *fama* is already on the way.

890. uiro : a clear example of substitution for *ei*; Conington's
suggestion is unnecessary, that it is put in for the sake of
juxtaposition with *bella*. For the omission of *sint* with *gerenda*
cf. 1. 752 'nunc quales Diomedis equi, nunc quantus Achilles'
(depending on *rogitans*).

891. Laurentisque . . . populos : cf. 7. 738 'Sarrastis populos'.
Virgil means Latinus' community in Latium; cf. 12. 24 'sunt
aliae innuptae Latio et Laurentibus aruis'. For the legendary
explanation of the name *Laurentes* see 7. 61 ff.; if a town
'Laurentum' ever existed it must have been early absorbed
by Lavinium, which was in the *ager Laurens*: for the problem
see Ogilvie on Livy 1. 1. 10, and for earlier discussions see
J. Carcopino, *Virgile et les origines d'Ostie* (Paris, 1919),
220 ff., C. Saunders, *Vergil's primitive Italy* (New York,
1930), 53 ff., B. Tilly, *Vergil's Latium* (Oxford, 1947), 83 ff.

892. Cf. 3. 458 ff., where Helenus prophesies of the Sibyl 'illa
tibi Italiae populos uenturaque bella / et quo quemque
modo fugiasque ferasque labores / expediet': obviously Virgil
would have revised one or other passage if he had lived; see
Norden, p. 347, Heinze, 440 n. 1, and Butler ad loc.

893–901. *Virgil describes the twin gates of Sleep and their func-
tions, one of horn, one of ivory. Through the ivory gate Aeneas
and the Sibyl leave the Underworld; and Aeneas returns to his
ships.*

Virgil adapts to his own purpose the description of the
Gates of Dreams in *Od.* 19. 562 ff.:

δοιαὶ γάρ τε πύλαι ἀμενηνῶν εἰσὶν ὀνείρων·
αἱ μὲν γὰρ κεράεσσι τετεύχαται, αἱ δ' ἐλέφαντι·
τῶν οἳ μέν κ' ἔλθωσι διὰ πριστοῦ ἐλέφαντος,
οἵ ῥ' ἐλεφαίρονται, ἔπε' ἀκράαντα φέροντες·
οἳ δὲ διὰ ξεστῶν κεράων ἔλθωσι θύραζε,
οἵ ῥ' ἔτυμα κραίνουσι, βροτῶν ὅτε κέν τις ἴδηται.

True dreams issue from the gate of horn, false dreams from
the gate of ivory. This became proverbial: so Plato, *Char-
mides* 173A ἄκουε δή, ἔφην, τὸ ἐμὸν ὄναρ, εἴτε διὰ κεράτων εἴτε δι' ἐλέ-
φαντος ἐλήλυθεν; *A P* 7. 42. 1 f. (on Callimachus' *Aetia*) ἃ μέγα
Βαττιάδαο σοφοῦ περίπυστον ὄνειαρ, | ἦ ῥ' ἐτεὸν κεράων, οὐδ' ἐλέφαντος ἔης;
Hor. *C*. 3. 27. 39 ff. 'an uitiis carentem / ludit imago / uana,
quae porta fugiens eburna / somnium ducit?' (Europa speak-
ing); Stat. *S*. 5. 3. 288 f. (a prayer to his father's spirit) 'inde
tamen uenias melior qua porta malignum / cornea uincit
ebur'; Ausonius, *Cup. Cruc.* 103 'euolat ad superos portaque
euadit eburna' (Cupid, after his horrid dream). Lucian's Isle
of Dreams (*Ver. Hist.* 2. 33) has two gates facing the sea,
ἡ μὲν κερατίνη, ἡ δὲ καθ' ἣν ἡμεῖς παρήλθομεν ἐλεφαντίνη.

The Gates of Sleep come now as a total surprise. Just as
Aeneas and the Sibyl entered the Underworld mysteriously
and imperceptibly, so they leave it by a strange and insub-
stantial path. They have been in the dwelling of Death,
Sleep's brother (278), the abode *somni noctisque soporae*
(390): its gates are a Virgilian localization of the Homeric
Gates of Dreams. The complexity of this book, both in its
purpose and in its art, made demands on Virgil that forbade
the simplicity with which Odysseus was made to leave the
world of the dead (*Od.* 11. 636 f.), at one moment encom-
passed by ghosts, at the next back at his ship and hurrying
away. These Gates gave him what he needed, to invest
Aeneas' departure with a mystery and awe which in turn is
communicated to the reader. But the Sibyl, it would seem,
had taken no account of them when she told Aeneas what he
must do 'si tanta cupido est / bis Stygios innare lacus, *bis*
nigra uidere / Tartara' (133 ff.): did the idea come to Virgil
in a flash of vision, or did he evolve it slowly as the book
shaped itself in his mind? The Gates of Sleep are as magical
in their own way as the Golden Bough which enabled Aeneas
to enter the Underworld. It is incredible that Ribbeck could
have been induced to believe that the lines are spurious
(second edition, 1895, with *auerna* for *eburna* in 898).

Aeneas and the Sibyl leave by the Ivory Gate. No one
knows the full implication of this. Servius certainly did not:
'uult . . . intellegi falsa esse omnia quae dixit' (with some

curious allegory as alternative). A view accepted by many,
including Norden, is that Virgil simply means that they left
before midnight, on a theory that 'true dreams' appeared
only after midnight (W. Everett, *CR* xiv [1900], 153 f.):
a dubious fact, and a comment by W. Clausen is apposite
(*HSCP* lxviii [1964], 'I have a sense, which I cannot quite
put into words, that Virgil was not merely telling the time of
night'. Others refer to the *uestibulum Orci* and the *somnia
uana* there (283 f.), noting Servius on 282 'intellegimus hanc
esse eburneam portam per quam exiturus Aeneas est': see
E. L. Highbarger, *The Gates of Sleep* (Baltimore, 1940),
71 ff.; H. R. Steiner, *Der Traum in der Aeneis* (Berne/Stutt-
gart, 1952), 91 ff. But to imagine that Anchises escorted
Aeneas and the Sibyl back across Styx to the *uestibulum* is
topographically absurd; the two contexts have no inter-
connexion. Both these views, with other improbabilities, are
rebutted by B. Otis, *TAPA* xc (1959), 174 ff.

Such speculations get nowhere. Anchises, himself an
umbra, cannot send his living visitants out through the Gate
of Horn, since they are not *uerae umbrae*. The Gate of Ivory
was his only choice. There is no means of knowing what
deeper significance this held for Virgil's mind for Aeneas'
experience in the Underworld (for some suggestions see R. D.
Williams ad loc.). Even the meaning of *falsa insomnia* is un-
certain (see below), and it must be emphasized that these only
provide the route, and that no direct equation is made be-
tween such users of the Ivory Gate and the travellers who are
now sent out by it. The matter remains a Virgilian enigma
(and none the worse for that).

Steiner (òp. cit. 88 ff.) and Otis (l.c.) are well documented;
see also Otis, *Virgil*, 304; G. Norwood, *CR* xxiv (1910), 212;
M. E. Hirst, *CR* xxvi (1912), 82; R. J. Getty, *AJP* liv (1933),
12 ff.; A. K. Michels, *AJP* lxv (1944), 135 ff.; T. J. Haarhoff,
Greece & Rome xvii (1948), 87 ff.; L.-F. Rolland, *RÉL* xxxv
(1957), 204 ff.; N. Reed, *CQ* n.s. xxiii (1973), 311 ff.

893. sunt . . . portae : cf. 7. 607 'sunt geminae Belli portae (sic
nomine dicunt)', where the parenthesis corresponds to *fertur*
here, implying a traditional allusion (see on 14).

894. ueris . . . umbris : apparitions such as those of Sychaeus
(1. 353 ff.) and Hector (2. 270 ff.).

895. candenti : cf. Cat. 64. 45 'candet ebur soliis'. It is com-
plemented by *nitens*, which is strictly superfluous but adds
to the radiance of the picture. The ablative *candenti . . .
elephanto* belongs both to *perfecta* and to *nitens*: the gate
'gleams with the sheen of wrought ivory'.

elephanto : cf. 3. 464 'dona . . . auro grauia ac secto ele-

phanto', *G.* 3. 26 'in foribus pugnam ex auro solidoque ele-
phanto'. These are the only examples in classical Latin of
elephantus used for 'ivory', like ἐλέφας, and the polysyllabic
endings are in the Greek manner.

896. The construction is carefully varied from that of 894:
sed is presumably intended to mark the contrast between the
loveliness of the gate and the unloveliness of falsehood that
issues from it. The ellipse of *hac*, to correspond with *qua*
above, is unexpected and rather difficult.

 insomnia : ἐνύπνια (cf. Macrob. *Somn. Scip.* 1. 3. 2), a Vir-
gilian innovation; but, confusingly, the word also occurs
as a plural form of the feminine singular noun *insomnia*,
'sleeplessness' (e.g. Prop. 2. 25. 47 'cum satis una tuis in-
somnia portet ocellis', Val. Flacc. 7. 6 'uertere tunc uarios
per longa insomnia questus'), and distinction between the
two is often difficult: see *Thes.L.L.* s.vv. *insomnia, in-
somnium*; Nettleship, *Contr. Lat. Lex.* s.vv.; Getty, *AJP*, l.c.

 Servius comments here 'id est somnia'; on 5. 840 he makes
the distinction '*somnium* quod dormimus, *insomnium* quod
uidemus in somnis', and then quotes the present line. Ti.
Donatus interprets 'quod autem uidemur nobis uidere dor-
mientes et quod nos plerumque facit non dormire per ebur-
neam mittitur'. Obviously the word caused difficulty. Virgil
has it once elsewhere, 4. 9 'Anna soror, quae me suspensam
insomnia terrent', of Dido, sleepless, with the figure and
form of Aeneas always before her (cf. 4. 83 'illum absens
absentem auditque uidetque'), a 'waking vision', ὕπαρ (*Od.*
19. 547 οὐκ ὄναρ, ἀλλ' ὕπαρ ἐσθλόν; Pindar, *O.* 13. 66 f. ἐξ ὀνείρου
δ' αὐτίκα / ἦν ὕπαρ): but there too the meaning is disputed (see
Pease ad loc.). Getty (*AJP*, l.c.), taking *insomnia* here as
'waking visions' (not 'dreams'), argues that they are *falsa*
from the point of view of the *Manes*; Reed (*CQ*, l.c.), assum-
ing that *insomnia = umbrae*, has a similar explanation of
falsa as 'not real', 'counterfeit', noting 3. 302 'falsi Simoen-
tis ad undam' (cf. 1. 684, with my note). These suggestions
are ingenious. But I doubt if they solve the problem of the
falsa insomnia in relation to Aeneas and the Sibyl as users
of the Ivory Gate, a problem which to my mind still remains
inscrutable.

 Manes : here plainly of the indiscriminate mass of the
spirits of the dead.

897. his : with *dictis* below. Manuscript support is divided be-
tween *ibi* and *ubi*; but *ibi* is clearly needed, to pick up the
ἔκφρασις of the Gates (cf. *hic*, 243), and with *ubi* the significant
portaque emittit eburna is relegated to a subordinate clause.
Norden, accepting *ubi*, adduces 7. 607 ff. 'sunt geminae Belli

portae ... / has, ubi certa sedet patribus sententia pugnae, / ... reserat stridentia limina consul'; but this is not a parallel, since *has* there picks up the ἔκφρασις, *his* here does not.

898. prosequitur : like a courteous host, showing out his guests; cf. 9. 308 ff. 'quos omnis euntis / primorum manus ad portas ... / prosequitur uotis'.

899. ille : Aeneas, in adversative asyndeton; the comma in OCT at the end of 898 is inappropriate, unless *ubi* is read in 897.

uiam secat : again, 12. 368; cf. Sen. *de ben.* 6. 15. 6 'certam secanti uiam': so Eur. *Phoen.* 1 ὦ τὴν ἐν ἄστροις οὐρανοῦ τέμνων ὁδόν, Ar. *Thesm.* 1099 f. διὰ μέσου γὰρ αἰθέρος / τέμνων κέλευθον πόδα τίθημ' ὑπόπτερον. There is no indication where the much-debated gate by which Aeneas leaves the Underworld is to be imagined, except that he seems to reach his ships on the shore under Cumae quickly enough. If *uiam secat* implies cleaving through obstacles, it may suggest that Aeneas makes his way through the dense forest into which he has emerged, presumably not far from Cumae and outside the crater of Avernus. But as usual Virgil has a short way with such considerations. Aeneas is to return to his ships swiftly, and all obstacles, the high rim of the crater, the dense wood, the sheer distance, are cut through κατὰ τὸ σιωπώμενον. His return to the upper world is as abrupt and imperceptible as his descent had been.

900. A quiet ending. Caieta (now Gaeta) is 58 km. north-west of Cumae; for the aetiology of the name see 7. 1 ff.

limite : the coast-line; cf. Val. Flacc. 4. 614 f. 'limite recto / puppis et aequali transcurrat carbasus aura', Stat. *S.* 2. 2. 84 f. (of a room with a view up the coast) 'quae tibi Parthenopen derecto limite ponti / ingerit'. The ancient manuscripts, Servius (on 3. 16, 8. 57), and Ti. Donatus read *litore*: *limite* (Bentley, Mynors, Geymonat) has only the witness of manuscripts later than the ninth century. The problem is bound up with the next line, which is repeated from 3. 277; Servius does not notice it, Ti. Donatus does; Bentley rejected it, followed by Ribbeck and Norden. If it is genuine, *litore* appears in both lines and in the same position, unless *limite* is accepted in 900. Such a repetition might perhaps gain support from 7. 653 f., where *esset* ends consecutive lines, or 8. 396 f. with *fuisset* similarly. If *litore* is retained in 900, and if 901 is accepted as genuine, it must be assumed that the latter is a temporary stopgap (cf. Sparrow, *Half-Lines and Repetitions in Virgil*, 150). My feeling is that 901 rounds off the book naturally, with a picture that balances the landing at Cumae with which it opens: and that in spite of all the ancient evidence *limite* is the proper reading in 900.

APPENDIX

THE CRATER OF AVERNUS AS A CULT-SITE

COLIN HARDIE

THE suggestion (above, pp. 108 f.) that there was never at any time a sacred cave for the consultation of ghosts or for a descent into the underworld within the crater of Lake Avernus may now be supported by stronger arguments, from two archaeological discoveries, both made about 1960: the first is the site of the Homeric nekyomanteion above the confluence of the rivers Acheron and Cocytus, near Ephyra in Thesprotia in northern Greece, the second, the Great Antrum excavated by Dr. Paget at Baiae.

The Cimmerians mentioned at *Odyssey* 11. 14 have caused trouble since the earliest times, as has their intrusion at Avernus.[1] They have been transferred to Avernus from Thesprotia and can now be eliminated from both places.

The Oracle of the Dead, mentioned by Herodotus (5. 92. ζ. 2) as consulted by Periander tyrant of Corinth in the early sixth century B.C. on the river Acheron in Thesprotia (cf. 8. 47), was identified and excavated in 1958–61 by S. Dakaris.[2] The massive and complex building is of Hellenistic third-century date

---

[1] Pliny, *NH* 3. 61 'Auernus iuxta quem Cimmerium oppidum'; Silius Italicus 12. 132; Festus p. 37 L. s.v. 'Cimmeri'; Strabo 5. 4. 5, quoting Ephorus; Lactantius, *Diu. Inst.* 1. 6. 9; *Origo Gentis Romanae* 10. 2; cf. Lycophron, *Alex.* 695, the *Orphic Argonautica* 1125 ff. Naevius has a Cimmerian Sibyl in Italy. The Cimmerians do not appear in the *Aeneid*, but *G.* 3. 349–59, by translating *Od.* 11. 16–18, implies that Virgil put Homer's Cimmerians in Scythia.

[2] *Arch. Delt.* xvi (1960), 2, 204; *Ergon* 1963; *Archaeology* xv. 2 (1962), 85–93; *Antike Kunst*, Beiheft i (1963), 35–55. See also N. G. L. Hammond, *Epirus* (Oxford, 1967), 63–9, and, for Cape Cheimerium, 446–7, and *Studies in Greek History* (Oxford, 1973), 452–6 (= *JHS* lxv [1945], 26–37); M. Brooke, *Illustrated London News*, 28. 11. 1970, 22–3; E. Melas, *Temples and Sanctuaries of Ancient Greece* (London, 1973).

and was destroyed soon afterwards (perhaps by Aemilius Paulus after Pydna in 168 B.C.), but there can be little doubt that the site goes back to the Mycenean age and was known to the Homeric tradition.[3] The 'confluence of two rivers' at *Od.* 10. 515, with the archaic literal meaning of ξύνεσις, seems traditional, but the poet has expanded the two rivers to four. Most Greeks would have approached the oracle by sea, to the territory of the people of Cheimerion (Χειμέριον), whether the town and cape are placed just north of the mouth of the joint river or further to the north-west. The difficulties of Κιμμερίων in the text of Homer, as regards both date and geography, have caused much dispute and an unusual variety of emendations, but before Dakaris' discovery G. L. Huxley[4] had already suggested reading Χειμεριέων, from Χειμεριεύς, which Dakaris accepts. Homer, who ignores everything after the Heroic Age, cannot have introduced the contemporary Cimmerians, but the Ionians in the seventh century, when Homer's poetry was widely diffused, had every reason to be preoccupied with the Cimmerians, who had destroyed Midas King of Phrygia and Gyges King of Lydia and threatened Ephesus.

The starting-point and core of the Odyssean Nekyia is then the Thresprotian sanctuary near Cheimerion, a place for the evocation of ghosts. But evocation has been fused, first with a descent into the Underworld, and then with a prophecy from Teiresias, who displaces Anticleia; Tiresias belongs elsewhere (mainly Boeotia) and could, as Homer candidly tells us, prophesy without blood. The setting as well as the nature of the Nekyia has been changed: it has been moved to the streams of Ocean, at the edge of Homer's disc-like world.[5] Impenetrable darkness, cloud, and mist belong to the Underworld that creeps up over the rim and are as absurd in Thesprotia and Avernus as in the Crimea. But in Greek mythological tradition the Ionian Sea on which Cheimerion stood *was* the Ocean, beyond which lay the world of the dead; here the souls took off westward by the Λευκάδα πέτρην (*Od.* 24. 11), whether that is the island of Leucas itself or Capo Bianco or Cape Leucimme. This

---

[3] E. Lepore, *Ricerche sull'antico Epiro* (Naples, 1962), 1–15.

[4] *Parola del Passato* xiii (1958), 245–8.

[5] This displacement was recognized by the ancient critics, whether they thought of it as moved from Thesprotia or from Avernus, e.g. Maximus of Tyre 14. 2, Eustathius 1667. 63, 1671. 31.

tradition survived long after Italy and Spain were explored and colonized.[6]

Cimmerians at Avernus can be explained if the Homeric Nekyia was localized there, however palpable the misfit. There is no archaeological evidence for any such pre-Greek population, living underground, nor for any single foundation in Italy by heroes from Troy, such as Diomedes, Philoctetes, and Antenor, and so no likelihood of Odysseus at Avernus.[7] The myth of Cimmerians at Avernus, living in caves from which they emerged only at night, was given currency by Ephorus,[8] who visited Cumae in the mid-fourth century B.C. when it was already Samnite, and it has been kept alive by the mistaken belief that the Campi Phlegraei are riddled with natural caves and underground passages. But caves do not form naturally in tufa (volcanic ash that solidifies with rain), as they do in the limestone of Sorrento or Capri, except where they are eroded by waves on the seashore.[9]

The Cimmerians are part of the Nekyia, and the Nekyia of Odysseus' voyages, and these have been variously localized. Serious critics and geographers have always been sceptical. Strabo is a special case with his desire to prove that Homer is the father of geography and that his fairyland is based on real places, though, with his contempt for Ephorus' mythologizing,[10] he rejects the Nekyia at Avernus.[11] Thucydides (3. 88. 1) and Aristotle (*Mete*. 2. 367a) are careful to add 'so-called' to e.g. the Aeolian islands, and Eratosthenes made fun of the whole notion: 'first find the cobbler who made the bag of winds',

[6] Aeschylus, *PV* 837, Euripides, *Alcestis* 591; cf. E. Wikén, *Die Kunde der Hellenen von dem Lande und der Völkern der Apenninenhalbinsel bis 300 v.C.* (Lund 1937).

[7] See D. Trump, *Central and Southern Italy before Rome* (London, 1966), 157–9; D. Ridgway, 'The First Western Greeks, Campanian Coasts and South Etruria', in *Greeks, Celts and Romans*, ed. C. and S. Hawkes (London, 1973), 5–38; 'Sugli inizi della colonizzazione greca in Occidente' (Ridgway, Johannowski, and others), in *Dialoghi di Archeologia* iii (1969); Ogilvie, op. cit. 33.

[8] Strabo 5. 4. 5.

[9] e.g. at Posillipo; the Grotta Dragonara at Miseno is artificial, and cf. Seneca, *Epist.* 55. 6, on the villa of Servilius Vatia at Torregáveta: the caves are *manu factae*.

[10] 9. 3. 12.

[11] 5. 4. 5; cf. 1. 2. 18.

quoted by Strabo (1. 2. 15).[12] Corcyra got its claim to Phaeacia (Thuc. 3. 70. 4) accepted so early that it had no rival claimants, but Calypso, who according to Hesiod was located in Cephallenia (fr. 150 M–W), was drawn into the westward drift to Italy and variously placed, in Ausonia,[13] Latium,[14] Avernus,[15] and Gaudos (Gozo, the northern island of Malta).[16] The localization of Heracles, Odysseus, and Aeneas on the west coast of Italy can be dated in the second half of the sixth century. About the middle of the century Stesichorus sent Heracles to Spain for Geryon's cattle, which had previously been placed in northern Epirus.[17] According to the Tabula Iliaca[18] Stesichorus brought Misenus also to his cape in the west, as Aeneas' companion, though he seems to have been originally attached to Odysseus.[19] Aeneas was localized in Latium about the same time as Odysseus, and appears in Hellanicus as 'after' or 'with' Odysseus.[20] It is not known where Eugammon of Cyrene about 600 B.C. placed his Telegonus, son of Odysseus and Circe, but

[12] For modern geographers and critics, see Sir Henry Bunbury, *History of Ancient Geography* (London, 1883), with map, p. 84; J. O. Thomson, *A History of Ancient Geography* (Cambridge, 1948), 23–7; T. J. Dunbabin, *PBSR* xvi (1948), 13; W. B. Stanford, on *Od.* 9. 18, 10. 1.

[13] Ps. Scymnus 228–30.   [14] Apoll. *Epit.* 7. 24.

[15] Dio Cassius 48. 50. 4.

[16] Callimachus, in Strabo 1. 2. 37.

[17] Hecataeus, Fr. 26 Jacoby. The foundation of Herculaneum at the foot of Vesuvius probably belongs to this period, and the via Herculea (Silius 12. 118) across the Lucrine lake on a causeway must be associated with the foundation of Dicaearchia (later Puteoli) about 525 B.C., when Cumae admitted Samian refugees from Polycrates' tyranny.

[18] *I.G.* 14. 1284, *CIL* 12. 1439; on these, and the others, see now A. Sadurska, *Les Tables Iliaques* (Warsaw, 1964).

[19] Strabo 1. 2. 18. Norden, pp. 180 f., ascribes the annexation of Misenus by Aeneas to Varro as the source of Dion. Hal. 1. 53. 3 and Solinus 2. 13, and he dates the story of Misenus' challenge to Triton (based on Marsyas and Thamyris) to the sixth century, when the Greeks got the trumpet from the Etruscans, its inventors; Triton was there before, with his conch, the prototype of the trumpet.

[20] 4F84 (= Dion. Hal. 1. 72. 2), where we have a choice of μετ' 'Οδυσσέα or μετ' 'Οδυσσέως, preferred by Jacoby. The complicated traditions of Odysseus in the West are examined by E. D. Phillips, *JHS* lxxiii (1953) 53–67.

the lines 1011–16 added to the end of Hesiod's *Theogony*, about Latinus, son of Odysseus and Circe, in Etruria, can be dated to *c.* 540–510 B.C.[21] The placing of Circe on Monte Circeo, half-way between Rome and Cumae, must be associated with the planting there of a Roman colony, ascribed to Tarquinius Superbus.[22] Monte Circeo is not an island, nor was it in antiquity, but it was rightly recognized as having been one.[23]

Circe, unlike Calypso, was firmly located, on the Tyrrhenian coast of Italy, and the Nekyia had to be placed within range of her. Why then was Avernus chosen, to which no alternative seems to have been suggested? Was there a sanctuary for evocation or descent there, as Norden supposed?[24] In support he quotes Strabo (5. 4. 5) and Maximus of Tyre (14. 2), who describes an evocation, but while the Homeric Nekyia is essentially an evocation (so Norden, pp. 200 n. 2, 356) Virgil's is a descent, and Naevius' Cimmerian Sibyl implies a prophecy. Dakaris' discovery in Thesprotia is of a place of evocation. A sanctuary at Avernus, whether pre-Greek or Greek, must have served one, and only one, of the three possible forms of cult. But all three elements are found in Homer, and each one has been separately developed by the Latin poets, prophecy by Naevius, descent by Virgil, evocation by Silius. They cannot have based their accounts on an actual ritual, but selected from Homer's amalgam. How could Virgil put the Sibyl in charge of two quite different cults unless there was nothing at Avernus to constrain him, while the literary precedent of Naevius suggested it? The double function of the Sibyl is an excellent literary device to unify the action. Further, there is in Virgil's account a certain incoherence which could not have existed in a specific ritual, that now Hecate and now Proserpina presides over the cult. This appears particularly in the Golden Bough, which belongs to Proserpina (142–3), but is not presented to her; instead it is awkwardly deposited at the threshold to the vaulted gate which Aeneas and the Sibyl do not enter (631–7).

[21] West, *Theogony*, 436.

[22] Dion. Hal. 5. 61, Livy 1. 56. 3 (with Ogilvie's note).

[23] Cf. A. C. Blanc, *Boll. Soc. Geol. Ital.* lxix (1950) 602–4; A. Segré, ibid. 604–8.

[24] pp. 199 f.: 'The ceremonies which Virgil here describes were really performed in the νεκυομαντεῖον until the region was given a quite different appearance by Agrippa in 37 B.C., which frightened the ghosts away.'

Secondly, we must reckon with the great Antrum of Initiation at Baiae which Dr. R. F. Paget discovered in 1960,[25] especially if it can be dated around 500 B.C. and connected with Aristodemus, tyrant of Cumae, as I have suggested.[26] If it is a place of ritual descent, its existence surely excludes the presence of another such place of descent hardly more than a mile away. Even if the Antrum was known only to initiates, yet some inkling of its existence and its uniquely extensive and complex structure may have contributed to the myth of Avernus.

Modern commentators have tended to assume that Avernus was chosen as an entrance to the Underworld because it was volcanic, that it was still smoking and boiling and birdless when the Greeks arrived. But the Greeks did not associate entrances to the Underworld with volcanic phenomena, but rather with lakes and caves.[27] Moreover, Avernus was much less active than many other craters nearby, such as Solfatara and Agnano, and the second and last eruption of Avernus was perhaps 40,000 years ago, when the floor of the crater was sealed from below in such a way as to form a lake. Our earliest commentator denies the alleged 'birdlessness' and the name has nothing to do with the Greek ἄορνος.[28]

The localization of the Odyssean Nekyia at Avernus had, however, great success, except perhaps at Cumae, where its defects were obvious. The oracle in Thesprotia was perhaps in abeyance, little known until its rebuilding. The first play in Aeschylus' tetralogy on Odysseus, the Ψυχαγωγοί, contains a lyric hexameter spoken by the chorus, Ἑρμᾶν μὲν πρόγονον τίομεν γένος οἱ περὶ λίμναν[29] and the λίμνα is more likely to be Avernus than the confluence of rivers in Thesprotia, and there is no doubt about the location by Sophocles of a νεκυομαντεῖον ἐν τῇ ἀόρνῳ λίμνῃ περὶ Τυρσηνίαν (Pearson fr. 748), probably to be connected with the play on Odysseus' death, Ὀδυσσεὺς ἀκανθοπλήξ.[30] The Cumaeans must have known that there were no Cimmerians

---

[25] *PBSR* xxxv (1967), 102–16; *Vergilius* xiii (1967), 42–50.

[26] *PBSR* xxxvii (1969), 17 ff.

[27] Volcanic activity was associated with the Gigantomachy, as the name Campi Phlegraei shows, and with the smithy of the Cyclopes, though the Ploutonion at Hierapolis in Asia Minor is certainly volcanic (Strabo 13. 4. 14).

[28] See note on 239 ff.

[29] Fr. 476 Mette.

[30] Frs. 453–61.

to be found, but they no doubt welcomed the localization at Avernus of Odysseus' Nekyia, difficult and embarrassing though it was. There were no rivers, but Homer's four had to be accommodated, and there was no agreement about them.[31]

Cicero's words at *Tusc. Disp.* 1. 37 must be mentioned and may be relevant to Sophocles: 'inde (from the error that incorporeal souls live on underground and have a corporeal shape) Homeri tota νέκυια, inde ea quae meus amicus Appius νεκυομαντεῖα faciebat, inde in uicinia nostra Auerni lacus,

Vnde animae excitantur obscura umbra opertae ex ostio,
Altae Acheruntis, salso sanguine †imagines mortuorum†.'

This might seem to confirm that there was an oracle of the dead at Avernus in Cicero's time,[32] but he speaks only of the literary tradition, 'errores quos auxerunt poetae', and he quotes a Latin tragedy, possibly an adaption of Sophocles' drama on Odysseus. The tradition became so strong that Avernus became synonymous with νεκυομαντεῖον, Πλουτώνιον, Χαρώνιον, and was even applied to the Thesprotian sanctuary.[33]

The account of Ephorus' visit to Avernus given by Strabo[34] is revealing. According to Strabo, Ephorus 'adapted the place to the Cimmerians' and said 'they live in underground houses, which they call *argillae*, and visit one another through tunnels, and admit visitors from abroad into the oracle which is established deep underground. They live by mining and what they get from those who consult the oracle and from the king who assigned them an allowance. Those employed with the oracle have an ancestral custom that no one may see the sun, but they emerge from their caverns only by night, and for this reason the poet said of them, "and the shining sun never looks upon them". But later the whole company was abolished by a certain king when the oracle did not turn out well for him. Yet the oracular site still survives after removal to a different place.'

'Such are my predecessors' fables' is Strabo's comment.

[31] Strabo, 5. 4. 5, identifies Acheron with the Lago Fusaro, the lagoon south of Cumae, but at 5. 4. 6 he mentions that some identified it with the Lacus Lucrinus, and Artemidorus with Avernus itself.

[32] His villa, the Academia, was very near Avernus (Pliny, *NH* 31. 6), probably where Monte Nuovo now rises.

[33] Pausanias 9. 30. 6; Hyginus, *Fab.* 88; Pliny, *NH* 4. 2.

[34] 5. 4. 5; cf. Diodorus 4. 22.

Ephorus was evidently not shown the different site, nor could he have seen any underground dwellings. The only place anything like his description is the Antrum at Baiae, which is not a dwelling. The suppression by a king (seventh century?) seems unlikely; if there was a restoration, why not at the same place and why was it not shown? Ephorus has added to Homer some wholly implausible local features: *argillae* is the Latin for 'clay', but the Cumaeans used clay from Ischia, presumably because they had none of their own (Pliny, *NH* 3. 82), and the mention of mining is likewise suspect, since metals, gold and iron, do not occur in tufa. Ephorus then was shown nothing to support the existence of an oracle of the dead at or near Avernus, and Strabo, far from being 'deeply impressed', as McKay says, is the strongest evidence against Norden's assumption, since he contemptuously refutes his predecessors and the local guides.

Almost everything then about the sanctuary of the dead at Avernus can be accounted for by the transference of the Homeric Nekyia from Thesprotia; this brought with it the Cimmerians, the rivers, the alleged sunlessness, the mixture of descent, evocation, and prophecy.[35] The Sibyl, Hecate, the Golden Bough, and the absence of birds are, however, peculiar to Avernus; the Sibyl comes from Cumae, the birdlessness from Greek etymologizing; Hecate and the Golden Bough remain enigmatic.[36] The Homeric Nekyia cannot be accounted for on the basis of Avernus, whereas Aïdonati (as the site is still called) in Thesprotia fits perfectly. Virgil has incorporated the fables about Avernus, such as the mephitic fumes and the absence of birds, but his Nekyia is a purely literary construction and not based on any cult and ritual that he had seen practised at Avernus.

[35] Propertius—and *a fortiori* Virgil—seems to know of the derivation of Avernus as a νεκυομαντεῖον from Thesprotia; his reference to *aequora Thesproti subdita regno* (1. 11. 3–4) has perplexed commentators, who take Avernus as parallel to the Thesprotian sanctuary and not derivative from it and fictitious. Virgil has dropped the Cimmerians (unlike Silius 12. 132), and he has been careful, after suggesting rivers at l. 8, to put Homer's four all underground (671; cf. 3. 386).

[36] It is strange also that the only person recorded as having sacrificed at Avernus is Hannibal in 214 B.C. (Livy 24. 12. 4), but without any indication of the nature of the cult or the identity of the deity.

INDEX NOMINVM

INDEX VERBORVM

INDEX RERVM